GOVERNMENT

A Public Administration Perspective

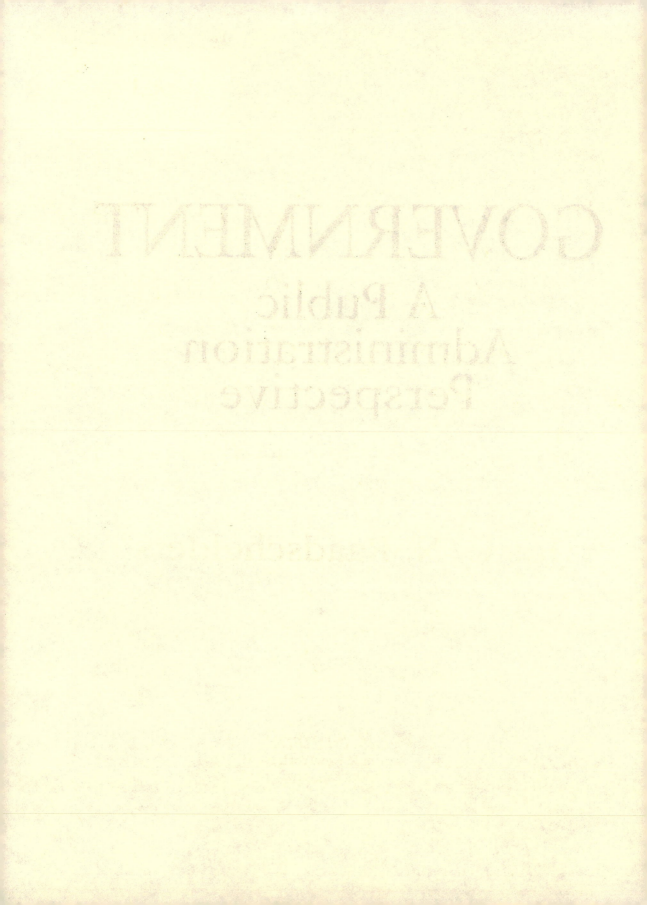

GOVERNMENT
A Public Administration Perspective

Jos C. N. Raadschelders

M.E. Sharpe
Armonk, New York
London, England

Library of Congress Cataloging-in-Publication Data

Raadschelders, J.C.N.
   Government, a public administration perspective / by Jos C.N. Raadschelders.
     p. cm.
   Includes bibliographical references and index.
   ISBN 0-7656-1125-2 (hc : alk. paper) ISBN 0-7656-1126-0 (pbk : alk. paper)
   1. Public administration. I. Title.

JF1351 .R249 2003
351—dc21

                                     2002030893

CONTENTS

LIST OF TABLES AND FIGURES

Tables

Figures

PREFACE AND ACKNOWLEDGMENTS

This book presents an approach to the study of government that draws from a variety of academic disciplines. Knowledge about government is so compartmentalized that it has become more and more difficult to develop a comprehensive view of this social phenomenon. I am convinced that such a more integral approach to government is beneficial to advanced students, middle and higher public servants, politicians, and interested citizens. Advanced students in public administration, political science, economics, history, international relations, law, and so forth whose major research interest concerns the public sector and who prepare for comprehensive exams need a summary overview that helps them connect the various bodies of knowledge together. Public servants, politicians, and citizens need a summary overview that also connects them to the larger body of literature on government. To my knowledge, few studies—if any—exist that attempt to provide a bird's-eye overview of government that draws from various bodies of knowledge. The challenges contemporary governments face in the twenty-first century require a holistic view that maps the role and position of contemporary governments in the context of their historical development.

The references in this book include literature that is generally regarded as mainstream to the studies of public administration and—to a lesser degree—political science. As much as one would like to, it is impossible to be complete. Simon's concept of "bounded rationality" is truly evocative. There are times that scholars are perhaps overwhelmed with the sheer number of studies annually published in their field and in related fields. If anything, this book represents an attempt to forget the urge of complete references in favor of the larger picture. The number of studies and specializations in the areas of public administration and political science, as well as in other disciplines, meanwhile is testimony to the central place that government has come to occupy in society and is certainly testimony to the various ways in which society and government are intertwined.

This book represents an attempt at creating that bridge between various disciplines and specializations that study, among other subjects, government. The study of public administration is the only study that takes government as its core interest. Casting the scope of the traditional study of public administration wider, that is, as the study of government, requires a framework to connect the dispersed knowledge about government. No false modesty is intended when I say that working on this book has humbled me increasingly, if only because of the ambition, perhaps even arrogance, to assume that the theories and wisdom of so many renowned scholars could be discussed in so little space. My thanks for their work and apologies for the often summary mentioning or even omission of them are sincere. Equally truthful, however, is my belief that we should try every now and then to show that the study of government would benefit from a more integrated approach.

The basis for the notion of an integrated approach to government was laid some twenty years ago. Each in their own way, Professor Emeritus Aris Van Braam,† Professor and Senator Marie Louise Bemelmans-Videc, and Professor Emeritus Hans Surie (all at the University of Leiden in the 1980s) have greatly influenced my outlook on the study. More than anyone, they can probably see where their lectures have provided an invaluable starting point for my further study. Their classes on politics and administration, organization theory, decision making, policy analysis, and sociology were insightful, structured, enthusiastic, and enticing because they tapped into the rich literature across disciplines. Two of my friends and colleagues in the Netherlands are likely to affirm my sentiments. Frits van der Meer and Mark Rutgers also took these classes, and I regard discussions we had about them as equally important. I am privileged to have coauthored various pieces with these colleagues. We also work together in research projects. Since 1990, Frits van der Meer and I have been members of the consortium on Civil Service Systems in Comparative Perspective that has produced several books (including my 1998 *Handbook of Administrative History*). Mark Rutgers invited me to be a member of the international panel of experts for his research project, The Renaissance of Public Administration (1998–2003; Rutgers 2003). This book is an attempt at differentiated integration of our knowledge of government and thus fits his research project perfectly.

After fifteen formative years at the University of Leiden (1983–98), I was so fortunate to be given the opportunity to work at the University of Oklahoma (OU). While my ideas about the nature of our study emerged in my final years in Leiden, this book was started at OU. It reflects the multidisciplinarity of the faculty in the department where I was and the department

---

† He passed away last April.

where I am now. Singling out people is always risky, but I would like to mention six OU colleagues and one former Leiden colleague. James Douglas (since August 2001 at the University of South Carolina) commented upon the entire manuscript, Larry Hill and Ron Peters commented upon several chapters, and Don Maletz, Jill Tao, and Marie Louise Bemelmans-Videc (Catholic University of Nijmegen) commented upon a chapter each. I am grateful for the time they took and have benefited from their insightful remarks. Without the extensive comments of OU colleague Aimee Franklin, however, this would not have been the book it is now. Richard Stillman of the University of Colorado was also so generous to read the entire text and provide valuable comments. In the end, though, the responsibility for its contents is mine. I am in Professor Stillman's debt for he introduced me to Harry Briggs, the acquisitions editor for M.E. Sharpe's books in public administration, whose enthusiastic support of this project was a source of inspiration. His colleagues at M.E. Sharpe, Elizabeth Granda and Susan Rescigno, have been equally helpful and instrumental in pushing this project forward.

This book will have a life of its own once considered and digested by readers from different backgrounds. It will be corrected, amended, critiqued, and possibly appreciated. Whichever it will be, I hope it will help people as citizens, as officeholders, and as students to find and explicate their outlook on and desires for government in the years to come. While this book has been written thanks to teachers and peers, it is dedicated to Julie Bivin Raadschelders, for reasons that cannot be expressed in words and certainly go beyond my gratitude for her careful editing, and to Kitty and John, who can still take everything for granted.

Jos C.N. Raadschelders
Norman, Oklahoma
July 2002

INTRODUCTION

1 GOVERNMENT: THE MOST CENTRAL SOCIAL PHENOMENON OF OUR TIME

You can fool all the people some of the time, and some of the people all the time, but you cannot fool all the people all of the time.
—Abraham Lincoln, 1858

The difference between a good manager and an extraordinary manager lies not in one's technical skills, but in one's sense of one's self and one's surroundings, a sense that can only be derived through thoughtful reflection, through theory.
—Robert Denhardt, 1984

Government and governance are as old as the human race. Every society that we know of through records had rulers, whatever their titles. At an abstract level, government is inherent to society. It is a constant in society. At a more concrete level, however, nothing about governance and government is constant. Society is always in flux, so styles of governing must change. The institutional arrangements for governance are a reflection of the dominant worldview(s), of the dominant theories about the interaction between citizen and government, and of the dominant ideas about organizational structures and processes. In short, government is a reflection of what is valued by its environment.

In the first section of this introduction, I consider the nature of contemporary government, and especially the fact that while government is bound by culture, it can be studied through more "universal" concepts. Given that government is always in flux, I briefly discuss what is new about government by means of a two-tiered approach to historical time: comparing contemporary government with that of 100 years ago, and comparing government of the late modern era (i.e., the twentieth century) to that of the early modern era (before the late eighteenth century) (section 1.2). This approach helps us understand why the study of government proliferated across the entire spectrum of the social sciences in the twentieth century (section 1.3). In section 1.4, I explore attempts to link knowledge about government and the integrative role that the study of Public Administration[1] can play in that endeavor. The conclusions of section 1.4 serve as the basis for the framework of this study, which is presented in section 1.5. In section 1.6, I outline the structure of the book, and in section 1.7, I discuss the audiences that could benefit from this effort.

1.1.   Government in an Ever Changing World: Universal but Culture-Bound

The internal structure and functioning of public organizations, which is the traditional focus of the study of Public Administration, reflect what citizens and society at large desire from government. As I argue in chapters 2 and 3, a definition of *government* involves the authoritative allocation of values by politics and administration. It has become fashionable to use the term *governance* instead as if it were a synonym (cf. March and Olsen 1995; Dror 2001). The concept of *governance*, however, refers to all organizations and institutions that are involved in the structuring of society. These include, next to governmental actors, also nongovernmental actors (e.g., churches, sports clubs, social movements, global networks, mass media), independent agencies (grant committees, health management authorities), and private industries and corporations (Dror 2001, 169–170). Without any doubt, government is the single largest actor in the governance of society.

This is a generic study in government, but since the traditions and customs of government very much mirror what society considers acceptable in a given period and culture, this is first and foremost a study of government in Western democracies (with illustrations from the United States and Western European countries). The contemporary concepts, theories, and models about government have been developed primarily in the Western world, which means that they are grounded in Western values. Western Public Administration has been accused of being ethnocentric, especially when its concepts, theories, and models are used as a blueprint for reform in non-Western countries. This use of Western Public Administration knowledge for non-Western reforms can be seen in two very different ways.

First, and most commonly, is the implicit assumption that Western models of government are an example to follow by others because they are better, more civilized, more democratic, and so forth. The (partial) failure of public sector reforms elsewhere often can be explained by the application of Western thought in societies with very different legal, social, moral, and ethical value systems. It is specifically in the functioning of governments in their respective societies that we can see the importance of culture and values. The *usable* or *practical value* of Western-based Public Administration may be limited, but the *substantive value* of comparing Western and non-Western administrative systems is indispensable for the understanding of our own and other governments (Dahl 1947, 11; Riggs 1998, 29).

Second, recognizing that the functioning of public administration and the content of its study are culture-specific, however, does not mean that the concepts, theories, and models used have no analytical value or relevance to other parts of the world. One could argue that at an abstract level, the various challenges of governing are more or less universal. These include establishing and maintaining (a) order and stability in society, (b) a balance of power between rulers and ruled, (c) a balance between the political and the administrative branches of government, (d) a balance between individual and collective arrangements, and—more specifically—a balance between service delivery by public and private institutions, (e) a balance between centralization and decentralization, and so forth. It is at the abstract level that the analytical tools (concepts, models, theories) of contemporary (Western) Public Administration can be useful (Heady 1996).

In contemporary Western democracies, government has assumed a place more central to their societies than ever before. Given the degree to which government has penetrated society, given the range of services provided and activities exercised by government, and given the degree to which individual citizens have come to depend upon government, it is arguably one of the most, if not *the* most, central social phenomena of our time. In the course of the twentieth century, many of the social sciences have included the study of this phenomenon because it is the only remaining institutional arrangement that truly binds society and—at least—has the capacity to serve as society's binding force.

In historical perspective, Western government as we know it—with its freedom of elections, welfare provisions, large bureaucracies, sense of fairness and equity as set in law, emphasis on government by and for the people—is of recent origin, dating back only 100 years or so. It is in the twentieth century that government began operating at a level (of activity, societal penetration, organizational size and complexity, and so forth) unheard of before. From early on, the study of Public Administration originated in the midst of the need to buttress the field with the kind of knowledge that helped government respond to the various social needs that emerged as a consequence of democratization, urbanization, industrialization, population growth, and (more recently) internationalization. And Public Administration has responded to the public demand for a more responsive and responsible government. While the choice of a particular public policy is ultimately political, the administrative structures and processes to implement these policies have been served very well indeed by both the field's (i.e., public administration) as well as the study's (i.e., Public Administration) attention to organizational structure, policy and decision-making styles, the management of human and financial resources, and so forth. Over time, a wealth of experience and knowledge has been accumulated in field and study, and while this has not always been of a problem-solving nature, it has certainly been enlightening.

The rapid development of the study of Public Administration in this century (Fry 1989) is an illustration of the importance that government, or, as Waldo (1984) and Chandler (1987) would say, the administrative state, has come to play in society at large. In fact, many scholars, including Woodrow Wilson, have expressed some weariness when observing that society and government change faster than the study can keep up with.

1.2. What Is New About Government in Our Time?

The major features of contemporary government, such as a wide range of public services, laws and regulations, and a fairly uncorrupted public workforce, have become so common that their existence is taken for granted and their origins forgotten. When we look only at the present features and future challenges of government, we lose sight of the fact that what we take for granted is really of very recent origin. A focus on the present, the day-to-day events, deprives us of the deeper understanding of longer-term developments (see also section 5 below). The study of government is generally limited to the twentieth century. Studies of the welfare state, for instance, often present current challenges (the short term) in the context of its emergence and proliferation from the late nineteenth century onward (the middle range). The uniqueness of the welfare state, though, becomes apparent only when we take an even longer time perspective that would include the changes from medieval to early modern and modern views about and institutions for private and/or public collective provisions for welfare.

We can look at contemporary government in different ways. One way is to look at our own day and age, circa 2002, and contrast that with government in the year 1900. We can then see remarkable and rapid changes. Government as we know it today is very different from government a century ago. Throughout this book, the reader will find illustrations of this change. The second way is to look at our era, the twentieth century, in comparison to government preceding the modern era. In this view, we recognize that between the 1880s and the 1900s a new type of government emerged that was very different from the earlier types and the foundations of which still exist today. Thus, the late nineteenth up to the late twentieth century is a coherent period, in sharp contrast with early modern times. The discussion of these two ways will be organized by four very simple questions: We will pay more attention to the past century, since the long-term perspective has been presented in an earlier study (Raadschelders 1998a).

A. Why Does Government Do Certain Things?

The major challenges in society at present are of such magnitude that no single institutional actor will be able to confront them. Among these challenges are growing population size and diversity, the technological revolution, increased connectedness among nation-states, regional and global environmental stress, and a growing disparity between the rich and the poor (both between countries as well as within countries).

While government is not necessarily the only actor that can and should muster the capacity to confront these challenges, it is the sole actor that has the legal and moral authority to serve as a binding and coordinating force in society. However, the representativeness, impartiality, and legitimacy of government are challenged by the increasing diversity of society in the Western world. Indeed, a century ago, demographic diversity was not at all relevant to the representativeness of government. At the same time, more people are somehow dependent upon government than ever before (through entitlements and social services, as well as through employment in both the public sector and in businesses and industries that produce goods and services for government). The technological revolution has not only accelerated the information flows but also, for instance, subjects the First Amendment to a more serious test than ever before. Should government monitor, restrict, or even ban Web sites that preach hate against minorities and that reach a potentially infinite audience? Yet another feature is that governments share—and at least pay lip service to—global responsibilities for peace, a cleaner environment, and a fairer distribution of welfare. International economic, military, political, and cultural cooperation have assumed enormous proportions.

A century ago, government's binding force was also grounded in legal authority, but local communities and churches served equally to bind people on the basis of social control and moral authority. Fewer people depended upon government for their livelihood. Environmental problems were not yet an issue, and few people were concerned with the gap between rich and poor. It was in the twentieth century that government and society penetrated each other. Government's role changed from being the political organization of society to providing the entire foundation of and framework for society. When we compare the past 100 to 120 years with prior decades and centuries, the differences are equally striking because early governments functioned in a rural and agrarian society in which a variety of collective services were provided by local and private actors. Government's intervention was thus limited to the maintenance of public order and safety and some economic regulation.

B. What Does Government Do?

Public organizations currently provide an enormous number of services. While the individual's rights are protected by law and while policies seek to meet the needs of individuals, laws and policies are first and foremost aimed at providing services to identifiable collectives (senior citizens, disabled, orphans, single parents, unemployed, youth, criminals, professionals, women, gays, native Americans, etc.). The fact that the public provision of welfare services (in the areas of social security, health, social services, education, housing, water, and so forth) is huge today in comparison to 100 years ago is largely forgotten. Insofar as collective services were provided back then by a public organization, it targeted individuals rather than collectives. Yet the innovations in government (in terms of new policies, new organizations, styles of functioning, etc.) in the last quarter of the nineteenth century link that period to ours and make it distinct from earlier times when the traditional tasks of government included maintenance of public order and safety (the military and the police), the judiciary, and taxation.

C. How Does Government Do It?

A century ago, government embarked upon new policies and programs in response to the equally new developments in the economy and the structure and concentration of labor (industrialization and urbanization). Given the growth of public services, we now have a government that is larger than anything that could be imagined 100 years ago. The impact of public service growth is visible, for instance, in personnel size and in the composition of the public workforce, in the high degree of organizational differentiation, in the annual revenue and expenditure, and in the percentage of public sector consumption of the gross national product. By every measure, government a century ago was small. Also, the various levels of government now are much more interdependent than ever before. Where public service delivery now largely rests upon shared and coordinated efforts in a system of intergovernmental relations, government and public service delivery were still fairly insulated by town and region a century ago. As a consequence, government today utilizes much more middle-range and longer-term planning. A century ago, the concept of social engineering did not even exist.

However, as different as the late nineteenth and the late twentieth centuries are in terms of the structure and function of government, much of what is now "normal" originated in the late nineteenth century. It was then that government started to grow in terms of public services, which translated into a growth of personnel size, organizational differentiation, and revenue and expenditure at a pace markedly different from that in previous centuries. Another important aspect of how government functions today is that it is more open, accessible, and accountable than a century ago. The technology needed for this openness and accessibility developed in the twentieth century (radio, television, computers, information networks such as e-mail and the Internet). Government attempts to inform the public through its own venues as well as through the media. Most public organizations have Web sites and informational brochures. The media also seek out government, especially to uncover abuse of power or unethical and immoral behavior. In this respect, it is even harder to fool the general public than in the days of Abraham Lincoln. But given its sheer size and complexity, a case can also be made that government is less accessible than before.

D. Who Governs?

Both the relative openness and the size of government have not only changed its position and role in society, but they have also had an impact upon those who work in the public sector. Nowadays, it would be inconceivable to conduct public affairs without the participation of various interested parties. As compared to 100 ago, the networks between citizen associations, lobby groups, industries, and corporate business on the one hand, and government officials (both elected and appointed public servants) on the other are extensive and indispensable. For centuries, government officials stood above society. There was a real gap between government and society—those who governed belonged to a privileged elite; those who were governed had little say in the business of government. From the mid-nineteenth century, the expansion of the franchise and the advent of civic associations, among other things, expanded opportunities for participation in government by the citizenry at large. The role and position of public servants have changed significantly. Both elected and appointed public officials (as political executives or civil servants) represent and safeguard our general *and* particular interests. They have to keep in touch with constituencies, interest groups, private enterprise, citizens, particular professions, voluntary associations, and so forth, in order to assure that policy making will meet the needs of the targeted communities. In terms of their position, public servants are still approached with some respect (the respect that individuals show to one another as well as respect for the authority invested in a particular office), but they no longer occupy a higher place in the stratification of society. Truly no one is above the law, as presidents and monarchs learned.

1.3. The Study of Government as a Multidisciplinary Effort

Given that government has become so central to the structure and functioning of contemporary society, it is no wonder that it has drawn attention in a variety of academic disciplines, especially in the social and the humanist sciences. Economists look at the role of government in the redistribution of scarce resources. They have also been leading the way in our understanding of decision-making processes from the rationalist and institutionalist perspectives. Political scientists look at the organization of power, at ways in which various communities have advanced their particular interests on the public agenda, and at the meaning of political parties for government (e.g., for interest formation, agenda building, and filling political office through elections). The political theorists among them focus on issues such as the foundation of government and civil society. Students of law are interested in how the administrative state deals with inequalities of justice through law as well as the balance between common law and statute law. Sociologists attempt to understand political-administrative behavior in the context of structure and culture. Psychologists study individual behavior in organizations as well as decision-making processes under pressure. Historians debate the influence of leaders in comparison to the influence of structural developments. Theologians focus on the underlying religious and moral values that help define our relation with society and with government. Philosophers consider the role of government in terms of the old question of how the good, the beautiful, and the just have been advanced against the forces of evil, ugliness, and injustice. Scholars of these disciplines have made invaluable contributions to the understanding of government. But to argue that the study of Public Administration is "left to feast on the leftovers" (Rodgers and Rodgers 2000, 441) would be too hasty a conclusion.

While it is unclear to what degree scholars of government have benefited from the scholarship in Public Administration, it is clear that students of Public Administration have profited enormously from the research conducted in other disciplinary contexts. The study of Public Administration is somewhat of a garbage can since in it we can find theories and conceptualizations that originated in other disciplines. This has given Public Administration a reputation of being intellectually underdeveloped. This is an incomplete—if not dead wrong—appreciation of what has been achieved thus far. More than any other discipline engaged in the study of government, Public Administration has striven toward a multidisciplinary approach, thus, of necessity, becoming the "Israel of academic disciplines . . . always squabbling over the precise (and priceless) boundary lines that define our identity" (Rodgers and Rodgers 2000, 436). For instance, students of Public Administration concentrated on and specialized in civil service systems and public human resource management, public organizations, public policy making, public budgeting, public management, intergovernmental relations, public sector ethics, and other fields. Indeed, Public Administration was long regarded a subfield of political science, but a growing number of public administration scholars no longer regard their study as a subsidiary to political science. However, given the amount of literature published by its scholarly community, the study has developed a standing of its own. Many of the areas of interest embraced by the study of Public Administration have long ceased to interest political scientists. Holden's observation about the state of political science, however, equally applies to Public Administration:

> Of course, our discipline is greatly imperfect. What discipline, profession, or human activity is not? Law? Medicine? Psychiatry? Economics? True, some other disciplines are logically more coherent. They have a dominant set of assumptions, theories, methods, and data, although none of the social sciences approach the coherence of physics, chemistry, or biology. Some are equipped with better mathematicians. Someday we may get closer to the standards in those fields. *But, as far as we are, we know more [public administration] than any other discipline.* It is our business to know public administration, however imprecisely we state it. (Holden 2000, 2–3; italics in original)

Although for some scholars Public Administration is nothing more, but also nothing less, than a professional degree that seeks to train practitioners (or "pracademics," as Waldo once called them), or a "subject-matter in search of a discipline" (Waldo, as quoted in Hood and Jackson 1991, 172), others believe that Public Administration has the multidisciplinary potential to arrive at a more complete understanding of government. Public Administration scholars have been trained in and recruited from a variety of disciplines. It is important for Public Administration to break free from the shackles imposed by the image of being only a professional study. As a professional study, it has to focus on instruments and techniques, and this is no doubt beneficial to the professionalism of its graduates. As an academic study, it is bound to look beyond "technocracy" because contemporary society not only needs professionals with technical skills, it also needs these professionals to be savvy in intellectual appraisal (Self 1979). It is, after all, the capacity for intellectual appraisal that elevates the technocrat and the specialist to the status of generalist. It is intellectual appraisal that marks the difference between a good and an extraordinary manager. A generalist perspective on government is not attained by focusing merely on the instruments and techniques of policy making, evaluating, budgeting, human resource management, organizing, and negotiating, all of which have so far dominated Public Administration. Instead, a generalist perspective explores the underlying values of choices made. These values do not surface in an instrumental-technical approach to government. In fact, in view of the various specializations and subfields that surfaced within the study since World War II, a Public Administration perspective is not easy to develop. It is, however, critical to strive for an overview since our understanding of governance and government is already more compartmentalized than it should be.

1.4. The Study of Public Administration as Integrative Framework

A perspective of government that focuses solely on what Public Administration has defined as its interests would be as incomplete as if government were studied only in a political science, international relations, economical, psychological, or theological perspective. Ideally, the complexity and challenges of contemporary government require that scholars draw insights from a variety of disciplines and studies and thus arrive at a fuller, deeper, and more nuanced understanding of this social phenomenon. It is not my ambition to "integrate" various disciplinary perspectives, theories, and concepts about government in the social and the humanist sciences, for two simple reasons. A practical reason is that no individual can pretend to have the ability to present such an overview (Barth and Green 1999, 537). Indeed, several handbooks in the study of Public Administration are the fruit of collaborative effort between editor(s) and authors. A more theoretical reason is that any discipline-transcending foundation for substantive integration of our knowledge about government is lacking. Instead, the understanding of governance and government is pursued from a variety of disciplinary perspectives. The Public Administration perspective is especially relevant to practitioners and students alike since that is the primary study whose explicit object of study is government and which thus could attempt to provide an integrative framework for all knowledge about government. Adopting a Public Administration perspective provides a foundation, a point of departure upon which one draws from knowledge generated in other academic disciplines and studies. Such an integration of knowledge, though, can be a major undertaking dependent upon the level of ambition.

Four types of integration can be distinguished and they are quite different by nature (the following is partially based on Raadschelders 2000a). The first type is *general* or *professional integration* of what is considered mainstream to the study. Throughout the twentieth century, handbooks and introductions invariably included the topics of organization and management, personnel, budget, policy, decision making, intergovernmental relations, and a wide array of concepts, theories, and models for analyzing them. What different bodies of knowledge must our graduates master and "connect" in order to be properly equipped for starting a career in the public, the nonprofit, or even the private sector? While we should pay attention to what the market needs, it is equally important to present the various discrete bodies of knowledge in a framework that includes the conceptual, technical, and normative competencies future academics and practitioners will need (Barth and Green 1999, 539). A framework to the study provides depth when it links the various specializations or subfields together. Often, however, this professional integration is left to the student. There are numerous examples of generic handbooks throughout the twentieth century, and they have mushroomed since the 1970s (e.g., Dimock, Dimock and Fox 1983; Gordon and Milakovich 1998; Henry 1999; Nigro and Nigro 1989; Perry 1996; Shafritz and Russell 2000; Starling 1998).

The second and equally common type of integration is *specialist integration*, which presents the study as a series of "miniparadigms," to use Robert Golembiewski's phrase. This type of integration occurs at the level of the various subspecializations in the study. The advantage is that students receive an in-depth discussion of the major themes within a specialization and thus acquire some overview. There are many examples of such specialized handbooks on, for instance, human resource management (Berman et al. 2001; Condrey 1998; Rabin et al. 1995), organizational theory (Rainey 1997), law and administration (Cooper and Newland 1997), intergovernmental relations (Wright 1988), local government (Gargan 1997), public sector ethics (Cooper 1992), comparative public administration (Farazmand 1991; Heady 1996), administrative communication (Garnett and Kouzmin 1997), public budgeting (Meyers 1998; Mikesell 1991), consultation (Golembiewski 2000), and strategic management (Rabin, Miller, and Hildreth 2000). (For a discussion of several of the generic and specialized handbooks, see Barth and Green 1999.) Anthologies are yet another example of specialized integration since these pull together classic or seminal texts in one particular area, as for instance, on personnel policy (Hays and Kearney 1995; Thompson 2002), organization theory (Shafritz and Ott 1996), and intergovernmental relations (O'Toole 2000).

There are more than fifty professional and specialized handbooks in print in the United States alone. With the exception of those that are explicitly devoted to comparative administration, they all have a distinctly American outlook on (P)public (A)administration. These handbooks reflect American traditions of and ideas about governance and government and then, it is surprising to see that several of these American-based handbooks have been translated and used as generic introductions to public administration, especially in countries that lack a national tradition in the study of Public Administration. Countries that do have such nationally well-developed studies (e.g., Western European countries, Canada, Australia) may use American textbooks in addition to but never instead of national textbooks that build upon the tacit knowledge readers have of their own country and its administrative traditions. Recently, an effort has been undertaken to develop a truly international handbook of Public Administration that considers differences in approach and conceptualizations within the various national traditions (Peters and Pierre 2003).

What the general and specialized handbooks of Public Administration have in common is that they lack shared concepts and a central theory. Of course, the editors and authors of these tomes generally do not claim to work on such a basis. Instead, they present the various themes relevant to the study at present with an eye for the challenges ahead. The major challenge for handbooks is to be complete, and the size of most of these textbooks reflects that desire. As a consequence, generic and specialized handbooks of or introductions to Public Administration perhaps appear to be somewhat eclectic in terms of approaches and fashions—of which there are so many—and even in terms of the subject matters selected. It may be clear that the various topics in a handbook have something in common: they all concern government, or, for instance, human resource management, and so forth. But how the various topics are related to one another is less clear for lack of a conceptual framework. The various specializations in the generic handbooks and the various topics in the specialized handbooks are presented as discrete and compartmentalized bodies of knowledge connected in terms of the locus or object of study (government) instead of connected through a substantive framework based on the focus of or approach to the study.

That type of framework is provided by *differentiated integration* (Rutgers 1997), which is an attempt to provide a coherent, cohesive framework at a practical rather than at an epistemological level. Differentiated integration is achieved when a text is organized around, for instance, *the core subjects of the study,* or *the core disciplinary perspectives of the study,* or *the major questions of the study.* In his introduction to *Public Administration*, Richard Stillman (1992, x) organizes knowledge about American government around the core subjects. The organizing model is introduced in the first chapter "The Scope and Purpose of Public Administration." The first ring around that core is concerned with the environment of public administration and contains six chapters on formal structure, general environment, political environment, intergovernmental dimensions, internal dynamics, and key decision makers. The second ring contains six chapters on decision making, administrative communication, executive management, personnel motivation, public budgeting, and implementation. The exterior ring has three chapters with discussions on the relationship between politics and administration, between public and private sectors, and between ethics and public service. What distinguishes Stillman's handbook from the other general handbooks mentioned earlier is that he presents an explicit diagram for the design of the book that suggests how the various core subjects can be related to each other. Such an explicit organization of the study helps students search for and develop their own framework for the study. What makes Stillman's book attractive to students and practitioners and unique among handbooks in general is the combination of a conceptual and a case-study approach.

An example of a handbook that departs from the argument that a Public Administration perspective should combine several core disciplinary perspectives is the one by Rosenbloom (1998, 1983). He argues that bureaucracy has to serve as a bridge for the three branches of government defined in the U.S. Constitution. Thus a proper understanding of public administration as coordinator and bridge between the executive, the legislature, and the judiciary requires a combined managerial, political, and legal outlook on government's structure and functioning. Rosenbloom's handbook is divided into four sections. In the first section, he maps the study and the field in the United States. The second part contains five chapters on core functions of public administration (organization, personnel, budgeting, decision making, policy analysis, and evaluation). Each of these chapters shows how we can understand the core functions when looking through the political, legal, and managerial lenses. Understanding governance and government is enhanced by integrating political science, law, and management approaches. Rosenbloom's third section serves to illustrate that mix of management, politics, and law in the practice of administration. In the fourth section, the same disciplinary approaches are used to discuss various aspects of public administration and the public. Rosenbloom's handbook is attractive and unique because it is the only one that explicitly approaches government from different disciplinary perspectives in the hope of arriving at a richer understanding of government.

The third subtype of differentiated integration takes core questions of the study as a point of departure in combination with a conceptual framework that organizes the material. These simple questions are less simple to answer: Why does government do certain things? What does government do? How does government do it? Who governs? A visual presentation or diagram of an organization of the *study of public administration* around core questions and of the *study of government* around core themes was published earlier (Raadschelders 1999, 2002a). The conceptual framework for this book, in terms of a differentiated integration approach, will be developed in the next section.

Stillman's and Rosenbloom's handbooks, as well as this book, lack the theoretical or epistemological coherence coveted in a positivist perspective, but have the advantage that they present a cohesive framework for the study of government. Handbooks such as those by Stillman and Rosenbloom show that differentiated integration is possible and desirable from both an academic and a practical point of view. Many handbook editors and authors do not present a framework of the study beyond the professional and the specialized levels, but do provide a useful overview of the study. At the same time, though, the debate about the academic identity of the study emphasizes its theoretical and methodological weakness and reveals hopes for a more natural-science type of framework for Public Administration (Perry and Kraemer 1986; White, Adams, and Forrester 1996).

This *theoretical* or *epistemological integration* is the most ambitious of all types since it departs from the basis of shared concepts and a central (explanatory) theory. Its approach is deductive-nomological, in which one or a few concepts are selected as a point of departure for an ever more detailed mapping of the study. In this approach, theoretical and methodological unification of the study is presumed possible and is characteristic of several general handbooks by continental European scholars (e.g., Debbasch 1989; Van Braam 1986). In the United States, Vincent Ostrom of Indiana University is one of the advocates of such an approach (i.e., Public Administration as a science of association). Epistemological integration can also be pursued on the basis of an inductive-empirical approach, and that is characteristic for the argument made in the United States that Public Administration research should be theoretically and methodologically more rigorous and also more cumulative. Both rigor (in terms of validity, but also in terms of shared concepts and theories) and accumulation of knowledge are central features of the natural sciences.

This type of integration, however, is not only impossible but also irrelevant to our understanding of government. First, it is impossible because the social sciences and the natural sciences employ very different "languages" and use very different research methods. Several of the natural sciences have the luxury of a universal consensus about at least part of their language (mathematical and chemical formulas, medical terms, and so forth), while most if not all social scientists find themselves debating the particular definition of concepts (on differences between both major fields of learning, see Raadschelders 2000a, 212–213). Second, as a consequence, the social sciences at large, and thus also Public Administration, operate much more from an interpretative perspective rather than a naturalistic perspective. Third, there is also a normative consideration at play here. While it may sound trivial to say that human beings perceive the world differently, that difference is certainly a factor in how we can pursue our understanding of, for instance, government. The impact of phenomena studied by social scientists is bound by time and place and not universal (as are gravity, magnetism, natural selection, etc.). Instead, social scientists are concerned with interpretations of social phenomena that, at a very abstract level, are universal (i.e., there is always governance and often government, people tend to associate and organize, populations have leaders and followers, etc.), but that varies with time and place, and thus culture, at a concrete level. Epistemological integration is not only impossible from a purely academic point of view, it is also irrelevant to our need for understanding and—from a normative point of view—it is possibly even dangerous because it would negate the variety of opinions and perspectives that are a source of wealth to society.

The pursuit of differentiated integration acknowledges the need for an explicit conceptual framework that provides coherence to the study while, at the same time, it respects the fact of human interpretation. As Waldo (1996) said: "I do not teach you what to think, but how to think" (Waldo Symposium, the Maxwell School, Syracuse, June 27–28). An explicit conceptual framework for understanding government that everybody will subscribe to is a theoretical and social dream, but it will hopefully enable individuals to develop their own perspective on government and possibly help generate competing conceptual frameworks. In the next section, an integrative conceptual framework for understanding the balancing act of government and the challenges of governance is developed.

1.5. Framing the Study of Government: The Challenge to Balance

This book is an attempt to present a generic outlook on government that is not specifically grounded in one particular political and administrative system. At an abstract level, some features and challenges of government are universal and they are what determines the content of this book, even though there will be frequent reference to particular countries. It is an attempt at differentiated integration of knowledge about government that is based on a series of fundamental conceptual perspectives. Purposefully, I do not speak of disciplinary perspectives, for the concepts that are used to organize Public Administration as a coherent body of knowledge are relevant in several, if not in all, of the social sciences. Thus, these concepts are not specific to the study of Public Administration, but they are relevant for understanding government. In this section, that multidisciplinary framework, which contains four elements or angles, is outlined:

1. balancing individual and collective desires: the political challenge;
2. balancing juridical and sociological perspectives: the fairness challenge;
3. the embeddedness of public choices and events in layers of meaning and understanding;
4. the embeddedness of public choices and events in layers of time.

In isolation, none of these elements can provide a full understanding of government. Together, they serve as facets of a diamond: turn it and we see the same issue from a different angle and in a different light.

The first element is basic to the public realm and can be defined, for instance, in terms of the individual versus a collective of people or in terms of local versus central government. The relation between individual and group is expressed in degrees of freedom enjoyed by the individual within the larger community to which he or she belongs. The United States is the land of individual freedom par excellence, while in advanced welfare states as well as in totalitarian and dictatorial regimes, the collective appears to be more important than the individual. In terms of local-central relations, the relevance of the individual-collective continuum for the United States, for instance, goes back to the debate between Federalists (i.e., centralists) and anti-Federalists (i.e., decentralists) in the late eighteenth century, which flared up again in the late nineteenth and late twentieth century. Comparable debates occurred in Europe as well, as is illustrated by the debate between Federalists (i.e., decentralists) and Unitarians (i.e., centralists) about how to organize the new Dutch Republic at the time of the French occupation (from 1795 onward). All Western governments have had to face the challenge of balancing individual and local needs with those of the collective and the national interests.

The second element is mainly concerned with the distinction between formal and informal patterns of interaction, relevant to understanding a government that has to balance between, for instance, bureaucracy and networking. The third element concerns the deeper lying parameters (one could also say perimeters) within which we act as well as the level of concreteness of our actions in and perception of the public realm. Finally, the fourth element draws our attention to the basic developmental features of government.

The Balancing of Individual and Collective Desires: The Challenge of Politics

The opening remarks of a prewar introduction to the study of American government clearly outline that a single perspective on government's role and position in society does not exist:

> Some people think they would be happy with the junglelike liberty of the lion and the tiger. Others urge an elaborately planned society with a government that restricts liberty but promises an equality of opportunity. Still others would take a middle course. Opinions range all the way from anarchism to communism. (Magruder and Seckler-Hudson 1936, 1)

In the view of these authors, anarchism and communism represent the extremes of a continuum in between which individualism, collectivism, and socialism (in that order) could be placed (2–5). It is revealing that they mention anarchism, socialism, and communism as types of political organization, but do not mention democracy. In a footnote, both capitalism and fascism are paraded as examples of individualism (2). More important, their continuum is inconsistent in containing three types of polities/ideologies next to two concepts (individualism and collectivism) that concern degrees of societal cohesion. It makes little sense to seek conceptual framing of the study of government on the basis of a continuum of existing types of polities or actual political ideologies, because we will simply differ on the question of whether fascism, for instance, is an expression of individualism or collectivism. Also, viewing the individualism-collectivism continuum solely in social and political terms (i.e., individual liberty) would blind us to its economic aspects (i.e., Darwinian-style competition, invisible hand of the market). The attention to individualism and collectivism was very strong during the early decades of the twentieth century, when authors considered the impact of collective bargaining, the cooperative movement, and government ownership of industries on the politics and economy of the United States (e.g., Tugwell, Munro, and Stryker 1930, 649–684) and of Europe (e.g., the development of the tripartite corporatist networks between representatives of employers, employees, and government in determining economic policy). The challenge of balancing individualism and collectivism is no less important today. In addition to the initial interest in determining what degree of government intervention in society and economy is acceptable, it now also includes much more attention to the role and position of each level of government in a system of intergovernmental or central-local relations that is far more institutionalized than seventy years ago.

Individualism and collectivism pose a very fundamental challenge to government, the nature of which can best be phrased as a question: How can the desires of a *collection of individuals* be balanced with those of the *communities of peoples* that live within one *state-society?* At the same time the answer is very simple and very complex: through a *government of citizens.* Both question and answer require some elaboration. The concept of a collection of individuals refers to a society that is highly fragmented and where individuals are not of necessity concerned with the well-being of others. In a society that functions as a collection of individuals, it is primarily self-interest and immediate gratification that drive public action. In a community of people, on the other hand, individuals have a sense of belonging to and being connected with a larger group. In this type of society, individuals first operate as members of a community, placing the collective interest before the self-interest. Ever since Tönnies in 1887 distinguished between *gemeinschaft* (community) and *gesellschaft* (society), the social development of Western societies has been characterized as a move from community to society, with loss of social ties and increased anonymity. Obviously, to argue that "society" superseded "community" is too simple an analysis. The link between people is nowadays based on citizenship rather than kinship, friendship, and proximity. The concept of state-society suggests that the link between territory (state) and people (society), which in our contemporary, secularized social and political system is established through governance, is established at a level far beyond that of the local communities in the premodern era. The more common concepts of *nation-state* or *national state* also assume a link between a territory (state) and a (homogeneous) population (a nation). However, the "nation"-element in the nation-state concept is increasingly less relevant (if, indeed, it ever was relevant) to contemporary state-society given its multinational, multiracial, and thus multicultural nature. Given this, the major challenge is to establish a basis for governance that is accepted by all. Governance through a collection of individuals might lead to a continuous Darwinian struggle for power in which the strongest will survive. Governance through a community of people might end in a tyranny of the majority and also in a continuous struggle for power between different communities. The particularist interests of individuals and peoples could prove detrimental to true collective and national interests. What connects individuals and peoples, though, is the fact that both interact with and in government as citizens. It is through citizenship that individuals and peoples converse with and act in government. It is citizenship that legitimizes government. In our modern state-society, the biggest challenge is to balance individual and collective desires through a *government of citizens.* In essence, this balancing of individual and collective desires is a political challenge.

The idea that governing is a balancing act between two extremes may seem a straightforward and even simple statement, but it is not. When looking at the Public Administration literature of the past century, the dominant way of looking at government was dichotomous. For analytical reasons, democracy and efficiency, market and state, fact and value, politics and administration, centralization and decentralization, individualism and collectivism, and many other such terms were paired and contrasted. Although for more than fifty years, for instance, the separation of politics and administration has been labeled as insufficient or outright wrong when describing reality, it is still difficult to leave the dichotomy behind. In the attempts to reform government, currently legitimized on the basis of a market-oriented managerial philosophy, we find another example of dichotomous thinking. When it comes down to choices in the public realm, the analytical frames of mind have been trained in an "either-or" mode rather than a "this plus that" mode. Yet another illustration is the famous Friedrich-Finer debate in the early 1940s about the nature of government and human nature. Friedrich believed that politics and administration could not be separated and that governance of society should proceed on the basis of discourse and science, totally trusting the human being. Finer, on the other hand, believed politics and administration should be separated, for one could trust neither the people nor the administrators (for a detailed analysis of this debate, see McSwite 1997, 29–50).

The paired opposites mentioned above do point to particular tensions ever present in society and are often presented as a zero-sum configuration (e.g., at present we have 40 percent centralization and thus 60 percent decentralization) rather than in terms of the extremes of a continuum in an "and-and" setting (e.g., elements of centralization and of decentralization both are visible in central-local relations; elements of individualism and collectivism both are visible in the welfare state).

Deep down, individualism and collectivism are not a dilemma but rather a continuum in which they coexist. While it is a platitude to say that the individual would not exist without the community or vice versa, it is nonetheless true. It is through the lens of this continuum that the debate about balancing state and market takes place. It is in terms of this continuum that we see immediate visible challenges and benefits. Individualist-oriented policies are more identified with the right end of the political spectrum in America and Europe and emphasize lower taxes, free markets, low degrees of government intervention, smaller government, and so forth. Collectivist-oriented policies, on the other hand, are the hallmarks of left-wing parties and focus more on welfare policies and higher taxes, extended government intervention in and control of the economy, and bigger government. These examples of individualist and collectivist orientations indicate that both of these concepts do not mean anything unless valued and specified in a specific ideological framework. They are valued differently in, for instance, Ayn Rand's philosophy of objectivism (1967) and in Mustapha Mond's observations of individual happiness in a totalitarian society (in Aldous Huxley's *Brave New World* [1996]).

This balancing act is performed by government within each state-society as well as in the international arena. Within state-society, individualism and collectivism operate as push-and-pull factors, visible in any public policy. From an economic perspective this push-and-pull process can be analyzed in terms of Pareto optimality (a change [in policy, in economic organization] that makes one or more members of society better off without making anyone worse off). In a legal-philosophical perspective, we can analyze it in terms of Rawlsian justice (1971). In the international arena, state-societies tend to defend the same perspectives. Individualism is apparent in the foreign policies of each state-society that reflect what is domestically valued most, while at the same time collectivism is visible in the solutions sought to international conflict (e.g., peacekeeping activities of the United Nations), in international economic, political, military, and cultural association, and in multilateral development aid.

The Balancing of Juridical and Sociological Perspectives: The Challenge of Fairness

The second element for the framework is a combined juridical and sociological perspective. The distinction between these two perspectives plagued Public Administration throughout the twentieth century. A juridical perspective dominated in the first part of the century. Politics and administration were conceptualized as distinct and this idea was given a legal expression. Comparative legislation and jurisprudence, international law and constitutional law, and all of these in a historical perspective were at the heart of the study of government at the beginning of the twentieth century (Hill 1992, 30). The second part of the twentieth century has been increasingly dominated by a sociological approach ("sociological" used as a generic term encompassing all of the social sciences including economics), within which some scholars sought to map structures and uncover regularities (structural-functionalists), others emphasized the interaction and differences between actors (behavioralists), and yet others pointed to the futility of earlier research by parading "interpretation" as a novelty (postmodernists). However, both structure (statics) and process (dynamics) of governance need to be understood. A juridical perspective draws attention to degrees of standardization and formalization of rules and interaction in society and to the role of government in this. A sociological perspective draws attention to the informal rules and interaction between various actors in and around the public arena. Throughout this book, the juridical and sociological perspectives go hand in hand because, as with the first two elements, each on its own provides only partial insight.

This element is also linked to the first. Public choices regarding the balance between individualist and collectivist alternatives are elaborated into rules with a certain degree of standardization and formalization. How can impersonal codification of rules be mixed with the more personal judgments public officials make? From a legal point of view, impersonal codification serves such important objectives as equality before the law, due process, and fairness. In a legal perspective, no individual or group should expect preferential treatment. The same rules apply to each, irrespective of particular individual circumstances. Fairness in a more sociological perspective strives to serve the objective of equality relative to need and individual characteristics. In this perspective, the public servant should have some amount of discretion to determine whether or not an individual should receive financial support. In this perspective, rules are not rigidly but rather flexibly interpreted. In this perspective, it is clear that tailor-made law that meets the needs of each individual is impossible. By nature, lawmakers must generalize at the level of fairly sizable collectivities (e.g., senior citizens, college students, orphans, unemployed, single mothers, physically and mentally disabled). The challenge here is to balance fairness from a legal and abstract point of view with fairness from a social and concrete standpoint. As it is, citizens expect both from government. Thus, government is caught between a rock and a hard place. Dwight Waldo captures the dilemma thus: "Why would an instrument [bureaucracy] designed to be impersonal and calculating be expected to be effective in delivering sympathy and compassion?" (as quoted in Gawthrop 1997, 210).

As with the first element, juridical and sociological perspectives are better seen as a continuum than as a dichotomy. Social reality is too complex to be framed in terms of dichotomies. Furthermore, there is ample empirical evidence that the judgment as to whether government is impersonal depends upon the level of abstraction at which that judgment is made. At an abstract level (where government is perceived as a bureaucratic monolith), it appears impersonal and neutral, while at the most concrete level (that of the interaction between citizen and public servant), civil servants do come across as compassionate.

Balancing the Concrete and the Abstract: Layers of Meaning and Understanding

The third element highlights the fact that we should acknowledge, at least for analytical purposes, that there are different levels of action, rules, perception, and so on. Referring to Hirschman's observation as that "sentiments for and against government activity wax and wane cyclically in the United States and other countries," Rainey observes (and thus mildly corrects Hirschman) that "Americans often support both positions simultaneously" (Rainey 1997, 6). But how can there be such ambivalence? Can we be for and against government at the same time? Government and its bureaucracy are stereotyped as too big, its public servants as lazy, its functioning as formalistic and so forth, while at the same time its services are appreciated, the attention of public servants in concrete cases of need is appreciated, and the tangible support of government is valued. Indeed, our shifting sentiments are testimony not to ambivalence, fickleness, or bounded rationality, but to the fact that in our attention to and appreciation of government, different levels of perception emerge.

Throughout this book, the reader will find how various authors have conceptualized their understanding of, for instance, the constitution of society, government structure and functioning, public management values, new public management, reform, governance, rules, policy analysis, planning, the politics-administration dichotomy, the perception of government (see above), ethics, and morality, as embedded phenomena. What is most visible is rooted in something deeper, in something that constitutes and legitimates. This is true for governance (i.e., the relation between society and government as expressed in, for instance, concrete policy, legitimated by more abstract political programs and longer-term visions, and ultimately legitimated by the Constitution) as well as for government (i.e., the internal structure and functioning of government: for instance, levels of planning, levels of organization, levels of public management values, and so forth). The embeddedness of social phenomena is expressed in the distinction between a most abstract, an intermediate, and a most concrete level, which will be used throughout this book.

The *most abstract level* provides the foundation upon which, as well as the outer limits within which, we act. This is the constituting level that serves as the foundation for the *intermediate level,* where action is conceptualized as ongoing process. The *most concrete level* is that of day-to-day action. In a variety of literature, it appears that scholars frequently conceptualize reality at three interconnected levels. In this book, some chapters concern a particular level while other chapters demonstrate the "reality" of three levels. Each of these levels on its own contributes to the understanding of government, but considering various characteristics of governance and government as layered phenomena provides a much richer insight. Government is then analyzed as a social system that is composed of subsystems (various organizations, groups, and subunits within these organizations) that are embedded in wider social systems (local community, society) (Parsons 1966; Mouzelis 1967, 149, 153). As Mouzelis argues in reference to Parsons, one cannot be satisfied with merely looking at one level and should strive for micro-macro integration (1967, 119; 1991, 107–108, 158). In a comparison of the various strands of "new institutionalism," it becomes clear that individual action cannot properly be understood without recognizing its embeddedness in institutions and environments, while institutional performance and durability cannot be understood without taking the individual into account (Peters 1999, 2, 26). In terms of this study, we conclude that analyzing the internal structure and functioning of government is valuable but only acquires real meaning when considered as a reflection of a larger societal context.

Balancing Short- and Long-Term Perspectives: Layers of Time

The fourth way that we can look at government is through comparing the present with the past (see section 1.2). There are different ways of looking at

present and past. Developments from the past toward the present can be un-
raveled and reconstructed, thus revealing how the past contributed to the
present. Or we can attempt to understand the present by looking at how it
differs from the past and how it is similar to the past. The last approach is the
one most frequently adopted by policy makers and, indeed, also by teachers
of policy makers (Neustadt and May 1986). Yet another way of understanding the interconnectedness of past and present is through considering time as
a layered phenomenon. The French historian Braudel (1958) refers to the
short-term perspective as the history of events (*histoire événementiel* or *du
temps court:* days, months, a few years: e.g., political events). The history of
events is embedded in middle-range developments (*la conjuncture:* decades,
sometimes centuries: e.g., economic cycles), which in turn are embedded in
long-term developments (*la longue durée:* centuries, millennia: e.g., climatic
change). In a similar fashion, the sociologist Sorokin conceptualizes development over time as a stacking of short upon longer and very long rhythms or
cycles (e.g., Sorokin 1962, 395). In an earlier study, I explored the development of government in the Western world up to the present day (Raadschelders
1998a). In this study, a contemporary outlook on government is presented,
and every now and then (more now than then) we will go back into the past in
order to clarify the present.

If we now look at what defines the public realm, the answer is no longer
simple and clear-cut (Figure 1.1). Our public realm is one in which we seek to
balance, all at the same time,

1. the needs of the individual with those of society (individualism and
   collectivism)
2. impersonal application of rules with a more personal application of
   them (juridical and sociological perspectives)
3. conceptualizations and legitimations of public action at three different levels of abstraction (most abstract, intermediate, most concrete)
4. continuity, diversity, and change (two time-perspectives: past and
   present)

Each of these angles provides valuable insight but, once combined, the complexity of contemporary governance and government emerges. The challenge
of government in society is not designing the proper mix of and division of
labor between public and private activities, but the continuous balancing within
the "quadrant" of desires, perspectives, and levels of understanding and of
time as discussed above.

While Public Administration may have been traditionally thought of as
rather technical and applied, a significant portion of the post–World War II

Figure 1.1 **Perspectives on the Public Realm**

	Individualism		Collectivism	
Juridical perspective				Historical perspective
		Public Realm		
Sociological perspective				Contemporary perspective
	Abstract level	More concrete level	Concrete level	

scholarship has shown more than a token awareness of the context presented in Figure 1.1. Studies such as those by Waldo (1984; a historical-cultural perspective), Marini (1971) and Frederickson (1980) (both on the Minnowbrook perspective), Wamsley et al. (1990) and Wamsley and Wolf (1996) (both on the Blacksburg Manifesto), Dror (2001; a vision for the future of governance), and McSwite (2002; a deep appreciation for public service) are testimony to the need for a more comprehensive understanding of government that is not limited to technocratic issues but includes attention for its foundations and culture and how these, in turn, influence politics, administration, and citizenship.

1.6. The Structure of This Book

The structure of this book follows from the "simple" questions raised in section 2 above: the why, what, how, and who of government's interaction with society. Part I of this book addresses the "why" questions in terms of the general foundations and environmental justification of government's role and position in society. Explaining government's intervention in society through particular environmental events (such as population growth, economic development, etc.) is reserved for the next part. In part I, I begin by arguing that people need governance and thus create a government of sorts and that government, in turn, needs people for its viability. The best way to demonstrate this is through the words of novelists who have advocated total individualism and self-governance (at the one extreme of the spectrum) as well as warned against the dangers of totalitarian government (at the other end of the spectrum) (chapter 2). Western societies and their governments find themselves gravitating toward the middle between these two extremes. Ideologically, the United States is closer to individualism while the social-democratic welfare states of northwestern Europe are closer to collectivism. However, these are differences in degree and they are rather superficial. Digging deeper, both the libertarian and collectivist polities of the Western world balance beautifully between total triumph of individual liberty and total triumph of the collective.

Western countries are successful doing so because the external and internal foundations for government are in near-perfect alignment. The external foundation of Western society and government is nowadays almost solely defined in terms of law, and more specifically in terms of constitutional law. I explore this aspect in chapter 3. If only, however, a constitution and the laws derived from it were enough to guarantee that socially unacceptable individual and collective behavior does not occur! Recognizing that externally imposed legal-rational authority (i.e., accepted power, legitimate government) does not guarantee self-restraint, but merely provides legitimacy to government's retaliation against deviant behavior, Western countries have relied to some extent also upon internalized guidelines such as those provided by religion and ethics. The meaning of religion and ethics for the foundation of governance and government will be explored in chapter 4.

In part I, the "why" of government action is outlined in terms of what constitutes that action at the ideational (institutional) level. That is the basis for a description in broad categories of the services government actually provides for its citizens ("what"). The chapters of part II cannot, of course, address all services in detail, but will address the major areas in which government provides services. The link between the "why" and the "what" is defined in terms of democracy as far as Western countries are concerned. In the name of democracy, Western governments provide fairly traditional collective/public services for the domestic and international preservation of order and safety (justice, the army, police) as well as rather new collective/public services aimed at improving the standard of living of their citizenry (education, health, social security, urban planning, etc.). In chapter 5, I briefly present some theoretical perspectives on democracy and then describe how democracy is organized at the societal level. I then discuss the traditional government tasks of law and justice (chapter 6) and of policy and the army (chapter 7). From our vantage point in time, these are the tasks of a limited government or nightwatch state. The services provided by a less limited or welfare state, such as public education, social security, public health (including environmental policy), and so forth, are explored in chapter 8. While building the welfare state, whether in the United States or in Western Europe, was initially a domestic issue, the ideology of redistributive welfare has spilled over to the entire world since the 1960s. This is why attention to development aid is given in chapter 8.

The expansion of public services both in depth (more detailed policies) and in scope (an ever larger range of policies) has had major impact upon the internal structure and functioning of government. Part III of this book is thus concerned with the organizational actors. In other words, organizational size and structure, procedures for financial and human resource management, and policy- and decision-making processes are expressions of the expanded government to which we have grown accustomed. In chapter 9, I continue the discussion about efficiency and effectiveness in the twentieth century that began in chapter 5. This discussion provides a foundation for the chapters on organization (chapter 10) and the implementation and evaluation of public policy making (chapter 11). These chapters are concerned with how government operates—that is, through organization and policy and decision making as well as through planning, implementation, and evaluation.

In the final analysis, organizations are composed of and policies are decided by people. Part IV deals with the individual actors in the "public" arena: political officeholders and appointees (chapter 12), civil servants (chapter 13), and interest groups (chapter 14). In the representative democracy so characteristic for the Western world, we cannot but think first of the elected and appointed political officials, but almost in the same breath we think of the civil servants who shore up the politicians' ambitions. Politicians and civil servants, though, are two sides of the same coin. After all, at least ideally, if the citizenry is not content with the delivery of, for instance, services provided by politics and administration, it might well revolt. Thus, in all Western governments, societal interest groups and networks have become involved in public policy and decision making, to varying degrees but in all countries to a degree larger than ever before. I therefore explore the role and position of these societal interest networks in the governance and government of society.

The topics of the chapters in parts III and IV are characteristic of the traditional handbook of and introduction to the study of Public Administration. These chapters together with those in parts I and II constitute a modern outlook on the study of Public Administration that emphasizes the interplay between institutional and individual levels of government (Figure 1.2).

In each of the chapters, the perspectives outlined in section 5 above and the metaframework presented in Figure 1.2 help to further identify the challenges that government presently faces. In chapter 15, I review and summarize the arguments made and conclusions drawn in each chapter. The why, what, how, and who of governance and government are then addressed. When outlining challenges, the "where to" of government action is also addressed. The "when," however, will not be discussed in the context of this book. The answer to the "when" question regards the desires and visions for the future, and the steps to realize these should be taken "when the time is right."

One final remark about the structure of this book is in order. As mentioned in the introduction to this chapter, government is bound by culture. This includes both the present state and administrative culture and how it is perceived by the population at large, as well as the historical legacy that helped to shape the present. It is widely recognized that history and culture are important in understanding the structure and functioning of contemporary government, but at the

Figure 1.2 **The Structure of This Book**

Institutions	Ideational level	People need government (ch. 2)	Legal constitution of society (ch. 3)		Moral and ethical constitution of society (ch. 4)
	Societal level	Democracy (ch. 5)	Justice and social justice (ch. 6)	Traditional services (ch. 7)	Welfare services (ch. 8)
Actors	Organization level	Efficiency (ch. 9)	Decision making, organizational structures and cultures (ch. 10)		Policy making (ch. 11)
	Individual level	Political actors (ch. 12)	Bureaucratic actors (ch. 13)		Citizen actors (ch. 14)

same time that message is dispersed. The theme that connects all the chapters in this book is the historical and cultural traditions that can become clear only in a comparative perspective. Inevitably, in various chapters I have to discuss the nuts and bolts (i.e., present knowledge) of the structure and functioning of government and of the relations between government and society (which is the subject matter of mainstream Public Administration), but I consistently apply a historical and cultural lens that provides understanding of the similarities and differences between state and administrative traditions.

Each chapter will open with one or more quotations to set the tone. The quotations for which there is no reference in the bibliography are taken from the *Oxford Library of Words and Phrases, Part I, Quotations* (1990).

1.7. The Audience for This Book

The primary audience for this book is graduate students in Public Administration and political science who are trained in a variety of subfields and approaches but are not necessarily exposed to ideas about the embeddedness of knowledge about government nor necessarily familiar with relevant contributions in other academic studies and disciplines. "Government" is taught, but knowledge about it is organized and compartmentalized across a variety of approaches within Public Administration (i.e., traditional public administration, public policy, public management) as well as a variety of subfields within Public Administration and across various disciplines. This book is an attempt to provide a holistic perspective on government and thus present graduate students with a generalist outlook on government in addition to the specialist pre-entry training they already receive.

This book is not a standard introduction to the study of (an aspect of) Public Administration. Excellent textbooks are available in the market (see section 4 above) and these do not need to be duplicated. Public Administration is focused on developing particular skills and specializations. Lengthy handbooks and introductions to Public Administration are comprehensive with regard to mainstream Public Administration. What is needed is a comprehensive book on government that is brief, useful for both pre- and post-entry education, and aims to develop generalist rather than specialist qualities. This book is therefore also useful to graduate students in other disciplines (economics, business administration, organizational sociology, social psychology, etc.) who are required or choose to develop a basic understanding of government. There are yet other audiences that could benefit from this book.

Would this study be useful to entrepreneurs in the private sector and to public managers? As Rainey reports, reviewers of the first edition of his *Understanding and Managing Public Organizations* indicated that his book was too detailed on research and theory to be attractive to managers and leaders. Rainey's response in the second edition of his book is worthwhile quoting: "This assumption underestimates many practicing leaders and managers . . . [An academic book can] provide a reference for busy managers who want a review of basic topics in the field, who might find a conceptual framework useful, or who might value the book in other ways" (1997, xvi–xvii).

The public manager may find this book useful especially in the explicit linking of motives and objectives of governing (parts I and II) to the consequences of public service delivery for the internal structure and functioning of government (parts III and IV). This book meets the needs of practitioners and managers for a generalist perspective next to the specializations they developed during their college years and early careers.

Democracy is also served by informed and involved citizens. Much of the literature in the various disciplines that study government has been focused on a particular issue and on a particular audience, such as students, scholars, or practitioners. Scholars have a duty to inform the public at large and the citizen who is interested in understanding government. Some of these citizens are reached through teachings in classrooms, some are reached through columns in newspapers and television appearances, but the majority can be reached through publications that are informative, enticing, and accessible. Citizens continue to perceive a gap between themselves and government. Popular stereotypes about the public realm include, for instance, references to the arrogance and distance of political officeholders and civil servants but also to the indifference and laziness of citizens. We should ask ourselves what academia has done to reach the public at large and help develop a critical understanding of government.

Perhaps it is too much to assume that this book can attract different audiences. And yet I believe that this book provides an approach to governing that challenges various types of readers to develop an informed opinion about the role and position of government in society for the sake of a more civil society (Raadschelders 2002a). It is a book that requires time for digestion. It does not provide ready-made answers to complex questions. Certainly in the public realm the solutions to complex societal problems are politically charged and will therefore vary. This book also does not provide detailed information about, for instance, the organizational structures, the budgeting or human resource management procedures, the managerial techniques, the leadership styles, the implementation instruments, and so forth, of specific political and administrative organizations and institutions. There is ample literature that provides such detail. The references in the various chapters will enable anyone who desires to pursue further in-depth study to locate relevant and more detailed publications. This book provides information on these traditional topics of Public Administration but only in a fairly general manner. What makes the book attractive to a wide readership is the comparative perspective through which we can see the degree to which governance and government in the United States are unique and the degree to which they are comparable to those in other Western countries. The comparative perspective invites the reader to step out of the American context.

This book is thus reflective rather than technocratic in its approach to government. The skills of the specialist are important to government and citizens. Government needs people who have knowledge of the budgeting process, personnel policy, environmental science, road construction, planning and zoning, and so forth. But government also needs people who can transcend disciplinary and ideological boundaries, who reflect upon the role and position of government, who have the courage to ask themselves why they made a particular choice, and who can explain that choice to any relevant group. This book provides neither a philosophy of government nor a detailed and technocratic discussion of public administration and its study. Rather, its objective is to fill the gap between the more theoretical philosophy of government (political theory, etc.) and the more applied Public Administration literature (specialized, focused on techniques and instruments). Perhaps this is an impossible goal, but the twenty-first century requires that public servants be technocrats as well as reflective practitioners.

Note

1. Only in this chapter will I follow Waldo's distinction between the study (in capital letters: Public Administration) and the field (in lower case: of public administration, i.e., government). In the remainder of the book I will use the word "government" when I speak about the field and use lower case when referring to the study of public administration.

PART I

WHY GOVERNMENT? THE IDEATIONAL (INSTITUTIONAL) LEVEL

The study of government starts with questions about the relation between population and ruling elites and about whom government is supposed to serve. By way of generalization, one could say that for most of history governments were run by elites and thus served the ruling elites. The population was merely subject and had little or no say in the structure and functioning of government. Bureaucracies served a monarch, a dynasty, and/or the various elites (military, clergy). Much has changed in the last 300 to 400 years. Governments have come to serve the citizen rather than a monarch or a state, and (political) theory pushed the dignity of the individual to the point at which all adults have at least the right to vote. We may argue about the degree to which there is a gap between democratic theory (individuals are citizens, not subjects) and ruling practice (king-philosopher notions about governance), but all Western democracies share this idea that government is the servant of the people. It is therefore fitting to start this part of the book with the people who discuss not whether to have government, but rather what kind of government they desire. Thus, in chapter 2, I discuss views of government as seen through the eyes of novelists. This is a useful approach since novelists command the art of expressing our deepest fears and desires.

The people are, at least in theory, the constitution of society and government. What makes contemporary Western democracies unique is that the people at large are the first in history who have a right to choose government and even to choose an entirely different government (as in the case of revolution). The basic choice is between a small, law-and-order government or a more interventionist, social activist government. Whichever is preferred, the choice of a particular type of government is rooted in the laws that government enforces and in the moral values that society holds. Both the legal and the moral constitution of society and government is a reflection of the people. My conception of constitution includes a legal and social perspective, but not as encompassing as, for instance, Giddens's *The Constitution of Society* (1989). He provides a social theory that includes issues relevant to Western society at large and thus deals with the nature of human action and people's relation to institutions. The book before you is more limited in scope, dealing only with human beings in their role as citizens in relation to societies' public institutions.

2 CITIZENS AND THEIR GOVERNMENT: WHO NEEDS WHOM?

The State exists for the sake of Society, not Society for the sake of the State.
—Woodrow Wilson, 1892

Ask not what your country can do for you, ask what you can do
for your country.
—from the funeral oration for John Greenleaf Whittier, 1807–1892;
also Lyle Boren, 1938; also John F. Kennedy, 1961

The novelist and the poet reflect the principal preoccupations of people
and their times.
—Edward T. Hall, 1983

Government is one of the most important institutions of contemporary Western society, yet it is among the least understood. There may be numerous reasons for this, but all of them essentially boil down to one: its size. Government in Western countries is bigger and provides a wider range and variety of public services than any other government in history. As a consequence, contemporary government employs more people in a highly differentiated set of organizations, raises more revenue, and requires much higher expenditures. This raises an important issue. Government does more for citizens than ever before, but that does not mean that they are necessarily more content with it than citizens in prior ages. Citizens do not tend to look at the past and therefore do not judge their own government in comparison to preceding governments. Rather, government is judged on the basis of its performance. At this point, two important questions arise. When is performance good or bad? Who determines when performance is good or bad? Good or bad performance is, for instance, determined in terms of the size of government. Government is too small or too big, should increase or cut budgets, should upsize or downsize. When is government too small or too big and who determines that? No matter what the answer, government is necessary. People need governments as much as governments need them.

In this light, the often quoted "Ask not what your country can do for you . . ." is a little one-sided and should at least be complemented with "Ask not what you can do for your government, but what your government can do for you." The reason for this is simply that in democracy both citizens and government have rights and duties. And, of course, citizens in their role as taxpayers can and should make demands upon government. In this chapter, I focus on the relationship between citizens and government (sections 2.1 and 2.2) and, more specifically, on what the role and position of government in society ought to be (section 2.3). It is on the basis of that actual relationship and the desired role and position of government in society that the concept of government is defined (section 2.4). There is, of course, no clear-cut answer to the question about the desired role and position of government because it all depends on where you are.

2.1. Do People Need Government?

Government is one of the oldest institutions in society and hence those working for it occupy one of the oldest "professions" in society. Even the oldest societies, the tribal hunter-gatherer groups, must have had some type of government. Most likely they had a chief, a shaman or priest, and a council of elders. Sometimes the same person would occupy the offices of chief and of shaman; in other cases these positions were clearly demarcated. But in whatever manner organized, and whatever positions existed, there was a government. Without it a *collection of individuals* could not ultimately survive interpersonal conflict. Without it a *community of people* would not be able to achieve goals regarded as crucial to the support of the entire group and not just to some individuals. A collection of individuals and a community of people create a *government of citizens* out of necessity. A government of citizens can act as mediator between conflicting individuals and groups in society. A government of citizens can also allocate scarce resources among the people in a community according to need. Government needs to cater both to individuals and to communities. Sometimes citizens emphasize and exercise their individual rights rather than their collective duties. In such cases they are guided by what differentiates them from their neighbors. At other times citizens emphasize their interests as a community, guided by a sense of togetherness. And, again, it is government that has to cater to both the individual needs and the community needs. This constant balancing of government between individual and collective needs is not always understood by citizens.

If people need government, how do they make it? Is it a conscious effort or rather a process of trial and error? What kind of government do people choose? Why would some types of government be preferred to others? Why is it so difficult to achieve a consensus about the type of government that suits us best? The choices made, and how these choices are motivated, can be placed on a continuum in which one side represents the triumph of the collective and the other side the triumph of the individual. In great world literature, both sides are explored in the condensed art of the novelist. The most extreme end of collectivism is well illustrated in Huxley's *Brave New World* and in Orwell's *1984*. In the brave new world, the individual is totally controlled by society, and the conditioning necessary to achieve such ultimate control starts at conception and is continued through life by means of communal love sessions and drugs. The brave new world is run by ten World Controllers, and its civilization is grounded in machinery, medicine, and happiness as organized by mankind rather than grounded in religion and God. Mustapha Mond, the World Controller for Western Europe, argues that in earlier days social instability was a constant threat to civilization. Nobility and heroism

> are symptoms of political inefficiency. In a properly organized society like ours, nobody has any opportunities for being noble or heroic. Conditions have got to be thoroughly unstable before the occasion can arise. Where there are wars, there are divided allegiances, where there are temptations to be resisted, objects of love to be fought for or defended—there, obviously, nobility and heroism have some sense. But there aren't any wars nowadays. The greatest care is taken to prevent you from loving anyone too much. There's no such thing as a divided allegiance; you're so conditioned that you can't help doing what you ought to do. (Huxley 1996, 198)

Huxley's world is truly a universal civilization in which the individual's place in society is determined from conception. It is a world with global governance, with one highly centralized government, in which the clash of civilizations (in terms of race, gender, culture, and so forth) has been eradicated. Orwell's world is not as "advanced" as Huxley's for it is dominated by three superpowers that are constantly at war. The one where Winston Smith works, Airstrip One (i.e., England) in Oceania, controls individuals through manipulated information and through communal hate sessions, drugs, and—if necessary—torture. Both Huxley and Orwell suggest that internalization of the denial of individuality is best guaranteed when love, a very powerful emotion, is directed not at other individuals (at least not beyond the sexual encounter) but at the state in its individualized image: "Big Brother is the guise in which the Party chooses to exhibit itself to the world. His function is to act as a focusing point for love, fear, and reverence, emotions which are more easily felt toward an individual than toward an organization" (Orwell 1961, 171). These novelists conceptualize collectiveness in terms of the totalitarianism that they witnessed emerging in Russia and Germany during the interbellum and in China after World War II. At the same time, their novels send a warning about "scientification" and industrialization in society carried to the point at which passion and religion no longer determine our values. Obviously, this is not the kind of collectivism fitting a democracy.

A more positive outlook on government at the collective end of the spectrum is provided by the so-called social protest or proletarian writers. From the turn of the last century onward and on both sides of the Atlantic, writers advanced the notion that a reformed government could well serve as the champion of social legislation and thus eradicate the many evils (hunger, poverty, usury, disease, etc.) of industrial and urbanized society. McCurdy even argues that authors such as Mark Twain, Emile Zola, and many others thus "helped to lay the groundwork for the modern administrative state" (1987, 550). In Western Europe, from the late nineteenth century on, collectivism has been expressed in the development of a welfare state for which government took the initiative upon the requests of citizens, professional associations, and labor unions. National and subnational governments together came to provide collective services in the area of social welfare hitherto left to private institutions (e.g., the church) and individual initiative. Where governments did not provide collective services themselves, they increasingly served as a mediator between various conflicting interests in society. At present, the states and their governments in Western Europe are very much the central binding force in society. Government is considered the main provider of a minimum standard of living. It is also government that is expected to protect the rights of the mentally and physically disabled, children, senior citizens, and the unemployed. In Europe, government is the people's champion. This is an interventionist government, providing detailed frameworks for the interaction between individuals, between individuals and private organizations, between individuals and private organizations on the one hand and government on the other, and so forth. It is a government of the welfare state and of the planned economy, both to varying degrees.

A welfare state developed in the United States as well, but following the Jeffersonian conception of the relation between government and society, the idea of self-governance remained a much more influential strand in American political thought than in Western Europe. The people's capacity for self-governance has been beautifully captured by John Steinbeck in *The Grapes of Wrath:*

> as the dark caught them, they clustered like bugs near to shelter and to water. And because they were lonely and perplexed, because they had all come from a place of sadness and worry and defeat, and because they were all going to a new mysterious place, they huddled together; they talked together; they shared their lives, their food. . . . At first the families were timid in the building and tumbling of

worlds, but gradually the technique of building worlds became their technique. Then leaders emerged, then laws were made, then codes came into being. And as the worlds moved westward they were more complete and better furnished, for their builders were more experienced building them. . . . The families learned what rights must be observed—the right of privacy in the tent; . . . the right to talk and listen. . . . And the families learned, although no one told them, what rights are monstrous and must be destroyed; the right to intrude upon privacy, the right to be noisy while the camp slept, the rights of seduction or rape, the right of adultery and theft and murder. . . . And as the worlds moved westward, rules became laws, although no one told the families. It is unlawful to foul water near the camp; it is unlawful in any way to foul the drinking water; it is unlawful to eat good rich food near one who is hungry, unless he is asked to share. And with the laws, the punishments—and there were only two—a quick and murderous fight or ostracism; and ostracism was the worst. For if one broke the laws his name and face went with him, and he had no place in any world, no matter where created. (1957, 198–201)

Wherever people live together in a group, they sit down together and make rules. They do so because of something that happened that day, or earlier, that they would rather have prevented. They want to encourage certain behavior and discourage other behavior. They desire to determine what behavior is detrimental to the society as a whole thereby demarcating public and private. Behavior that threatens the stability of the society as a whole is punished.

John Steinbeck is one of the champions of the so-called proletarian school in American literature. He places special importance on a government that protects a community of people. Indeed, his basic social units are families who establish self-governance when living in the ad hoc tent camps that mushroomed along the roads from Arkansas and Oklahoma to California in the days of the dust bowl. The individual is part of a larger group, the smallest unit of which is the family. In Steinbeck's perspective, both individual misbehavior and collective needs make people act as a community and thus organize governance. Where Steinbeck is illustrative of a style of self-governance that is rooted in the community rather than in the individual, other writers conceptualize self-governance in terms of absolute individualism. In such an individualist society, individuals do not need government, other than for providing the most basic services. The next quotation comes from one of the most forceful advocates of this position.

The only proper purpose of government is to protect man's rights, which means: to protect him from physical violence. A proper government is only a policeman, acting as an agent of man's self-defense, and as such, may resort to force *only* against those who *start* the use of force. The only proper functions of government are: the police, to protect you from criminals; the army, to protect you from foreign invaders; and the courts, to protect your property and contracts from breach or fraud by others, to settle disputes by rational rules, according to *objective* law. (Rand 1957, 1054)

Ayn Rand was a Russian citizen who emigrated in 1926 to the United States. She authored several books, novels as well as philosophical works, all passionately advocating individualism. In *Atlas Shrugged,* gifted individuals and entrepreneurs, such as Hank Reardon and John Galt, confront the establishment and ultimately bring it down. In *The Fountainhead,* the architect Howard Roarke follows his own interpretation of beauty rather than that of the masses. Ayn Rand's perspective was inspired by her youthful experiences in communist Russia. The quotation above is followed by her definition of what a perverted government is:

> But a government that *initiates* the employment of force against men who had forced no one, the employment of armed compulsion against disarmed victims, is a nightmare infernal machine designed to annihilate morality; such a government reverses its only moral purpose and switches from the role of protector to the role of a criminal vested with the right to the wielding of violence against victims deprived of the right of self-defense. Such a government substitutes for morality the following rule of social conduct; you may do whatever you please to your neighbor, provided your gang is bigger than his. (Rand 1957, 1054)

Rand's definition of perverted government, cast in strong words, describes not only the totalitarianism of her day and age, but also the government of much of history as well as the type of government foreseen by Huxley and Orwell. She is probably the strongest defender of individualism, and thus she places special importance on a government that protects society as a collection of individuals. The basic social unit is the individual. Nothing else matters. In fact, if everybody lived up to her or his fullest potential, then government would not be needed to support people in any other way but through the maintenance of public order and safety and the defense of the territory. When she argues that "the protection of individual rights is the only proper purpose of government" (Rand 1964, 110), she means that government is definitely not responsible for the redistribution of scarce resources in order to promote the welfare of the less advantaged in society. In this perspective, support for those who are unable to provide for themselves is probably left to caring individuals and private associations such as the church. In this perspective, government is the individual's champion. In Rand's words:

> The source of the government's authority is "the consent of the governed." This means that the government is not the *ruler,* but the servant or *agent* of the citizens; it means that the government as such has no rights except the rights *delegated* to it by the citizens for a specific purpose. (1964, 110)

This is a restrained government, withdrawn into the core functions and services that neither a collection of individuals nor a small community of people can provide. It is a government of the nightwatch state and the free market economy. It is a government that intervenes only when asked to. Rand's observations about individualism, the role of government and what perverts government, are not unique to the twentieth century alone.

As far as individualism is concerned, it is startling to see how much Ayn Rand's philosophy is an echo of Nietzsche's philosophy of strength and reliance on self-development and on the belief in the superior individual: "My opinion is *my* opinion: another person has not easily a right to it" (Nietzsche 1980, 295). According to her biographer, Rand rejected Nietzsche's ultimate consequence that a superior man (*Übermensch*) could use force against another person (Branden 1986, 45, 114–115). With respect to government, Nietzsche was equally clear: "And how could there be a 'common good'! The expression contradicts itself; that which can be common is always of small value" (Nietzsche 1980, 296). Nietzsche was alarmed and distressed by the decline of individuality and free expression in the machine age. The warning against loss of individualism was not one of the last hundred years. The sentiment of Thomas Jefferson and that of many after him was that the best government is one that governs least. Jean-Jacques Rousseau argued that the law protects the powerful and destroys natural freedom. Herbert Spencer envisioned only a nightwatch state as a role for government. Ralph Waldo Emerson believed firmly in the self-reliance of the frontier man. Walt Whitman believed that the most important function of government was preparing mankind for the time that they would rule themselves. In the second half of the twentieth century, the political theorist Vincent Ostrom embraced the idea of self-government more or less along the same lines (Ostrom 1987).

The novelists agree about one thing: government provides a degree of order and stability in society. The question is, of course, to what degree order and stability have to be organized through government. Naturally there are other institutions that also provide order and stability in society, such as the family, the church, voluntary associations (sports clubs, senior citizens' groups, service organizations, etc.), but also marriage, friendship, and shared values. When the question of whether people need government is raised, a universal answer is not possible. Instead, we should ask: which people need government and when and under what circumstances do they need it? Americans are likely to respond to this question in a different manner than the French or the Swedes. In a world with ever increasing international cooperation and with globalizing economies that also enhance our sensitivity to cultural differences, a comparative cross-national perspective is no luxury for it shows that the answer is dependent upon national traditions and administrative cultures. A comparative cross-time perspective is no luxury either. We can quote Paine, O'Sullivan, and Thoreau ("most order is not the effect of government," "the best government is that which governs least"), but we must not take their opinions out of context. Paine wrote at the time of the Atlantic Revolutions, the end of centuries of rule in which European countries were rarely focused on the needs of the people. American novelists and poets of the nineteenth century wrote during a time when government was very small and when one could not but rely upon individual initiative for meeting collective needs. Nowadays, on both sides of the Atlantic, much of the order and stability of society is to varying extent a consequence of government's intervention through formal and informal ways.

In addition to asking which people need government when, we should also ask what type of order they desire. Is an informal order preferred, handed down from generation to generation, internalized through socialization, and reliant upon self-governance, or an order that is more or less formalized, where rules are codified to some degree and more reliant upon government? To what degree should the rules that are intended to safeguard order and stability in society be left to self-governance and to what degree should they be developed and monitored by government? Perhaps, deep down, people need government because they need the predictability that it provides; they need people to step forward and assume leadership; they need something that helps them to protect their society and community against threats that go beyond their individual ability to counter. Indeed, self-government is certainly an option for *specific purpose local governments* (e.g., school boards and fire districts in the United States, water boards in the Netherlands). There are, however, not many *general purpose local governments* (e.g., municipalities) that would be able to operate on the basis of self-government since what affects their constituency is often beyond their control (economic crisis, natural disasters, crime, etc.). And those that do are small in terms of the territory governed (the small states).

What government is like in the Western world differs from country to country, but fortunately it is not the government that Aldous Huxley, George Orwell, John Steinbeck, or Ayn Rand envisaged. Rather, government represents a mix of both extremes. What is more, government sometimes leans toward Steinbeck's ideal and at other times toward Rand's ideal. But whichever direction, it is somehow closer to the middle of the continuum than to either extreme of collectivism or individualism.

2.2. Does Government Need People?

The answer is very simple. Whether government plays a restrained or interventionist role in society, government needs people. The first, and most important reason, is that people legitimate the existence of government.

While this is true to some extent for all types of government, it is most true for representative democracy. Representative democracy requires the voluntary support of all its citizens. The citizenry is the largest possible clientele a government can have, and thus the challenge to meet its varying needs is greatest in the government of representative democracy. When under a single ruler (dictatorship) or a government by a few (aristocracy, oligarchy), the group of people considered relevant to government's legitimacy is smaller than the entire population. However, these types of government, too, need the support of some people. A ruler or governing elite that has lost all support will quickly go out of business. And from prehistoric times to the present, people have replaced those who abused power, and individuals have defended the right to do so in treatises of political theory. As soon as we believe that those in power no longer represent our interests, they are considered illegitimate.

Government also needs people as a human resource in at least three different ways. First, government needs individuals who are willing to take up political responsibility. In contemporary government, these officeholders are elected as our representatives. Through election they are not only invested with the authority to meet the responsibilities of office, they can also be held accountable for what they do. *Political officeholders* or *politicians* usually occupy the top positions in any government organization. Government also needs individuals who seek employment in the public sector, whether for reasons of job security (a good reason in the past), or as a call to public duty (always a good reason), or for sheer interest (an equally commendable reason), or out of habit (family tradition). Our type of government requires *civil servants*. Government nowadays employs individuals in a great variety of capacities. Government hires medical doctors, social workers, street repair people, psychologists, plumbers, nurses, carpenters, and so on, in a wide range of positions, with a wide range of skills and experiences required. However, neither politicians nor civil servants would be able to achieve much on their own. Government needs *citizens* as well, not just for legitimation, but for actual consultation and participation in the decision making about public policy and for the production of public services. Government needs volunteers in the school boards and in the many other types of (voluntary) associations that exist in society and serve a collective purpose. Without the voluntary input of citizens, a variety of services that we regard essential for our society and community would not be available. Genuine concerns with civic duty, civil society, and dwindling citizen participation on the one hand, and theorizing about coproduction, public-private partnership, referenda, and so forth, on the other hand, indicate that government needs citizens for more than abstract legitimation.

2.3. What Type of Government Do Citizens Want?

Throughout most of history, government was an instrument in the hands of the few, the wealthy, the well-bred, and the well-connected. It is only recently that government has become more responsive to the needs of entire populations. While it may not always cater to our individual needs, it does somehow manage to meet collective needs. Would it be too much to suggest that if citizens are truly and fundamentally discontent with government they would dispense with it? Indeed, when citizens display discontent with government, they usually do so in stereotypical and generalized manners. Government is too big (as compared to what?), civil servants are lazy (as compared to whom?), there is too much red tape in bureaucracy (are Microsoft, IBM, and Boeing not bureaucracies?), there is too much formalism in government (as compared to where else?), government costs too much (who else would pay?), government could be much more efficient (than, say, any private business going bankrupt?), etc. Stereotypes and misconceptions are difficult to disregard, but there is a difference between general opinion and personal experience. Judged by general opinion, citizens apparently are discontent; in terms of personal experience, though, they must be quite content indeed.

Given that human beings are political animals, as Aristotle argued, the issue is not whether to have government but to determine what type of government citizens want (Mansfield 1993, 133). The answer depends on where one stands. The choice between an interventionist or a restrained government varies from individual to individual, a variation explained by role and position occupied in society, educational background, career development and experiences, character, degree of dependence upon others (e.g., children, senior citizens, the physically and mentally disabled). Any discussion about an interventionist or a restrained government is far too general, because it does not relate to the real world where government is both interventionist in some areas and at the same time restrained in other areas. A discussion about the role and position of government in society would look at what is wanted from government and what is not. However, is it possible to set up such an enumerative list of tasks, a division of labor between government, individuals, and people? It would probably take much negotiation to little avail.

The most sensible discussion, therefore, is likely to be one about the functions of the state. Should the state limit itself to the bare necessities of public order and safety services (Ayn Rand's option)? To what extent should government assume social welfare responsibilities (somewhere between the limited welfare state of the United States and the extended ones of Western Europe, but avoiding Huxley's and Orwell's total government)? To what extent should government rely upon the people's capacity for self-governance (Steinbeck's angle)? Assuming that total agreement about that choice cannot be achieved, citizens can start negotiating what belongs to the public sector and what does not. Most will agree that the army, foreign relations, the police, and justice should be in the public sector, but even parts of these tasks and services are considered for some degree of privatization. What about welfare tasks? Would a government creating some minimum standard of living for all not also create conditions contributory to the maintenance of public order and safety, such as accessible and affordable (public) education and health care? Would social welfare arrangements of some kind enhance the legitimacy of government action?

Individuals may know what type of government they want, and they may substantiate their arguments eloquently. Individuals may, secretly, be pleased that collective needs are met, without too much direct involvement by themselves. People are probably only able to say that they prefer democracy to dictatorship. Citizens will vote about the division of labor between individual, community, and government responsibility. Citizens also know that such division of labor is not for all time.

At the most general level possible, governments can serve and have served three basic functions. First, they may operate as mediators between society/community and the divine/supernatural. This function is still important to countries where the government is closely linked to a religious order (e.g., Nepal and the Vatican). In most Western countries, that mediating function has passed solely into the hands of churches and other religious organizations. The second function of government is to regulate the interaction between individuals, between individuals and institutions/organizations, and between institutions and organizations. Willingly or reluctantly, government has slowly taken over tasks in this area. It usually does so willingly if it derives material gain, such as in the regulation of the exchange of goods (an interaction) between private individuals (as producer or as consumer), an activity for which government could levy taxes from both parties. The judiciary, too, is nothing but an institution that regulates interactions of various natures. Government is usually more reluctant if there is less material gain, such as in the regulation of the housing and health care markets. A third role of government concerns the distribution of proceeds. This is an old function. We know there were granaries in ancient Egypt, in the Hebrew kingdoms of the seventh century B.C.E., and in ancient Rome, ready to be used in times of famine and disappointing harvest. Nowadays we have elaborate mechanisms of redistributing wealth, both among the communities in our own countries and among communities of different countries (for instance, development aid).

2.4. Definitions of Government from the Juridical and Sociological Angles

A proper, unambiguous, and objective definition of government is not possible since such a definition needs to express the desired relation between government and the individuals and peoples it seeks to serve in a particular time and place. Aldous Huxley, George Orwell, John Steinbeck, and Ayn Rand had important and legitimate reasons to be concerned about the balance between the individual, the people, the citizens, and their government. Their personal experiences made them define a particular choice, and none of the choices are right or wrong, but they cannot dissociate their personal experience from what they believe government should be. And why would we expect them to do so? We all have an opinion of what government should be just as much as we all have an opinion about what it now is.

Some kind of definition is possible when we focus on what makes government (and thus, public organizations) different from other organizations in society. The only reason that "government" needs to be defined is for the purpose of analysis. Scholars are able to analyze only when they have identified and defined the object of their interest so it is clearly demarcated from other more or less comparable phenomena. But in doing so they may have to be content with less than what was wanted: "it is better to be vague than nonrelevantly precise" (Easton and Easton 1969).

For a long time, the definition of government has been dominated by a presumed distinction between politics and administration. In 1887 Woodrow Wilson defined *administration* as the most obvious part of *government,* as government in action, and as the executive (Wilson 1992, 7). Four decades later, Luther Gulick, one of Franklin Roosevelt's advisers, had the same distinction in mind when he defined public administration in terms of principles of organization and management: "Public administration is that part of the science of administration which has to do with government, and thus concerns itself primarily with the executive branch. Public administration is thus a division of political science" (Gulick 1967, 3). And even though disagreement and uneasiness about the distinction between politics and administration increased during the twentieth century, and the managerial approach to administration was increasingly considered proverbial, it seemed difficult to go beyond that managerial and technocratic perspective. Thus, Frederick Mosher in a contribution to the *Encyclopaedia Britannica* in 1974: "Public Administration, traditionally defined, comprises those activities involved in carrying out the policies and programs of governments . . . public administration focuses principally on the planning, organizing, directing, coordinating, and controlling of government operations" (reprinted in 1982a, 4). This distinction between politics and administration was first made in Europe and elaborated upon in the United States. The French scholar C.J. Bonnin in 1812 believed that "administration" was separate from "state" and from "government." In the middle of the nineteenth century, Bonnin's countryman C.-J. Vivien defined the political and the administrative as two branches within the executive (Martin 1987, 298). Deep in the twentieth century, an English scholar reasoned that the "political process deals with the input of demands and the administrative process with the output of services" (Self 1979, 5). A German professor defined the function of politics as legislative and that of administration as executive (Mayntz 1978, 43).

In the past two decades, politics and administration have been presented less in terms of a dichotomy and more as if they are two sides of the same coin. For Garvey, public administration and politics are more or less synonymous, although he does provide a qualifying distinction between politics and administration: "Public administration is politics—not the 'obvious politics' of high-stakes electioneering and policy making, but the 'other politics' of small-scale, behind-the-scenes problem solving" (1997, 9). If politics and administration are two sides of the same coin, what is it that unites them? For one, it is the concept of *government.* Government, we believe, has a political as well as an administrative function, and these two are not as easy to separate as definitions appear to suggest. We could define "politics" in terms of its formal function of legislation and in terms of its incumbents, the politicians. In the same vein, we could define "administration" in terms of its formal function of execution, and in terms of its incumbents, the civil servants. The dominant perspective in this type of definition is legalist and juridical, emphasizing formal roles and positions. Indeed, the distinction between politics and administration as made in Europe and the United States was legalist. If we move to a more sociological perspective, though, these legalist definitions are shaky at the least. The literature is full of examples of civil servants exercising power, of politicians following procedures, and yes, of politicians becoming civil servants and vice versa. From a sociological perspective, it is not the formal roles and positions of individuals and organizations within government that are central to the definition of it; it is the objectives of government that define what it is. While we may argue about the practicalities and the concrete choices to be made, probably few would disagree with the following definition: "The study of government is thus the study of the 'elements' in society that jointly (in conjunction but also more than occasionally in opposition) produce [an] 'authoritative allocation of values' " (Blondel 1990, 8).

Blondel does not distinguish between politics and administration. What substantively unites them is not that they are simply two sides of the same coin, but that they both are involved in the "authoritative allocation of values." Policies are not developed and decisions are not made only on the basis of the values of those politicians and civil servants directly involved. Indeed, we like to think that societal values are taken into account. We like to believe that values shared by the population are taken into account. That is what is suggested in Denhardt's definition of public administration: "public administration is concerned with managing change processes in pursuit of publicly defined societal values" (Denhardt 1984, 17). In this definition, "politics" is the realm where societal values are publicly defined, while public administration manages the implementation of these values in policies. In David Easton's original and often repeated quotation, the "authoritative allocation of values" was the definition of politics only. Given the interpenetration and interdependency of politics and administration, I would argue that the authoritative allocation of values occurs in both. Government is both politics and administration, and as such, it is deeply involved in the selection and realization of publicly defined societal values and policies. The concept of values in relation to Easton's definition will be discussed further in the next chapter.

2.5. Concluding Remarks

In this chapter, I explored the various ways in which people express their need for government. This was done, first, by presenting novelists' perspectives on various options in the collectivist and individualist continuum. What makes the use of novelists attractive is that in their invented societies they present us with "extreme" cases of collectivism and individualism. Thus, they are able to present a much clearer picture of what potential course existing societies may take. Second, the people's need for government is also expressed in the fact that as citizens, they are part of government on the basis of election, appointment, and voluntary involvement. However, no matter the degree to which society and its people feel that they are part of the institutional arrangements for government, there will not be a consensus about the type of government that citizens want. Thus, we briefly discussed more interventionist versus more limited government options. Finally, definitions of government and public administration were explored in terms of their juridical and sociological content. This last theme will be further explored in the next two chapters.

3 THE LEGAL CONSTITUTION OF SOCIETY AND GOVERNMENT

This country, with its institutions, belongs to the people who inhabit it. Whenever they shall grow weary of the existing government, they can exercise their constitutional right of amending it, or their revolutionary right to dismember or overthrow it.
—Abraham Lincoln, inaugural address, 1861

What is valued by family and friends, by the society and its government to which we belong, and ultimately by mankind, is protected by means of written law and unwritten custom. The things people most value, the values truly shared, are the foundation upon which society rests and which the individual and the institutions are expected to respect. Individual and institutional actors are considered legitimate as long as they act within the boundaries of law and custom. Actors who violate these shared values are subject to sanctions proportionate to the violation. The ultimate sanction for the individual is ostracism, for in many ancient, early modern, and contemporary societies the expulsion of the individual from society, which involved loss of all property and loss of all contact with spouse, children, extended family, and so forth, was considered far worse than capital punishment. The ultimate sanction for the institution is the overthrow of those who govern abusively.

In contemporary society and government, law plays a central role. It is through law that the boundaries are set for almost any type of interaction in the public as well as in the private sector: the transfer of products from producers to consumers, the transfer of property between equal parties or from the deceased to the living, the transfer of anything that is regarded valuable—whether it is material or intangible—but also the joining of property, the joining into marriage, the redistribution of wealth and the sharing of surplus, and so forth. There is more. Not only are laws and regulations created about what is considered valuable for all, but laws and regulations for what is regarded as valuable to specific groups also exist. The balancing required of government between individual and collective needs is certainly visible in the law. This concept, the law, refers to a body of legal regulations of varying status. Our society, as any Western society, is bound to thousands and thousands of laws, all securing that both our individual as well as our collective interests are met. The law is an institution and what it means to society can be and is appreciated differently.

In the first section of this chapter, I briefly explore these differences and conceptualize law as solidified or codified values. This helps in understanding that famous phrase: "the authoritative allocation of values." In section 3.2, the legal foundations of society and government are discussed by looking more closely at the juridical and sociological interpretation of "constitution" and how this translates into a particular understanding of authority. Law and authority are not static by nature. Indeed, one of the major features of our time is that law is artificially created and thus subject to change and that authority can rest only in the willingness to compromise. Thus in a juridical sense, we very much operate on the basis of legal-rational authority, while in a sociological sense we expect *negotiable authority*. This concept is defined in section 3.3 and is very important for the justification of resistance against government (section 3.4). Abraham Lincoln's remark in his inaugural speech is concerned with the ultimate consequence of negotiable authority.

3.1.   The Meaning of Value and of Authority

When did the human race start to think in terms of values? Scholars are not sure, but once people did, so several authors would argue, civilization or civil society began. Values and society go hand in hand. Not only do values provide the individual with the motive to act or not to act, but the decision to act is reviewed, consciously or not, in terms of societal acceptability. Values provide the individual with a yardstick to judge the nature of the action experienced or employed. The motive to act is found in the protection of the life, liberty, and property of the individual and of the collective. When any of these three is invaded in a way that is harmful to the individual or the collective, it is met with defense or even retaliation. In this sense, value is useful (as yardstick) and comes at a price (effort, money). Action is justified only if a yardstick exists to determine when the invasion of life, liberty, and property is good or bad. The concept of value refers to a distinction between good and bad. As simple a distinction as this may seem, what is considered good or bad, useful or useless, valuable or not valuable, varies with time and place and from individual to individual. In other words, in different societies—and even within one society—different appreciations of value are likely to exist. The law then seeks to satisfy the greatest number in a way that, at least in our society, prevents harm to others whenever and wherever possible. Inequality between individuals may be a fact of life, but the type of government created in the twentieth century indicates that citizens want to mitigate the consequences of this inequality to a greater or lesser extent.

Following this line of reasoning, civil society is necessary only if inequality exists between individuals. One of the most famous quotations from Rousseau's reflections about the origins of inequality concerns the birth of civil society: "The first man who, having enclosed a piece of ground, bethought himself of saying 'This is mine,' and found people simple enough to believe him, was the real founder of civil society" (1986, 84). Rousseau then proceeds to elaborate this statement through descriptions of how our ancestors arrived at ever higher planes of awareness, starting from a point at which they were little more than animals up to a point at which they considered themselves masters of nature. Somewhere in that process, Rousseau argues, the first step toward inequality was made when people compared their looks, their performance, their strength, their possessions, with those of others and found some of these others to be prettier or more handsome, to be better dancers, to be stronger, to be wealthier. And he continues:

> As soon as man began to value one another . . . arose the first obligations of civility even among savages. [And] . . . as every man punished the contempt shown him by others, in proportion to his opinion of himself, revenge became terrible, and men bloody and cruel. [However] . . . so many writers have hastily concluded that man is naturally cruel, and requires civil institutions to make him more mild; whereas nothing is more gentle than man in his primitive state, as he is placed by nature at an equal distance from the stupidity of brutes, and the fatal ingenuity of civilized man. (90–91)

Rousseau considers civil society an expression of the cruelty inherent to mankind. Thus he longs for the natural state of the "happy barbarian," the primitive man who did not need to be restrained since he was not inclined by nature to harm others unless he was harmed by them. Rousseau then quotes John Locke: "There can be no injury, where there is no property" (91). But Locke arrived at a different appreciation of civil society than Rousseau: "I easily grant that civil government is the proper remedy for the inconveniences of the state of Nature" (Locke 1986, 123). More than two centuries after Locke, American author Will Durant would also advocate social organization as a mark of civilization. He did so in ways reminiscent of Locke's argument and of Rousseau's style:

> Here are two men disputing: one knocks the other down, kills him, and then concludes that he who is alive must have been right, and then concludes that he who is

dead must have been wrong—a mode of demonstration still accepted in international disputes. Here are two other men disputing: one says to the other, "Let us not
fight—we may both be killed; let us take our difference to some elder of the tribe,
and submit to his decision." It was a crucial moment in human history! For if the
answer was No, barbarism continued; if it was Yes, civilization planted another root
in the memory of man; the replacement of chaos with order, or brutality with judgment, of violence with law. (Durant 1963, 251)

In this quotation life is valued, perhaps as a commodity with a price (the
economic angle) or perhaps as a mysterious gift that is good (the religious
angle), but either way it is the value of life that urged the mediation of an
elder considered wise.

Values are the very fabric of society and possibly the most basic reason for
the existence of government. Sociologists define values as part of *culture:* the
entirety of values, norms, goals, and expectations in a given society. The *values* refer to general, hence shared, opinions about good and bad. From these
values *norms* are derived: more specific and concrete guidelines for behavior,
the written and unwritten rules that guide social interaction and communication and that determine the ways in which we associate and act. Law is a set of
(formalized) norms. Privacy is an informal norm protected by law. The secret
ballot is a norm in our society based upon the value we place on freedom of,
for instance, speech. *Goals* are equally important to society, for it is in these
that we define a desirable situation. And, finally, we hold *expectations* about
what shall or may happen. Together, values, norms, goals, and expectations
constitute culture and society. They may even become *ideology,* a system of
values that serves as justification of the position and interests of a particular
group. That particular group can be the citizenry of an entire country. Americans support an ideology in which freedom and the sanctity of the individual
(two values) determine the norms (such as a secret ballot and institutional
checks and balances), the goals (such as a smaller but better government),
and the expectations (such as lower taxes when the economy is in decline).
The particular group can also be a substratum of the larger society defined by
gender, race, education, social background, and so on. The substratum may
also be defined in terms of political ideology. Communism *values* the absence of property; sharing and redistribution of surplus is the *norm* (but remember Locke: no one shall take more than one needs, which is the guiding
rule of hunter-gatherer societies such as Eskimos, native Americans, and Aus-
tralian Aboriginals in their relation to nature); the proletarian state is a *goal;*
and the decline of capitalism an *expectation.*

People value different things. They also may interpret the same values
differently. It is in the public realm that choices are made about collective
values as well as about the discretion with which individuals can pursue

their own values. What is valued in terms of price, and what is valued in terms of quality of life, are subject to regulation. Such regulation is left to the discretion of government. Government is synonymous with the elder in Durant's quotation above. It is government that will propose how much revenue will be spent on social services instead of on defense. It is government that will decide whether or not a particular interest in society will receive access to the policy-making arena. More than four decades ago, Easton defined the study of politics as the "understanding how authoritative decisions are made and executed for a society" (originally 1957: Easton 1968, 87). A few years later, he defined politics in another publication as "those interactions through which values are allocated authoritatively for a society" (Easton 1965a, 2) and in yet another as the "*authoritative allocation of values*" in society (Easton 1965b, 50). Easton explains allocation is necessary because "scarcity prevails with regard to most of the valued things" (Easton 1968, 89). It is the individual that provides government with the authority to allocate.

In the state of nature favored by Rousseau, the only thing that individuals lack is an authority that guarantees that they can exercise their individual rights. That is where the elder or government steps in. Government is invested with that ultimate authority in society, in the sense that a decision made is considered binding, authoritative. Although Blondel observed that Easton's definition of politics is attractive because it avoids using the ambiguous concept of power (Blondel 1990, 11, note 11), the concept of power is, however, present in the definition of authority. Max Weber, the German scholar of law, sociology, and history, one of those few scholars who fundamentally influenced the twentieth century social sciences in their entirety, defined power as the chance that one person can pursue his or her wishes against the desires of someone else. Authority, he argues, is the chance that an order will be followed because it is considered legitimate. In other words: *authority is the legitimate use of power* (Weber 1980, 28).

In Western governments the use of naked power or physical violence is solely, or at least mostly, the prerogative of the state. Authority may be found in a variety of social institutions. We recognize and acknowledge the authority of the Immigration and Naturalization Service, the authority of an tribal chief, the authority of a priest or minister, and the authority of the elected officials (chair, treasurer, secretary) of any voluntary association. Every actor or institution in society that governs or rules something wields authority. Dependent upon role and position in society, that authority is lesser or greater. Thus, the authority of the minister or priest concerns a more limited realm or jurisdiction in society at large than the authority of the American president. Whatever the scope of the authority, however, its use must be perceived as legitimate by those individuals who are influenced by it, though the source of that legitimacy can vary.

Weber argued that there are three pure types of authority (Weber 1980, 124–148). *Charismatic authority* rests in the charisma of the individual ruler. Gifted with unique and extraordinary qualities, such a leader is able to rally entire populations behind a cause. Charisma is a powerful instrument in the hands of a charismatic ruler. It is dangerous in the hands of such charismatic rulers as Adolf Hitler and Ayatollah Ruhollah Khomeini. It is beneficial in the hands of a ruler such as Nelson Mandela. A charismatic ruler (not necessarily a head of state, but also a general or, in fact, any leader in a community) is often considered a hero with supernatural, if not divine, powers, someone you want to follow till kingdom come. Charismatic authority is the type wielded in unusual times. It is the kind of authority that may make revolutions. It therefore comes to an end. Once the charismatic ruler dies, the formal authority may pass on but not necessarily the charisma. Or, once a charismatic ruler has been in office for a while, his or her authority can lose that charismatic glow and may transform into traditional authority (see below). Only in a few cases is charisma attached to a position instead of to a person and can actually be passed on by means of ritual (for instance, the election and coronation of a Pope and the reincarnation of the Dalai Lama).

Traditional authority is based in the belief that its legitimacy is derived from a predetermined order and stratification in society, the belief in the sanctity (Weber speaks of *Heiligkeit*) of status and of everyday routine. In this situation, the leader is invested with authority by tradition of birth, family, wealth, and so forth—a leader by tradition. Often such traditional authority is grounded in a higher source. Thus the doctrine of the divine right to rule (in medieval Europe) basically held that any secular and temporal authority of kings was ultimately instituted by God and thus could not be challenged by the ruler's subjects. After all, to challenge the monarch's authority would be equal to doubting God's divine plan. In a society structured by traditional authority, the order and rules are considered sacred and inviolable except in cases of grave abuse (see section 3.4 below).

Legal-rational authority is the type found in modern societies, and its legitimacy rests upon the impersonal and standardized application of established rules in the most democratic and the most efficient manner possible. Anyone acting on the basis of legal-rational authority is legitimate when not pursuing his or her own interests. While under charismatic rule there are followers and believers, and under traditional rule there are subordinates and subjects, it is only under legal-rational authority that there are real citizens who interact on the basis of equally sharing and participating—at least in theory—in the governance of society. The ideal organization for legal-rational authority to thrive is the bureaucracy. While many recognize Weber for his contribution to our understanding of bureaucracy, his thesis on bureaucratization is but part of his more general theory about the rationalization process in Western society since the early modern period (say, since the 1500s). This process has had major consequences for the way we look at our world and thus for the way that we constitute our world.

3.2. The Basis for and Regulation of Interaction

The foundation of many modern societies is believed to be the constitution, which, ideally, provides the ultimate codified framework for societal interaction. Used in this sense, the concept of a constitution refers to a legal, written document, from which other legal documents and regulations may emanate and by which they are justified. In addition to this juridical understanding of the concept, it is important to point to a more sociological approach in which the constitution refers to the actual principles or maxims in terms of which the country is governed. In this perspective, the constitution refers to the set of fundamental public institutions. In the first meaning, the study of constitutions is concerned with law and the interpretation of various related documents, precedents, and conventions. In the second meaning, the study of constitutions is more focused on the actual politics and administration of a country (Lane 1996, 9–10). It is both in this juridical and in this sociological sense that the concept of constitution has to do with values in society and with authority or authorities. For this reason, the study of law is necessary for understanding government. The understanding of constitutions from both the juridical and sociological angles can be further refined when viewed as a layered phenomenon. The level of constitutional rules serves as the foundation for the level of collective rules, which in turn serve as the foundation for the operational rules. The day-to-day activities (i.e., operational rules) are embedded in an institutional arrangement about who decides what and when (i.e., the collective rules), which decisions, in turn, must be embedded in and legitimated by constitutional rules. This understanding of rules as being embedded has been advanced by Kiser and E. Ostrom (1982; also E. Ostrom 1990). To be sure, at first sight, their conception of rules as embedded phenomena may appear to emphasize a juridical perspective, but in fact does not exclude sociological substance. Indeed, E. Ostrom's research, for instance, provides a wonderful illustration of how both the juridical and sociological aspects of common pool resource management need to be explored as embedded phenomena. Furthermore, these juridical and sociological aspects are not only synchronically but also diachronically embedded. Real understanding of the revolutionary nature of constitutions as they are generally defined, a founding document for a society, requires a historical perspective.

The American Constitution is among the first of such documents in the world. In all fairness, the Swedes were first (1772), followed by the Americans (1787), the French (1793), and the Dutch (1798). The legalist approach to constitution was adopted in an age when *political economy* and *constitutionalism* became important. The concept of political economy, dating back to seventeenth-century France, was intended to distinguish the economy of the state from the economy of the private household. This was an important step in demarcating the public sector from the private sector. As a study, political economy developed further in eighteenth-century Germany, under the name of cameralism. In the nineteenth century, this became the study of public administration, which had long been concentrated on practical concerns of administration only.

Central to the idea of constitutionalism is a separation of church and state, for the constitution as a legal document is a human-made, secular document. This separation did not come about overnight. In fact, it took centuries to unfold. Just how long it took is admirably and concisely captured in the following opening remark of an article initially published in 1928–29: "The Reformation superseded an infallible pope with an infallible Bible; the American revolution replaced the sway of a king with that of a document" (Corwin 1955, 1). The hierarchical organization of the Roman Catholic Church was replaced by the more horizontal organization of the Protestant denominations that emphasized the Word of God rather than the (medieval) image of God. What the Reformation prepared was concluded in the American Revolution: no one, not even a king, is above the law. Technically speaking, no one was above the law in medieval Europe either, but that was a law of divine, not of positive, origin. And until the end of the eighteenth century, divine law would— at least in theory—be the universal authority in society, although decreasingly so. The American Revolution heralded the end of the theory of divine law, and with it the divine right to rule was replaced with the constitutional authority to rule. To appreciate the major difference between the pre-1800 and post-1800 world, we turn again to a novelist.

Generally, a movie has to be more concise than the book upon which it is based. This is the case, for instance, with Victor Hugo's *Les Misérables*, a large novel about two men in early nineteenth-century France. The one, Jean Valjean, is a convict, who escapes prison and builds a new, productive life but is never able to escape his pursuer, the police inspector Javert. During a lifetime, Valjean is the hunted, Javert the hunter. When they finally meet in the sewers of Paris, Javert has the chance to kill the man he has hunted all his life but does not for a reason that he cannot quite grasp. Valjean also has the chance to kill Javert, but he does not. In the movie, Javert asks Valjean why he does not kill him. Valjean answers that once a man bought his soul for God, whereupon Javert replies, "There is no God; guilt or innocence only exists before the law." Javert's struggle to solve the tension between two contradictory worldviews ends in his suicide (Hugo 1987, 1319–1330). In Javert's answer one can find all of what the French Revolution brought to a conclusion. Centuries of slow change, increasingly separating state and church in practice, increasingly separating office and officeholder in practice, increasingly balancing political powers both within the state (e.g., Locke and the division of power) and between states (e.g., Grotius and the idea of international law), finally culminated in a full-fledged theory on the sovereignty of the people. What happened during the French Revolution justified what had happened in prior centuries, which is namely the undermining of traditional authority and the slow ascent of legal-rational and negotiable authority.

Central to the notion of legal-rational authority is that people themselves can make the laws that rule society. While political theorists had always paid much attention to the relation between *natural law* (the laws of nature), *eternal law* (the law known to God only), and *divine law* (as revealed in, for instance, the Old and New Testaments), it was positive law that would ultimately prevail in the public realm. *Positive law* is made by human beings. It is the enacted will of the people, and it is grounded in reason and legitimated through consensus-seeking social interaction from the start (the negotiation process) to its application (the implementation and/or enforcement of law). Equally, if not more, important is that positive law is, by nature, not static but always subject to renewed negotiation if environmental circumstances so require.

3.3. Negotiable Authority

What occurred around the 1800s should be more closely examined for its nature (this section) and in its consequences (see section 3.4). We have to go back in time, though, for a better understanding of the magnitude of the changes in the theory and the practice of authority around 1800.

Throughout medieval Europe, the central theory or frame of reference that defined social relations was *universal authority*. The world was God's creation and so social stratification must have been equally God-given. In that society, all, from the monarch to the slave, occupied a predetermined place. A king or queen held office upon a divine right to rule (*droit divin*). The ultimate authority was God. On earth, God's authority was invested in the pope of Rome and the emperor of the Holy Roman Empire. The king's authority was derived from that of God and as such theoretically subordinate to that of the church's spiritual leader. Such being the case, who would challenge the king's authority? What could one do in case of clear abuse of power (see next section)? From the high Middle Ages up to the seventeenth century, scholars struggled to solve the tension between a divinely appointed king turning abusive and a people's right to resist. Many a ruler in medieval and early modern times encountered the gap between the theory of the right to rule and the practice of the chance to be discharged. While the theory supported universal authority, the practice proclaimed the *expendable authority* of a ruler as demanded (in most cases) by another (new) power elite or (sometimes) by the people.

Between the sixteenth and eighteenth centuries, several strides were made toward the closure of the gap between theory and practice, the capstone of which we now recognize as the time of the Atlantic Revolutions (the American, the French, and—humbly added—the Dutch). Rarely mentioned in the political theory or the sociological literature is the fact that the Reformation, prepared for by Jan Hus and John Wycliffe and advanced by Martin Luther and John Calvin, changed people's understanding of religion and thus of the world from one based in the heart and its emotions (as is the case with the Roman Catholic Church) to one based in the mind and its rationality (as in the Protestant denominations). Emotion was superseded by reason and with it came a renewed appreciation for learning and literacy. While the religious experience of the Middle Ages rested largely upon the stimulation of the senses (stained-glass windows, Gregorian chant, incense, recitation), the religious experience of the Reformation and after rested upon the Word and the Word alone. It brought the Word to the people in the vernacular. The Reformation required the people, not just the elite, to read. A medieval Rembrandt would never have painted his mother reading the Bible. What is more, most common people, let alone women, would not have been found reading before the 1600s. As a consequence, authority came to rest with the Word of God rather than with the word of those who represented God's interests on earth. This is how the first part of Corwin's opening sentence ("The Reformation superseded an infallible pope with an infallible Bible") can be understood. And this is how Weber summarized Western history since early modern times: as the unfolding of rationalization, as the triumph of reason over emotion.

In the course of the seventeenth century, the secular notion of authority found new momentum in the effort to establish checks and balances in government. Clearly uncomfortable with any blunt overthrow of government, theorists attempted to both justify such events and advance a rather medieval solution (tyrannicide or forced abdication) or a more modern one (balance of power within and between states). Thomas Hobbes thus justified the decapitation of Charles I of England, but he was locked into belief in a world order where the struggle was between unified leadership and disintegrated society.

A few decades later, John Locke escaped that dilemma by introducing the idea that power within the state could actually be divided and thus balanced, so as to prevent any possible abuse that could arise if all power and authority were vested in one person or body. Locke's division between an executive (the king and courtiers) and a legislative (Parliament and its constituents) was carried one step further by Montesquieu, who added a judiciary to the equation. In the realm of international politics, the notion of a balance of power between states had already been developed by Hugo Grotius and Samuel von Pufendorf and was finalized by Emmerich de Vattel. What else can be concluded but that universal authority, resting in and emanating from God, had been transformed into *negotiable authority*, resting in and emanating from the people. Neither the law between nations nor the law within societies could possibly be other than positive law, a law that is negotiated by the people, a law subject to reconsideration whenever changing environmental circumstances (and the people's response to those) deem such necessary.

At the time of the Atlantic Revolutions, negotiable authority became the value (i.e., the collective rule) that determined the day-to-day structure and functioning of society and government (i.e., the operational rules) and that required legitimation (i.e., the constitutional rules). To date, negotiable authority is the central norm in contemporary society and government. Kiser and Ostrom argue that constitutional rules not only flow downward to more concrete levels, but are in turn influenced and changed by feedback from these more concrete levels. This indicates that negotiable authority is not only defined at the constitutional level. Whether through textual change of the constitution (as is common in continental Europe) or through amendments added to the constitution (as is the case in the United States), the constitution itself is negotiable authority and an expression of changes at more concrete levels of rules.

3.4. Tyrannicide Justified: The Ultimate Price for Abuse of Authority

It could be argued that a system of negotiable authority (the value), as expressed in institutional checks and balances (the norm), prevents social discontent from getting out of hand. Since social order is not considered God-given, we do not have to wait until the waters have risen beyond our lips before we explode in wrath (which is what Thomas Aquinas advised us to do; see below). All authority is negotiable since it emanates from the people. Corwin's conclusion that the Ninth Amendment to the American Constitution points to the existence of a "law superior to the will of human governors" (Corwin 1990, 434) assumes a law that is antecedent to the Constitution. Such a higher authority could be God, but could also be the people and even the law. While at an individual (spiritual) level God can still be accepted as a higher authority, at the societal (secularized) level the only recognized authority is that which people have invested in themselves as a community, the use of which can always be negotiated. With respect to the authority of the law, the notion that no one is above the law would suggest that the law is a higher authority than the people (which is the medieval understanding of law). If law refers to natural law only, then such a line of reasoning is logical. If, however, the concept of law also includes positive law, then that line of reasoning is flawed. After all, when people are the source of the law, how can they be its subject at the same time? Hence, in a community-of-people perspective, the people-as-collective are above the law while in the collection-of-individuals perspective they all are subject to the law.

Acting as a collective, the people have assured that a collection of individuals, let alone an individual, cannot usurp power. Instruments have been created to deal early with potential abuse of power. Given all the institutional checks and balances, it is virtually impossible for any government in the Western world to corrupt and pervert the governance system in the core for years on end. We no longer need a theory of justified tyrannicide because political offices are filled with individuals who are elected by vote rather than selected through clientele relations. Moreover, most elected offices can be held for a specific and renewable (but controlled) term of office rather than held *ad vitam.*

The theory of justified tyrannicide is older than the existence of negotiable authority and received some renewed attention in the twentieth century. In the aftermath of World War II, scholars, especially in Germany, wanted to understand the collaboration of civil servants with the Nazi regime and on what grounds they should have obeyed or resisted collaboration. The study by Herbert von Borch (1954), an excellent example of this sociology of resistance, serves as the main source for the following discussion.

The struggle to develop a theory of resistance, and which could even be a defense of tyrannicide is understandable when one considers the way in which the Bible, and especially the New Testament—for medieval society, *the* document that constituted society and government—demands obedience of individuals to government. Two quotations will illustrate this:

> Everyone must submit himself to the governing authorities, for there is no authority except that which God has established. The authorities that exist have been established by God. Consequently, he who rebels against the authority is rebelling against what God has instituted, and those who do so will bring judgment on themselves. (Romans 13:1–2)

> Submit yourself for the Lord's sake to every authority instituted among men: whether to the king, as the supreme authority, or to governors, who are sent by him to punish those who do wrong and to commend those who do right. (1 Peter 2:13–14)

This advice was given to Christians living in a non-Christian world and under a government that was suspicious—to say the least—of Christianity. In this context, Paul and Peter provided sensible advice. Only in late antiquity and the early Middle Ages, when European governments embraced Christianity as the state religion, could government itself become sacred. The rulers of Christian governments have a duty to do good and be loved by their subjects. What could the subjects do, though, if rulers abused their God-given power, but obey the New Testament that so clearly stated that everyone was subject to secular authority? We have no way of knowing whether Paul and Peter intended their advice to be followed for all centuries and under all political conditions. I suspect this is not the case, though. The tension between the duty to obey and the right to resist emerged as soon as Christianity had won the day, and it came from three sources. First, from the Germanic tradition came the notion that the central concept was not obedience to the sovereign, but loyalty to the sovereignty of the collective. Any ruler trampling that loyalty should expect resistance. Second, the idea that the church itself could serve as a source of resistance against tyrants came from the Roman church. And third, feudalism gave the vassal the right to resist the temporal lord (*diffidatio*). Sacral kingship was never more than a theory for, in practice, rulers could be and were deposed (e.g., the last Merovingian king before Charlemagne). A king not true to the law could be forced out of office, and in extreme cases tyrannicide was justified, as John of Salisbury argued as early as 1159. Thomas Aquinas also supported tyrannicide, but—like John of Salisbury—only in the most extreme cases. Aquinas distinguished two types of tyranny. He spoke of *tyrannus secundum titulum,* when a ruler had illegally acquired power (as is the case when one country invades and occupies another country), and of *tyrannus secundum regimen,* if the ruler had legally acquired power but turned tyrannical after that (a modern example would be the German Reich, after Hitler became chancellor in January 1933). In Aquinas's thought, resistance was possible, but to decide upon such action was the prerogative of the Pope and the Holy Roman Emperor, who together held universal authority. But resistance was an avenue open only to the privileged among the subjects. The population at large, Aquinas advised, had better be patient, for the use of violence often leads to more violence.

Resistance was pulled away from the established church by Luther and Calvin, who argued that all administrators, from high to low, belonged to government and all thus had the right to resist oppressive laws and rulers. A public servant, Luther argued, had a right to resist, but for his loved ones he had the duty to resist ("Aber als obrigkeitliche Person hat er zum Widerstand für sich ein Recht, *für die Seinen ein Pflicht*"; italics in original). Calvin was more pronounced than Luther. Perverted government, the Apocalyptic Beast, should be resisted, not by the individual, but by those near the center of power. In Calvin's view, public servants work upon delegation by God and, thus, resistance of government could not be legitimated in a concern for the people but only in a concern for God's law. Calvin was a staunch supporter of the right to freedom of the estates (clergy, aristocracy, people) that had found early expression in the Magna Carta of 1215. It was further expressed in the parliamentary right to resist a monarch, upon which grounds Edward II in 1327, Richard II in 1399, and Charles I in 1649 would be dethroned. The English Bill of Rights of 1689, its American equivalent of 1776, and the French Declaration of Rights of Man and the Citizen of 1789 owe much to Luther and certainly to Calvin, for both brought the right to resist under positive law. The English or Glorious Revolution of 1688, the American, the French, and the Dutch Revolutions elevated positive law to the central organizing element that it still is. Positive law provides the structure, while negotiable authority is the mechanism that makes it function.

3.5. Concluding Remarks: Relevance for Today

It is very likely that the discussion above, in sections 3.3 and 3.4 especially, may appear to be of more intellectual rather than practical value. And yet it does help to see beyond the surface when appraising the nature of today's relation between society and government. If a gap between citizen and politics is perceived, if declining citizen participation in the provision of public services is a concern, and if government faces its greatest legitimacy crisis ever, we should not only point to decreasing voter turnouts at elections, or address in generalist terms the deteriorating morale and ethics in society, nor should we refer to big bureaucracy without qualifying "big." Instead we should consider that, as De Tocqueville observed, democracy has loosened social ties, leaving responsibility for the sick, the young, the elderly, the disabled, and so forth, to government instead of to local communities and their associations (churches, guilds, clubs, etc.) and also leaving the responsibility for externalities (the unwanted consequences and byproducts of, for instance, industrial production, such as pollution) to the visible hand of government intervention. Today's government is society's creation. People can no longer blame God or the elite. The ever increasing demand of citizens for collective public services has created an ever increasing government. Research so far has amply demonstrated this demand. And in the course of the rationalization process, as Weber called it, in the move from the heart to the mind, in the shift from a firm belief in universal authority—at least in theory—to the disenchanting (Weber's word: *Entzauberung*) revelation of negotiable authority, we have settled for a system of human-made checks and balances. If anything, we are still learning how to balance between powers at the institutional level and between options of exit, voice, and loyalty at the individual level. From the mid-eighteenth century up to the present, and probably well into the twenty-first century, we have been learning to cope with the merging of theory (balancing powers at the collective institutional level and acknowledging freedom at the individual level) with practice (again: balancing powers and protecting individual freedom). In the concept of negotiable authority, the institutional needs (balance of power) are complemented and merged with the individual needs (freedom, equality, brotherhood). There may be discontent with government (as expressed in the legitimacy crisis literature). Some citizens may feel suffocated by government (as expressed in the stereotypes: red tape, formalism, big bureaucracy, etc.). Deep down, however, people are quite content with how things are. For some reason, there are no revolutionaries in Western society today who are convincingly leading us into different avenues of governance. Of course, revolutionaries do not exist until after a turnover has been established and there has been sufficient time to ascertain the impact of otherwise, at best, enlightened individuals or, at worst, blind and angry young men. Indeed, so far, there is nothing in Western society at large that suggests that we are heading for a major departure from negotiable authority. Indeed, most of the future-probing literature still extrapolates from the current situation (how could it otherwise?). The present concerns include adequate responses to demographic growth, environmental waste, globalizing economies, and so forth. The road to solving these concerns, negotiating for the future now, is still based on the theory that authority is neither absolute nor God-given but earned and tolerated by the people.

What constitutes society can be analyzed at three levels. At the most fundamental level, there is the kind of authority that supports a society, authority that can be traditional, charismatic, or legal-rational or, more likely, a mix of these. It is the nature of this authority that determines at the intermediate (collective) level the degree to which power is concentrated or not. Where legal-rational authority constitutes society, the institutional structure (collective level) is based on pluralism and checks and balances. By its nature, legal-rational authority is the juridical expression of that which constitutes society. How legal-rational authority is manifested in reality becomes clear through the more sociological lens of negotiable authority. The outcome of negotiations is first visible at the operational and collective levels and subsequently codified at the constitutional level. At the most concrete level, that of the day-to-day choices, what constitutes society becomes apparent in how collective and individual needs are balanced.

If a convincing case is made that negotiable authority characterizes contemporary Western societies, communities, and governments, neither the rulers nor the constituents should ever delude themselves into thinking that the best ideology, the best organization, or the best policy exists. Ideology, organizational structure, and policy styles are all negotiable. And when negotiation fails, we can always keep Abraham Lincoln's remark, quoted at the opening of this chapter, in mind. We are left to wonder whether the notion of negotiable authority will serve our understanding of contemporary governance and government. If it does: Great. If it does not: Would Hobbes smile in his grave?

4 THE MORAL CONSTITUTION OF SOCIETY AND GOVERNMENT

Of all the dispositions and habits which lead to political prosperity, religion and morality are indispensable supports. . . . reason and experience both forbid us to expect that national morality can prevail in exclusion of the religious principle.
—George Washington, farewell address, 1796

Without a behavior-controlling religious institution, they will believe that civilization will sink into moral anarchy, where might becomes the final arbiter of right.
—John Shelby Spong, 1998

Good government in Italy is a by-product of singing groups and soccer clubs, not prayer.
—Robert Putnam, Robert Leonardi, and Raffaella Nanetti, 1993

Ethics cannot be delegated.
—Lloyd Nelson, as quoted by Deming, 1994

Order and stability in society are increasingly defined in terms of law as a restraint to behavior. Law, however, is external to the individual and is certainly not intended to create social bonding or a sense of social responsibility. If every relationship in society becomes reduced to a legal relationship that is expressed in an adversarial manner, then, Nisbet argued in 1975, the very juices of social bonds dry up (240). It was a concern that many shared with him at the time (Bellah 1975; Crozier et al. 1975; Lipset 1979) and has never quite left us. These and many authors since then have voiced their concern about declining citizenship and civicness, increasing self-serving individualism, and an increasing appreciation of materialism. The individual's sense of social responsibility is allegedly expressed and satisfied by giving time and money (Bellah et al. 1996, xxiv) rather than by actively working in society for the common good. If anything, positive law, as negotiated by people, shores up and thus reflects moral values that reside in and are hence internalized by the individual.

Moral values provide the social foundation of society and government, and they are generally defined in religious and/or secular terms. First, the notion that religion is indispensable to society and government requires some attention (section 4.1). Undeniably, religion has played a role in the emergence of modern government (section 4.2). It has done so in a rapidly secularizing society where the role of religion is limited to the level of the individual (and her or his comfort and salvation) while its role in society at large has been debunked and unmasked as elitist (section 4.3). It is in this secular context that public sector ethics and morality (section 4.4) and civil religion and civic culture (section 4.5) have been defined. It has been argued that "In the American experience, the secular state and the religious society are not to be seen as contradictions, but as complementary (Wood 1991, 4–5). This observation is also relevant for large parts of Europe, but in an entirely different way, as we shall see when we discuss three types of social-political systems (section 4.6). I conclude with optimistic remarks about the future of society and government (section 4.7) that provide some counterpoint to the pessimism that has dominated the past thirty years or so. In this chapter I demonstrate that the public and the private realm are intertwined. In chapter 3 law is presented as the foundation for government's authority over the private sphere, while in this chapter we see society's morality, whether defined in a religious or secular context, as foundational to government's authority in society as a whole.

4.1. Religion as Foundation for Society and Government

Scholarship, especially rich in sociology and political science, has approached the crumbling of civicness and the decline of internalized morality from various angles, but there is a consensus about the two main causes: religion is relevant to the individual but no longer to society, while that same society is less and less a community. Crozier et al. argue that churches have lost their moral authority (1975, 26). Nisbet remarks how a sense of community is provided by the political society rather than by the church (1975, 3). A secular utilitarian individualism has superseded the spiritual community of old (Bellah 1975, 4; Bellah et al. 1996, 37). Increased interest among political scientists in recent years in the relation between politics, religion, and society indicates the importance of establishing and/or maintaining a moral foundation in a massive, largely secularized society (for an overview of recent literature, see Hertzke 1987; Hertzke 1995; "Divining the God Factor" 2000).

The decline of religion and of community as sources of morality and as binding forces in society and the concomitant rise of secular worldviews is a concern of the last two centuries. In the late eighteenth century and the early decades of the nineteenth century, a variety of observers (Burke, de Tocqueville, Burckhardt) argued that the rise of the national and political state increasingly came to safeguard social stability, which hitherto had been within the realms of church, guild, and kinship. They also prophesied that this trend would end in alienation from the state (Nisbet 1975, 6). Primary and direct identification of the individual with society through such social institutions as local community, religion, voluntary association, and so forth gave way to indirect identification with a more imagined community embodied by the state. A century later, various scholars expressed their concern about the impact of urbanization and industrialization. In the early 1880s, Ferdinand Tönnies described this momentous social and economic change in terms of an evolution from *gemeinschaft* (community) to *gesellschaft* (society/association) that resulted in an atomization of society. In the 1890s, Emile Durkheim analyzed the alienation of the individual from work and from community by contrasting the *organic solidarity* of small-scale societies to the *mechanic solidarity* of the industrial age and the urban environment. In the early twentieth century, Max Weber (1980) warned against the threat that bureaucratization posed to democracy. All three concluded that the economic and social changes they witnessed had resulted in the breakdown of morality and social order. In large-scale modern society, churches were no longer able to address the immediate needs of the deprived and the poor on the basis of charity and membership. The gap between rich and poor was increasing, as Karl Marx in Europe and Orestes Brownson in the United States had earlier pointed out (Bellah 1975, 119), and has continued to expand since then (see De Long 1988, 1148).

Throughout the early and high Middle Ages, religion and the church as its organizational expression had occupied a dominant place in Western society. From the late Middle Ages onward, government and church together served as constitution to society, with the state increasingly the dominant partner both in Catholic and Protestant countries. The church was actively involved in governance through the provision of a variety of collective services (health care, care for the poor, care for the elderly, etc.), and its representatives (priests, ministers) were actively involved in government. In early modern times, priests continued to be appointed by the church hierarchy. In the dominantly Protestant lands of the United States and northern Europe, the ministers of Protestant churches were appointed by the local government and thus worked de facto as public servants (on the United States, see Bellah et al. 1996, 220; on the Netherlands, see Raadschelders 1994, 436).

While religion was an important source of community building both in Catholic and Protestant countries, by the late eighteenth century the church and state were legally separated (e.g., in the American, French, and Dutch constitutions). The advent of a formal written constitution, important as the start of a new era, also marks the end of a period in which church and state attempted to define their own territory. Ever since the high Middle Ages, the state had slowly become the more powerful of the two institutions. The constitutionalism of the late eighteenth century merely codified what had increasingly become practice. Once church and state were formally demarcated, clergy were no longer considered public servants and the church was relegated to the private realm of the individual. The emerging division of labor made the church responsible for the salvation and morality of the individual as a human being, while the state was more concerned with the morality of the individual as a citizen.

While separated by law, in practice church and state continued to be regarded as a powerful tandem. In his farewell address, George Washington considered religion an indispensable support to society's morality. A national morality, so he believed, could not be maintained without religion. Washington and the other founders of the republic shared a deistic conception of religion that holds that God does not intervene in society and that people have the freedom to shape society in accordance with their wishes. However, the deists also realized that such an abstract understanding of religion would not create the morality and sense of community that the population at large needed. Religion and the church were—and still are—considered by many as behavior-controlling institutions without which society will sink into anarchy. The Episcopalian bishop Spong believes we have moved beyond a God-oriented, theistic experience of religion into a more individualized religiousness, but, while more than 200 years have elapsed since George Washington finished his terms as president, the substantive differences between Washington and Spong are small. In America and in the northern European (Protestant) countries, for at least two centuries a small section of the population, generally the educated elites, have share a rather abstract perception of religion (i.e., the God of the philosophers), while the public at large feels more comfortable with a concrete image of religion (i.e., God the Father). It is interesting that the educated elites still recognize that religion with its morality is an instrument of social control useful in the effort to uphold the laws of the state.

While de Tocqueville observed that the American nation as a whole believed religion to be indispensable for the maintenance of its republican institutions, he noticed that the older biblical and republican traditions of individualism that emphasized community and self-governance had been complemented with a utilitarian individualism. This assumes that social good emerges automatically (as if through an "invisible" hand) when people pursues their interests in society (these concepts of individualism from Bellah et al. 1996, 29–33, 37; see section 4.6 below). The American version of individualism was deeply rooted in Protestantism, which, since the time of the Pilgrim Fathers, had focused on the moral rather than on the contemplative and mystical elements so characteristic of Catholicism. Protestant religious attitudes were concerned with Christian morality and the creation of a debating community where a genuinely ethical and spiritual life could be lived rather than with transcendental beliefs and salvation in the afterlife (Bellah et al. 1996, 29; Lipset 1979, 158).

What de Tocqueville had observed was not a passing fad but proved to be a lasting feature of American society. By the mid-nineteenth century, the judge of proper behavior was no longer the minister or (local) community but individual conscience (Coontz 1992, 48, 98). American religion had become part of the private world. By the 1880s, the role of religion in American society and government further changed under the influence of major social-economic developments. In the words of Richard Stillman: "The old, limited set of classical Judeo-Christian beliefs that worked well for a rural, self-sufficient society would swiftly be supplemented by another, a set of secular-democratic-rational beliefs" (1991, 48). As correct as this observation is, it does not mean that religion and these Judeo-Christian beliefs ceased to play a role in the public arena (see section 4.2 below). But by that time, the late nineteenth century, religion had become a source of guidance vested in and limited to the individual. Church life became part of the weekly schedule. More or less the same happened in the northern parts of Western Europe.

Churches are still partners in the distribution of welfare, and Western governments are generally supportive of their efforts. Berns wonders whether government can support religion, naturally on a nondiscriminatory basis, given the constitutional separation of church and state (1986, 208–209). American government indeed supports religion, perhaps not in as direct a manner as in the European welfare states (subsidizing denominational schools), but certainly indirectly, for instance, through substantial tax exemptions (Barker and Barker 1978, 21). Are faith and religion a public issue, an entirely private matter, or something in between? (Hertzke 1995, 484). As much as rugged individualists may dislike it, there is a public element to religion, but it has nothing to do with one's individual appreciation of religion. As in most Western governments, the American government does not prescribe a particular religion nor a particular ritual and certainly does not prescribe what road to take to personal salvation or material gratification. The public aspect of religion has to do with the development of societal bonds, the sense of collectiveness and a foundation of morality. In this sense, religion is not a threat to public civility but a support, much as George Washington advocated.

In addition to the church, it is in the family, the sports club, and so forth that vehicles can be found to internalize morality and establish community, for "without mediating institutions that inculcate and reinforce civic duty, moral restraint, and compassion, all we have is *carnal capitalism*" (Hertzke 1995, 83; emphasis added).

The question is, of course, whether or not religious and other types of associations help in building morality. In view of the mounting concern about a declining sense of morality among the generations since World War II, we might cautiously consider the possibility that collectives in the private sphere do not and, in fact, cannot meet that challenge because the lives of the associations' memberships are not intertwined but highly fragmented. Even in the nuclear family, considered to be the core of American society but only encompassing 25 percent of the population, the family becomes rapidly fragmented once the children reach some level of independence. Citizens are members of one society, but individuals are members of different and rarely overlapping associations. The only social institution that overarches these different associations and thus combines individuals as citizens is government. Every other social institution includes only a small part of the nation's population and thus cannot provide a foundation to society at large.

The need for moral guidance has become all the stronger in the past four to five decades since the secularization of worldview is no longer limited to the elites (and their God of the philosophers in the eighteenth century). The secularization of society at large combined with growing demographic diversity and hence with a religiously and ethnically heterogeneous society has generated a strong sense of individualism with regard to moral standards. While we celebrate multiethnicity, we also recognize that the crumbling of a homogeneous (Judeo-Christian) moral standard might potentially jeopardize the legitimacy of public authority. It has been argued: "A society that cannot agree what values to teach its young—and thinks it can teach value-free education—is courting disaster" (Hertzke 1987, 829). At the same time, however, it would be wrong to assume too much divergence among values. As a United Nations' survey in the late 1940s showed, there is remarkable similarity between the basic values across cultures and religions (respect for the elderly, respect for life, respect for property, respect for marriage, respect by and for children, etc.). Where cultures vary is on the more concrete platform of nationally held values, and there the differences may lead to clashes between countries or even within countries. In this sense, the more timeless values of religion provide a better and more neutral constitution for multiethnic societies than do the nationalistic values of particular states. Religion itself is not volatile: it is the political use of religion that creates havoc. Also, religion is not synonymous with social control: it is people who use religion as an instrument of social control. One does not have to be religious to acknowledge that there is at least some truth to this. In his newspaper column, the developmental psychologist John Rosemond appears to argue in favor of religious education when he observes that

> where the pre-1960s child had no excuse for misbehavior, today's child is given one excuse after the other. . . . Although secularists accuse religion of producing guilt, the secular view of children and child-rearing is far more likely than the scriptural view to result in parental guilt. The scriptural view holds that knowing the difference between right and wrong, a child chooses to misbehave. His parents are responsible for dealing properly with the misbehavior, but the scriptural view does not presume that they caused it through parenting sins of omission or commission. But that is exactly what the secular view implies. The child's parents have but two means of escaping this trap. They can escape by successfully pointing the finger of blame at some other agent: teacher, playmate, the school curriculum, a television show the child watched. . . . Or they can escape by finding an expert who will tell them that the problem is biological, not psychological. In other words, it has nothing to do with them. (Rosemond 1998, 4)

The religious education provided by Sunday schools is fine but, of course, adheres to the dogmas of a particular denomination. What is needed in a society where the collective level is generally defined in the secular terms of law is a civics education that makes the student aware of and appreciate both the Judeo-Christian and Greco-Roman foundation of Western society at large and the interpretation of these traditions from the religious and secular angles. This is important in a time when the baby boomers allegedly have little or no sense of taking responsibility for their actions. Public officials are expected to have a strong sense of right and wrong, which can only be rooted in a secular and/or a religiously inspired ethic internalized from early on. Thus, formal education, whether through public and private schools or through Sunday schools, is not enough. It is in the family and in the local community that morality, a sense of community, and, hence, an education for democracy begins.

4.2. The Role of Religion in the Creation of Contemporary Government

There can be little doubt that religion has played a role in the making of modern government and society, and in this section I illustrate this briefly with the United States and the Netherlands. How religion continues to play a role in reforms of government and in government-society relations is illustrated with examples from the United States, Germany, and Italy.

What role has religion played in the shaping of American government? De Tocqueville noticed how religious values dominated far more in the United

States than in Europe, but how did they help shape America's government? In a study of some of the major innovations in the 1870–1940 period, Stillman (1998) argues that some government reforms were advanced by principled men and women with a small-town Protestant background. While this insight is not new (e.g., Hofstadter 1955, 204; Hofstadter 1968, 161), Stillman's biographical approach is unique. In seven biographies, he outlines the moral considerations of reform-spirited individuals in their social and political context.

Five of these reformers stressed the need to improve the internal structure and functioning of public organizations and their personnel. George William Curtis (1824–1892, Rhode Island) chaired the 1873 committee that recommended the creation of (a) an independent commission to administer civil service, (b) a *merit system*, (c) open competitive exams, (d) position classification, (e) probationary period for candidates, (f) rule of three, (g) prohibitions against political activity and other influence upon civil service, (h) methods for internal procedures and for examination practices, and (i) enforcement mechanisms (Stillman 1998, 36). Curtis was a close friend of Dorman Eaton, who traveled to England in 1877 to study the Northcote-Trevelyan reforms of the 1850s. Emory Upton (1839–1881, New York) shared Curtis's interest in *public professionalism,* but he focused more on clear lines of authority, top-down command, and provisions for control as exemplified in the U.S. military, in which he rose to the rank of major general during the Civil War and served as a lieutenant colonel after it (70–71). The pursuit of professionalism was not a passing fad. Like Curtis and Upton before him, Louis Brownlow (1879–1963, Missouri) matched their appetite for professionalization at all levels of government. He became most known as the chair of the Brownlow Commission (1937), where he, Charles Merriam, and Luther Gulick laid out the principles of *administrative management* that had major influences upon the shaping of the American presidency (155, 157). Frederick Taylor (1856–1915, Pennsylvania) hardly needs introduction. He is widely known for the study and application of *scientific management.* It was on the basis of his ideas that the New York Bureau of Municipal Research further developed its study of public administrative institutions that in turn served as the model for the establishment of comparable agencies in other cities (111, 114). Equally interested in local government, Richard S. Childs (1882–1978, Connecticut) is credited with the elaboration of the *council-manager plan* that, since its first adoption in Sumter, North Carolina in 1912, has become the dominant model of local government organization (131, 133).

The two remaining reformers in Stillman's book helped define the role of government in society. Charles Francis Adams (1835–1915, Massachusetts), the great-grandson of John Adams, advocated the creation of a *regulatory commission* as the government's way to deal with the unrestrained growth of the power of private corporations. He was one of the three commissioners in the first state regulatory board (the Massachusetts Board of Railroad Commissioners, 1869), and his ideas served as the model for the first federal regulatory commission (the Interstate Commerce Commission, 1887) (46, 61). Jane Addams (1860–1935, Illinois) was one of the early champions of *social reform*. Her work in the settlement movement helped in creating the maternal welfare state, to use Skocpol's (1992) phrase, that is based on compassion, self-help, and local volunteerism (Stillman 1998, 82–91). Addams and other well-educated middle-class women have been instrumental in the innovation of social welfare policies for the urban poor. Experiments that they started in infant health, education, and welfare programs culminated in the 1935 Social Security Act (SSA). The SSA codified what had been in the making for more than forty years and, in turn, continues to serve as the foundation to the American welfare state.

Stillman's concluding analysis emphasizes that all seven of these reformers were raised in the "galaxy of Protestant morality," that they pushed for reform with as much zeal as the Puritans had two centuries earlier, and that they emphasized such Protestant values as merit, calling, service, public interest, and mission. Befitting Protestantism and adhering to an American state that was built from the bottom up, they rejected European-style centralization and embraced capitalism. They also shared in the Protestant preference for the written word over ritual and, hence, they wrote extensively about their ideas for reform. Finally, and perhaps most importantly, they confronted opposition with great organizational leadership skills and a persistence that gave the various reforms something of a "crusades" flavor (165–169). On the basis of Stillman's text, we can infer that they also shared a civic-religious conception of justice (see Bellah et al. 1996, 218) that regards work as a calling, where the individual as a member of the civic community is morally obliged to contribute to the common good, and where one should respond to the needs of others. A final element that these seven reformers share is their geographic area of origin. Five out of the seven were reared in New England states and two in Midwestern states, which emphasizes the influence the Northeast had upon the creation and subsequent innovation of the American administrative state. The link between religious beliefs and programs should not be carried too far, though. There is little doubt that religious upbringing and beliefs influenced these reformers' behaviors and attitudes in later years, but that is not the same as saying that there is a causal connection between their programs and their personal beliefs. In fact, the substance of their reforms is purely secular and thus perhaps only indirectly inspired by their religious background.

The Netherlands provides another example of how religion has influenced the formation of modern government. During the two centuries of the Dutch

Republic and well into the nineteenth century, Protestants dominated the public sector. From the middle of the nineteenth century on, Catholics succeeded in acquiring public office and could thus influence public policy making. The defining moment of denominational influence in government and public policy was when the Protestant and Catholic parties both managed to secure public funding for private, denominational schools in return for the Socialists' achievement of universal suffrage for men (in 1917). This package deal institutionalized a system of political and organizational *pillarization* of society that would last well into the 1960s (Lijphart 1968). Even though the religious parties (since 1976 united in the Christian-Democratic Appeal) have dwindled in importance since then, they are still one of the major players in Dutch politics and government.

While these are brief descriptions and concern only two countries, it does not seem too far-fetched to generalize that religion has played a role in the shaping of modern government. And naturally, it has played a role in the discussions about socially divisive issues. In the United States, the politics of religion played a role in the debate about Mormon polygamy and slavery in the nineteenth century, in the civil rights movement of the 1960s and after, in the election of public officials up to the present (Hertzke 1987, 10–11), and, of course, in a variety of policies. It seems obvious that religion plays a role in debates about abortion, euthanasia, divorce, gay marriage, and other issues. Less obvious is that it also may explain differences in, for instance, the structure and functioning of local governments.

Since World War II, a policy of amalgamating local governments has been pursued in the United States as well as in a variety of European countries. In the United States, the number of general- and specific-purpose local governments declined between 1942 and 1992 by almost 45 percent (Henry 1999, 411). Between 1950 and 1992, in Denmark, Sweden, and Norway the number of local authorities declined by 80 percent, 87 percent, and 41 percent respectively. We see quite different figures, however, when looking at France (–5 percent), Italy (+ 4 percent), Spain (–12 percent), and Greece (–0.6 percent) (Council of Europe 1994, 8; Sancton 2000, 63–66). It appears that in the predominantly Protestant northern European countries, local amalgamations have been pursued with much more zeal than in the Catholic south. We can explore this by looking at Germany and the Netherlands. Both are countries with a dominant Protestant population, but each has a strong Catholic south. In Germany, the number of municipalities declined by 67 percent overall between 1965 and 1977, but many municipalities in the three southern, Catholic states (Bavaria, Baden-Württemberg, and Rhineland-Palatinate) were not forced to rescind their legal status and could thus keep their own mayors and councils. By the end of the 1980s, these three states held more than 65 percent of the total number of municipalities in Germany (Hesse 1991, 366–367). In the Netherlands, the number of municipalities declined by 36 percent in the 1950–1992 period, first in the secular and mainly Protestant provinces north of the Rhine. Local amalgamations in the southern Catholic provinces of Noord-Brabant and Limburg were not pursued until the mid-1980s. While this is peculiar in itself, it does not tell us anything about why Protestant local communities have been more inclined toward larger jurisdictions, while the Catholic countries in southern Europe prefer administrative reforms at the regional or provincial level.

The Norwegian political scientist Stein Rokkan has provided a starting point for understanding this through his thesis about an east (agrarian)–west (industrialized) and north (Protestant)–south (Catholic) axis in the political makeup of Europe that has deep historical roots. Especially in the Protestant countries, elementary education for all children in the native language has been enforced since the late sixteenth, early seventeenth century, and "the established national churches simply became agents of the state and had no reason to oppose such measures" (Rokkan 1970, 103). In a coauthored study he said it thus:

> Protestantism strengthened the distinctiveness of each territorial culture by integrating the priesthood into the administrative machinery of the state within the confines of the local language. In terms of the paradigm suggested by Hirschman (1970), the Reformation raised a wall against cultural "exits" into other territories. This barrier was not only an important strategy in legitimizing the territorial state; in the long run it was also a crucial step forward in preparing people for the use of "voice" within their system. (Rokkan and Urwin 1983, 26)

In the south the Catholic church largely maintained the supraterritorial orientation it had developed since the early Middle Ages and was therefore much less if at all a factor in nation building (Rokkan 1970, 33; see also Rokkan and Urwin 1982).

The administrative consequences in terms of service delivery were further explored by the British political scientist Edward Page. In his cross-time study of central-local relations in Europe, he argued that in the Protestant territories, major efforts at local government reform had been under way since the mid-nineteenth century. These countries generally had strong traditions of local self-governance reaching back deep into the early Middle Ages. Protestantism, with its preference for local chapters that operate on a decentralized basis within an overarching, but nonrestrictive, synod or conference, was a natural match. In the Catholic parts of Europe, a more hierarchical system of central-local relations persisted (Page 1991, 133). In time, the strong government-church partnership at the local level in the north provided the basis for the welfare state bureaucracy (143) that still characterizes these parts of Europe. What is more, welfare state expansion in the United States also coincided with extensive reforms at the local level (144–145). Further support for the thesis of Rokkan and of Page can be found in two empirical studies on the origin and development of public health (Archer 1979) and of public education (Immergut 1992) in Western Europe.

But as with so many social science theories, the distinction between a Protestant and industrialized north versus a Catholic and more rural south is not perfect, as the case of Italy illustrates. Italy is a predominantly Catholic country with a thriving, industrial north and an impoverished, agrarian south. In his analysis of the relation between civic, political, and economic trends in the course of seven centuries, Putnam and colleagues attack the notion that religion has anything to do with state building. Their study, in fact, provides a challenging counterpoint to the idea that religion is a necessary pillar for government. While the major thesis of their work is that civicness precedes economic growth and not vice versa (1993, 152), they also conclude that religiousness is not related to good government nor to civicness: "Organized religion, at least in Catholic Italy, is an alternative to the civic community, not a part of it. . . . Vertical bonds of authority are more characteristic of the Italian Church than horizontal bonds of fellowship" (Putnam, Leonardi, and Nanetti 1993, 107). There is one important question, however, that Putnam did not explore, and that is the question of tacit knowledge. What does it mean to be reared in a Catholic or Protestant country and in an industrialized or agrarian community? How does that influence an individual's outlook on life? More particularly, what is its impact on an individual's visions of civicness and of government's role and position in society? Stillman provides us with some clues as far as the United States is concerned, but more research that adopts a biographical method is needed on Europe. The desire for generalizations in the social sciences stands in the way of proper assessment of the impact of religion in the making of European government.

As sketchy as the illustrations above may be, it appears that the regional and national differences in governance in Europe can be at least partly explained by the role of religion. There is one major objection to carrying the importance of religion too far. Most theories that include attention for the role of religion in the shaping of the state and of government do not go further back than the Middle Ages and they therefore pay no attention to the fact that Western governance and government are grounded in the intellectual heritage of the Greeks and the Romans. Waldo observed that "our politics are Greek, but our administration is Roman," and that many of the concepts, techniques, and institutions of administration have come to the Western world from the ancient empires through Rome. Roman administrative technology was to an extensive degree adopted by the Roman Catholic church (Waldo 1987, 96–97). What Waldo calls the "civic-culture tradition" of the Western world, which concerns politics and political theory, is based in the experience and thought of classical Greece and of the Roman Republic about "government and deciding what it should and will do" and in some of the medieval and early modern city-states in northern Italy, the Germanic principalities, and the Low Countries (Flanders, the Dutch Republic). What Waldo calls the "imperial tradition" of the Western world, concerning administration and management, goes back to the Roman Empire's attention to "organizing and executing government functions" in a large territory (98). Hofstede's work supports and expands Waldo's observations. In his empirical work on organizational cultures, Hofstede observes that "it is not this religious split which is at the origin of the cultural differences between North and South but the inheritance of the Roman Empire" (1997, 16). When analyzing the differences between countries, he draws attention to the fact that Protestantism especially struck root in those parts of Europe that had not been part of the Roman Empire (131, 135). What characterized government during the Roman Empire was centralization, hierarchical organization, and departmentalization of "public" organizations, while in the nonoccupied Germanic parts, governance was organized under local, tribal groups (42–43). These two traditions of centralized and fragmented government are not only visible in the current traditions in central-local relations (see above) but also in theories about organizations.

Hence, when assessing the impact of religion on the shaping of modern government, we have to go back to antiquity. It is in this distant past that the advent of secularization in Western society since the sixteenth century emerges as an alternative explanation for the role and position of Western governments today. Antireligious or indifferent attitudes toward religion provided fertile ground for a return to the more secular Greco-Roman ideas about governance, government, morality, and civicness (see sections 4.3 to 4.5 below) as well as to secular Roman Empire traditions of administration and management.

4.3. The Secular Challenge: Religion in the Economic and Psychological Perspectives

The secularization of Western society since the Renaissance has been the object of many studies in the twentieth century. Secularization can be seen as a consequence of the evolving de facto state-church separation, which demarcated spiritual from secular authority, since the early twelfth century. It can be seen as a consequence of the de jure separation of church and state since the late eighteenth century in order to establish a truly impartial government. It can also be considered a consequence of the great scientific discoveries of

Galileo, Newton, and Darwin that not only did much to demystify the forces of nature but also raised doubt about the Bible as a true history of mankind. These are three explanations of secularization that would, however, be rather simple if not linked to a deeper reason that also connects them: the increasing sense of individualism since the late Middle Ages and the Renaissance.

During the centuries that the Catholic church was truly universal in Europe, its populations lived in highly stratified societies. Both church and government organizations operated on a hierarchical basis. An individual was born in a particular station in life and accepted it fatalistically as the will of the Divine. It is not that the individual was discounted. In fact, all three monotheistic religions (Judaism, Christianity, Islam), that, together with Greek thought, shaped Western philosophy (Solomon and Higgins 1996, 104) emphasized the dignity of the individual but as a member of a community. From the late fifteenth century on, the individual claimed higher status than the community. Artists began signing their own work; secular rulers distanced themselves from Rome; discoveries in physics, astronomy, and biology challenged the worldview that the church had peddled for centuries and suggested that people could think for themselves; and, of course, the church schisms in the eleventh (Eastern Orthodox Church) and sixteenth centuries (Protestant Reformation) did much to challenge the unified stand of the church. These were developments in practice, but they also found increasing support in philosophy and political theory. Increasingly, this "individualizing sense of will" (Nisbet 1975, 171) led philosophers away from theories that everything and everyone in society was predestined to theories that considered society as a social contract between free and equal people. Scholars such as Hobbes, Locke, Hume, Rousseau, and Kant thus further supported this shift toward individual will and self-rule (Solomon and Higgins 1996, 199). And, as we saw above, a strong sense of utilitarian individualism had developed by the middle of the nineteenth century in the United States (Bellah et al. 1996, 33). It was not as strong in Europe, but there too individualism found further support in Protestantism and secularization. Individualism since has only gained in importance, prompting Nisbet to observe that our sense of community is at stake and that we should strengthen the citizen's image as a member of a community rather than as a political subject (1975, 160, 284–286).

Ever since the seventeenth century, government was increasingly considered in a secular context that emphasized contract rather than association, starting with the Quakers in the England of the 1640s and traveling to the French philosophers and the New World rebels. Economic and class theory and psychological explanations of religion in particular have advanced the secular outlook upon public life. Economic and class theory precedes Karl Marx by some 130 years. By the end of his life in 1729, the French priest

Meslier had become convinced that religion is a device of the rich to oppress the poor (Armstrong 1993, 392). Karl Marx, going one step further, argued that religion is the opium of the people, that it turns individuals into herdlike animals who accept their station in life and believe in the inevitability of social stratification. In his *Age of Reason,* Thomas Paine wrote that as a system of religion, Christianity was too absurd for belief, too repugnant to reason, too derogatory to the Almighty, too unedifying and inconsistent, and that the Bible was a book of fables (Paine 1794, 248; Berns 1986, 222). Economic and class theories therefore argue that religion negates the individual and deprives entire classes of sharing in material welfare. Religion is, in fact, a political instrument used by the elites to appease the economically disadvantaged large majority. These thoughts have not lost their significance.

During the eighteenth-century Enlightenment, religion increasingly came to be regarded as inferior to science, which is observable and factual. Religion rested upon too many assumptions about a supernatural world. This attitude provided the basis for a search for human-centered and psychological explanations that emerged in the nineteenth century. While churches present religion through a ritual in reverence for a higher, divine order, Ludwig Feuerbach argued in 1841 that religion and God were nothing but human projections of selfish hopes for happiness. The history of thought, so he reasoned, was a history of progressive disenchantment that would ultimately demythologize religion (see Bell 1961, 394). Two decades later, J.S. Mill would write that Christian morality as devised by the Catholic church centuries after Christ and the apostles was negative rather than positive, passive rather than active, striving for innocence rather than nobleness, and attempting to avoid evil rather than pursuing good (Mill 1984, 117). In more strident terms, Friedrich Nietzsche wrote that the Christian God is a crime against life (see Paine), that it encourages people to fear their bodies, their passions, their individuality, and that it promotes a morality of compassion that weakens the individual. In all fairness, there were then and there are now deeply religious people who firmly believe(d) that religion actually helps them to live life passionately and to the fullest (Sören Kierkegaard in the nineteenth century; Spong 1998). Max Weber's concept of the *Entzauberung der Welt* (disenchantment of the world), reminiscent of Feuerbach, further testifies to the debunking of the role of magic and religion in society. Sigmund Freud argued that God is not a lie, but an exalted father figure, an expression of an infantile need for a powerful, protective father. Religion belongs to the infancy of mankind; with maturity comes independence and individualism. These eighteenth- and nineteenth-century secular perceptions of religion echoed into the twentieth century.

Ayn Rand's conviction that religion is an obstacle in the path of science and in the development of the individual mind has its roots in Nietzsche's philosophy. Jean Paul Sartre's argument that God negates individual freedom is also reminiscent of Nietzsche. Ironically, the existentialism of the agnostic Sartre is not rooted in Nietzsche but in the ideas of the deeply religious philosopher Kierkegaard, who is credited with being the forerunner of existentialism (Solomon and Higgins 1996, 227). We can also easily recognize the ideas of Meslier and Marx in the observations of Governor Jesse Ventura of Minnesota about religion as a political instrument. And finally, Freud is clearly visible in Spong's observation that once the human spirit comes of age, it cannot return to the image of God as a heavenly father (1998, 70).

Secularization has increasingly turned people to material gratification instead of pursuing eternal salvation (Berns 1986, 226–227). It brings out an egotistical trait inherent to human beings but suppressed by religion in the name of community and charity. Paradoxically enough, the Judeo-Christian traditions of social justice and humanism helped Western governments to rediscover the secular versions of these values as rooted in Greco-Roman thought. Meanwhile, given that for a long time, religion was an important—if not the only—source of ethics and morality, what impact did secularization have upon public sector ethics?

4.4. Ethics and Morality in the Secularized Public Sector

According to Aristotle, the family, the tribe, and the village serve to preserve life, much in the same way as the mother, the herd, and the cave protect the animal. Human beings, however, desire to be more than animals, so they engage in the establishment of political community and use the faculty of reasoning to distinguish just from unjust. It is an ethical need, and ethos is defined as the distinctive character (morals, rules of conduct) of the group. In chapter 6 we see how laws were considered to be character-building in antiquity. In Aristotle's belief, firm laws "with teeth" would build character and thus ethical excellence. Indeed, ethics and politics (and we should mention administration separately) are thus very closely related (Diamond 1986, 78–80). What is different between antiquity and the premodern and modern eras is that the idea of association has been replaced by that of contract. The consequence is that, while in antiquity, participation in civil society was regarded as positive and coming from desire, under modernity and in "the 'condition of mere nature,' man is driven by fear, especially the fear of violent death. . . . The social-contract thinkers argued that fear would drive men into civil society in order to protect their lives, liberty and property" (Peters 1990, 284). Mass democracy with its strong sense of individualism and egalitarianism calls for an ethics that may be quite different from that which was useful in antiquity.

Laws are as important, used not to build character but to protect property and to establish rules for proper interaction. Because laws serve huge numbers of people, there is a risk that "a representative system operating in a mass society combines the very worst features of direct democracy (the tyranny of opinion, passion, and ignorance) and of elitism (the tyranny of wealth and power)" (Barber 1986, 55). The difference between continental European countries and the United States is that in the former, government intervention slowly accelerated in the seventeenth up to the nineteenth centuries, to arrive at full speed in the late nineteenth and early twentieth centuries. Against this background, an ethics of public intervention reemerged (as it had emerged in the sixteenth and seventeenth centuries) when (local) governments took over church tasks in response to pressing health and housing needs in the urban areas. An ethics of public intervention did not exist in the early United States. In its original structure, the U.S. government almost appears to have been thrown into the deep without much of a swimming diploma. After all, "a properly designed state, the Fathers believed, would check interest with interest, class with class, faction with faction, and one branch of government with another in a harmonious system of mutual frustration" (Hofstadter 1986, 6). The founders did not discuss what government ought to do for its population in terms of public services, but what it should avoid in terms of concentration of power. In such a system, an ethics of public intervention ideally "aimed to create a government that would act as an honest broker among a variety of propertied interests, giving them all protection from their common enemies and preventing any one of them from becoming too powerful" (Hofstadter 1986, 69). One probably wonders what an ethics of public intervention really is? It is not concerned so much with what Rohr calls the first level or high road ethics because that is basically concerned with moral integrity and behavior that is internalized and at the heart of the individual (Figure 4.1).

This could also be called the constitutional level of ethics because it serves as the basis for organizational and professional ethics, for instance. Ethics today is as strongly related to politics as in antiquity, but now understood to serve primarily the education in democratic behavior. In the words of D.F. Thompson (1992, 255): "The main business of government ethics should be what may be called education in democracy. Government ethics should be seen as a way of reminding officials that they are accountable to the public, that they primarily serve not their administrative superiors or even their own consciences but all citizens." Striking in this quotation is that the concept of ethics is almost invisibly sliding into Rohr's second level or low road ethics, which is concerned with obedience to rules and which is external to the individual. Taken out of context, this quotation seems to reinvoke the notion that administrators are oblivious to their own value judgments and thus perfectly

Figure 4.1 **General Themes of the "High," the "Low," and the "Lower" Road in Public Sector Ethics**

High Road: first level, moral integrity	Low Road: second level, obedience to rules
The ethics of citizenship and democratic theory; the ethics of virtue; ethics education; philosophical theory and perspectives on governance	The ethics of personal integrity and public managerial practice; self-conscious study of public administration; organizational approach to ethics; ethics codes, ethics legislation, corruption
The ethics of societal responsibility grounded in internal morality	*The ethics of bureaucratic responsibility grounded in external morality*
⇩	⇩
Lower Road: third level, rules of interaction	
The ethics of interaction; ethical foundations to hiring, promoting, firing, etc. of personnel	
The ethics of managerial responsibility grounded in internal and external morality	

Source: Rohr 1989, 60–61; Bruce 1995, 112, and adapted by author.

neutral in applying the rules of government. The contemporary understanding of politicized bureaucracy and street-level bureaucracy seems to refute that statement.

Bruce suggests a third level of ethics concerning the relation between supervisor and subordinate (Bruce 1995, 115). At this level, attention to such issues as cultural diversity, gender, and affirmative action is raised. It appears that at this third level the main concern is operational or managerial ethics and the nature of the interaction between supervisor and subordinate. Bruce argues that this requires attention from different disciplines, such as anthropology, sociology, moral philosophy, human resource management, and even theology. Henry (1999, 459) speaks of organizational humanism (i.e., third level ethics) and contrasts this with bureaucratic responsibility (i.e., second level ethics). It is not appropriate, though, to suggest a third level ethics as a category distinguishable from Rohr's two levels. Bruce's third level concerns the material object of ethical involvement (i.e., internal management), while Rohr is more focused on the type of involvement (internal vs. external). Each of Rohr's levels provides a different lens through which one can look at Bruce's category.

There is nothing wrong with education for democracy and representative bureaucracy but using public ethics to remind officials of their duty is only one step away (if that) from approaching ethics as something that can be regulated externally and thus imposed rather than internalized through various other ways of socialization (the family, the church, etc.) and disseminated by exemplary behavior. Indeed, once ethics are codified, we continue with the order of the day and appear to be shocked if our well-meant effort to regulate does not work. Furthermore, "public administrators may take the low road not because it is easier, but because that is all they know to do. They have not generally been taught to engage in moral reasoning" (Bruce 1995, 114). At present, the literature exploring the state of public ethics and critically discussing the lack of a deep foundation for administrative action is growing fast (e.g., Adams and Balfour 1998; Applbaum 1999; Cooper 1998; Van Wart 1998). None is more forceful than Louis Gawthrop, who observed that "the evidence is mounting that the current cadres of public-sector careerists are . . . immature in their comprehension of the ethical-moral democratic values that are integrally related to the notion of public service" (1998, 19). His study is a call and a challenge for us to reacquaint ourselves with the deep philosophical, historical, and theological foundations of Western democracy. Without such grounding of administrative action, ethics is reduced to operational ethics (Cooper 1998, 6), procedural ethics (Gawthrop 1998, 157), or professional ethics (Applbaum 1999, 64), which is a consequence of the fact that we have compartmentalized the various roles we play. Such a limited understanding of ethics has had an undesired consequence in the public realm. As Gawthrop remarks: "far too often the *appearance* of a commitment to duty is sufficient to fulfill the demands of service, and as a consequence the individual who is successful in *appearing* to be a dutiful public servant is most frequently viewed as an exemplary bureaucrat" (41). This observation appears to feed into the stereotype we have of bureaucrats, and Gawthrop does continue along these lines, for he argues that "in attempting to maintain the artificial appearance of duty, many public administrators have sought to link their commitment of service to the amoral pretense of detached objectivity, neutral competence, and dispassionate loyalty" (41). His analysis, though, does not stop there, and he is deeply sensitive to the fact that "the enormous expansion of public policy activity by the federal government during most of the twentieth century has imposed an almost intolerable burden on those who bear the responsibility to ensure that the laws are faithfully executed" (75). It is sad and a bit startling to conclude that apparently a fair number of public servants have little understanding of political theory that goes beyond attention to ideas about power and ideas about the relations between citizens and government. One of the explanations that has been suggested is the following: "One of the prices we had to pay for democracy was a decline in the intellectual quality of American political life and an eventual separation between ideas and power. As the common man rose to power in the decades following the Revolution, the inevitable consequence was the displacement from power of the uncommon man, the man of ideas" (Wood 1986, 110). In this quotation we can substitute "Western," for "American," which is also relevant for the second explanation as to why so little attention is paid to the first level of ethics. Attention to ethics emerged in the United States at the end of the nineteenth century in the desire to call widespread corruption to a halt (Maletz and Herbel 1998, 4). In Europe, corruption raised its head as a consequence of the growth of the welfare state, especially after World War II. On both sides of the Atlantic, ethics codes and ethics legislation were developed and became more strict and explicit in the course of time. We now even have an independent organization in Berlin by the name of Transparency International that annually compiles a corruption perception index ("Emerging Market Indicators," October 3, 1998, 120). There has been an unforeseen effect, though, for "the pursuit of comprehensive defenses against corruption leads to multiple levels of control and regulation, to meticulous supervision and review of employees, and to defensive management techniques—in short, to the opposite of creative, risk-taking, entrepreneurial methods of public management" (Maletz and Herbel 1998, 17). By its very nature, bureaucracy cannot but respond in a standardized manner. What we create with all those ethics codes is just more regulation (i.e., bureaucracy), and this is then yet another example of the vicious circle of bureaucracy. Maletz and Herbel conclude that ethics legislation in the United States is aimed more at preventing corruption rather than at inspiring public servants. The current emphasis on managerial and bureaucratic responsibility does not particularly inspire public servants to do good for society. It merely tells them how to behave within an organization. Such a regulatory approach reduces ethics to merely another text among so many. Approaching ethics as if it is law is equal to delegating responsibility for ethics from the individual to the organization (through, e.g., ethics codes). But just as the individuals cannot dissociate from their moral autonomy, an organization cannot impose an inner sense of morality. Hence, ethics-as-law obscures the fact that ethics must be embedded in an individual's sense of social responsibility.

An individual does not develop a sense of ethics and morality overnight, and upon that assumption a series of developmental stages can be recognized. The three main stages Kohlberg distinguishs in the development of moral reasoning from childhood to maturity are illustrative (taken from Kalat 1996, 423–425). The first main stage is *preconventional morality,* wherein the basis for the choice between right and wrong is determined by immediate consequences (punishment) and/or self-interest. At the next stage, *conventional morality,* a sense of right and wrong is based in public opinion and—at least in part—determined by an interpretation of civicness (i.e., what is my duty to and my role in society?). At the third main stage, *postconventional or principled morality*, judgments are rooted in the combination of legalistic social contract notions and universal ethical principles. It is not difficult to see the parallel between Rohr's first level and Kohlberg's third stage. More importantly, when focusing on Rohr's high road ethics in combination with Kohlberg's principled morality, it is clear why efforts to regulate ethical and moral behavior can have only limited success. Regulation of second and third level ethics does not guarantee ethical behavior. Regulating for moral integrity is an absurdity and impossibility. The idea that ethics can be regulated rests on the assumption that societal responsibility is disconnected from bureaucratic and managerial responsibilities; the idea thus is oblivious to the embedded nature of ethics. Regulated ethics can never be so effective that it actually constrains the choices we make at the level of principled morality. At Kohlberg's third level, law is no longer absolute for it is subject to what people consider important at a given point in time. The law should change in response to changing environmental circumstances, and when it does so, the activity of changing the law is an illustration of negotiable authority. Also, law is not absolute when it conflicts with higher ethical principles.

The insight that our attempts to regulate ethics are limited at best is good reason to briefly discuss Kohlberg. However, there is another reason, which has immediate bearing upon the understanding of government. A decision made by government is generally judged in terms of right and wrong while less attention is paid to the reasoning that supported and legitimated that decision. Kohlberg's schema, though, suggests that it is not the morality or immorality of a decision itself that is at stake, but the morality or immorality of the line of reasoning supporting and legitimating the decision. Rohr, however, argues that individual morality in general is not particularly instructive for public servants. Instead, he proposes that we have to look at the moral foundation in a specific role, and for the public sector these are the regime values. These regime values are constitutional values that can be found in the public law of a regime and are thus normative to public servants because they have sworn an oath to uphold the law (Rohr 1989, 68). Rohr's regime values are those that have been elaborated by political theorists since Locke: freedom, equality, and property (Rohr 1989, 217, 225). They are protected in the administrative state by the legislature, the executive, and the judiciary. In Rohr's words: "The three constitutional masters of the bureaucracy resemble the Olympian deities when they deign from time to time to intervene in administrative affairs through legislative oversight, executive orders, and judicial review" (284). These regime or constitutional values are defined at the highest level of abstraction possible for those seeking to cater to a population that is united in citizenship but divided in concrete policy choices.

Much of the public sector ethics literature in recent decades adopts a secular approach (e.g., Adams and Balfour 1998; Applbaum 1999; Cooper 1998; Frederickson 1993; Van Wart 1998) that is implicitly rooted in Greco-Roman thought about citizenship (see the next section). It is striking to see that only a few authors within the study of public administration (e.g., Gawthrop 1998; Golembiewski 1962, 1992; Raadschelders 2002b; and Stillman 1998) include the Judeo-Christian foundation of public sector ethics and thus of our society in the attempt to understand the ethical challenge of government. It appears that in a secular frame of mind, public sector ethics is concerned with bureaucratic and managerial responsibilities only. This implies that public sector ethics is different from ordinary ethics, for bureaucratic and managerial considerations are only relevant to public servants. That conclusion has been challenged, however. The separatist thesis, which claims professional ethics to be different from ordinary ethics, does not appear to hold up under empirical investigation. While the separatist thesis is descriptively true (as testified by the existence of ethics codes), the differences between professional ethics and ordinary public morality are negligible (Overman and Foss 1993, 130). Furthermore, professional occupation and organizational context have no significant impact upon the ability to identify ethical challenges (Stewart and Sprinthall 1993, 210–211). When Rohr argues in favor of developing a morality for specific roles instead of relying on more encompassing theories such as the one by Kohlberg (Rohr 1989, 64–68), I take that to imply a separate public sector ethics. I argue, however, that a public sector ethics in itself is meaningless when not seen as embedded in personal morality. This is not to say that a public sector ethics is useless, for it serves as external motivator and constraint of professional behavior. Also, we cannot assume that a sense and understanding of public sector ethics (as different from a general sense of ethics) develop within the more general context of the family and the school system.

4.5. Civil Religion, Civic Culture, and Citizenship as Secular Sources for Moral Guidance

The initial focus in the 1970s and 1980s on second and third level ethics has been supplemented with renewed, although still limited, attention to first level ethics in the late 1990s. More than ever before, policy makers have become aware of how past, present, and future are connected. They are aware that they have an obligation to the future. In an eloquent discussion of what he calls intergenerational social equity, Frederickson observes, "Many of the routine decisions of policy makers and the implementation of public administrators appear to support the existence of a vertical moral community in which present generations act favorably on behalf of both near-term and long-term future generations" (1994, 461). While the bureaucratic and managerial ethics of the second and third levels mainly serve to ensure accountability for public actions in the present, the concept of "vertical moral community" draws upon a sense of societal responsibility that resides in the individual. Furthermore, it is a sense of ethics that not only travels forward in time (i.e., what is my/our moral obligation to the next generations?) but also is reconstructed backward in time, because public administrators are coming to the realization that "while present decisions cannot affect the past, they can be ignorant of the past and therefore badly informed" (Frederickson 1994, 464, note 5). The literature on public sector ethics has grown substantially since the first edition of Rohr's study (1978), but it remains too focused on the second and third levels. Henry—like Bruce—points out that "public administrators do make political decisions, but no effective moral and philosophical guidelines (as opposed to *mechanisms* for correcting "bad" decisions) exist for their making these decisions in the public interest (Henry 1999, 459). Second and third level ethics do not provide moral and philosophical guidelines because they should not. If they did, the public sector's claim to impartiality would be jeopardized. Nor can moral and philosophical guidelines be found in nationalism, in the imagined community of a citizenry, or in our civil religion. Civil religion is not connected to a specific denomination or a specific political ideology, instead centering on civic life while welcoming the religious support for public institutions (Zuckert 1986, 182). All countries have a civil religion, and it is expressed in symbols (the flag), in language ("In God We Trust," the Pledge of Allegiance), in buildings and monuments (the White House, the Lincoln Memorial), in documents (the Declaration of Independence, the Constitution), in rituals (the Fourth of July, Memorial Day, Thanksgiving), and in heroes (George Washington, Abraham Lincoln, Martin Luther King) (Fowler and Hertzke 1995, 293). This type of civil religion, however, is not strong enough in itself to make the individual voluntarily restrain behavior. The fear of God, however, would, and that was at the heart of many a (pragmatic) political theory in the seventeenth and eighteenth centuries. In his sober analysis, Locke held that society can never rest on strictly philosophical foundations, because people at large cannot philosophize. Only a few aim at something higher and nobler (theirs is the God of the philosophers), while the many are attracted to superstition and passionately (instead of rationally) embrace religion as believers (Zuckert 1986, 199, 203). George Washington believed in an "invisible hand" and looked upon religion as a politician, believing it was necessary to sustain civil society (Berns 1986, 212–213). Likewise, de Tocqueville and Abraham Lincoln were convinced that liberty could not govern without faith and that religion is needed more in democracy than in any other type of polity (Berns 1986, 214). This is because democracy as we know it is the open polity of "a pluralistic culture based on communication and persuasion, a culture of consensus and diversity, a culture that permitted change but moderated it. This was the civic culture" (Almond and Verba 1963, 6). In this civic culture, the individual is neither only a member of a community (i.e., the parochial political culture) nor only a passive subject in an elite government, but also plays the active political role of the participant in governance and government (339). The civic culture is a political culture where individuals alternate between their roles as citizens, as subjects, and as parochials (19). Almond and Verba argue that it is very important that participation in a civic political culture is neither purely instrumental nor solely emotional. Political commitment cannot be totally unemotional for then the effectiveness of the political system would be judged only in terms of performance and could give way to opportunism. Too much passion, though, will blind politics to reason (353–355). How to maintain the balance between passion and reason in a society where there are potentially as many opinions as there are people is the major challenge of democracy in a secularized society. Schattschneider voiced it thus: "how can we organize a society of [280 million] ordinary people so that it remains sensitive to their needs? This is a problem of *leadership, organization, alternatives, and systems of responsibility and confidence*" (as quoted in Almond and Verba 1963, 342). It is intriguing that Schattschneider perceives the problem of the allocation of values mainly in bureaucratic and managerial terms, which is the core of the study of public administration. This turns civic culture into a celebration of human engineering and provides societal stability and consensus through negotiation. From this it follows that political choices are embedded in civic culture. Is civic culture, in turn, embedded in something or is it the secular foundation of a diversified society?

Almond and Verba argue that civic culture is transmitted through socialization in a variety of social institutions, such as family, peer group, school, work place, and the political system (367). They do not mention religious institutions as a source of socialization, and nowadays religion is perceived more as a divisive rather than a uniting force. One can make a case, however, for the argument that religion could be brought back into public sector ethics, but for that we need to make a distinction between religion as an organized, hence, negotiated ritual and religion as a source of guidance. At the more visible level of organized ritual and negotiated dogma, it is clear that Protestants, Catholics, Muslims, Buddhists, and so forth, reach different conclusions about how to pursue what they value. Clearly, policy choices grounded in an identification with a particular denomination do not necessarily serve the needs of a society at large. In other words, a particular interpretation of ethics and morality will not help to define public sector ethics. Bringing organized religion back in the public sector is dangerous to society as a whole.

But religion (as a source for moral guidance) is already back when we recognize that the Judeo-Christian values are part of the fabric of Western society next to the more secular ethics of ancient Greece and Rome. In the Judeo-Christian and in the Greco-Roman traditions, respect for the individual is defined in societal and relational terms: love and respect (honor) your neighbor as yourself; give to the community what has been given to you; respond to the needs of others. In this sense, the Protestant values Stillman identified as important to public sector reform in the 1860 to 1940 period (section 4.2 above) may just as well be called secular. The least one can say is that Protestantism enabled the revival of secular Greco-Roman thought about civicness. What both the religious and secular approaches to morality emphasize is the membership in a community which makes the individual into a citizen. Citizenship in the liberal tradition provides an identity that is crucial for the development of the individual's moral maturity (see discussion of Kohlberg above). It is in a community, whether religious or secular, that a person grows as a social being and becomes aware of the needs of others. Equally important is that the citizen identity rises beyond the other social identities as they are defined by gender, religion, social class, race, and culture (Heater 1990, 183). Citizenship based in reason balances the emotions generated by other social identities and by naked nationalism. At the same time, however, citizenship should not gobble up these other identities, for that is the way to totalitarianism. In Huxley's *Brave New World* there are no citizens because the essential citizen right of freedom is violated (Heater 1990, 184).

It is in citizenship and civic culture that group cultures can be embraced, which is all the more important in the multiethnic societies of the Western world. Education for citizenship should thus establish not only responsibility and respect for such procedural values (to use Heater's phrase, 1990, 202) as freedom, toleration, fairness, respect for truth, and reason, but also a sense of loyalty to different levels of community (Raadschelders 2002a). From antiquity well into the Middle Ages, citizenship was primarily located at the local, city-state level. With the advent of the nation-state, where the sovereignty encompassed different localities, citizenship also became a matter of national identification. Finally, globalization in our own age also makes us aware of global responsibilities (e.g., to develop policies protecting the rain forest and endangered species, decreasing the hole in the ozone layer, redistributing wealth through development aid). Building upon Thomas Paine's argument that individuals recognize each other as neighbors, as townsmen, or as countrymen, dependent upon circumstances of contact, Heater advances a multilayered sense of citizenship that includes responsibilities to the locality and region, to the nation, and to the international community (Heater 1990, 318–323).

With all due respect, the churches no longer and can no longer reach each of these communities as a whole. They can only reach their membership and pursue selected missions. The only institution that does have the "universal" authority to act on behalf of the entire population, even under circumstances of distrust and legitimacy crisis, is government. What public sector ethics needs to be complete—and this argument is far better advanced by Gawthrop and Stillman—is the recognition that the ethics of bureaucratic and managerial responsibility are once again seen as embedded in a personal ethics that, as far as Western society is concerned, is rooted in both the Judeo-Christian religious and in the Greco-Roman secular traditions. This implies that we should balance our teleological bureaucratic and managerial ethics (focused by necessity upon output) with the more deontological societal and relational values. The latter cannot be codified through law nor expressed in codes of ethics. They can be inscribed upon the individual only through socialization from very early in life. This does not mean there is no place for public sector ethics education. In fact, it is necessary not only to instill a particular organizational morality but to teach that other viewpoints are as respectable and legitimate as the ones we were taught by parents, peers, and teachers. Ethics education will help in developing respect for other viewpoints, and that is what a public servant needs to be able to truly serve *sine ira et studio* (without anger or passion).

4.6. Western Political Cultures: Same Philosophical Roots, Different Policy Choices

Why is it important to dig beyond the bureaucratic and managerial ethics and look at their Judeo-Christian and Greco-Roman roots? Part of the answer has been given above: second and third level ethics disregard too much the personal ethics. The other part of the answer is that both the Judeo-Christian and Greco-Roman traditions have influenced Western political culture at large, but that the specific geographical context made for different choices with respect to, for instance, policy. In this section, I describe three different social-political cultures (Table 4.1) and compare the United States to Europe.

Bellah et al. (1996) distinguish three strands in social-political systems. While their study focuses on the United States, the more general argument is relevant to European countries as well. In the *politics of community*, individuals are by nature involved and strive for a consensus. The position of the individual in society is defined in terms of biblical individualism, which is the freedom to do what is good, just, and honest. That freedom, in turn, is defined on the basis of religious (Protestant) principles that stipulate production for the common good and in response to need. In those local communities, welfare depends upon individual and local institutional (church and government) charity. No or little government intervention is deemed necessary since all members of the community are aware of and adhere to the rights and duties of citizenship. This type of social-political culture is characteristic of the self-governing small towns in the early American colonies and

Table 4.1

Three Major Types of Social-Political Systems

Social-political system	Community	Nation	Pluralism
Understanding of individualism	Biblical individualism	Republican individualism	Utilitarian individualism
Style of governance	Consensual, local	Consensual, national	Conflictual, semi-legitimate bargaining
View of politics	Natural involvement	National purpose	Art of the possible
View of leaders	Wise and meritorious, amateur politicians	Servants, impartial statesmen, pursuing nation's interest	Professional politicians as mediators and brokers, pursuing self-interest
View of citizenship	Independent and holding to religion and to rights and duties of citizenship	Independent and symbolic; public office is a calling	Independent and holding to image of self-made man
Perspective on economy	Produce for common good and in response to needs	Government assistance to private economy	Triumph of competitive market
Perspective on welfare	Depends highly upon individual and local institutional charity	Depends much more on government intervention on behalf of the poor	Neocapitalism produces welfare for all through an "invisible hand"

Source: After Bellah et al. 1996, 28–33, 200–201, 218, 262–266.

the small (city-state, provincial) governments in Europe between the fourteenth and the eighteenth centuries (specifically, the German principalities and cities, the Low Countries, and Northern Italy).

The *politics of nation* is focused on national purpose, and politicians are wise and impartial statesmen who serve the nation's interest. Republican individualism embraces a self-governing society where all participate as relative equals. In this social-political culture, it is not private charity but government that produces welfare through targeted intervention (e.g., taxation policies, entitlement programs) on behalf of the disadvantaged. Citizens are involved in politics not because they are members of a physical community, but because they seek to serve a national purpose. This type of social-political system fits the emergent nation-state and appears when nationalism becomes defined. For the United States and France, this happened in the second half of the eighteenth century; for the Netherlands and Germany, this mainly happened in the course of the nineteenth century. In Europe, the politics of nation is more or less a continuation of the politics of community but on a larger scale. Social-democratic, socialist, and religious understandings of government's role in society have largely determined that European governments are the prime providers of welfare services. This generally goes back to a past wherein such services were provided through both private (guilds, churches) and public routes (e.g., public health and public education services at the local level). In the United States, the politics of nation is a departure from the past in the sense that a national government exists next to local and state governments. This political tradition in the United States becomes most visible in the New Deal policies of the 1930s and subsequent social welfare policies as generally pursued by the Democratic party.

Finally, in the *politics of pluralism,* different interests are pursued by professional politicians who need to mediate between overlapping and conflicting interests. The style of governance is much more conflictual than in the other two political cultures, and politics is reduced to being the art of what is possible. This political culture has its counterpart in the economic culture of the competitive market. In this neocapitalist competitive market, government does not need to intervene on behalf of the disadvantaged, for the market produces welfare for all. Benjamin Franklin's belief that when we all work hard, we all will, albeit to varying degrees, harvest, is embraced most recently by George W. Bush ("all boats will rise"). In the United States, this social-political culture clashes with the politics of nation, for the Democratic and Republican parties hold very different views of the role of national government vis-à-vis that of the states. In Europe, on the other hand, there is a politics of pluralism (certainly in countries that generally rely on coalition governments: the Netherlands, Belgium, Germany, France, Spain, the Scandinavian countries, Italy), but this is not perceived as conflicting with the politics of nation, probably because there is a much stronger state tradition in Europe than there is in the United States. Relations between various tiers of government are in Western Europe generally regarded as complementary rather than conflictual, as in the United States.

All Western countries share the same foundation in Judeo-Christian and Greco-Roman thought about civicness, civil religion, and civic culture. However, the geography, the history, and the place of individuals within each country make them respond differently to comparable policy challenges. Hence, most if not all readers of this book will agree in general terms to definitions of civicness, civil religion, and civic culture. Where they will disagree is what these mean in terms of actual policies, and no education can teach that. Also, most readers of this book will agree that it is very difficult to determine what the role of religion in the public sphere is or can be beyond the statement that it helps to shape a personal outlook on life and thus on government. It appears that in the past some type of congruence existed between the local political and the local religious community. The increased interdependence between local government and higher levels of government raised awareness of cultural and religious differences, so government at present emphasizes the secular basis of its policies. The role of Judeo-Christian moral values in the public sphere is now strictly limited to the individual. This means that religious background and roots are important for understanding people's motives: they are no longer important as a basis of government at the local up to the national levels.

4.7. Concluding Remarks

There can be little doubt that the nature of society, and thus of its government, has changed. Living in the midst of such momentous changes, scholars such as Tönnies and Durkheim resorted to fairly simple dichotomized conceptualizations of social and industrial change. In this chapter, we have seen that the loss of community continued to be a concern throughout the twentieth century. In addition to the pessimism about the future of society among a variety of authors, there are also some optimistic views. Thus, forty years ago, Daniel Bell wrote that the from-community-to-society thesis is too romantic and slightly false for creating the idea that in the past people lived in organic, close-knit communities that were shattered by industrialism and urbanization and replaced by a cold, impersonal, and atomistic society. Bell reminds us that this process did not happen overnight and that this thesis disregards the human capacity to adapt to and be creative in new social forms. Furthermore, if society is that impersonal, self-centered, and barren, how can the flourishing of social bonds in urban and metropolitan areas be explained? (Bell 1961, 27–28, 33).

Putnam and colleagues also argue against Tönnies' evolutionary thesis for it is a perspective that assumes the disappearance of the civic community and the advance of the modern metropolis, technologically advanced, but dehumanizing, inducing civic passivity and self-seeking individualism (Putnam et al. 1993, 114). Through their empirical work in Italy, they found an unusual concentration of overlapping networks of social solidarity and webs of civic community in the northern regions where the community values solidarity, civic engagement, cooperation, and honesty (115). This sense of community and civicness is, in large part, explained by community traditions that go back to the late Middle Ages and thus built substantial social capital (167). Northern Italy's civic communities are secular communities (109). Religion functions next to these and is not a necessary condition for civicness.

Comparing the United States with Europe and Japan, Crozier et al. (1975) discuss the breakdown of traditional authority (politics, church, education) in their countries and regions. Responding to Crozier's discussion, Ralf Dahrendorf acknowledges that a general political public no longer exists, but that there is no reason to be pessimistic about the future of democracy, community, and citizenship (in Crozier et al. 1975, 191–193). Reflecting upon both arguments, Samuel Huntington sketches two future scenarios (in Crozier et al. 1975, 196). In the pessimistic scenario, the self-destructive tendencies and mounting accumulation of citizen demand dominate and result in a demand overload. The optimistic scenario relies on the flexibility and openness of democracy. To Huntington's view, I would add that a pessimistic scenario rests upon the assumption that individualism will triumph over collectivism, but that, combining the arguments made by Bell, the evidence presented by Putnam, and the hopes outlined in Crozier et al., there is reason for optimism because although the moral foundation of society and government is expressed differently than it was 100 years ago, in terms of substance, it is quite the same.

PART II

WHAT SERVICES DOES GOVERNMENT PROVIDE? THE SOCIETAL (INSTITUTIONAL) LEVEL

Having explored the constitution of society and government in part I, we can now focus on the institutional superstructure of government in society and the services that it provides. The institutional superstructure can be analyzed in terms of both political theory and in terms of basic administrative structure. The legal and moral foundations of society and government (see chapters 3 and 4) find their expression in the political culture of representative democracy in mass society and in the political-administrative structure of intergovernmental relations (chapter 5). Democracy as political theory is the foundation and democracy as intergovernmental relations is the framework for the provision of a wide range of services. Public service delivery is the most immediate and visible link between society and government (hence, societal level of governance). It is part of the institutional framework because it is an expression of the division of labor between public and private providers of collective services. It expresses which collective services we value so much that we do not entrust them to the market. In chapter 6, I discuss the development of law, justice, and social justice in Western society and the challenges that the judiciary and its various functions face at present. In chapter 7, I focus on the maintenance of public order and safety through the services of the military and the police. Here too, the historical perspective serves to highlight how much their current role and challenges differ from those of the past. In the course of the past 120 years, the nightwatch state services discussed in chapters 6 and 7 have been supplemented with a wide range of services that now identify most Western democracies as welfare states. These services will be discussed in chapter 8 both in terms of their origin and development as well as in terms of their future.

5   DEMOCRACY: BETWEEN LOCAL COMMUNITY AND NATIONAL GOVERNMENT

Many forms of government have been tried, and will be tried in this world of sin and woe. No one pretends that democracy is perfect or all-wise. Indeed, it has been said that democracy is the worst form of government except all those other forms that have been tried from time to time.
—Winston Churchill

Democracy dies five miles from the parish pump.
—H.G. Wells, as quoted in Durant, 1963

The effective public administrator . . . will be like a skillful architect-builder who realizes that IGR [intergovernmental relations] in the United States is like a huge, complex building under continual construction and reconstruction.
—Deil S. Wright, 1988

Democracy as rule (in Greek, *krateoo*) by the people (in Greek, *demos*) is institutionalized as a particular division of labor between public and private institutions as well as a division of labor between public servants and citizens. The first division of labor refers to the balance between government intervention and self-governance. The second concerns the balance between direct citizen participation and indirect citizen representation. Together, these conceptualizations of democracy serve the understanding of the size and the overall institutional structure. Making democracy work in mass society is a major challenge. The modern concepts of coproduction, public-private partnership, participative democracy, corporatism, and so forth are expressions of the desire to somehow better organize the interaction between government and its citizens. How difficult it is to organize citizen involvement becomes clear when looking at the changing meaning of the concept of civil society. While in the nineteenth century this generally referred to "family, social relationships . . . , churches, schools, professions and crafts, and economic organizations" in the late twentieth century it "presents itself as a structure of control and discipline rather than as a paradigm of freedom and spontaneity. . . . Civil society now represents structures of power which self-consciously exercise disciplinary functions that erase the differences between state and society" (Wolin 1989, 27–28). This statement can be true only if civil society is merely regarded as a means to offload government by recasting the division of labor between citizens and government. Recasting that division of labor is prompted in part by the perception that the gap between democracy as we desire it and democracy as we perceive it has been widening. Why is this so? Is it a consequence of population growth or are there deeper reasons, such as a fundamental crisis of government's legitimacy? Another question is whether this crisis is at all relevant to public administration. Mainstream public administration literature has given substantial attention to this legitimacy crisis. The legitimacy crisis of government was the playground for the political theorist. And yet, democracy and the administrative state are inseparable. Modern democracy would not work without the extensive resources offered by the administrative state. Within the context of the administrative state, democracy assumes a particular manifestation. Direct participation is embedded in a system of representation that is tailored to serve large populations (sections 5.1 and 5.2) who identify with their community in powerful symbols that evoke emotion yet at the same demand rationality (section 5.3). Given mass society, the major challenge of government is to assure democracy as well as effectiveness and efficiency, the classical dilemma (Self 1979, 277–278) (section 5.4). Democracy thus requires an *institutional superstructure*, a concept first coined by Herbert Croly (1914, 53). That superstructure includes the nature of interaction in the political culture between public and private elites and citizens (i.e., models of democracy) (section 5.5) as well as the interaction between tiers of government (section 5.6). With respect to the latter, I view central-local or intergovernmental relations as an expression of the horizontal and vertical divisions of labor in contemporary democracy.

5.1. Democracy Theory and Center(s) of Power

Democracy can be defined at two levels at least (Van Braam 1986, 326). At the level of *theory and ideology*, democracy refers to a state system in which sovereignty is formally invested in the citizens. In this context it may, more specifically, refer to a system of guaranteed civil rights and freedoms. Among the classic civil rights are freedom of speech, freedom of association, and freedom of the press, while the human and social rights are of more recent origin. Democracy in this sense supports a society in which individuals, in principle, have their rights revoked only if their actions have been in some way harmful to others. At the level of *day-to-day practice*, democracy refers to the actual influence and participation of citizens in policy and decision making.

Democracy as we know it is of relatively recent origin. While the concept has traveled from ancient Athens to our time, it is only in the past 200 years that we actually speak of *liberal democracy*. The earliest advocates of this were Charles Lennox, third duke of Richmond (1735–1806), Jeremy Bentham (1748–1832), and James Mill (1773–1836). In a speech on June 2, 1780, before the English House of Lords, the radical duke advanced a proposal developed by the Society for Constitutional Information, which had been established earlier that year, with local branches throughout England and Scotland by 1790 (Plumb 1980, 157). He proposed annual elections, equal electoral districts, secret ballots, abolition of property qualifications for members of Parliament (MPs), payment of MPs and male suffrage (Heater 1990, 41–42). His ideas were echoed by Bentham and Mill, who advocated a secret ballot, political party competition for leadership, frequent elections, separation of powers, and freedom of speech and association, which together would ensure the interest of the general public. With that phrase, they did not refer to all people, but rather to the greatest happiness for the greatest number. They believed this to be the only scientifically defensible and ideologically acceptable criterion for liberal democracy (Held 1985, 15–16). In order for this principle of utility to work, government should be efficient in its service delivery, which could be achieved only through a centralization of authority. Bentham was very suspicious of local government (Carnoy 1984, 250). In his view, democracy should abolish inefficient local self-government and embrace national, centralized government (Hill 1974, 26). Local government would then function as an administrative extension of national government. These sentiments could be found in the United States as well. Hamilton acknowledged that the affection of individuals started with the family and then "traveled upwards, from their neighborhood, to local government, to state and finally the Union" (cf. Heater's conception of multilayered citizenship). This would be so "unless the force of that principle should be destroyed by a much better administration of the latter" (*Federalist,* no. 17, 1982, 81). Similar remarks are made in several other places (*Federalist,* nos. 27, 37, 45, and 46; 1982, 131, 178, 233, 238).

The emphasis on efficient government was countered by calling attention to democratic government in itself. In his *Local Government and Centralisation* (1851), Toulmin Smith nostalgically referred to a happy past in which the local government was truly a haven of community. Support for the idea of local self-governance in the more distant manner of the scholar came from John Stuart Mill (1806–1873). In his conception, democracy ought to provide the framework within which individual capacities could be channeled and developed. In his view, local government was the school for democracy that not only gave individuals the chance to act as citizens, but would even serve to emancipate people who would otherwise not have a chance:

> in the case of local bodies, besides the function of electing, many citizens in turn have the chance of being elected, and many, either by selection or by rotation, fill one or other of the numerous local executive offices. In these positions they have to act for public interests, as well as to think and to speak, and the thinking cannot all be done by proxy. It may be added, that these local functions, not being in general sought by the higher ranks, carry down the important political education which they are the means of conferring to a much lower grade in society. (Mill 1984, 378)

Contrary to his father, James Mill, and to Jeremy Bentham, who were reluctant to promote universal suffrage, J.S. Mill accepted the consequences of his reasoning and advocated voting rights for all men and, later (1869), for women. However, considering the elitist arguments of Bentham and James Mill, he did consider a plural voting system in which the wiser and more talented would have more votes than the ignorant and less able (Held 1985, 19). While J.S. Mill defended individualism and individual responsibility, he also recognized that some people were simply not able to adequately care for themselves (the senior citizen, the mentally or physically disabled, very young and orphaned children, etc.). It was for this group that government could and should provide a safety net (*social liberalism*). In general, though, state intervention was to be limited for three reasons. First, when individuals can do something better than government (a subsidiarity argument), then government should not intervene. Second, when an individual may not do a particular task as well as a public official, but the necessity of "mental education" is still to be recommended (e.g., jury duty), then government, again, should not interfere. Third, one should not unnecessarily add to the power of government (Mill 1984, 178–180).

Mill's reluctance to advocate universal suffrage stemmed from a fear of the tyranny of the majority. This was a serious consideration throughout the nineteenth century, when voices that supported government intervention in favor of disadvantaged groups were increasingly heard, while at the same time the logical consequence—expansion of the franchise—was suspect. Bentham and James Mill excluded the labor class and women; J.S. Mill qualified their suffrage. All considered suffrage to be a right that ought to be exercised by those of a high station in life. Theirs was a *representative democracy* or *indirect democracy,* not just in a numerical sense (the greatest number) but also in an ideological sense (the greatest happiness). A *populist democracy*, as one could call Rousseau's ideal of *direct democracy,* should be avoided. The ideal direct democracy was one where all citizens would meet in one place and discuss and decide matters of public interest. From a practical point of view, such direct democracy is possible only at the city-state level. Larger populations and larger territories in a democracy can be governed only indirectly through representation. The downside of representative democracy in the nineteenth century was considered to be the tyranny of the majority. The downside of representative democracy under expanded suffrage was voiced by Durant:

> The larger the number of voters, the more ordinary must be the man or the qualities that will appeal to them. We do not demand greatness or foresight in our elected officials, but only bare-toothed oratory and something this side of starvation. . . . In a nation where the few who really rule must get some show of popular consent, a special class arises whose function it is, not to govern, but to secure the approval of the people for whatever policy may have been decided upon by that inevitable oligarchy which hides in the heart of every democratic state. We call this class of men politicians. (Durant 1963, 293–294)

There is perhaps a sense of resignation in the first part of this remark, because rule by the people is expected to have a detrimental effect on the intellectual quality of those who rule. One can even read this as an elitist observation about twentieth-century democracy. What is interesting about this remark is that it was originally published in 1929, years before the Italian elite theorists (Michels 1966; Mosca 1972; Pareto 1935) were translated and had become available to the American readership. Thus, Durant's observations are likely to have a different source, namely in the ideas of the Hamiltonians and the reformers of the Progressive Era, who heralded efficiency and sought to control corruption: "Bureaucracy remains, as it always will; oligarchy remains, as it always will; but it is trained and responsible bureaucracy, a highly constitutional and limited oligarchy. Democracy remains—in elections—aristocracy is joined with it—through the restriction of the office to the best; but it is a democracy without incompetence or corruption, and an aristocracy without heredity or privilege" (Durant 1963, 316–317). Ideas of centralization for efficiency had met resistance among the Jeffersonians in the late eighteenth and among the Populists in the late nineteenth century. Both strongly supported a decentralized, if not almost confederate institutional structure on behalf of democracy. Aspirations and needs of democracy had to steer between the need for access at the local level and the need for efficiency at the national level. The sheer size of the American territory, even 200 years ago, defied any simple and clear-cut solutions.

5.2. Size and Democracy

The main challenge, then and now, is to protect the interests of democracy in society at large without too much concentration of power and to advance the needs of the local communities without too much loss of efficiency. Large-scale democracy was protected against the evils of centralization and inefficiency in two ways. First, of course, there was a division of labor between the executive, the legislative, and the judiciary authorities at the apex of the state and administrative system. The second was a separation of politics and administration, which goes back to the time of the Atlantic Revolutions. Without the changes during the decades between 1780 and 1820, modern government would not have been possible. These changes included the formal separation of office and officeholder so as to avoid ownership of office, the distinction between a public and a private sector, and, as a consequence, the legal separation of state and church. Given the separation of public and private, and the identification of what was public with the state, civil servants became public servants. The challenge was to avoid abuse of office by the top administrators—which had been fairly normal for most of history. The solution was found in determining who was accountable to whom. Political office would henceforth be reserved for the absolute top of the public service and could be acquired only through popular election (instead of through co-optation on the basis of relations of kinship or friendship). In the administrative offices, individuals were to be appointed upon merit and subjected to the authority of the elected official, instead of being invested with office on the basis of kinship (nepotism) or friendship (favoritism). There is no denying that favoritism and nepotism still play a role in politics and in the allocation of high offices (the "old boys network"), but it is far more restrained than ever before.

In the United States as well as on the European continent, politics and administration came to be perceived as separate realms: "Energy in the executive" is as essential to good government as is the "steady administration of the laws" (*Federalist,* no. 70, 1982, 355). The executive has to be concentrated in one office only and not in a collegial body such as a council, in order to prevent that "an artful cabal in that council would be able to distract and to enervate the whole system of administration. If no such cabal should exist, the mere diversity of views and opinions would alone be sufficient to tincture the exercise of the executive authority with a spirit of habitual feebleness and dilatoriness" (*Federalist,* no. 70, 1982, 358). Hamilton's choice of the word "cabal" is an example of how the American political theory drew upon experience with English government. The acronym "cabal," as developed in late seventeenth-century England, referred to a group of individuals that dominated English domestic and foreign policies in the 1660s: Clifford, Arlington,

Buckingham, Ashley-Cooper, and Lauderdale (see Lockyer 1982, 358). Unity of administration (i.e., of bureaucracy) would be served by the duration (i.e., tenure) in office, which in turn would add to the stability of the system of administration (*Federalist,* no. 71, 1982, 362). Administration in the larger sense, so Hamilton reasoned, was concerned with government in its entirety and included not only the executive but also the legislative and the judiciary. In its more limited meaning, administration referred only to the executive in all its responsibilities. Following the unity of command principle upon which the executive rests, "The Persons therefore, to whose immediate management these different matters are committed, ought to be considered as the assistants or deputies of the chief magistrate; and, on this account, they ought to derive their offices from his appointment, at least from his nomination, and ought to be subject to his superintendence" (*Federalist,* no. 72 1982, 366). Stability, however, is not provided only through the executive. In *Federalist* no. 70 it is also a function of the legislature, which will come to a consensus after deliberation and according to wisdom. It is in the legislature that the people can voice various opinions, thus avoiding the tyranny of the majority. But stability is also provided by unity of the administration, which concerns not only the highest executive office but all executive departments. It is in that sense that, in the young American republic, politics and administration for all practical purposes were considered separate spheres in which "administration stands above the partisan, interest-dominated conflicts of politics" (Wolin 1989, 98). The legal-theoretical foundation for the politics-administration dichotomy was further explored in the late nineteenth century (Stillman 1992; Goodnow 1900). The distinction between the *energy* of the executive as a uniting force under political leadership and the *stability* of the legislature in combination with the *stability* of the administrative departments echoes in the model of political-administrative relations at the top that Aberbach, Putnam, and Rockman (1981) developed. Finally, an independent judiciary is important to stability for it functions as mediator between opposing interests, as interpreter of laws, and, to use de Tocqueville's phrase, as a moral force (Maletz 1998, 610, 614). Together, the executive, the legislative, and the judiciary serve as center(s) of power carefully balanced vis-à-vis one another, and all are supported by bureaucracy.

While the basic institutional framework is not often challenged or changed, its structure and functioning respond to a constantly changing society. These changes have both a territorial and a functional aspect. I further explore the territorial aspect in this section. The functional aspect, what government does for society, will be more extensively discussed in chapters 6 to 8.

The increasing consolidation and concentration of power in one territory, the connecting of hitherto isolated communities into a nation (see section 5.3), and major changes in the economic structure of society (e.g., urbanization, industrialization) together heralded a major transformation of the social structure. The political consequence of the emancipation of the masses was democratization along the lines of indirect representation. In the United States and in Europe, these democracies were established in a matter of decades. The major difference between European and American developments is that in America a representative democracy was designed, defended, and negotiated in a very brief period of time. For both the young American and European democracies, the challenge was to overcome the problem that geographical distance imposed on government and citizen. In the words of the *Federalist:* "As the natural limit of a democracy is that distance from the central point, which will just permit the most remote citizens to assemble as often as their public functions demand; and will include no greater number than can join in those functions" (no. 14, 1982, 64). That is, the natural limit of direct democracy is determined by geography (i.e., how much distance can be traveled on horseback in a day) and by population size (i.e., how many people can effectively be involved in decision making). This limitation is basically overcome by means of representation. In the words of the *Federalist:* "The two great points of difference between a Democracy and a Republic are, first, the delegation of the Government, in the latter, to a small number of citizens elected by the rest: secondly the greater number of citizens, and greater sphere of country, over which the latter may be extended" (no. 10, 1982, 46). According to the *Federalist,* democracy can be exercised directly only by the people. The idea that true democracy can exist only in small-scale government the size of a city-state is phrased even more clearly in the following observation:

> in a democracy, the people meet and exercise the government in person; in a republic they assemble and administer it by their representatives and agents. A democracy consequently will be confined to a small spot. A republic may be extended over a large region. (no. 14, 1982, 63)

One could argue that the *catchment area* of early democracies was quite a bit smaller than that of today. Forces of centralization and decentralization were perhaps much more visible and more directly felt than nowadays. Even though, today, citizens in Western societies continue to express concerns about creeping centralization, it is also true that the various tiers of government rely more upon each other than ever before. In this sense, the intricate system of intergovernmental relations prevents extreme (de)centralization. Also, thanks to the communication revolution, citizen participation no longer depends upon the health and speed of a horse. The catchment area of a government is no longer defined by geography and population size but by speed of information exchange.

Once a representative democracy is established, the challenge is to develop a political-administrative system that can deal with majorities and minorities through institutional checks and balances. Dahl and Lindblom reject the idea that the only choice possible was one between representative (Bentham, Hamilton) or populist democracy (Jefferson, Rousseau). What they have termed *polyarchy* focuses on the nature of the control that the citizenry at large can exercise over the leaders. Characteristic of polyarchy are: secret ballots, equal weight of votes, subordination of administration to politics, subordination of politics to citizenry, availability of information resources, and freedom of opinion (Dahl and Lindblom 1953, 277–278). Dahl and Lindblom's approach is, in Mansfield's analysis, behavioralistic and thus ignorant of the formal role of the Constitution (1991, 151–153). The chapter in which Mansfield discusses Dahl is worthwhile reading because Mansfield's analysis of the social sciences' approach to the study of the U.S. Constitution makes a case that an adequate understanding is not possible from one disciplinary angle only.

From the beginning of modern government, around 1800, size was a consideration at various levels. In one way or another, all democracies in the making increasingly experienced a tension between local and central government. In nineteenth-century northwest Europe, this was apparent in the various municipal acts that sought to define local government's relation to central government. In the United States, this tension was visible in the conscious effort, during the adoption of the Constitution, to somehow reconcile the need for stronger national government with the colonial tradition of local self-government and of loosely connected states. De Tocqueville's analysis of this tension represents an early foreign appreciation of the novelty of the new American political theory (Maletz 1998, 602, 606). The problem of size in modern democracy is not addressed through reconfiguring constitutional foundations, but through reinforcement of national identity (section 5.3 below) and through piecemeal engineering of central-local or intergovernmental relations (section 5.4 below).

5.3. Basis for Contemporary Democracy: Collective Identity, Memory, and Morality

The consequence of enlarged territory for governance is that people may not identify as easily with a far-away government as they would with their local community. Yet H.G. Wells's remark quoted at the opening of this chapter is cynical and not entirely correct. In modern society, the geographically contained communities of the "olden days" are supplemented with citizen-communities that do not operate in a small geographic area. In a representative democracy or extended republic, the citizen identifies with something more abstract. The collective identity in modern societies is not based on kinship, friendship, or neighborly care, but builds upon shared symbols such as a national anthem, a national hero, a flag, a currency. In this sense, modern populations are indeed imagined communities (Anderson 1995) where the sense of togetherness is elaborated as equality before the law, which is an abstract rather than a tangible brotherhood. Public education, geared to making the new generation emotionally sensitive to national symbols and familiar with the geography of the land, the history of its people, and the current social stratification, is a major vehicle in the perpetuation of this collective identity. Toward the end of his brief and elegant study, Anderson remarks: "Because there is no Originator, the nation's biography cannot be written evangelically, 'down time,' through a long procreative chain of begettings. The only alternative is to fashion it 'up time'" (Anderson 1995, 205). The idea of fashioning history "up time," so characteristic of modernity, is echoed forcefully in Wolin's introduction and first two chapters on collective identity and memory, where he argues that the bicentennial, celebrating the 200th anniversary of the American Constitution, is like other

> rituals organized to promote a mythic history. They appear to be celebrating the past, but their most important function is to fix the collective identity in the present. A bicentennial might be thought of as an official story that narrates a past to support an image of collective identity that confirms a certain conception of the present. The narrative is designed to privilege a certain past in order to legitimate a particular present. (Wolin 1989, 3)

The Populists and early Progressivists did the same when revering the self-governing and happy past of village life and community in colonial America. We still act as a people but no longer in a village community. The closest we can get to that ideal is when we act as volunteers, the midpoint between the passive citizen and the permanent revolutionary. Mansfield argues that without volunteers, free governments will not survive (1991, 133–134). Wolin reasons along the same lines when he argues that the gains in level of democracy are made by civil society rather than by government (1989, 78). But how these gains are made is not clear-cut. Some people support a democratic morality in terms of individual realization, where the administrative state exists solely to expand opportunities for the pursuit of individual material well-being. Others advocate a more interventionist role of government upon a strong belief in egalitarianism. And then there are those who argue that all citizens should have the opportunity to participate in public decision making (after Howe 1998, 49). In this latter instance, democracy is direct and there is no distinction between those who govern and the governed. In representative democracy, individuals and community are distinguished—but as two sides of the same coin. *E pluribus unum* (one out of many), the proverb on the American penny, refers both to the individual and to the collective. With respect to the first, it concerns the fact that one person will be elected to lead the country (one from among many). With respect to the latter, it refers to the fact that as individuals we belong to a society (one in many).

The growth of the administrative state, as expressed in the size of government, places democracy under stress. The more national power increases, the more it may seek inroads into the (local) community and the more all actors involved operate in and through institutionalized networks. These networks, with private and public individual and institutional actors, behave according to more or less standardized processes. It is in this sense that one could speak about a bureaucratization of the world, as Jacoby did (1976) and as Weber feared. The tension between democracy and bureaucracy is thus understood as a tension between fraternal, horizontal and patriarchal, vertical types of institutional structures and organizations, between a humanitarian and a technocratic approach to government.

5.4. Democracy's Desire: To Serve Multiple Communities Efficiently

The legacy of the French Revolution for contemporary government was the elevation of liberty, equality, and brotherhood to sacrosanct status. Today *liberty* represents individualism, emphasizes citizen and human rights, and advances a notion of upward mobility in society. Self-help literature as published from the mid-nineteenth century on, especially in the Anglo-American state-societies (see Raadschelders 1998a, 169), would have been unthinkable even a century earlier. Liberty also represented a distancing from a feudal (in Europe) or a colonial (in the United States) past. But liberty had to be constrained, because—unlike in Nietzsche's argument—citizens in most state-societies would not reason in terms of "my freedom should start where I want that of my fellow citizen to end." Rather, the dominating interpretation of liberty became the one associated with John Stuart Mill: "my freedom is limited by your freedom." Political education in a state-society thus requires that individuals are taught how to restrain themselves, without jeopardizing their own opportunities of self-advancement. In the concept of liberty, we see again this balancing between individualism (individual advancement) and collectivism (the needs of others).

The contemporary understanding of *equality* includes the notion of equal opportunities and equal conditions. It inspires, for instance, equality before the law, universal suffrage and a system of public education accessible to all, equal pay for men and women, but also welfare services. In the extreme, equality means complete or reasonably complete equalization of people. However, even the socialist and communist political systems could not avoid a situation where some were more equal than others. The concept of equality cut through—at least in theory—the rather fixed social stratifications that had determined the relationship between those who govern and the governed during the Middle Ages and early modern times. In this sense, equality also helped to establish that a sense of social mobility was at least conceivable. And, again, the question is whether government should play a facilitating or an active role in advancing equality. If only facilitating, some individuals will not share in the progress of society. In a more active role, government helps those who are unable to help themselves. While government cannot make people equal, it can at least be instrumental in creating a minimum set of equal conditions.

The welfare state is also built on the notion of *brotherhood,* the third legacy of the French Revolution. Brotherhood or fraternity, of course, no longer refers to the real brotherhood based on kinship or friendship, but rather to the artificial brotherhood of imagined relations. In the departure from the past with respect to brotherhood, social relations have evolved from being direct or face-to-face and occurring in a local community to indirect social relations occurring in multiple communities. Contemporary citizens act and exist in multiple communities: the nuclear family, the neighborhood, school or work, the church, the sports club, women's guild, and so forth. The memberships in these communities overlap but they never overlap the way they did in the older "real" communities. The changed interpretation and appreciation of the concepts of liberty, equality, and brotherhood have had major consequences for politics and for the structure and functioning of government.

Contemporary Western governments not only have to balance somehow the different interpretations of democracy (i.e., liberty, equality, and brotherhood in the individualist and collectivist approaches), but they also need to balance democracy with efficiency. Time and again the *Federalist* hammers upon the necessity of efficiency. The rationale for the new Constitution is laid out in the opening sentence of *Federalist* no. 1: "After an unequivocal experience of the inefficacy of the subsisting Federal Government, . . ." (1982, 2). The objective of the new Constitution is repeatedly stated as "efficient government" (no. 11, 51; no. 14, 64; no. 23, 112; no. 44, 228 and 231). The efficiency of a government with a unified executive is praised many times: it will provide quicker means of communication (no. 28, 137), it will establish uniform command of the army (no. 29, 138), it will enhance revenue through a unified taxation system (no. 30, 145), it will be a necessary counterforce to the state's politics (no. 36, 172), and it will save expenses related to the meetings

Table 5.1

Almond's Typology of Political Systems

		Political culture	
		Homogeneous	Fragmented
Differentiation of	High	Anglo-American	Continental European
political system	Low	Totalitarian	Preindustrial

Source: After Almond 1968a, 55–66.

of the representatives in the federal political bodies (no. 84, 442). Democracy and efficiency cannot do without each other. Efficient government legitimates democracy, and democratic government requires some effort toward efficiency.

5.5.   The Institutional Superstructure I: Models of Democracy

Liberty, equality, and brotherhood together constitute democracy. Practicing democracy requires an institutional superstructure that varies with culture and that can be characterized in terms of both the *separation of powers* between political bodies (*trias politica*) and *society-politics relations*, hence the dominant type or model of (liberal) democracy, and in terms of *intergovernmental relations* (IGR), hence the dominant division of labor between tiers of government (vertical) and between governmental organizations (horizontal). I first discuss models of democracy from a political and from an economic point of view. Both approaches emphasize that democracy is important for societal stability, but they do so along different lines. The discussion below is not meant to be exhaustive in terms of references. Instead, I present some of the major arguments that have been made. While models of (liberal) democracy are concerned with the external relations of government and society, styles of IGR are concerned with the interorganizational relations in government.

Gabriel Almond classifies political systems according to the degree of consensus in the population about political values (e.g., homogeneous vs. fragmented) and according to the degree to which political institutions are differentiated from each other and from other societal institutions (Table 5.1). Obviously his classification includes more than only democratic systems, but from his typology it is clear that political institutions in democracies are highly demarcated from other institutions. Implicit in his text is that the *homogeneous, secular political culture* is the most stable for people who share the basic values of freedom, mass welfare, and security but who also have extensive opportunity to exercise their freedom of association (unlike in totalitarian regimes). However, the United States and the continental European

Table 5.2

Rankings of Four English-Speaking Democracies According to the Strength of Four Pattern Variables (4 = high, 1 = low)

	United States	Australia	Canada	Great Britain
Elitism—equalitarianism	3.0	4.0	2.0	1.0
Ascription—achievement	4.0	2.5	2.5	1.0
Particularism—universalism	4.0	2.0	3.0	1.0
Diffuseness—specificity	4.0	2.5	2.5	1.0

Source: Lipset 1979, 249. Reprinted with permission from the author.

countries have more contrasting political subcultures (old, religiously oriented vs. new, secularized middle classes; urban vs. rural areas) and are thus not quite homogeneous yet fairly stable societies.

What constitutes political stability is further explored in Lipset's *Political Man: The Social Bases of Politics* (1963) and *The First New Nation* (1979). Societies are more stable when the value system emphasizes individual ability and performance (achievement) rather than birth or rank (ascription), when people are treated according to the same standard (universalism: equality before the law) rather than on the basis of personal qualities and/or membership in a specific group (particularism), when people are treated in terms of their specific positions (specificity) rather than as individual members of a community (diffuseness), and when the differences between low and high status are not stressed in social relationships (equalitarianism vs. elitism) (Lipset 1979, 209, 211). Lipset considers the United States, Great Britain, Canada, and Australia examples of stable democracies, while he regards France and Germany as more unstable (213). Within that group of Anglo-American countries, though, differences exist (Table 5.2).

The United States appears as the country where achievement, universalism, and specificity triumph more than anywhere else, and it is almost as equalitarian (or egalitarian) as is Australia. Lipset concurs with Almond that homogeneity fosters stability.

This conclusion is challenged by Lijphart. From Almond he borrows the distinction between a homogeneous (England, United States) and a fragmented (or pillarized) political culture (France, Germany, Italy). A fragmented political culture, however, does not necessarily imply instability. While cleavages in society, such as those of language, race, religion, class, and so forth, may be reflected in the political party system, they do not automatically mean that in its functioning the political party system seeks conflict rather than consensus as the avenue for problem solving. Lijphart himself develops the distinction

Table 5.3

Typology of Democratic Systems

		Political culture	
		Homogeneous	Pillarized
Elite behavior	Cartel (harmony model)	Cartel or depoliticized democracy	Pacification or consociational democracy
	Competition (conflict model)	Centripetal democracy	Centrifugal democracy

Source: Reprinted from Arend Lijphart, *The Politics of Accommodation: Pluralism and Democracy in the Netherlands,* 2d rev. ed. (Berkeley: University of California Press, 1968), p. 229. Copyright © 1968 by The Regents of the University of California. Reprinted with permission.

between two types of stable democracy: that in which stability is based in horizontal divisions (e.g., England, United States) and that in which it is based on vertical divisions (e.g., the Netherlands) (Table 5.3).

In one of his earliest publications, he distinguishes between four models of democracy. A *cartel democracy* is the most stable of all. Fragmentation of the political culture is low or nonexistent and there are no political subcultures. Lijphart reasons that the Netherlands is in a state of transition toward this type, when dealing with the aftermath of being a *consociational* (or *pacified*) *democracy.* In this type, the political culture is potentially unstable, but controlled because the elites of the various political subcultures pursue consensus-style politics while the membership of their respective electoral bases/pillars (in the Netherlands: Catholic, Protestant, socialist, and to a lesser extent, liberal) does not interact with other pillars. The *centripetal democracy* is stable in terms of political culture and is therefore able to handle conflict between elites fairly well (e.g., the Scandinavian countries). Finally, the *centrifugal democracy* is highly unstable because of competition between and fragmentation of the elites (e.g., Italy, Weimar Republic). In a later study, Lijphart departs from this fourfold matrix and develops a more complex one in which there are five intermediary next to four principal types of democracy (majoritarian-unitary, e.g., Great Britain; majoritarian-federal, e.g., United States; consensual-unitary, e.g., Denmark; consensual-federal, e.g., Switzerland) (1984, 216, 219; 1999, 244–246).

Almond, Lipset, and Lijphart explain political stability specifically in terms of political culture and elite behavior. Indeed, democracy is most often defined as a political method for choosing a society's leadership. This emphasis on *political democracy* provides a rather limited understanding of democracy. Given that all Western countries are welfare states, the definition of democracy should be broader and include government's responsibility for social justice and for support of the disadvantaged. Various authors have pointed out that the existence of an affluent economy provides a better explanation for a stable representative democracy. Comparing various theories about societal stability, Lane and Ersson conclude that a high level of affluence is a necessary condition for a viable democracy even though the exact relationship between both phenomena is not yet determined (1994, 214–215). David Held (1987) has argued that political democracy is a first step, but "without a welfare state that prevents extreme material poverty and steep socioeconomic inequalities, it is not possible for the poor sections of the population to fully enjoy their political rights" (Sørensen 1998, 14–15). Hence, the formal rights and liberties granted under political democracy ought to be expanded with the substantive benefits and entitlements of the *welfare democracy*. Only then are the people at large truly liberated. The welfare democracy, thus, constitutes an expansion of political democracy along the dimension of liberalization. Political democracy can also be expanded along the dimension of participation. Held argues that the formal rights and liberties invested in and emanating from public institutions can be extended to include social institutions and the economy as well. When this happens, a *social democracy* is established. When political democracy is extended along both dimensions, a *democratic autonomy* is created (Sørensen 1998, 10, 16). Following Held, Sørensen defines democratic autonomy as

> the very broad concept of democracy. . . . It includes direct participation in local community institutions, active control of elected politicians through the party system, and social as well as economic rights to ensure adequate resources for citizens' political activity. It also foresees self-management of cooperatively owned enterprises. (1998, 160)

In the ideal democratic autonomy, the political and economic class differences are negligible since the people share not only political power through universal suffrage but also the ownership of enterprises. Democratic autonomy does not exist in any of the Western countries (and one could argue whether it ever existed; former Yugoslavia comes closest), but the idea of institutionalized cooperation between, say, employers and employees in private enterprise (with a mediating role for government) has been a normal feature of the decision- and policy-making process in the so-called corporatist or neocorporatist countries (e.g., Germany, the Netherlands).

5.6. The Institutional Superstructure II:
Intergovernmental Relations

All of these political and economic models of democracy are theoretical and abstract and in general characterize the relations between society at large and government. More specifically, they point to a limited or an expanded role for government. Government is limited in the case of a political democracy because, in that model, the welfare of all—or of the greatest number—is left to an "invisible hand." In this situation there is little need for an intricate system of local-state-federal relations. Indeed, deep into the nineteenth century, the national levels of government in the United States and in Europe were hardly intertwined with the subnational levels. In the United States, this was the age of *layer-cake federalism* (see below) and of *distributive policy*. In Europe at that time, central-local relations were defined only in terms of the organic acts prescribed by the constitutions. There, too, the national levels were hardly involved with local politics and policy. In a welfare democracy, however, national government's role in society is much larger in terms of active regulation, legislation, and the actual delivery of collective services. What makes the welfare democracy work is an intricate web of vertical and horizontal intergovernmental relations. Democracy at the practical and concrete level is a division of labor between the various tiers of government and between various governmental organizations at one level.

Whether unitary or federal, all states have a system of intergovernmental relations (United States) or central-local relations (Europe). The characteristics of its functioning are distinctly national, but at a conceptual level comparisons between countries are fruitful (Page 1991). In the analysis of intergovernmental relations, three levels have been distinguished: federalism (Wright 1990) or intergovernmental constitution (Toonen 1990), intergovernmental relations, and intergovernmental management (Agranoff 1990; Wright 1988). The *intergovernmental constitution* (IGC) concerns the entirety of legal, political, social-cultural, and economic conditions, rules, norms, and values that provides the foundation for governance and government. The IGC level of government's structure and functioning serves as a normative framework defined in terms of state and administrative law, the (party) political system, historical circumstances and legacies of the past, civic culture, public perception, public ethics, and administrative culture. The elected politicians are the most important actors at this level since they determine policy objectives in the political environment (Wright 1990, 174). The concept of *intergovernmental relations* (IGR) points the attention to the system of juridical, financial, political, and organizational relations between the various organizations and units that together constitute government. Hence, at the IGR level we emphasize, for instance, the number of governmental units (see below), the administrative framework and organization, the tax system, central-local (financial, juridical, etc.) relations, recruitment and career patterns of office-holders, and regional disparities. This is the level at which the generalist civil servants or top public managers play the most decisive role since they are most involved in coordinating policy between various branches and organizations. Finally, *intergovernmental management* (IGM) is the concept with which we refer to the problem-solving activities, procedures, techniques, and types of administration employed within the constitutional and intergovernmental framework. At this level we can situate the techniques for guidance, evaluation, and control of government activity, leadership and legitimacy, and human resources. This is the level at which the specialist civil servants or policy professionals are most important.

The Intergovernmental Constitution Level

Each of these levels can be further analyzed in terms of theoretical and abstract models as well as in terms of concrete relations between levels and organizations of government. With respect to models of national, state, and local relations, Wright proposes to distinguish between three basic types.

The model of *coordinate authority* (dual federalism or layer-cake federalism) assumes that the responsibilities of the national level are clearly demarcated from those of the state and local levels. In legislative terms, the state and local levels operate more or less autonomously from the national level, but the local level is a creation of the state (i.e., Dillon's Rule as outlined by the Iowa judge John F. Dillon in the 1860s). In terms of service delivery, this model operates upon a more or less exclusive delegation of legislative and executive tasks and competencies to various tiers of government. In the developmental models of IGR in the United States (see, e.g., Wright 1988, 67), the period up to the nineteenth century was conveniently described as the phase of dual federalism. However, most scholars nowadays acknowledge Grodzins's and Elazar's arguments that even in the nineteenth century such a demarcation between national and state or local levels was a theory (and, indeed, acted upon by the Supreme Court) but never a reality (Dinan 2000, 133; Elazar 1966, 33; Elazar 1993, 55; Nice and Frederickson 1999, 89; Schreiber on Grodzins 2000, 66; O'Toole 2000, 6; Wright 1988, 41).

At the other side of the spectrum, Wright finds the *inclusive authority model,* where both state and local governments are essentially creatures of the national state. This model is useful for analyzing central-local relations because it not only emphasizes the formal, hierarchical nature of authority in the constitutional democracies but it also suggests that in practice state and local public servants have little impact upon the major national political questions. This latter observation is suggested by Dye's definition of the elite in the governmental sectors as including individuals in authoritative positions in the civil and military branches of *national government* (Dye 1986, 11). However, of the three main branches of U.S. government, it is the executive (including the presidency as well as the heads of the departments) and the judiciary that operate nationally, whereas the legislature provides for state influence through the Senate and for local influence through the House of Representatives.

The most realistic of Wright's three models is that of *overlapping authority* (cooperative or marble-cake federalism). In this model, the states not only implement their own legislation, but are also charged with the execution of regulations, programs, and projects of the federal government. There is another feature of this third model that is important. In the coordinate authority and the inclusive authority models, a vertical relationship is assumed between state and local levels and between federal, state, and local levels. The overlapping authority model, on the other hand, includes both the vertical as well as the horizontal (local-local, state-state) relations.

State and administrative systems can also be characterized according to whether they are *federal* or *unitary states*. This distinction rests mainly upon the constitutional foundations. In federal states, the territorial autonomy is rooted in a constitution of each of the parts. In a unitary state this constitutional relation is reversed since the component parts derive their legal autonomy from the national state (e.g., the United Kingdom, the Netherlands, France, Sweden). In federal systems, the division of labor between various levels of government is often expressed enumeratively and constitutionally and subject to supervision and preemption by national government and by or appeal to a constitutional court (e.g., judicial review). The access of the various states to the constitutional decision-making process in a federal system is institutionalized through representative bodies such as the *Bundesrat* in Germany and the Senate in the United States. Unitary states usually lack such an institutional arrangement, but there are exceptions. Thus, in the Netherlands, the members of the First Chamber of Parliament (comparable to the U.S. Senate) are elected by the members of the Provincial Councils. It is important to note that in actual functioning the component parts of a unitary state may be as important to the structure and functioning of the whole as those are in a federal state.

Above we have seen that federal systems have been conceptualized in three different ways. Unitary states can be subdivided into two different types: Westminster versus consensus unitarism (see Lijphart above). To some degree, the *Westminster model* represents the pure case of a unitary state. The English unitary state is based on the principle that the autonomy of the component parts rests upon delegation of authority by Parliament. The English system of *sovereignty of Parliament* is often presented as the opposite of the American model of *separation of powers*. The English model works upon the assumption that unity of state authority as expressed in parliamentary sovereignty, a district system of elections, and a two-party system are necessary conditions for a viable and stable democracy. In the case of *consensus unitarism,* we are dealing with more pluralistic, fragmented, and divided societies with a system of proportional representation and a multiparty system. This often necessitates coalition governments (e.g., Belgium until 1994, the Netherlands, Sweden). Despite the degree of fragmentation, these systems can be quite stable liberal democracies because their stability is grounded in so-called *consociational devices* or rules for a politics of pacification. These provide arrangements for mutual adaptation, strategies, and tactics for redistributive justice and institutional arrangements for negotiation and decision making focused on continuously achieving a consensus and pacifying differences of opinion within the political-administrative system as a whole.

The Intergovernmental Relations Level

Federal and unitary states can also be categorized at the level of intergovernmental relations. A first distinction is that between *cogovernment* and *deconcentration.* At what level of government is legislation decided and are policy programs executed? In horizontal systems, we may find a *nonexecutant role of the center*, as in the United Kingdom. In the Netherlands, we speak in this case about *cogovernment.* In systems where vertical relations dominate, we speak about *administrative deconcentration*, as in France.

A second distinction, between *governing-from-a-distance* and *administrative intertwinement,* can be used to characterize the type of mutual relations between administrative organizations. In international literature, this distinction is often referred to as between non-Napoleonic and Napoleonic systems (Wunder 1995). Non-Napoleonic systems with *government-at-a-distance* are characterized by regulations via general norms and frameworks that can be enforced through the use of courts (*statutory regulation*) (e.g., Scandinavian countries, United Kingdom). The Napoleonic model of administrative intertwinement is characterized by direct administrative relations between various government levels in terms of supervision (*tutellage*), strong functional and sectoral administrative ties, and detailed administrative steering and control via memos, directives, and other types of direct administrative interference from the center (*administrative regulation*) (e.g., France).

The basic structure of intergovernmental relations after World War II was not sacrosanct even though administrative traditions are deeply rooted. Most Western countries have pursued territorial and functional reforms. In the United States, we see especially changes in the number of special-purpose governments. In the 1942–1997 period, the total number of governmental units in the United States declined by some 44 percent (see Table 5.4).

This decline is almost solely the consequence of massive amalgamations of school districts and would have even been greater if most of the municipalities and special districts had not grown. Of these, the special districts have grown the most. Two-thirds of these special districts are those for natural resource development, fire protection, urban water supply, housing and community development, cemeteries, sewerage, and parks and recreation. Also in this period, the number of municipalities, which are general-purpose governments, has increased by 16 percent. The emphasis in Europe has been much more on the amalgamation of general-purpose governments because generally there are not so many overlapping territorial and functional jurisdictions as there are in the United States. In Europe, most local and regional government is organized as general-purpose government. Functional IGR reforms in both the United States and Europe include decentralization, the development of neighborhood councils, and the development of formal arrangements of intermunicipal cooperation (in the United States, for instance, Unigov for Indianapolis and Marion County; in Europe, the intermunicipal joint provisions).

The Intergovernmental Management Level

The intergovernmental management level is often the one at which administrative reforms are aspired and pursued. This is a consequence of three particular qualities or aspects of IGM as identified by Wright: *problem solving*, *coping capabilities*, and *networking* (1988, 450; 1990, 170). With respect to problem solving, there are limitations to what administrators can do in terms of IGM since this is not the level where fundamental social problems are addressed. As far as coping capabilities are concerned, IGM is "a means of understanding and coping with the system *as it is*, including strategic perspectives that address how and why interjurisdictional changes occur, as well as guidance on how to cope with the system" (Agranoff 1990, 23). It is in the networking that the "major and immense social, political, and administrative organizations, with associated larger powers, must be managed" (Wright 1988, 451; 1990, 171). What has made IGM attractive as an area of interest is that it "emphasizes collaborative decision making and dispute settlement rather than the traditional win/lose judicial or elective systems" (Nice and Frederickson

Table 5.4

Number of Governmental Units in the United States, 1932–1997

Type of government	1932	1942	1952	1962	1967	1977	1987	1997
Total	182,651	155,116	116,807	91,237	81,299	79,913	83,237	87,504
U.S. government	1	1	1	1	1	1	1	1
State	48	48	50	50	50	50	50	50
Local	182,602	155,067	116,756	91,186	81,248	79,862	83,186	87,453
County	3,062	3,050	3,052	3,043	3,049	3,042	3,042	3,043
Municipal	16,442	16,220	16,807	18,000	18,408	18,862	19,200	19,372
Township and town	19,978	18,919	17,202	17,142	17,105	16,822	16,691	16,629
School district	128,548	108,579	67,355	34,678	21,782	15,174	14,721	13,726
Special district	14,572	8,299	12,340	18,323	21,264	25,962	29,532	34,683

Source: Statistical Abstract of the United States, 1999, table 500; figures for 1932 from Ostrom et al. 1988, 52.

Note: Adjusted to include units in Alaska and Hawaii, which adopted statehood in 1959.

1999, 191). Underlining that the IGC-IGR-IGM construct not merely describes an intergovernmental structure or division of labor but also sheds light on how this structure functions, Wright quotes Pritchard:

> The public administrator will be an intergovernmental specialist who . . . comprehends that intergovernmental relations is not a seminar topic, an academic study [but] are in fact intergovernmental "negotiations" in which the parties are negotiating in dead earnest for power, money, and problem-solving responsibility. He will be fully aware that in virtually every major policy issue the elements of power, money, and responsibility are on the bargaining table. (Wright 1988, 467)

O'Toole observes the same (2000, 20). Intergovernmental relations is an embedded phenomenon where IGC determines IGR which in turn determines IGM, but also where new practices at the IGM level may be translated into institutional arrangements at the IGR and IGC levels. It is in this assumed built-in feedback mechanism that intergovernmental relations appear to be dynamic rather than static and as such provide an illustration of what I earlier referred to as negotiable authority.

Intergovernmental arrangements have grown and become more complex in all welfare states. Wright describes this development for the United States in seven phases (1988, chapter 3). The first phase, that of *conflict,* was the one most characterized by layer-cake federalism (up to the 1930s). During the second phase, *cooperation* came to the forefront (1940s–1950s). Each of the next five phases partially overlapped the previous phase. In the third, *concentrated phase* (1940s–1960s), the focus of IGR became much more specific and functional. During the fourth, *creative phase* (1950s–1960s), government took a leading role through program planning, project grants, and citizen participation. It was during the fifth, *competitive phase* (1960s–1970s) that "the administrative consequences of executive and legislative policy whirlwinds" (Wright 1988, 81) became the focus of attention in view of, for instance, the proliferation of grants and the gap between (political) promise and (administrative) performance. It was in this period that the concept of *picket-fence federalism* was coined to denote the fragmentation of IGR visible in the separateness of one program from another as well as in the autonomy of program specialists vis-à-vis the generalists. The enhanced need for coordination gave rise to the sixth, *calculative phase* (1970s–1980s), which was the period that separate attention for the IGM level emerged.

Managerial concerns were threefold. First, there was the increased need for *calculation,* which included weighing the costs and benefits of grants, establishing who benefits from distribution of funds via conditioning formulas, and assessing the risk of noncompliance with requirements versus the costs of compliance (Wright 1988, 90–92). Second, there was concern about the increased capability to transfer or shift resources received for one purpose in order to accomplish another goal (also called the game of *fungibility*). Block grants and General Revenue Sharing funds in particular enabled state or local governments to reduce their own financial commitment to a particular program (Wright 1988, 94–95). Third, there was the perception of *political overload,* which stressed the enormous increase of government's responsibilities and thus created excessive costs, ineffectiveness, and overregulation (94). During this phase, the concept of *facade federalism* underlined that federalism is a formal structure (i.e., as expressed in laws and in intergovernmental organization) as well as an artificial front (e.g., expressing the sharing of responsibility while silently embracing the golden rule of "He who pays the piper calls the tune" (see Wright 1988, 485). In this latter sense, facade federalism refers to the fact that power had become too concentrated at the federal level.

During the last, *contractive phase* (1980s–1990s), attempts were made to correct the perceived imbalances between federal and subnational governments through *deregulation* and *decentralization,* through *cutbacks* in federal expenditure, and through *reductions* of personnel at the federal level (e.g., the National Performance Review). In this listing of reform efforts, I do not include *privatization* since that, by definition, involves the transfer of services *and* of authority to actors outside the public arena.

In the sections on IGC and IGR above, I have frequently referred to European countries. National-subnational relations are not an exclusive feature of federalism in the United States but are as relevant to federal and unitary systems in Europe. We will not provide European illustrations of the characteristics and challenges at the IGM level of central-local relations. In terms of their objectives (off-loading from the center, cutbacks, contraction, amalgamation of local government, etc.), intergovernmental structure and functioning in European countries experience the same challenges as in the United States, as is testified by some of the literature in the 1980s (Dente and Kjellberg 1988; Rhodes and Wright 1988; Page and Goldsmith 1987; Smith 1985). With respect to managerial reforms, we can assume that the differences between Western countries are much larger. While the ideas and "jargon" of managerial reform are the same (think, for instance, of "New Public Management" and of the frequent references to the "public manager" instead of the "public servant"), administrative traditions and cultures mean that they play out differently. In the context of this book and chapter, the detail about actual IGM practices and developments would not contribute much if anything to our understanding of the institutional superstructure.

5.7. Concluding Remarks

In this chapter I discussed democracy and intergovernmental relations as the elements of the institutional superstructure that, together, further the objectives of the legal and social constitution of society. Democracy and IGR are best understood as layered phenomena, both in levels of abstractness and in developmental perspectives.

All Western democracies have evolved from merely political to welfare democracies and, as a consequence, have developed extensive and intricate intergovernmental or central-local relations. Political democracy is a necessary condition for welfare democracy, and welfare democracy in turn is the ultimate expression of *true* political democracy. While the development of democracy in each of these Western countries is, of course, unique, the general trend is the same. The expansion of public services requires the legal and abstract relations between national and subnational governments to be supplemented with a variety of financial and coordinative relations.

From the discussion in section 5.6 we can conclude that the attention to federalism in the early days of the independent United States was mainly concerned with the IGC level—that is, determining the basic structure within which the various branches of government independently and together contributed to the growth of democracy. Given increased federal support for state and local activities in the nineteenth century (especially for public education and for the construction of railways and highways), the understanding of federalism came to include the IGR level. Finally, in the course of the twentieth century and as a consequence of the advent and proliferation of welfare services, the definition of federalism (or, in more neutral terms, national-subnational relations) necessarily encompassed attention for the managerial challenges. A parallel development occurred in Europe. Central-local relations were initially defined in constitutional terms only (i.e., municipal and provincial acts). From the 1880s onward, national governments gradually but surely penetrated subnational levels with legislation that required some degree of subnational implementation (e.g., national public housing and public health legislation). This fueled a more systematic and comparative study of centralization and decentralization in the early twentieth century. In Europe since World War II, welfare services have grown to proportions beyond what Americans are familiar with. Hence, the attention to the managerial challenges is as large as it is in the United States.

This most recent object of study, the IGM level of national-subnational relations, provides us with just another indication of the importance of and attention to the fact that efficiency is the counterpart to democracy. In their combination, efficiency and democracy legitimate government. Sole emphasis upon efficiency of the public sector leads not only to an impoverished under-standing of the role and position of government in society but also to the misguided idea that managerial reforms will be sufficient when attempting to make public service delivery more efficient. The public manager at the higher levels is not a faceless technocrat, to borrow U.S. senator E.L. Bartlett's phrase (as quoted in Price 1965, 57), but a generalist who is able to make decisions with an eye for the needs of democracy, efficiency, and efficacy.

6 EQUALITY BEFORE THE LAW: SOCIAL JUSTICE AND THE ADMINISTRATION OF JUSTICE

Laws are like spiders' webs: if some poor weak creature comes up against them, it is caught; but a bigger one can break through and get away.
—Solon

. . . a just constitutional order, when adjoined to the smaller social unions of everyday life, provides a framework for these many associations and sets up the most complex and diverse activity of all.
—John Rawls, 1971

Man's capacity for justice makes democracy possible, but man's inclination to injustice makes democracy necessary.
—Reinhold Niebuhr, 1994

The administration of justice is among the oldest of public services. Initially this mainly concerned the resolution of conflicts between individuals and between individuals and organizations or institutions. In Western welfare democracies, justice involves much more than mere adjudication. Niebuhr's suggestion that man's inclination to injustice necessitates democracy (see quotation above) not only refers to justice, the modern—but limited—sense of equality before the law and individual responsibility, but also hints at the egalitarian principle of social justice and collective responsibility in the context of the welfare state. In Western welfare states, justice in the limited sense concerns the passing of judgment, while in the extended sense it includes care for the weak and the oppressed. Social justice rests upon equity and, more specifically, upon "the correction of existing imbalances in the distribution of social and political values" (Denhardt 1984, 112). It is in equity that governments seek to create greater benefits from public programs for the most disadvantaged.

In this chapter, I briefly discuss the modern sense of social justice that has deep roots in the monotheistic religions that together helped shape the ethics and morality of the Western world (section 6.1). This subject is of relevance to chapter 8, but is also discussed in this chapter since the foundation of social justice, and thus of public services, is in law. I then discuss how public law developed from common law to Roman law and statute law (section 6.2) and how equality can be served by avoiding injustice (section 6.3). One of the unforeseen consequences of the growth of the welfare state is that the independence of the judiciary, so central to the separation of powers, has come under pressure. This will be examined in section 6.4. Also, the judiciary is no longer the only institution with the power to adjudicate. Since the early twentieth century, regulatory powers have been increasingly invested in independent agencies (section 6.5). Given the changes in the law and the organization of justice, I look at the foundations of international law and justice for the simple reason that they have gained increasing influence on policy making at the domestic level (section 6.6).

6.1. Ancient Roots and Modern Expressions of Social Justice

Equity and equality in their current secular meaning became fashionable theory in the latter part of the eighteenth century, and they materialized in public programs from the end of the nineteenth century onward. The idea of government care for the disadvantaged, however, is much older and rooted in the Judaic, Christian, and Islamic religions and value systems. These three monotheistic religions share a strong egalitarian and even socialist spirit that requires the believer to contribute to the creation of a just and equitable society wherein the less fortunate also may expect decent treatment (Armstrong 1993, 60, 157, 167, 183). All three advocated the primacy and importance of individual charity through almsgiving, but they also supported and operated facilities for the sick, the elderly, and the orphaned, in synagogue, church, and mosque or in separate buildings. All three had a tradition of private endowments for foundations or charitable work (Gil 1976, 9–39; Stillman 1975 and 2000). Specific for Judaism were provisions concerning the harvest that show a deep sense of social justice:

> And when you reap the harvest of your land, you shall not reap your field to its very border, nor shall you gather the gleanings after your harvest; you shall leave them for the poor and for the stranger. (Leviticus 23:22)

> When you reap your harvest in your field, and have forgotten a sheaf in the field, you shall not go back to get it; it shall be for the sojourner, the fatherless, and the widow. (Deuteronomy 24:19)

The secularization of the eighteenth century did not obliterate this sense of social justice. If anything, it was a cornerstone in the emerging political theory of governance and government. Marquis de Condorcet (1743–1794) wrote in his *Outline of the Progress of the Human Mind* (1793) that the state was the prime instrument for progress, and he and his contemporaries (Montesquieu, Rousseau, Voltaire, etc.) firmly believed the state to be the best guarantee for social welfare (Palmer and Colton 1971, 335). Montesquieu was especially taken by the English limited monarchy model of king-in-Parliament. Rousseau favored the direct democracy of the republican commonwealth. Voltaire and many of the other philosophes advocated an "enlightened despotism" with a powerful, well-disposed government (Palmer and Colton 1971, 336). A case can be made that the welfare state democracies of today are not that much different from what Voltaire desired.

The difference between the secular and religious approaches to social justice is that the former places much more emphasis on collective services organized by and provided through the state. The ideological connection between, for instance, Jesus Christ and Voltaire, the two servants of humanity, as Victor Hugo labeled them, was that they both attempted to protect the weak and the oppressed. In Hugo's words:

> The completion of the evangelical work is the philosophical work; the spirit of mercy began, the spirit of tolerance continued. Let us say it with a sentiment of profound respect: Jesus wept; Voltaire smiled. Of that divine tear and that human smile is composed the sweetness of the present civilization. (Hugo 1997, 187)

What would Victor Hugo have written had he lived at the beginning of the twenty-first century when few know the meaning of the Atlantic Revolutions for the modern era and when the welfare state in cross-time perspective must represent an even sweeter civilization? In terms of law and justice, it was during the Atlantic Revolutions that a de jure separation of church and state was pursued that also restrained both church and state. Neither justice nor religion could be instruments of vengeance. Again, in the powerful words of Victor Hugo:

> Never, I insist upon it, will any wise man shake those two august supports of social labor, justice and hope, and all will respect the judge if he is embodied justice, and all will venerate the priest if he represents hope. But if the magistracy calls itself torture, if the Church calls itself Inquisition, then Humanity looks them in the face, and says to the judge: I will none of thy law! And says to the priest: I will none of thy dogma! I will none of thy fire upon the earth and thy hell in the future! Then philosophy rises in wrath, and arraigns the judge before justice, and the priest before God! That is what Voltaire did. It was grand. (Hugo 1997, 187)

Dramatic, perhaps, but it conveys the mood of the postrevolutionary age. What is more, law and justice in the modern conception are necessary conditions for a welfare state. Law is always rule and changing it is only possible after thorough consultation and deliberation by a qualified majority. Law is not an instrument in the hands of some whimsical power seeker. Nor is justice, for, ideally, its standard-bearers judge within the framework of the law as it is designed by men.

6.2. Common Law, Roman Law, Statute Law, and the Functions of Law

Law is as important a moral force in public life as religion used to be in earlier societies. Law is a set of rules that applies to individuals and to institutions alike. It is human-made upon an almost completely secularized foundation. The standard it sets for behavior is negotiated rather than derived from a supernatural authority. However, contemporary law is based on the laws of nature, which provide us with a sense of right and wrong. This *natural law* (the rules that govern humankind in a state of nature, for instance, the survival of the fittest) envelops humankind in its entirety and comes before *negotiated* or *positive law,* which is the law of a particular community. Consequentially, there are, in principle, as many positive laws as there are identifiable communities (tribes, nations, states).

Positive law comes in two basic types, often found concomitantly, sometimes not. The first type is *common law,* which is mostly concerned with adjudication in one-to-one or one-to-society conflicts (i.e., on contracts, loans, torts, property, domestic issues) (Hurst 1977, 138). Under common law, the judge who rules in a particular conflict sets precedent for any comparable case thereafter. The ruling serves as law and so under common law *justice precedes law.* Common law could be found everywhere in the Western world until approximately the twelfth century. The English government and society continued to operate on the basis of common law, while the countries on the European continent changed toward Roman law. Well into the nineteenth century, the United States judiciary basically functioned under a system of common law, but from the end of the nineteenth century, Roman and statute law have gained in importance and have, in fact, pushed common law to the background.

In a system of *Roman law,* the legislator makes the law, which then will serve as a standard for the judiciary. Under Roman law, then, *law precedes justice.* Roman law may apply both to one-to-one and one-to-society conflicts as well as to problems for groups and society at large. Roman law is not synonymous with *statute law,* for the latter is concerned only with large groups or society at large (the organization of government, public education, environmental law, etc.) (Hurst 1977, 139).

Under a common law system, judicial power is not limited to making and applying law (via setting precedents and contributing to jurisprudence) but may very well include judicial policy making. The difference between "judicial" and "policy" is what determines the difference between justice in the limited sense and justice in its more expanded meaning. Justice in the limited sense concerns a comparison of (usually) an action against an existing standard, whether in jurisprudence or in law. Sometimes even legislation is compared to an existing standard. The purpose of *judicial review* as it exists in Germany, the United States, and—in a way—the European Union, is to compare new state or national legislation to existing and higher legislation (e.g., a constitution, European Union law). In the case of *judicial policy making,* however, the judiciary goes beyond its conflict resolution role and assumes the responsibilities of a problem solver (Cramton 1982, 150–151), even when this role is acknowledged only with hesitation (Chase 1982, 4, 160; Feeley and Rubin 1998, 340; see also section 6.4 below).

According to Hurst, in the twentieth century we witnessed a shift from common law and judicial policy making to *legislative* and *executive-administrative policy making.* There are a variety of reasons why this occurred, but a central reason is the growth of welfare services that, in turn, prompted a rapid expansion of the administrative and executive branches of government. The resources for this growth of public services were provided by the legislature, not the judiciary, and were a response to three types of demands. First, the growth of the executive required that, in some areas, existing expertise and techniques were brought into the public sector, such as through the hiring of pharmacists and chemists to facilitate drug regulation. Second, the growth of the executive also required the incorporation of new expertise and knowledge, such as in the regulation of public utilities, collective bargaining, and corporate security issues. Finally, the specific handling of certain policies during implementation required specialized organizations, such as for the administration of the social security system (Hurst 1977, 140; see also section 6.5 below). In countries where a Roman law tradition already existed, such a shift could not occur by definition, since through their legislative action, parliaments made law and thus policy. However, legislative and executive-administrative policy making have grown in importance to equal or even surpass judicial policy making. But in countries with a common law background, judicial policy making is more important than in Roman law countries.

The functions of law in contemporary society are both more limited and more expanded than ever before. Law is less important than it used to be in classical political theory. In Aristotle's view, good laws, together with religion, education, family life, and morality, have teeth so that they develop character. His *idealist approach* to the function of law is quite different from the more cynical and *realist* observation of Solon, who argues that law serves the powerful and oppresses the weak. Under modern political philosophy, law in the hands of government channels individual passions and interests so that these do not interfere with the passions and interests of others (Diamond 1986, 80, 83, 106). Law thus fulfills one important political role in society: it protects individual freedom. However, in contemporary society, law also serves to protect the equality of rights. Under the constitutional order that government provides, law protects equality of rights, and, while it cannot eradicate the inequalities one inevitably finds in society (McWilliams 1986, 300), it does seek to serve equality of opportunity. In that sense, the role of law has expanded. Finally, law (with or without tradition, morality, and religion) serves as a restraint on government, which is a novelty in the history of government. Most contemporary democracies may be called a *Rechtsstaat* (for lack of a better translation: a constitutional state). The idea that no one is above the law, not even government itself, or rather the representatives in government, is the cornerstone of the contemporary theory of governance. But this is only half of the story, because we are subject to the law as individuals, but the people as a collective are above the law. It is at the collective level that law can be negotiated and can become positive law.

6.3. Serving Equality Through Avoiding Injustice

This modern outlook on the functions of law, the regulation of relations, the service to social justice, and the restriction on government, is visible in the following quotation from one of the speeches of Martin Luther King:

> We must continue to struggle through legalism and legislation. There are those who contend that integration can come only through education, for no other reason that morals cannot be legislated. I choose, however, to be dialectical at this point. It is neither education nor legislation; it is both legislation and education. I quite agree that it is impossible to change a man's internal feelings merely through law. But this is really not the intention of the law. The law does not seek to change one's feelings; it seeks rather to control the external effects of those internal feelings. For instance, the law cannot make a man love—religion and education must do that—but it can control his efforts to lynch. So in order to control the external effects of prejudiced internal feelings, we must continue to struggle through legislation. (1992)

Legislation serves as the most important formal guarantee against injustice. Moral guarantees, which grow on the basis of religion and education, cannot be the object of the law. And yet the contemporary notion of law takes an important moral position with regard to the role of government in society. In a *Rechtsstaat,* equality is as important as liberty. It is the duty of government to protect the weak and the oppressed, and thus justice comes to include social justice.

Among Western governments, the religious nature of social justice has given way to a more secular interpretation. It is clear that governments cannot eradicate inequalities for, in that attempt, government would overstep the limited boundary that Locke defined for government, which is to protect the equality of rights. Equality of rights in a restricted sense refers to *individual equality,* and government is restricted to equal treatment of citizens. In the expanded variant, equality of rights is a political action sentiment considered vital to society and referred to as *communitarian* or *civic equality* (Diamond 1986, 283–284). It is in this expanded understanding of equal rights that public policy making intends to mitigate some of the consequences of social inequalities.

Inequalities become more apparent when changes in the social and economic fabric of society appear to be more advantageous for some people than for others. The advent of the industrial-capitalist mode of production served, among other things, to emphasize differences between social groups rather than to diminish them. Such inequalities, Marx believed, would ultimately result in the downfall of the capitalist exploiter and the victory of the proletariat. John Rawls has argued, however, that social inequalities could actually be advantageous and, at least, permissible. In Rawls's two principles of justice for institutions, liberty and equality are closely linked. The first principle, the *equal liberty principle,* holds that each person in society has an equal right to maximum liberty which then is compatible with the same amount of liberty for everyone else. Under the second principle, which Rawls labeled the *difference principle*, inequality is permissible when it serves everyone's advantage and when it occurs under conditions of equal or fair opportunity. From these two principles, he derives two priority rules that support the lexical order of the two principles. The *priority of liberty rule* stipulates that liberty can be restricted only for the sake of liberty. The *priority of justice over efficiency and welfare rule* stipulates that fair opportunity is prior to the difference principle of everyone's advantage (Rawls 1971, 302; 1980, 432–433).

However, as Wolin has pointed out, the situation of the least advantaged may improve, but "it does not follow that in doing so inequality is reduced, much less eliminated" (Wolin 1989, 142). Wolin qualifies what justice means in a political culture that embraces liberty, equality, and fraternity. Consider his remark quoted below in relation to Solon's observation at the opening of this chapter:

> What does justice look like in the era of the political economy? The answer is that although for Locke and Hobbes justice meant first and foremost that political authority should protect each person in his or her rightful possessions, this is no longer

a primary concern. Instead, the principal preoccupation of the state is to protect and nurture the economy. This takes the form of policies for money supply and credit, taxation, investment, and trade. Justice means that which forms the basis of national power, security, and prosperity. (Wolin 1989, 43–44)

When discussing the four branches or rather functions of government, Rawls links concern for the economy to concern for individual and, by implication, for societal needs. The *allocation branch* serves to "keep the price system workably competitive and . . . prevent the formation of unreasonable market power." The *stabilization branch* "strive[s] to bring about reasonably full employment . . . and the free choice of occupation." The *transfer branch* "take[s] needs into account and assign[s] them an appropriate weight with respect to other claims." Finally, the *distribution branch* "preserve[s] an approximate justice in distributive shares by means of taxation and the necessary adjustments in the rights of property" (Rawls 1971, 276–277). Contemporary government provides social justice through intervention in the economy and thus prevents the deterioration of the standard of living of the masses Marx predicted.

It is instructive to elaborate somewhat on Wolin's usage of Hobbes and Locke. As Wolin points out, Hobbes is radical when arguing that the human is a commodity with a price (Wolin 1989, 41). In Hobbes's words a human being's "*Value,* or WORTH, is as of all other things, his Price; that is to say, so much as would be given for the use of his Power: and therefore is not absolute; but a thing dependant on the need and judgment of another" (Hobbes 1989, 151–152). Hobbes proceeds by arguing that an honest and learned judge is worth more in a courtroom than on a battlefield. Man's value therefore depends upon and is related to a particular circumstance. What can be inferred from Hobbes's statement is that value is negotiable and that professional capacity is a property that can be taken away by the state. Some forty years after Hobbes, Locke too underlines that the political sphere is concerned with the protection of property: "Political power, then, I take to be a right of making laws, with penalties of death, and consequently all less penalties for the regulating and preserving of property, and of employing the force of the community in the execution of such laws" (Locke 1986, 118). Hobbes and Locke certainly did not write only about the political economy as they knew it, but also advocated, respectively, an omnipotent government (Hobbes) and a heavily restricted government (Locke). In the political economy that emerged from the eighteenth century onward, government increasingly intervened in society, most dominantly in the regulation of the economy (*mercantilism*). In its original meaning, *political economy* referred to the "government household" vis-à-vis the "private household"—that is, the private economy of the king (Zimmerman 1987, 5). When Wolin speaks of a political economy, he refers to "an order in which the limits of politics are set by the needs of a

corporate-dominated economy and of a state organization that works in intimate collaboration with corporate leadership" (1989, 147). Wolin's *economic
polity,* as he also calls it, is thus not the same concept as that of *political
economy* in the eighteenth century. The contemporary political economy is
one in which government and the business sector penetrate each other. The
one-way-street relationship Wolin appears to suggest, which goes from the
corporate sector to government, owes more to some intelligible suspicions
than to empirical research. There are ample conceptions available that point
to the mutual penetration and intertwinement of the corporate sector and government: the military-industrial complex, union mediation between employers and employees, and iron triangles and issue networks. There is also antitrust
legislation (e.g., the Sherman Antitrust Act of 1893), legislation regulating
banks and insurance companies, and the various government programs to
stimulate the economy (in the United States, the Tennessee Valley Authority,
the Hoover [originally Boulder] Dam, the Panama Canal, and so forth). Political economy is one concept, but in our day politics and economy have
become separated, if only because economic relations are subject to political
negotiation (see also Zimmerman 1987, 363). Where Wolin's sense of justice
is that of a realist, Rawls's is more that of an idealist.

There is one area about which one could argue that government and not the
corporate sector takes the lead, or at least takes collective responsibility, and
that is in the legislation of social justice. In a rapidly industrializing and urbanizing society, inequalities become starker and require a type of legislation
that would deal with the consequences of social and economic change. The
realist view on the development of the welfare state is thus nothing more but
the dry observation that it alleviates some of the most atrocious circumstances
(remember the etchings of Gustave Doré) and so prevents public outrage of a
scale and intensity the authorities could not possibly handle (Marx's hope).
Bismarck's social insurance legislation is the case in point. The idealist view
of the welfare state is of course the material manifestation of this sense of
social justice in all of the Western societies. One could, however, just as easily argue the other way around, namely that it is still the corporate sector that
determines the limits. But it is no longer the corporate sector within the nation, but the transnational elite that sacrifices social justice for the "Gods of
the Global Economy," as was recently argued (Friedman 1998).

6.4. The Idea and Organization of Justice: Changes in
the Independent Judiciary

The specific nature of our contemporary idea about and organization of justice acquires meaning only in a cross-time perspective. Berman's monumental

study of the origins of the Western legal tradition (1983) provides one of the best summaries. Berman focuses primarily on ideas about justice, but each of his stages of development can also be elaborated upon in its organizational consequences. Berman distinguishes between six revolutions (1983, 18–21). During the *papal revolution,* from A.D. 1050 to 1200, the period his book mainly analyzes, church and state became de facto separated (de jure not until the time of the Atlantic Revolutions). Justice was associated with the Last Judgment. In the spiritual realm, justice was organized under one body: that of canon law. In the secular realm, on the other hand, a variety of bodies of law developed (feudal law, urban law, royal law, manorial law, merchant law, etc.) (Berman 1983, 531–532), and justice was an instrument in the hand of the ruler, and at least in the hands of the elite. During the *Protestant Reformation,* from 1517 to 1555, justice became associated with Christian conscience and the first public efforts at social justice were organized (poor laws, poorhouses, public education). In terms of organization, the judiciary had not yet developed into an independent body. Law had predominantly been perceived as order, but from the *Glorious Revolution* of 1688–1689 on, law was increasingly equated with justice and associated with public spirit, fairness, and past traditions. The contribution of the fourth and fifth of these revolutions, the *American Revolution* (1775–1789) and the *French Revolution* (1789–1792), is that justice became related to public opinion, reason, and human rights, and it would be organized as a separate branch of government. Justice, or better, the judiciary, had been severed from the hands of the legislator and executive. And finally the *Russian Revolution* (1917) can be portrayed as organizing the consequences of the third, fourth, and fifth revolutions: justice associated with collectivism, planned economy, and social equality under the total control of the state. While most people in the Western world dissociate themselves from the Marxist-communist body of thought, it cannot be denied that in the welfare state, collectivism, planned economy, and social equality have assumed greater proportions than ever imagined.

Ideally, the judiciary in the Western world operates as a branch independent of government and the people so as to guarantee its objectivity and neutrality. The United States represents a somewhat different case. The federal judiciary in the United States is not entirely independent in the sense that court officers are appointed by the executive upon approval by the legislature. After that, their independence is secured through lifetime tenure. The judiciary at state and local levels is not independent of the people, since it is the latter who elect court officers. Also, in criminal proceedings at the local, state, and federal levels, the defendant is judged by a jury of peers rather than—as is the case in continental Europe—by one judge (for lesser crimes) or a collegial body of judges (as is the case for major crimes). In general, in countries with a long Roman law tradition, the legislative by nature will ultimately meet the challenge of developing law. If a particular social issue is highly politicized, the law that can be developed may be a weak compromise, but it still precedes justice. In countries with a common law tradition, the judiciary by nature is more likely to be used for solving political "hot potatoes." The best case in point is the judiciary system of the United States, especially the U.S. Supreme Court, which has assumed a legislative role in the twentieth century that none of the Founders could have foreseen. The public has come to expect quicker and more decisive action from the judiciary than from the legislative or the executive branch. Also, American politicians tend to avoid issues that cause deep social divisions, thus shifting the burden of decision making to the court system. Courts have been hesitant to take that role, but have taken it up nonetheless. Their reluctance springs from the realization that such legislative responsibility would be at the cost of neutrality. More fundamental, though, is the question "how government by nonelected, lifetime officials can be squared with representative democracy" (Cramton 1982, 154). So far the courts have been successful, which may be explained by "the magic of the robe, the remnants of the myth that law on these matters is discovered by an elaboration of existing rules (rather than by personal preference), and the prudence of the judiciary in picking issues on which it could command a great deal of popular support" (Cramton 1982, 154; see also Scheb and Lyons 2000). And then, of course, the court's popularity is protected by the fact that only the final judgment is publicized. As a rule, the public will not be privy to the deliberations and will see only the outcome, including dissenting opinions. Even a recent publication by Edward Lazarus (1998) does not really provide new insights into the workings of the Supreme Court, at least not in the eyes of Sullivan (1998, 15).

6.5. Dispersion of Regulatory Powers

There is one part of government that deals with lawmaking and adjudication that is organized independently from the executive, legislative, and judiciary. The *administrative agencies* perform tasks that all the other three branches of government also perform: making laws (known as rules), monitoring these laws, punishing a violation of them by means of trial, and providing services (Cann 1995, 15). Administrative agencies are a relatively young phenomenon in government. In the United States as elsewhere, they made their first appearance around the turn of the last century, and they grew in number as the welfare state expanded. For most of the nineteenth century, the expansion of the executive in the United States had taken the route of creating yet another government department, befitting a system of congressional dominance under which the executive is held in check through fragmentation of bureaucracy (Arnold 1998, 137). Under the growth of the presidency's role from the end of the nineteenth century on, administrative agencies became increasingly attractive because they were more directly linked with the executive.

In general, the development of administrative agencies has gone through three spurts. First, around the turn of the last century, the Interstate Commerce Commission (1887), the Food and Drug Administration (1906), and the Federal Trade Commission (1914) were created. Second, during the take-off of the welfare state in the 1930s, the Federal Home Loan Bank (1932), the Tennessee Valley Authority (1933), the Federal Deposit Insurance Corporation (1933), the Federal Communications Commission (1934), the Securities and Exchange Commission (1934), the National Mediation Board (1934), the National Labor Relations Board (1935), and the Social Security Board (1935) were created. And, third, the maturation of the welfare state in the 1960s and 1970s saw the creation of four new government departments (the Department of Housing and Urban Development in 1965, the Department of Transportation in 1966, the Department of Energy in 1977, and the Department of Education in 1979) and several agencies, such as the Equal Employment Opportunity Commission (1964), the Occupational Safety and Health Administration (1970) and the Federal Mine Safety and Health Review Commission (1977) (Cann 1995, 12–13).

In the postwar era, the notions of social justice and welfare state had not only become global (e.g., development aid), but also went beyond the helping of individuals who were harmed by market imperfections. In a way, one could say that the welfare state became collectivist because, from the 1960s on, it also endeavored to correct market failures that would strike at society at large. The creation of the Peace Corps in 1961 is an example of a globalizing welfare state that targets individuals, while the creation of the Environmental Protection Agency (1970) is an example of a welfare state meeting social justice at the collective level. Cann (1995, 13) reported that by 1992, fourteen cabinet-level agencies (i.e., government departments) existed with 2 million employees in addition to sixty independent agencies, government corporations, and independent regulatory commissions or agencies with another million employees. Thus, about one-third of the federal workforce is employed in the independent agencies. Through their administrative rule making, they fulfill an important function, especially as the "purest expression of the adversarial system" (Garvey 1997, 237). They are important because in the administrative agencies, administrators legislate, execute, and adjudicate, becoming in effect truly a fourth branch or power of government. By all accounts, this is a combination of powers that the Founders would probably have found atrocious, but it became possible in the government system they invented. The various branches of government significantly overlap (Hill 1999). To be sure, at every stage, administrators are required to inform the public and the appropriate political bodies of their activities (Garvey 1997, 134). Hence, appropriate action can be taken if an administrative agency assumes too much independence. Since the 1970s, agencies have been required to substantiate their decisions more than ever, whether affecting an individual or society at large, and to argue their constitutional justness before the regular courts (Hill 1995, 338). Many of these court actions have been pursued by individuals who felt that they had been unjustly treated and thus disadvantaged by a particular agency (including universities). The effect is something the public does not want: more bureaucracy. For in their sometimes justifiable pursuit of justice, citizens have also been the prime instrument of the phenomenon that "agencies have become increasingly concerned with proceduralism over the last quarter century. As a consequence of court intervention, agencies become more rigid, slower, more concerned with documenting action, and less concerned with the substantive needs of their clients" (Hill 1995, 338). As a result, the growth of bureaucracy is a consequence not just of megalomaniacal civil servants (on the size of organizations, cf. Downs 1967 and Niskanen 1971, 1973) or of a vicious circle of bureaucracy (on the number of rules, cf. Crozier 1964), but certainly also of the citizen's demand for due process.

The administrative agency is not just a cultural and national feature in the United States linked to the strengthening of the presidential office. In fact, throughout the Western world, administrative agencies emerged from the turn of the 1900s onward—an international phenomenon occurring wherever and whenever governments expand their scope of services. This growth of government had consequences for the degree to which political officeholders could hold the reins of government, and so they could not but address the apparent loss of control and the need for more expertise. One way was to enhance the civil service's professionalism through new training programs and the hiring of new experts. Another way was to strengthen, formally or informally, the role and position of the head of government, either by creating or strengthening the authority invested in the office itself or by enhancing the executive control over the bureaucracy through the creation of administrative agencies. Both happened in the United States and several European countries (Raadschelders and Van der Meer 1998, 29–30). More recently, independent administrative agencies have been regarded as the organizational solution to the need to downsize government; they thus operate between the extremes of completely public and completely private organizations. Whether or not this is desirable depends entirely upon the question of how much control citizens would like government to have over various activities that are collective by nature.

6.6.   The Foundations of International Law and Social Justice

At the domestic level, the scope of government has expanded and state and society have become highly intertwined, to such a degree that lawmaking would not suffice if it was merely concerned with regulating interactions between individuals and between individuals and organizational entities. Indeed, contemporary lawmaking meets both the individual as well as the collective needs of society. The same development has occurred at the international level.

The foundations for this internationalization of social justice were laid back in the seventeenth century, when scholars started developing a body of international law to establish order between the sovereign states. John Locke distinguished between two domestic powers, the legislative and the executive (in that order), supplemented with a federative power that concerned the protection of the state's interest in the international arena. The federative power had to be effective and thus invested in the executive or at least very close to it:

> Though, as I said, the executive and the federative power of every community be really distinct in themselves, yet they are hardly to be separated and placed at the same time in the hands of distinct persons. For both of them requiring the force of the society for their exercise, it is almost impracticable to place the force of the commonwealth in distinct and not subordinate hands, or that the executive and federative power should be placed in persons that might act separately. (Locke 1986, 192)

The federative power is therefore concerned with foreign relations that were well within the authority of the executive into the mid-twentieth century. Foreign relations did not really concern the public at large and were conducted by means of diplomats and ministers of foreign affairs. During the centuries of a balance-of-power politics (1648–1989), there were both domestic as well as international reasons to focus attention on how to formally regulate international relations. At the domestic level, positive law became the major means of assuring tranquility, and in the process statesmen and jurists became aware that a counterpart in international law was missing. Thus, a body of international law slowly developed from the mid-seventeenth century on. This body of law was, however, limited to regulating the interaction between states and would not infringe in any way upon the sovereignty of a state. In the international arena, the prevailing sovereignty theory prohibited regulation beyond the state (Raadschelders 1998a, 218–224).

That situation has drastically and rapidly changed in the twentieth century, at least in theory, if not so much yet in terms of practical consequences. Even during the final decades of the balance-of-power period, the signs that a new era was emerging were present. While state and economy had already become highly interdependent at the domestic level, the same was happening at the international level from the 1940s on. The expansion of multinational private corporations and the emergence of a globalizing economy meant that increasingly, and certainly more visibly, domestic policy making was influenced by fluctuations in the world market. The Great Depression of the 1930s made this clear, and a variety of international agreements and treaties from the mid-1940s on were testimony to this enhanced awareness of global intertwinement of hitherto more or less isolated countries and regions.

This global intertwinement was not purely economic, for the international community started to operate in communion on a more or less shared basis of social justice. As limited as it is, development aid is an expression of welfare state ideology at the international level and thus an illustration of international social justice. More basic and truly encompassing the globe is the development of human rights as part of the body of international law. It is here that formal international agreements are having an impact upon domestic policy and politics that would have been unthinkable even sixty years ago. The League of Nations was nothing but an international forum for debate, although it was more formal than the nineteenth-century Concert of Europe had been. The United Nations (UN), on the other hand, is not simply a forum organization. The UN actually delivers services through its auxiliary organizations.

We have come a long way from the Bill of Rights and Thomas Paine's *Rights of Man.* The body of international law that deals with a political regime's impact upon individuals (e.g., all human rights agreements) has been slowly expanded to the collective level of the states together. It is almost unbelievable that crimes committed by state leaders against humanity can now be prosecuted. The fact that the international community calls independent states or their representatives to justice is a clear sign that the old sovereignty theory has been eroded. At the same time, it is too early to conclude that the era of the state is drawing to a close because of the human rights issue, the mushrooming of international agreements and treaties, and, in parts of Europe, the far-reaching international cooperation realized in the European Union.

From a Western perspective, three things are remarkable about this internationalization of social justice. The first concerns the Western world as a whole. In 1946, the UN appointed a committee of philosophers, historians and lawyers to develop a list of human rights shared by most if not all cultures ("The World Is Watching" 1998, 8). Remarkably, the lists submitted by various cultures were strikingly similar, although differences of opinion were apparent about the conditions under which a particular human right was protected and when a violation was pursued. These lists underline the fact that cultures may very well be comparable to each other at a deep level, while disagreement about means and methods may emerge at a more superficial level. Huntington's *Clash of Civilizations* (1996) is certainly not the kind of clash in which the various cultures must crash on each other as tectonic plates from the deepest to the surface levels.

The second remarkable fact is that the United States has simultaneously been a staunch and a reluctant supporter of international law and enforcing organizations. The United States generally ratifies human rights treaties long after other countries have done so, but also supported the international tribunal for war crimes and genocide in Rwanda and former Yugoslavia. At present, it opposes the creation of a permanent international criminal court that has met with quite substantial support from other states ("The World Is Watching" 1998, 6). However, this is only remarkable at first and very superficial sight. First, the foreign policy of the United States wavers between the domestic forum of the isolationists and the international forum of those who envision the United States fulfilling a leading and guiding role in the international community. Second, as the only remaining superpower, the United States is not only the policeman of the world, it also supplies a large part of the budgets of the international organizations of which it is a member. The United States is also reluctant to accept the jurisdiction of an international criminal court because it desires immunity for its peacekeeping forces especially when they can be subjected to politicized proceedings. Obviously, the United States would prosecute blatant war crimes as much as any other. The problem is, of course, to determine what exactly a war crime is.

The third and final remarkable fact is that the internationalization of social justice has made clear that the relation between the corporate sector and the government is not a one-way street, but resembles rather the structure and functioning of an issue network that includes nongovernmental organizations and international advocacy groups. Governments have helped lay the legal foundations for the international human rights movement since they are, after all, the only bodies that can make binding decisions on behalf of an entire constituency. Organizations such as Amnesty International, the Red Cross, the Red Crescent, and Human Rights Watch have been very important in persuading international private corporations to refrain from dealing with political regimes known for their violation of human rights. The antiapartheid campaigns in the 1980s proved that multinationals are not the only ones that hold the reins of power ("The World Is Watching" 1998, 13). The hopeful sign here is that both economic as well as humanitarian considerations increasingly play a role in determining domestic and international welfare policies.

6.7. Concluding Remarks: Social Justice Domestically and Internationally

In this chapter I explored the complex nature of justice in Western government. While the justice of settling conflicts between individual parties has been a public task throughout history, it is only in the past 500 years or so that the primary responsibility for social justice has transferred from private charity to public policy. For some 300 years, the inclusion of social services in the public realm was the practical response to the overload of private associations. From the Atlantic Revolutions on, however, social justice as government's responsibility was shored up in political theory, then expressed in law, and finally materialized into a wide range of social services. With the expanding conception of justice, government moved from being mere adjudicator to being the largest, most encompassing redistributor of wealth. Initially, the theory of social justice depended upon the practice of private charity—the extent of which was unpredictable. In contrast, the developments in the past 200 years have turned social justice into a coordinated effort, the objectives of which are expressed in, for instance, prospective budgeting so the outcome is thus much more predictable.

Domestically, this shift has drawn the judiciary into policy-making roles unthinkable 100 years ago. At the same time, its traditional role has fragmented and it has, perhaps, even been eroded by the other branches of government. More than ever before, the theory of separate branches of government is complemented not just with the practice of intertwinement but with the practice of each branch exercising the authority of the other branches. It is perhaps in the melting of judicial, legislative, and executive authorities that social justice is served best. The theory and organization of a division of power are sacrosanct. Western democracies would not accept concentration of power in one person or body. However, the practice of today's governing is not a concentration of power in one person or body but rather the distribution of these primary legislative, executive, and judiciary powers according to function or process. As it is, in practice the three branches are separated at the political summit (Congress or Parliament, head of state, Supreme Court). It is at the administrative level, however, that these three distinct functions collapse into one. The government departments and agencies can issue regulations, execute policy, and monitor compliance through the imposition of sanctions. The work of the Internal Revenue Service as a unit of the Treasury Department is an example. The various independent regulatory agencies are another. Democracy with accountability and efficiency with frugality are served by the separation of powers at the political level and by the collapsing or intermingling of powers at the administrative level.

The Western theory and practice of social justice have been exported to other parts of the world. The democracy of equal rights and opportunities is no longer the prerogative of Western states. While the member-states are the constituting elements of, for instance, the United Nations, international organizations have also acquired a life of their own. They may not enjoy the same legal standing as sovereign states (i.e., the legal authority to make binding decisions), but in practice they combine the legislative, executive, and judicial functions that serve the cause of human rights and social justice and that exercise influence through moral authority. They are generally understood as political bodies, but they resemble national administrative organizations in their functioning. The volume of bi- and multilateral aid and the much larger domestic effort for social justice are simply expressions of the fact that the utilitarian individualism of the nightwatch state has given way to redistributive justice for the collective in the global welfare state.

7 THE NIGHTWATCH STATE: EXTERNAL AND INTERNAL SAFETY

Governments need to have both shepherds and butchers.
—Voltaire

Little else is requisite to carry a state to the highest degree of opulence from the lowest barbarism, but peace, easy taxes, and tolerable administration of justice.
—Adam Smith

The protection of the territory by means of an army against foreign invasion and the maintenance of public order and safety through law enforcement are, like justice, very old and basic functions of government. Together, the existence of an army and a police force in the modern era indicates submission of the territory under the single authority of the civil state. During those few decades between the 1810s and the 1860s that we know as the nightwatch state, Western states withdrew from a variety of functions in the economic and social spheres but retained their coercive powers. Men's inclination for violence makes the services of the military, the police, and the justice system necessary under public sector authority. Calls for a government that works better and costs less, massive privatization, massive personnel layoffs, and so forth, are underpinned by the idea that government is too big and that the state ought to be rolled back. The particular reform objective of a smaller government has not stopped at these most basic functions of government. During the Middle Ages and most of the early modern period, military and police functions developed from being exercised by and organized through private arrangements to being completely incorporated in the public sector. Their function was mainly repressive and reactive. In the twentieth century, both for military and police, preventive action in the domestic and international arenas is increasingly important. In the past few decades, the developments of military and police diverged. Notwithstanding the existence of private militias, the military is still a solely public force. Policing, on the other hand, is increasingly becoming a shared public-private responsibility that also includes the prison system.

In this chapter I look at the protective and corrective functions of the state. The existence of a standing army and of professional police forces under civil authority indicates how strong the state must be. When Adam Smith wrote that little else was necessary for progress than peace, taxes, and justice, he assumed that these would be provided by a strong state whose governing authority is uncontested. In section 7.1, I first briefly define concepts of state and of government and then describe the advent of the state in Europe and theories of state making. This section concludes with a discussion on the future of the state. Next, the development and role of the military in the past (section 7.2) and in the present (section 7.3) will be outlined, followed by a description of the development and role of the police and of the prison system in the past (section 7.4) and in the present (section 7.5). The changing roles of the military and of the police and penitentiary system are best understood against the background of the changes from the nightwatch to the welfare state (section 7.6).

7.1. State Making as Theory and in History

The juridical aspect of the concept of state originated in the Dutch Republic and the French monarchy of the early seventeenth century when it came to be linked with the authority, the privileges, and the property of government (Dyson 1980, 26–27). The *state* is merely a territory within which *government* organizes the formal institutions and processes through which binding decisions are made for society. The current definition of a state in international law is provided in Article 1 of the Montevideo Convention on Rights and Duties of States (1933) that qualifies a state as an international actor if it has "(a) a permanent population; (b) a defined territory; (c) a government; and (d) a capacity to enter into relations with other states" (Shaw 1986, 127). The Conference of Westphalia (1648) is usually considered the starting point of the modern state in the international state system. In the juridical definition, a political entity is or is not a state. States, however, differ in their degree of "stateness" (Nettl 1968), and a sociological definition of state not only allows a variety of states to be included (Vincent 1987, 7) but also captures something about the nature and sources of the relationship with the domestic population. Badie and Birnbaum have distinguished four types of political systems. France is an example of a country that has a center and a state. Italy is a state but has no center. In France and Italy, the state dominates civil society (but see Putnam et al. 1993, on northern Italian civic associations). The United

Kingdom and the United States are systems with a center but without a true state, while Switzerland has neither a center nor a true state. In these more stateless systems, civil society is much more at liberty to organize itself (Badie and Birnbaum 1983, 103; see also Vincent 1987, 10).

A crucial element for what constitutes a state is the degree to which, as Max Weber argued, it has a monopoly over the use of physical violence through military and policing functions (1980, 822). In Weber's footsteps, Tilly defined the state in terms of four elements: control over a well-defined, contiguous territory; a relatively centralized administration; differentiation from other societal organizations; and a monopoly over the use of violence (Tilly 1975, 27). Basically, a state is a territory under one sovereignty. The concept of *nation-state* refers to a territory that is occupied by a people (nation) that totals up to 95 percent of the population. Few states were ever in that situation. Tilly (1990, 3) mentions that Sweden and Ireland came close and one could probably add Iceland. With that in mind, Tilly's later preference to speak of *national states* rather of nation-states was intended to solve the fact that most sovereignties have a multinational population. Not satisfied either with the national state concept, Tilly later withdrew to a definition of state that solely emphasizes the centralization of power within a territory: the *consolidated state* (1994, 5–6).

The historian McNeill (1999) has argued that the (nation-)state is a rather new and young phenomenon in the history of political regimes. He argues that empires and city-states have been the most common types of political regimes, with the (nation-)state being an actor of any significance only in the past 500 years. The contemporary state showed itself first in the less contested territories at the fringes of Europe that were defended by the sea and/or mountains as natural barriers: the Scandinavian countries, Iceland, England, France. A state such as Poland between the tenth and the fourteenth centuries could exist for it was surrounded by fragmented polities. In the late fifteenth century, Spain and Portugal developed statehood. Russia and the Dutch Republic followed in the sixteenth and seventeenth centuries. In the middle and most contested part of Europe, the hundreds of small principalities and city-states did not amalgamate into large entities until the middle of the nineteenth century.

The (nation-)state as the most dominant actor in the international arena is only a feature of the past 100, maybe 150 years. The facts are simple. Around 1500 C.E. Europe was fragmented into at least 500 territorial units, from city-republics, principalities, and a few (nation-) states (France, England) to kingdoms (Hungary) and empires (Ottoman empire) (Tilly 1990, 40–43). By 1815, the number of states worldwide was twenty-three and their numbers gradually increased to forty by the year 1900 (Wallace and Singer 1970, 272). At present, there are more than 190 states in the world. The (nation-)state as

Table 7.1

International and Domestic Dimensions of State-Society

	Exogenous	Endogenous
International	Sovereignty; independence vis-à-vis other states	Declining independence; sovereignty loss; integration of states
Domestic	Political centralization; relation between government and society	Administrative centralization; political-administrative relations

principal unit of territorial government is larger than the city-state and quite a bit smaller than the empire. It is not merely a unit of territorial government, but also identified by a particular dominant population. The state as we know it is one of the export products of Western governments to the rest of the world. On the international stage, it is the state that acts as representative of a population and as the prime decision maker. The state may have to compete with other internationally operating actors, such as nongovernmental organizations, but only the state can engage in international treaties that are legally binding for its population. In this sense, the end of the state is certainly nowhere in sight. We will get back to this point later in this section.

Theories of state making can be categorized in terms of international and domestic dimensions and in terms of exogenous and endogenous dimensions (see Table 7.1 above).

The exogenous dimension focuses on the state as the link between the domestic and the international environment. From an exogenous point of view, it is the independence of states that counts, as expressed in their sovereignty. At the domestic level, it is the relation between government and society that is the main concern. Can subnational government, for instance, interact directly with international and supranational bodies (as happens in the European Union)? What combines both dimensions from an exogenous point of view is the theme of political centralization. The studies by Rokkan (1970, 1975) and Tilly are examples of works that depart from an exogenous model of state making. From an endogenous point of view, one would have to look inside government. At the international level, the far-reaching but voluntary cooperation between states may result in a loss of independence. This is certainly the case in the European Union, where integration of sovereign states has advanced the farthest. At the domestic level, the endogenous dimension concerns the political-administrative relations. How are the boundaries between levels of government and between the political and administrative branches drawn? Administrative centralization is relevant to the structure and functioning of government. Studies that focus on endogenous patterns of state making usually look at, for instance, the development of the civil service or the development of central-local relations. Together, political and administrative centralization are to some degree necessary conditions of state making and for any further development of public services at the domestic level.

Empirically we can distinguish between two major types of state making processes. The first type is characteristic for most of Europe and for the United States, where the state emerged as the outcome of war. In Europe, individuals mobilized to win rights from the state and the political elites. The Americans, on the other hand, revolted against a crown that took their rights away. In the words of James Madison, the American Constitution in comparison to European examples was a "charter of power granted by liberty rather than a charter of liberty granted by power" (Morone 1990, 3). In the second type of state making, the state is imposed on a territory from above as the result of an internationally negotiated agreement. This is what happened to some parts of Europe (e.g., Yugoslavia) and to large parts of Africa, Latin America, and, to a lesser extent, Asia. Whatever its origins, the state is an instrument for the concentration of power and is subject to internal forces of centralization and decentralization and to external forces of cooperation and isolation. Elias's model of state making (1982) describes that process in terms of centralization and decentralization. The last phase in his model is international integration, which has given rise to discussions about the future of the state.

Koch (1993), elegantly summarizing this debate as it takes place mostly in the studies of political science and international relations, expressed surprise that neither field was in much communication with the other. It is equally surprising that the future-of-the-state debate has not yet spilled over into the study of public administration, because the various theories that authors outline about the position of the state in society naturally must have consequences for the size, structure, and functioning of domestic government.

In the political science and international relations (IR) fields, Koch distinguishes between a theoretical, an empirical, and an institutional-normative line of argument (see Table 7.2).

The *theoretical debate* is focused on the usefulness of the state-concept. Within political science, the pluralists make a case for continuous fragmentation of state power and are opposed by those who support a strong role for the state. In the IR field, the theories of transnational relations point to alternative centers of power, while the realists continue to see the state as the primary actor in international relations. The *empirical debate* is much more concerned with the question of whether state power actually increases or decreases. Within political science, some authors believe that statelessness is becoming increasingly important, while others point to increased state

Table 7.2

Three Dimensions to the State Debate in the Studies of Political Science and International Relations

	National political science		International relations	
Theoretical debate	Pluralists	State centrists	Transnational relations	Realism
Empirical debate	Statelessness	Increased societal complexity; increased state intervention	European integration	Continuity of state; global state
Institutional-normative debate	Privatization, deregulation, downsizing	Strong state intervention	World government; central guidance system	Functionalists; networks of international organizations instead of states

Source: After Koch 1993, 3–6.

intervention as a consequence of ever increasing societal complexity. In IR, the loss of sovereignty is central to the argument. Some see a supranational state emerging, as in the European Union, while others point to the continuity of the state in a global state context. Finally the *institutional-normative debate* centers its efforts on what the state should be. Should the state retreat and give way to privatization, deregulation, downsizing, and so forth, or should it instead increase its efforts at holding society together? In the IR field, some dream about a possible world government or, at least, international steering systems, while others advocate an interlocking network of international organizations.

Central to the political science discussion is the degree of political centralization. The core in the IR debate is the question of whether state sovereignty as we know it has a future. What connects the debates in political science and international relations is the choice between private, individualist, and isolationist, or public, collectivist, and cooperative arrangements. In reality, there will be a mix of individualist choices in some policy areas and collectivist choices in others. In reference to both the last and the next chapters, this means that the proper placing of traditional and welfare services needs to be considered in the context of state traditions.

The relevance of state theory and debate about the future of the state is clearly relevant to the study of public administration. Network theorists, for instance, emphasize government's mediating role amidst other equal actors. The focus of their analysis is the process of decision making. Students of bureaucracy, especially in Europe, emphasize government's leadership and are more focused on structure and formal procedures.

On the European continent a tradition of fairly strong and centralized states suggests an active role of the state in providing traditional services and in reshaping welfare policies. Such interventionist action befits these countries that at some point in the twentieth century have all had socialist governments or coalition governments with socialists. The United Kingdom and the United States, on the other hand, are often considered to have a weak state tradition (Vincent 1987, 2). British authors such as Frederick W. Maitland and Harold Laski and American authors such as Mary Parker Follett and Arthur F. Bentley emphasize that civic associations had to be based in the free action of individuals (Vincent 1987, 183, 195). The state's role was to maximize the conditions in which individuals could pursue their desires. However, the United Kingdom and the United States are not totally individualist societies because, as these authors argue, freedom can develop only in the context of multiple semi-independent groups (Vincent 1987, 196). The American libertarian or pluralist view of the state is partially rooted in these ideas as well as in, for instance, Adam Smith's and Benjamin Franklin's conviction that society and economy can take care of themselves. In a capitalist democracy, the state is a neutral arena for debate that unfolds between competing interests. Free market, minimum state, elimination of social programs, and antibureaucracy are keywords that characterize the most extreme manifestation of this approach to state (Carnoy 1984, 48, 248–250).

7.2. The Military for the State in the Past

The military has always been closely related to those in power and as such could be considered a political force, if not *the* political force, of most governments throughout history. In the early centuries of Western history, armies did not really exist as a continuous presence in society. Indeed, armies emerged only whenever there was an outside threat, and their existence was based on a system of mutual obligation known as feudalism. The *feudal armies* of Europe disappeared with the advent of the state, which was a political entity whose sovereign sought to expand power into territories that had hitherto been governed more or less independently of the "high" king. The new states in the late Middle Ages required larger armies to fight wars against each other and to defend the sovereign against the regional lords who resisted the political centralization under the state. The feudal army thus gave way to the *mercenary army:* war as hobby or as obligation became war as profession for the lower rank and file. From the mid-seventeenth century on, those mercenary armies were replaced by *standing armies*, first in Sweden and Prussia, then in France, Austria, and Russia. What is interesting about this development from a public administration point of view is that a standing army is a sign of a strong state, a state in which the army is firmly controlled by those who rule. That control was not too difficult to establish in a society where any position of command, whether civil or military, was privileged to the aristocracy, for whom such positions were a pastime befitting their stature. Up through the late eighteenth, early nineteenth centuries, armies were part of the center of power because their officers were recruited from the same elite as high officials in civil government (Parker 1988; Roberts 1955).

The military as we know it came into being from the 1800s on, when the officer corps turned from amateur to professional. That change is generally explained by four factors: a strengthening of civil authority over the military (further centralization of state power), increased functional specialization and division of labor in society, the advent of democracy and political parties (including the decline of the nobility), and technological innovation (Huntington 1957, 32; Abrahamsson 1972, 37). While the thesis about the declining influence of the nobility in the nineteenth century was convincingly challenged some years ago (Kinneging 1994), it is a fact that recruitment for civil and for military positions was based increasingly on achievement and increasingly less on ascription. In the light of history, this change was so abrupt that Mosca remarked at the turn of the last century how unusual a noninterventionist and apolitical army was (Abrahamsson 1972, 41). Indeed, by the end of the nineteenth century, the army was clearly subject to government and separate from politics, with the exception that most ministers of the army and navy were recruited from among the highest in the military ranks. During the first four decades of the twentieth century, scholars of political science and public administration conducted little research that specifically concerned the military, even though the elements of classic administrative theory with its emphasis on efficiency, its unity of command, and its neutrality vis-à-vis politics would have made it an interesting case (Perlmutter 1977, 3). This apolitical position of the military befitted the times. In the context of democratization and growing government intervention into social welfare, the military could not have overcome what Finer calls its two politically crippling weaknesses: its technical inability to administer any society beyond the most primitive, and its lack of legitimacy to rule (Finer 1975, 12). Finer elaborates this as follows: "Thus as an economy advances, as the division of labour becomes more and more sensitive, as the secondary and then the tertiary services expand, and as the society requires the existence of a trained professional bureaucracy, of technicians, labour organizations, and the like—so the army ceases to be able to rule by its own resources alone" (1975, 14). Mosca highlighted the apolitical nature of the military, but this did not mean that the military was no longer an influential factor in government and politics. Indeed, in the first half of the twentieth century, a pattern of civil-military relations emerged that was quite different from the old, but not less influential. Some spoke of a convergence of military and civil organizations (Janowitz 1971, xi). Others spoke of a garrison state in which the military dominates because of the likelihood of war (Lasswell 1941; for discussion of Lasswell, see Huntington 1957, 346–350) and—related to the garrison state thesis—a military-industrial complex was "discovered" supported by government (Lang 1965, 841–842). In terms of research, during the 1950s the social sciences rediscovered the military as a social force to reckon with, which resulted in an outburst of studies in the 1960s and 1970s that attempted to analyze the social geography of the military in its relation to politics. Books that focused on the extreme features of political-military relations, such as revolution, guerrilla and psychological warfare, covert operations, and the military role in civil disorders (see, for instance, Little 1971) were outnumbered by those that zoomed in on the mundane, day-to-day interaction between military and civil powers that changed the military. As Lang observes: "the increased reliance on civilian experts for technical advice on internal problems (like training and manpower management) and on external policy exemplifies a civilianization of the military rather than the other way around" (Lang 1965, 842). The military could not and would not dominate policy in a pluralist system (Lang 1965, 841). Still, though the political power of the military was substantial enough, it was not a power wielded through an identifiable aristocracy but through a more amorphous political body. The Kennedy administration found that there had been too much focus on spending (fiscal control) during the Eisenhower years and that policy choices regarding defense programs were a consequence of budget decisions rather than the other way around (Kanter 1983, 59, 61). McNamara's planning-programming-budget system (PPBS) as a new method for resource planning and budgeting at the Defense Department may not have generated the changes desired (Kanter 1983, 70), but it did bring the focus back to the primacy of politics. To be sure, politics sought out the military just as much. Congressmen lobbied for military employment, especially in their electoral backyards, and as the size of military establishments declined, the House Armed Services Committee became increasingly dominated by congressmen representing military districts (Arnold 1979, 95, 128).

The contemporary military is apolitical in the sense that it is an instrument in the hands of civil government. In Western society, a military seizure of power would not be considered legitimate, nor is coercion believed to be an efficient way of securing obedience (Finer 1975, 16). The contemporary military is, however, a political force in the sense that it actively interacts and "networks" with representatives from business, industry, politics, academia, and labor unions, as well as with the police and civil guard groups (Abrahamsson 1972, 141). This networking presents the military in a way that is far removed from the image of a military-industrial complex, suggesting rather the kind of actions undertaken by any interest group in a large and complex state-society. In other words, the basis of the military's relation with politics has changed, but not its influence.

That influence should not be measured in terms of its budgets because military expenditure has declined steadily since World War II. In absolute terms, military expenditure in the United States, for instance, increased from almost $46 billion in 1960 to more than $300 billion in 1991 (Peters 1993, 323). Large cutbacks in the major source of expenditure, that of arms, were, however, possible and did not meet with much public opposition (Peters 1991, 88). In relative terms, defense expenditure declined as a consequence of strong increases in welfare policy expenditures. Rose calculates that the average defense expenditure as a percentage of the GNP in seven Western countries (Denmark, France, Germany, Italy, Netherlands, United Kingdom, and the United States) and Japan declined from 6.3 percent in 1954 to 3.2 percent in 1980. The decline in the United States was above average: from 11.3 percent to 4.6 percent. Expenditures in welfare programs for the same period at least doubled (Rose 1989, 213). Peters presents a relative decline of defense expenditure from 7.9 percent in 1960 to 5.2 percent in 1991 (1993, 323).

7.3. The Widening Scope of the Military: International Policing in a Multipolar World

The military fulfills an important function domestically since it is often called to help, for instance, with natural disasters and urban riots. As an interest group, it exercises influence over public policy. The military also plays an important role in the international arena. Government changes under both domestic as well as global pressures. What makes both kinds of pressure challenging is that there is little consensus either about their nature and direction or about the best way to deal with them. The domestic pressures concern the real need to recast the welfare state (see section 7.6) and the perceived breakdown of law and order, while the international pressures concern the adjustment to a multipolar world. What connects both, in the view of Huntington, is

a global crisis in governance. The rise of transnational corporations producing economic goods is increasingly matched by the rise of transnational criminal mafias, drug cartels, and terrorist gangs violently assaulting civilization. Law and order is the first prerequisite of Civilization and in much of the world—Africa, Latin America, the former Soviet Union, South Asia, the Middle East—it appears to be evaporating, while also under serious assault in China, Japan and the West. On a worldwide basis Civilization seems in many respects to be yielding to barbarism, generating the image of an unprecedented phenomenon, a global Dark Ages, possibly descending on humanity. (Huntington 1996, 321)

It is impossible to argue against such sweeping generalizations without presenting an elaborate analysis of countertrends such as the development of common programs between different countries without too much reference to the conflicts of the past, as happens, for instance, in the European Union (Malitza 2000, 8). The individualist-collectivist dilemma in the international realm plays out as a choice between isolationism within the boundaries of one's own society or, at best, the civilization to which one belongs versus international cooperation that potentially encompasses the entire world.

It is in the scenario of international interaction and cooperation that the military has come to play a role that goes beyond its traditional function of protecting the territorial integrity of the state. In various parts of the world, international armies have been deployed to fight (e.g., the Gulf War), to stabilize regional unrest (e.g., former Yugoslavia), and to help on the road to permanent peace. In doing so, the military moved from traditional war making into international policing, and international military presence is increasingly accompanied by international civil involvement (supervising free and fair elections; international civil servants temporarily working on behalf of the countries' administration as in, for instance, Cambodia). Thus foreign affairs is less and less a playground for diplomats and national armies but has become the playground for national politicians who support an international counterpart of the national patterns of civil-military relations. A case can be made for some international political centralization on the basis of an international civil-military complex. As long as the various cultures of the world are willing to look beyond the fault lines Huntington so vividly describes, such an international civil-military complex, rooted in the national societies that legitimate it, may be an investment in the future. At the international level, the emergence of a civil-military complex can provide a hopeful counterweight against the forces of blind, fanatic regionalism and nationalism. That civil-military complex functions on the basis of a negotiated cooperation that constitutes a fairly weak political centralization between state-societies.

7.4. Policing Between Repression and Prevention in the Past

For centuries, the military was crucial to the perpetuation of the state in two ways. It defended the territory against any foreign aggressor and could also be used domestically at the regional or local level. In the case of outside threat, the town's civic militias (semiprofessional but permanent troops) could be mobilized, or temporary semiprofessional troops (such as the *waardgelders* in The Hague, the Netherlands) could be established (Wagenaar 1997, 211). These same semiprofessional troops were also used for policing duties, especially when civil disorder rose to levels that disrupted civil government. In the early modern states, there were no national and subnational police forces, with the possible exception of the secret police, such as in France around the 1800s. The police as we know it, a uniformed corps of professionals trained to maintain public order and safety by means of persuasion and physical force, generally did not exist until the late nineteenth century (the London police force of 1829 is the exception). In most Western countries, policing was a local affair in the towns and cities and the responsibility of a sheriff who was usually also the presiding judge of the local court and the public prosecutor. He was aided by some deputies. In general, the police were conspicuously absent during the day. At night, the streets were patrolled by night watchmen, male citizens who performed this duty on the basis of conscription. In the rural areas, a police force was usually absent or insufficient, and policing was provided through the regional level of the bailiwick and county.

In the course of the nineteenth century, policing underwent major changes in its structure and functioning, mainly because in most Western countries the existing situation of an insufficient police force in the towns and an absence of police in the rural areas was increasingly considered undesirable. Civil government could no longer deal with the rising crime rates, especially in the urbanizing areas that experienced major demographic growth. As a consequence, national governments stepped in and reorganized the police structure for the entire country, as in Europe, or at least came to regulate the police on a firmer basis, as in the United States (Szymanski 1999). The night watchmen in Europe and the small sheriff's departments with deputized officers and night watchmen in the United States were replaced by regular police forces in uniform. The civic militias were abolished.

At that time, the basic function of the police force was law enforcement in general and crime prevention and detection in particular. The repressive functions were emphasized, no longer limited to action only in case of major civil disorder (as the semiprofessional armies had been) but including a general daytime presence on the streets. In the past fifty years or so, police activity has shifted its focus more and more to crime prevention, seeking collaboration with the citizens in the neighborhood where the precinct is located. Generally, the civil authority over the police is invested in the highest elected officeholder at local government level, such as the mayor. Law enforcement is, though, also an area of major interest for most central governments, either under the jurisdiction of a Ministry of the Interior, Ministry of Justice, or Ministry of the Police.

When police and justice have done their work, the prison system is in place to hold those who have been sentenced to the punishment of being deprived of their freedom. This is a quite recent phenomenon. Before the sixteenth century, prisons were not used as a means of punishment and only provided space for torture or execution or for holding alleged criminals until trial. In the face of rising crime rates, increasing public disturbances, and increased poverty, all as a consequence of economic depression, modern prisons were built in most of Western Europe from the late sixteenth, early seventeenth century on. Their function was purely repressive (Koch 1993, 105–106) and would remain so until the middle of the twentieth century, when in most Western countries, prison life was humanized: better food, more meaningful work, rehabilitation schemes, education possibilities, and so forth. Thus, the prison system also came to emphasize the preventive function. In the United States, the prison system was organized at federal, state, and local levels in a manner comparable to the police. In addition to state and local prisons, a national prison system was created in 1930 through the centralization of the federal prisons into the Federal Bureau of Prisons in response to a congressional report in 1928 about major abuses on the part of prison wardens (Boin 1998, 150–167).

With regard to police and prison functions, one can choose between a centralized system, as in Europe, and a more decentralized system, as in the United States. In the case of police forces, one may have to consider whether they should be totally in the hands of public authorities or if some or all functions could be contracted out or privatized (see the next section). The same questions arise with respect to prisons. What type of prison can be privatized—maximum security or only minor prisons? And what type of criminal can be left to the control of the private sector—those in death row or only the up-for-parole model prisoners? (Ryan and Ward 1989).

7.5. Complementary to Safety: Community and Private Policing, Imprisonment, and Civic Militias

At the domestic level, the individualist-collectivist dilemma with regard to public order and safety seems to go in a direction opposite from that in the military—namely, to a fragmentation of policing activities between public and private providers.

At the domestic level, the state's monopoly over the use of violence is apparent in the concentration of law enforcement and of crime prevention and detection under public authority. While private policing never really disappeared, it was mainly limited to surveillance (private detectives) and protection of property (private security companies). Private policing was thus supplemental to its public counterpart. In recent decades, private security and policing agencies have grown rapidly (Jones and Newburn 1998). Private agencies hire their employees out to organizations and have their personnel patrol the property of a variety of usually corporate clients: the modern equivalent of the nightwatch. A fairly new phenomenon is hybrid policing, where regular police officers offer their services to private agencies when off-duty (Johnston 1992, 114).

The growth of private policing may support an argument in favor of privatizing some public police functions, but there are at least three objections to that argument. First, private organizations regard policing as a profitable business and thus will not monitor general safety. Government needs to maintain a police force of some size, given its general-purpose task. Privatization of the police may appeal for budgetary reasons, but at the same time it is a short-term policy. In a longer term perspective, the consequences for democracy (who controls the private police? to whom are they accountable?) as well as for social stability (safe vs. unsafe areas) need to be taken into consideration. Second, in the state-theory perspective, we should wonder whether or not further decline of the state's monopoly over the use of violence is desirable. While this is an important consideration in most Western states, it is especially relevant to the United States, given its liberal policies on the access to and ownership of firearms. Will that be the paying clientele or the public at large? What kind of public law basis can we provide to private policing? Third, the economy-of-scale perspective brings us to the question of whether private police can be as effective as their public counterparts. For this to be so would require equal jurisdiction and authority. If this is unacceptable to public authorities, how then can we circumscribe and limit the authority of private policing without jeopardizing its effectiveness? It is clear that government can benefit only from private policing that uses trained professionals, but it is also clear that such requires cooperation between and thus demarcation of the authority of both types of forces.

Policing is not only limited to trained professionals in the public and private sectors but has also emerged as an initiative of lay citizens. Neighborhood watches and civic militias can be found everywhere in the United States. These initiatives can be applauded as a sign of strengthening civil society, especially when civilian groups cooperate with public police forces. Community policing, as sponsored by federal funding since 1994, has become quite prominent, including projects such as neighborhood policing (foot patrols, local ministations) and the development of advisory committees of community members to review and discuss police services and local problems (Rochefort et al. 1998, 553–554). Concern with crime rates and violence motivates collaboration between neighborhoods and the police. At the same time, though, these citizen efforts may indicate a lack of trust in public police officers and signify a fragmentation of the public sector's monopoly over the use of violence.

The same can be said with respect to reforms of the prison system. Privately run prisons are feasible but that does not make them desirable. To no small degree, the legitimacy of government rests in its monopoly over the use of coercion, even in the United States. When an individual is incarcerated in a public prison, government exercises that coercion on behalf of a violated individual and the public itself (DeIulio 1991, see also Garvey 1997, 229). The value of efficiency may well support privatization, but the symbolic value of the legitimacy of public action should not be surrendered to the market too quickly. With respect to privatization of prisons, it is again important to consider the consequences. As a profit-seeking institution, a private prison benefits from full use of capacity, which can only be guaranteed by a government and judiciary that prescribe prison terms rather than consider other types of sentences. Already, the United States incarceration rate is far higher than in Western Europe. At the same time, crime rates are higher than in Western Europe. Perhaps this is a function of the kinder and gentler society, as Lijphart suggested (1999).

7.6. From Nightwatch to Welfare State and Beyond

In sections 7.2 to 7.5 above, I outlined the changes from early modern to modern defense and police. Whether these most recent changes will be definite remains to be seen. So far, society and government since the mid-nineteenth century could be comfortably characterized as changing from a nightwatch state with restricted government to a welfare state with interventionist government. Table 7.3 focuses on that change in terms of state functions, indicating the changes in the underlying philosophy of governance.

Government has become the largest provider of collective services in Western states, developing elaborate systems of coordination, communication, and policy and decision making in order to live up to that responsibility. In view of the discussion above about the changes in the basic functions of government, the change in the "philosophy of government" can be summarized as a change from repressive to preventive and caring government (Table 7.4).

The visible structural manifestation of that change is the public organization whose base changed from collegial administration and parochialism (more or less isolated local government and weak central-local relations) to bureaucratic administration and a complex network of central-local and public-private relations. The consequences for the distribution of power are great, because

Table 7.3

Nightwatch State and Restricted Government Versus Welfare State and Interventionist Government

Nightwatch state and restricted government	Welfare state and interventionist government
Limited number of public functions	Large number of public functions
Mainly protective functions	Protective, organizing, stimulating, and development functions
Public order and safety, defense, foreign affairs, poor care, some health care	See left, plus public housing, labor protection, social security, energy supply, technological development, environmental protection, etc.
Limited intervention, and, if necessary, only when *subsidiary* (i.e., to private initiative), *after the fact* (principle of repression), *ad hoc*, and *short-term*	Large intervention in economic, social, and cultural life; state action is *primary* (proactive), *preventive* (creating favorable conditions), *systematic* (rational decision making), and *prospective* (through planning)

Source: Van Braam 1986, 124–125.

Table 7.4

Development of Government Between 1850 and the Present

	Mid-19th century	Present
Size and nature of state functions	Nightwatch state	Welfare state
Dominating governance strategy	Laissez-faire state	Interventionist state
Dominant governance model	Repressive governance	Preventive and caring governance
Type of public organization	Collegial and parochial	Bureaucratic and complex
Distribution of power	Mainly with governing political bodies	Shared—at least—with bureaucracy

Source: Reprinted with permission from A. Van Braam (in cooperation with M.L. Bemelmans-Videc), *Leerboek Bestuurskunde* (Muiderberg: Coutinho, 1986), p. 351.

power is no longer concentrated in the bourgeois and/or an aristocratic elite that populated the political bodies. Instead, it is shared with the public bureaucracies in continuous consultation with representatives from various societal actors. If, indeed, we are tearing away at the foundations of the welfare and interventionist state as we know it, we are obliged to at least attempt to consider what lies beyond.

7.7. Concluding Remarks

In his monthly column in the *PA Times*, the 2000–2001 president of the American Society of Public Administration, Marc Holzer, argued that "government is a necessary, productive and efficient investment of our scarce resources" and that "government is the vehicle for our security." That security is provided by the military, police, and correctional officials. Perhaps the military is not underfunded, but "many police and correction departments would argue compellingly that they are severely underfunded" (Holzer 2000, 13). Holzer recognizes that he is speaking to the converted and that it is the task of those who teach public administration and political science to convince the political practitioners of the worth of government. From the late eighteenth and early nineteenth century on, there has been support in the political leadership for the idea that the best government is the smallest government, especially in the United States. What distinguishes the current politicians from their predecessors is that the latter did not really tamper with the most basic functions of the state. In this chapter, I have argued that the use of violence, while never totally under public control, could be controlled more by government, especially in densely populated areas.

The dimensions of our analytical framework in chapter 1 that are most relevant to the topics of this chapter are the historical-contemporary and the individualist-collectivist perspectives. With these we can see how defense, police, and correctional functions moved from the private and individual sphere into the public and collective sphere and that the present policies to develop public-private partnerships and even to privatize certain services represent a break with the past. This is not necessarily bad because new times may well need new types of governance. However, we should not be too quick to throw the baby out with the bathwater. Creating a government that works better and costs less is fine, but it should not be done without carefully considering what that may mean to government's most basic function: protection of life, liberty, and property. It also requires attention to potential problems of coordination and authority. We must assure that public organizations will maintain some type of control over private initiatives and set certain standards for how police and prison services should be provided.

8 THE WELFARE STATE: NOVELTY AND TRIUMPH OF THE TWENTIETH CENTURY

There is no art which one government sooner learns of another than that of draining money from the pockets of the people.
—Adam Smith, 1776

. . . perhaps, the richer the nation, the more apparent is this inability of its average inhabitant to survive unaided and alone.
—Robert Heilbroner, 1962

When I pay taxes, I buy civilization.
—Chief Justice Oliver Wendell Holmes, as quoted in John Gaus, 1947

Contemporary Western government stands apart from all its historical predecessors because of its welfare state. While several early modern governments provided some poor care, health care, and education, such services were basic and supplemental to equally basic services provided by other societal institutions, among which most notably were the churches. Most such services were organized at the local level and provided support in kind (food, clothing, housing, firewood, and so forth). What really makes the contemporary welfare state unique is that services in kind have been almost totally replaced by financial aid. The availability of unemployment and health care benefits and elaborate pension schemes has become so normal that it is hard to realize how unique and unusual this is in light of history. In terms of organization, what it takes to make large-scale redistribution work effectively is rarely considered. This is no reason, of course, to praise government without a sense of criticism. Indeed, had government been beyond criticism, there would probably never have been a welfare state.

It is impossible to fully understand the welfare state from a single theoretical and disciplinary angle. From an economic point of view, the welfare state is a gigantic economy of scale that works like an hourglass whose waist is the government. Without this hourglass, nationwide redistribution of surplus would not be feasible. The welfare state is a large apparatus for matching costs and benefits without donors and recipients being connected to one another. In terms of political theory, the welfare state can exist only under mass democracy, where the citizen identifies himself with the state rather than the local community. A political scientist focuses on how political centralization is a necessary condition for the welfare state. The same can be said for massive bureaucracy, the topic highlighted by administrative scientists. Sociologists and psychologists have pointed to the declining meaning of primary social relations, the alienation from work as a consequence of industrialization, and the shift from community to society (Tönnies's *Gemeinschaft* and *Gesellschaft*). The anthropologist of Western civilization marvels at the degree to which human beings have come to define themselves as members of an imagined rather than of a real community.

The literature on the development of the welfare state is rich, both nationally and comparatively. It would be futile to attempt to duplicate it in the context of this book. In this chapter, the policies characteristic for the welfare state are not detailed, but I pay attention to their size in relation to total government expenditures. For the purposes of this book, it is necessary to elaborate upon the theory of multiple and imagined communities that was briefly mentioned in chapter 5. Thus, in section 8.1 I discuss nation building as a process that resulted in an imagined togetherness in multiple communities. We can then see how government slowly took over tasks in this imagined community that had been largely or solely provided by other societal actors for centuries. The municipalization and subsequent nationalization were important steps toward the public welfare system as we know it. This increase of (central) government intervention happened everywhere (section 8.2). There are, however, significant differences between welfare states or regimes. These are discussed in section 8.3 with special attention to the degree to which they are successful at alleviating poverty. A welfare state requires large-scale redistribution of wealth, which, in turn, requires a taxation and budgeting system that generates enough revenue. The professionalization of the budget and the various mechanisms for large-scale redistribution are discussed next (section 8.4). What started locally and became national acquired global proportions after World War II. Development aid is highly relevant to any society. In section 8.5, I also briefly ponder the changes in international relations, thus tying in some of the remarks in the previous chapter with those made here. In section 8.6, I discuss limits to welfare. Should we pursue more collectivism or more individualism? Is collectivism or individualism off balance?

8.1. Nation Building: Imagined Togetherness in Multiple Communities

We have used the concept of the nation-state for so long that it will not disappear any time soon, even though the inadequacies of the concept are recognized by most scholars. The major inadequacy is revealed when the "nation"-element of the nation-state concept is defined in terms of a population's togetherness (Dyson 1980, 129; Weilenmann 1966). A nation is a people that shares heritage, language, and religion and is the dominant ethnic group in the territory, comprising (as theory has it) more than 95 percent of the population. The nation-state concept rapidly loses meaning in our increasingly multicultural societies. It makes sense to define a nation as a large community of people living together under one government whose actions are considered to be representative of all. While common descent and shared heritages of various nations in one country are important as sources of values, at the same time, individuals as citizens are expected to have grown beyond these.

When Americans speak of "this great nation," they do not think of the ethnic group to which they belong, nor of the variety of cultures and nations that created the American nation. Instead, they think of the country as a whole, in which collections of individuals or multiple communities live together in an imagined community of the citizens of the United States. Such a nation did not come about overnight. Under the impact of major societal changes that reinforced each other, such as rapid population growth, industrialization, and urbanization, many people left their real communities for a life in or near the city, driven by the promise of work and enticed by those who had gone before. Countries almost literally opened up. Newspapers, the telegraph, and later the telephone connected communities across regions. In the new urban environment, people were thrown back upon their immediate relatives; the larger supportive community was no longer the village but the civil government. Is it true that democracy loosens social ties, as de Tocqueville argued (2000, 233)? When people moved to the cities, the type of representative welfare democracy of today was, at best, in *status nasciendi*. There is, however, ample evidence that the loosening of social ties made the cries for universal suffrage and government support of the unfortunate stronger and stronger. The swelling urban populations had to be housed and general basic living conditions had to be improved so as to avoid the massive outbreaks of epidemics that had occurred in mid-nineteenth-century urban America and Europe. Housing programs for the working class, sewage systems, running water supply, water closets, and the like were introduced in the 1880–1920 period. In these decades, the first attempts at social insurance were made in Germany, starting with sickness insurance, insurance against work-related accidents, pension schemes, and disability insurance. This example was followed by England around 1910, the Netherlands between 1890 and 1920, and France and the United States mainly in the 1930s.

What tied these new urban people, strangers to each other, together went beyond sharing the same housing and general living conditions. The discovery of common cause found an outlet in various sorts of associations, among which labor unions and civic associations are most known (Skocpol et al. 2000). What ultimately bound these different collections of people together as a nation was symbols such as a flag and an anthem. This is what finally transformed villagers into citizens. The villagers knew each other and shared each other's joys and hardships. They knew less of the outside world. As newborn citizens, they did not know all others, but came to share an emotion evoked by symbols of national unity. Their nation was an imagined community and in that imagined community mere symbols carried the transformation from neighbor aid to anonymous welfare services. We have now reached a point where "the overwhelming proportion of government responsibility is the administrative operation of facilities and services that a century ago were left primarily to family, neighborhood, local church, guild, and individual initiative" (Lowi 1979, 24). It is important to understand that the nation of an imagined community is based on citizenship. Membership in that civic community is open and voluntary in contrast to membership in an ethnic group into which one is born. *Civic nationalism,* a concept coined by Greenfeld (1992, 11), can be individualistic or collectivist by nature. In some countries, such as the United States, the emerging nationalism was individualist by nature, because it was based in the idea that people who exercised sovereignty should, as much as possible, govern themselves. In the exercise of sovereignty, they became members of a nation (i.e., the civic tradition of nationalism). In other countries, the idea of a nation was connected to a sense of people's uniqueness, and the nation was more perceived as a collective (e.g., France).

The idea of a nation in its modern connotation emerged in sixteenth-century England, which, possibly with the province of Holland (in juridical terms a state between 1588 and 1798), was to be the only ethnic nation until the eighteenth century (Greenfeld 1992, 14). The bond between the peoples of the Seven United Provinces of the Dutch republic was based in the rebellion against Spain, and, at best, a sense of civic nationalism. The bond that the inhabitants of each of these provinces felt may have been closer to ethnic nationalism. Joost van den Vondel, poet, playwright, and citizen of Amsterdam in the province of Holland, referred to ethnic nationalism when he wrote in one of his most famous plays: "The love for one's country is born unto all" (*De liefde voor zijn land is ieder aangeboren*). Nationalism spread in the eighteenth century, especially in France and Russia, and by that time had come to separate nation from people. The United States developed its sense of nationalism partially in the decades immediately preceding and following the year 1800 and partially after the Civil War. The American idea of nation is distinctly individualist, and the concept of people is used in the plural sense of a collection of individuals. The nation became related to the federation, referring to generality, commonality, and the centralized sovereignty that united a group of states (Greenfeld 1992, 426–427).

The idea of nation emerged and spread in a Europe divided into states but sharing the culture of Christianity. Whether Protestant or Catholic, that suprastate culture of Christianity was a major condition that allowed nationalism to spread easily on the European continent and ultimately permeate the rest of the world (Greenfeld 1992, 495, note 9).

8.2. Municipalization and Nationalization: Toward Public Welfare

The domestic consequence of the merger of the civic nation with the territory was the welfare state. In the late nineteenth and the early twentieth century, the provision of welfare services changed first from private hands to local government and later became a shared responsibility between national and subnational governments. The pattern everywhere was the same, although the particular moment that it happened, and the degree to which central government stepped in, varied with the administrative traditions. The redistribution of surplus, increasingly generated through direct instead of indirect taxes (see next section), expanded to include the entire sovereignty. Periods of war (1914–1918 and 1939–1945) and of economic depression (especially the 1930s) accelerated the state's intervention in society and economy. Government intervention was the only possible response to social needs of a scale that no private charity or private actor could have effectively served. It is the same reason why in Europe the responsibility for some health services (e.g., care for those with pestilence, almshouses) and for elementary schools shifted from mainly a church operation to a local government task in the fifteenth and sixteenth centuries. Churches, and possibly guilds, simply could not assist the fast-growing numbers of the needy. What is more, they served only their own constituency, while local government served the entire population.

The motive supporting and thus legitimating this government intervention may have been humanitarian (charity), political (mass emancipation), elitist (avoiding an uprising of the discontented masses), or legal-constitutional (equal rights). Whatever the motive, a consensus emerged that the state was responsible to provide a minimum standard of living for all. There was obviously much less consensus about the definition of a minimum standard of living or about when and where government should intervene.

Table 8.1

Public Functions, 1985, in Percentages of Total Public Expenditure in Seven Countries

	Social	Health	Education	Defense	Interest	Other
United States	24	11	14	18	12	21
United Kingdom	30	6	5	11	10	38
France	37	13	11	8	5	26
Germany	31	16	9	7	6	31
Italy	19	11	10	2	16	43
Netherlands	36	11	10	5	10	28
Sweden	36	13	12	5	12	22

Source: Reprinted with permission from B. Guy Peters, *The Politics of Taxation: A Comparative Perspective* (Cambridge, MA: Blackwell, 1991), p. 82.

Table 8.2

Trends in Social Transfer Expenditures, 1950, 1975, and 1992, as a Percentage of the GNP in Seven Countries

	1950	1975	1992
United States	3.3	11.5	20.6
United Kingdom	5.7	11.1	27.2
France	11.3	20.0	29.2
Germany	12.4	16.7	19.3
Italy	9.3	19.6	25.6
Netherlands	6.6	26.1	31.3
Sweden	6.3	16.6	40.0

Sources: 1950, 1975 from Flora and Heidenheimer 1990, 317; 1992 U.S. from *Statistical Abstract of the United States* 1997, 372; 1992 EU from *Eurostat Yearbook* 1995, 230.

In Table 8.1 we can see the degree to which public sector expenditure is concentrated in welfare state rather than in nightwatch state tasks. With the exception of the United States, defense accounts for around 10 percent or less of total public expenditures, while the welfare state portion of public expenditures (social policy, health, and education) accounts for almost 50 percent in the United States, 41 percent in the United Kingdom, and between 40 and 61 percent in the other five countries. Italy represents the low end of the welfare state spectrum. Table 8.1 contains figures from 1985 but does provide at least an idea of the relative importance of the traditional versus modern government tasks.

In Table 8.2, we can see how social transfer expenditures developed between 1950 and 1992. Since the numbers for 1992 are taken from two different sources and together may also have a different basis than the numbers for 1950 and 1975, Table 8.2 only provides an impression. Furthermore, the data of European Union (EU) countries include all expenditures that the EU defines as *social protection expenditure,* which includes benefits for the unemployed and expenditures for promoting employment, benefits for the physically and mentally disabled, benefits for disabilities as consequence of work-related accidents and diseases, public health, benefits for old age and survivors, and benefits with respect to maternity and family. It is not clear to what degree the figure for the United States includes the same types of services, but from the legend in the *Statistical Abstract* it does not appear to differ too much.

France, Germany, and Italy already had fairly sizable social transfer expenditures in the 1950s. Since then, the French and Italian budgets only increased with a factor 2.5 to 3, while the German budget increased with a factor less than 1.0. In the United States, the United Kingdom, the Netherlands, and Sweden, social transfer expenditures increased five to six times. It is clear why Sweden is considered the ultimate welfare state. These social transfer expenditures are part of what has been called the uncontrollable budget (Gordon and Milakovich 1998, 332).

Both the national and subnational governments play a role in developing and implementing welfare state policies. One of the major consequences of the emergence and growth of the welfare state has been that national and subnational governments have become highly intertwined. This occurred for reasons of both efficiency and equity. The linking between social/welfare services and intergovernmental relations developed gradually over time. Based on earlier research, I distinguish seven phases (Raadschelders 1988, 277) that are formulated as hypotheses:

1. The smaller local government is in terms of administrative size (personnel, public expenditure, and so forth), the larger the need for and possibilities of private action with respect to social services (e.g., through churches, labor unions, and voluntary associations);
2. A sizable private initiative in social services increases the chance that local government is asked to intervene by means of regulation (e.g., for regulating lobbying by private groups);
3. Increase of local government initiative may ultimately lead to a downplaying of private initiative, which then is reduced to private participation;
4. Increased local government intervention may ultimately lead to incorporation of services within the local government organizational structure (especially public utilities in order to fight corruption, abuse, usury, etc.; the equity and efficiency arguments);

Table 8.3

A Typology of Welfare States

		Redistribution and equality			
Social Security	National minima: socialist ethic	Sweden Netherlands Germany	England New Zealand	Regulation of markets and industrial relations	Insecurity
	Equality of opportunity: liberal ethic	France Spain Italy	United States		
	Inequality and meritocracy				
		State	Market		

Source: Adapted from Flora and Heidenheimer 1990, 26.

5. Increased local government activity enhances the possibility that the quality and quantity of social service delivery between local governments start to differ;

6. Increased differences in quantity and quality of service delivery between local governments may lead to a standardization of local ordinances as a result of state and national government intervention (the equity argument);

7. The greater the degree of centralization, the more a division of labor develops in which national government is mainly concerned with policy making and regulation, while local governments are mainly involved in the execution of public services.

By and large, this is what happened in most Western countries, even though the differences in organization, degree of centralization, expenditure levels, and so forth between, for instance, the American and Swedish welfare states are large.

We can probe a little further into different conceptualizations of welfare between countries. In general, the welfare state came about as a response to the desire to create social and economic equality and to institutionalize social rights in addition to civil and political rights (see Marshall 1965, 78). But what started as a pursuit of socioeconomic *equality* and social security became increasingly a demand for socioeconomic *security* (Flora and Heidenheimer 1990, 23). By means of these two dimensions, equality and inequality and security and insecurity, Flora and Heidenheimer developed a typology of welfare states. In Table 8.3 above, the original model of Flora and Heidenheimer (1990, 26) has been expanded by including countries and by a more explicit definition of the place for state and for market.

On the horizontal axis of this table, the security-insecurity continuum is positioned, while the vertical axis represents the equality-inequality continuum. From this figure it is clear that the Western concept of equality has two contradictory meanings (Flora and Heidenheimer 1990, 25). The *socialist ethic* emphasizes equality of results so that social policy seeks to establish social minima via the means of redistributing welfare (poor relief, minimum wages, national pensions, compulsory education, progressive income tax, etc.) (e.g., Verbon 1988). Sweden, the Netherlands, and Germany are considered countries where the state is given a substantial role in establishing these minima. In view of large-scale privatizations, the United Kingdom and New Zealand have introduced more market into their system of social welfare. The abolition of socialized medicine in the United Kingdom is illustrative of this. The United States provides the case of a country with a market-oriented liberal ethic. In all welfare states, markets and industrial relations are regulated by government, but to varying degrees. Another aspect of the welfare state has to do with the role and position of the individual. It has been said that "public bureaucracies take over many of the functions formerly filled by smaller social units, and their services and transfer payments tend to become more and more individualized" (Flora and Heidenheimer 1990, 24). This is true, in the sense that welfare policy in general attempts to develop tailor-made solutions for social problems. Naturally, this does not mean that there is a policy for every individual, but it does mean that circumstances under which public financial support is considered are standardized and made to fit various different groups: the unemployed, the mentally and physically disabled, single parents, senior citizens, the homeless, and so forth. A welfare state government seeks to develop social programs in a way that balances the needs of efficiency (via categorizing and standardizing) with those of democracy and social justice (support of individuals in need). The transfers in money or in kind alleviate some of the most tragic circumstances.

8.3. Types of Welfare Regimes and the Alleviation of Poverty

The data presented in the previous section are neither the most recent nor the most consistent, but they do provide some impression of the differences between welfare states. It is only in the past ten years that comparative theoretical and empirical studies of the welfare state have really been done. The 1990 study of Flora and Heidenheimer, already a classic, is one example. The 1990 study of Esping-Andersen, equally classic, is another example. Flora and Heidenheimer's study provides an overview of welfare state development from the mid-nineteenth century and tracks welfare expenditures from 1950 to 1975, in some cases providing data going back to the 1880s. Like Flora and

Heidenheimer, Esping-Andersen compares eighteen welfare states, but instead of distinguishing them according to their placement in a two-by-two matrix (see Table 8.3), he distinguishes between three welfare regimes. The *liberal welfare state* provides means-tested assistance based on demonstrable need. Transfers and social insurance plans are modest and states encourage private social insurance plans (e.g., United States, Canada, Australia). In the *corporatist welfare regime*, the state displaces the market as provider of welfare, but the regime primarily facilitates group-based mutual aid and risk pooling (e.g., Germany, France, Italy, Austria). The corporatist model is profoundly shaped by a long conservative and Catholic tradition. Finally, the *social democratic welfare regime* assigns a powerful redistributive role to the welfare state; it is the regime that most promotes equality of condition (e.g., Scandinavian countries, the Netherlands) (Esping-Andersen 1990, 2, 26–27, 52; Goodin et al. 1999, 39). While Esping-Andersen provides examples of these three types, he points out that

> we must recognize that there is no single pure case. The Scandinavian countries may be predominantly social democratic, but they are not free of crucial liberal elements. Neither are the liberal regimes pure types. The American social-security system is redistributive, compulsory, and far from actuarial. At least in its early formulation, the New Deal was as social democratic as was the contemporary Scandinavian social democracy. And European conservative regimes have incorporated both liberal and social democratic impulses. (1990, 29)

The key concept in his analysis is that of the *decommodification of labor:*

> It is as markets become universal and hegemonic that the welfare of individuals comes to depend entirely on cash nexus. Stripping society of the institutional layers that guaranteed social reproduction outside the labor contract meant that people were commodified. In turn, the introduction of modern social rights implies a loosening of the pure commodity status. (21)

Hobbes, who argued that labor was a commodity and that an individual's worth depended upon the need and judgment of others, was a very early advocate of commodification, preceding capitalist-industrial society by more than a century. He wrote at a time, however, when at least two social arrangements had existed that helped to prevent commodification. The first was feudalism during the high and late Middle Ages, a system in which markets were not important and labor only marginally important to someone's well-being. Feudalism is not something of the past, for Haiti is a contemporary example of a society and economy that function on the basis of feudal arrangements (Esping-Andersen 1990, 38). The second arrangement, from the late Middle Ages through the early modern period, was corporatism, which thrived in much of Europe. In this system, artisans and merchants were members of guild and fraternal organizations that shared the burden of welfare and that existed to the end of the eighteenth century (Esping-Andersen 1990, 38–39; see also Putnam, Leonardi, and Nanetti 1993). In the second half of the nineteenth century, they would emerge again but as mutual benefit societies.

With the advent of the capitalist industrial society, individuals ran the risk of being treated as commodities, "captive to powers beyond their control; the commodity is easily destroyed by even minor social contingencies, such as illness, and by macro-events, such as the business cycle" (Esping-Andersen 1990, 37). Esping-Andersen is careful to point out that decommodification is not synonymous with the eradication of labor as a commodity. Rather, it refers to the degree to which people can maintain a decent standard of living independent of market participation. Generally the decommodification scores for the liberal welfare states were the lowest, while in the social democratic states, they were the highest. The high scores on the European continent, though, were not solely the product of left-wing politics, but also rested in a legacy of conservatism and Catholicism, while low scores could be found in countries with a fairly strong labor movement (e.g., Australia, New Zealand). Also, some nations with conservative and/or Catholic legacies moved to a social democratic regime with very high scores (e.g., the Netherlands, Austria, Belgium). Among the countries with a liberal tradition, some moved toward social democracy (e.g., Scandinavian countries) while in others, labor failed to realign the national political economy (e.g., United States, Canada). (Esping-Andersen 1990, 52–53). Esping-Andersen's analysis leaves no doubt about the importance of paying attention to state and administrative traditions and to deep-seated societal and religious values when trying to understand the various policy choices made by welfare state governments.

The rationale of the welfare state is that it supposedly serves several moral values through objectives such as the *reduction of poverty,* the *promotion of economic efficiency, equality, social integration* (avoiding social exclusion), *social stability,* and *autonomy* (personal independence) (Goodin et al. 1999, 2, 123). Various policies help these objectives materialize: for example, "to avoid unwarranted manipulation and exploitation of the most vulnerable members of society, welfare assistance should be run by state agencies rather than private charities" (Goodin et al. 1999, 34). Building upon Esping-Andersen's work, Goodin et al. seek to determine how successful the social policies of various types of regimes are. Using panel data that tracked tens of thousands of individuals over a ten-year period in the United States, Germany, and the Netherlands, they conclude that all three types of welfare regimes produce about the same sort of economic growth and prosperity for the citizenry (Goodin et al. 1999, 151). The regimes differ, markedly, however, with respect to the other

Table 8.4

Extent of Postgovernment Poverty as Percentage of the Total Population

Year	United States	Germany	Netherlands
1987 (85)	18.0	7.6	4.3
1992 (90)	18.2	8.9	6.8*
1985–89 (83–87)	14.7	6.2	1.1
1990–94 (88–92)	16.3	7.1	1.4
1985–94 (83–92)	13.0	5.8	0.5

Source: Reprinted with permission from Robert E. Goodin, Bruce Headey, Ruud Muffels, and Henk-Jan Dirven, *The Real Worlds of Welfare Capitalism* (Cambridge: Cambridge University Press, 1999), p. 276, Table b.

*Postgovernment poverty should be a bit higher in the Netherlands, given the weak Dutch economic performance in that year.

five values. We will only discuss their findings for "reduction of poverty" since they are representative of the conclusions for the other four variables.

Goodin et al. distinguish between *pregovernment income* (market income plus private transfer income) and *postgovernment income* (adjusted for government taxes and transfers). Their data indicate that pregovernment poverty in all three countries hovered around 20 percent, remaining high over a one- to five-year period and decreasing slightly over a ten-year period. Postgovernment poverty, on the other hand, varied dramatically (see Table 8.4).

On an annual basis, postgovernment poverty in the United States averaged around 18 percent, dropping to 15 to 16 percent over two five-year periods and further dropping to 13 percent over a ten-year period. Postgovernment poverty on an annual basis was less than half the U.S. figure in Germany and less than that in the Netherlands. Measured over two five-year periods and a ten-year period, the German welfare regime saw its poverty rates drop to around 7 percent, while in the Netherlands they dropped to a little more than 1 percent for both five-year periods and to 0.5 percent over a ten-year period (Goodin et al. 1999, 154). The researchers' conclusion was that the social democratic Dutch system outperformed the corporatist German and the liberal American systems (see also Bok 1996, 345).

What does this mean? Is the conclusion warranted that the United States is far less successful at, for instance, alleviating poverty than the other two countries and, by implication, that its welfare regime is much worse than the other two regimes? The Goodin et al. data do suggest that with respect to poverty, individuals at the poverty level or below are much better off in the Netherlands and even in Germany. However, the data also suggest that the social democratic welfare regime at large is overall far better than the other two. The data do not allow for generalizations beyond these three countries, yet they do suggest that the study's conclusions are representative for each of the welfare regimes at large. A recent study by Lijphart does suggest that consensus democracies (i.e., generally found in continental Western Europe) are "kinder and gentler" than majoritarian democracies as shown in the quality of social welfare, greater environmental responsibility, a less punitive criminal justice system, and generosity with foreign aid (Lijphart 1999, 294–298). When we combine the analysis of Goodin et al., Esping-Andersen, and Lijphart, we arrive at a more balanced picture (see also De Swaan 1988).

The question as to whether the United States is worse, or better for that matter, can be countered with "in whose context?" For an answer to that question, we can consider Hofstede's work (1997) on national organizational cultures. His discussion of the dimensions of, for instance, individualism and uncertainty avoidance is not just relevant to organizations but characterize societies at large. It is only when these deeply rooted normative values are taken into consideration that we can begin to understand the different welfare systems. That understanding prohibits any ranking in terms of better or worse welfare systems. Social welfare traditions cannot be judged on their input (e.g., welfare expenditures) and output (e.g., poverty reduction) alone. Taxes, size of welfare expenditure, and types and size of output are expressions of how theory and conceptualizations at the most abstract level (i.e., that which constitutes society) drive decisions at the intermediate, more concrete level and produce outcomes at the most concrete level. I do not discount the work of Goodin et al. and am certainly not able to challenge their data, but what the data mean is open to interpretation and leaves room for different future scenarios, as Esping-Andersen shows. He argues that the "contemporary welfare state is not merely a passive by-product of industrial development. With its institutionalization, it becomes a powerful societal mechanism which decisively shapes the future" (Esping-Andersen 1990, 221). He then argues that for a long time social theory emphasized that industrial and economic progress had occurred independently from the state, which from the late eighteenth century on had moved away from the interventionist, absolutist and authoritarian styles of governance. Many scholars had come to believe that economic forces determine societal change (1990, 222). Esping-Andersen basically arrives at a conclusion not that much different from Putnam's. Of course, their focus differs: Esping-Andersen presents material on the welfare state, while Putnam discusses civic associations. In their conclusions, however, there is complementarity. Putnam argues that civics precedes economics and affluence, and Esping-Andersen concludes that government intervention does alleviate at least some of the consequences of market

Table 8.5

Public Expenditures 1902–1962 in the United States in Billions of Dollars and as Percentage of the GNP

Year	Federal		State/local		Total	
	$	%	$	%	$	%
1902	0.6	2.6	1.1	5.0	1.7	7.6
1913	1.0	2.5	2.3	5.8	3.3	8.3
1922	3.6	4.9	5.5	7.5	9.1	12.4
1932	4.0	6.8	8.3	14.2	12.3	21.0
1942	34.3	21.6	10.3	6.4	44.6	28.0
1952	62.2	18.8	29.2	8.4	94.4	27.4
1962	89.0	23.3	65.3	11.7	154.3	27.7

Source: From Mosher and Poland 1969, 155, 157.

competition. What connects both ideas is that social institutions (e.g., a civic association, a welfare state) influence the market (economy) and not the other way around. Given the different traditions and constituting societal values, the impact of state intervention in various countries is different. Thus, in Sweden or the Netherlands, it is government itself that provides equal opportunities and guarantees employment, while in the United States government encourages the private sector to take responsibility in that area (Affirmative Action, Equal Employment Opportunity). And, in the case of the U.S., "the egalitarian impulse has been noticeable" for diminishing class differences between sexes and races and at the same time increasing class differences within those categories (Esping-Andersen 1990, 226, 228).

8.4. Public Sector Size: Expenditure, Personnel, and Regulation

The growth of welfare services is reflected in public expenditure, public personnel size, and type and volume of regulations. When looking at the development of public expenditure in the United States, we can see that in 1902 federal public expenditures were roughly half of those of state and local governments (Table 8.5).

This proportion remained more or less the same until the end of the 1940s, when federal expenditures for defense rose to unprecedented levels as an immediate consequence of World War II (Mosher and Poland 1969, 26). Defense expenditures continued to be substantial because of the Cold War, but added to federal expenditures were extraordinary increases for social security and other insurance trust funds (Mosher and Poland 1969, 30). In

Table 8.6

Public Expenditures 1950–1996 in the United States in Absolute Figures and as a Percentage of the GNP (000 omitted)

Year	Federal		State/local		Total	
	$	%	$	%	$	%
1950	44,800	15.7	25,534	8.9	70,334	24.6
1960	97,280	19.2	54,008	10.7	151,288	29.9
1965	110,129	16.0	92,553	13.4	202,682	29.4
1970	208,190	21.2	124,795	12.7	332,985	33.9
1975	341,517	22.5	218,612	14.4	560,129	36.9
1980	576,700	20.0	432,328	16.4	1,009,028	36.4
1988	1,215,000	24.9	827,000	15.8	1,920,000	39.4
1990	1,197,200	22.0	1,016.200	19.5	2,213,400	41.5
1996	1,705,486	23.5	1,397,634	19.2	3,103,120	42.7

Sources: From Peters 1993, 32; data for 1996 from *Statistical Abstract of the United States 1999*, tables 504 and 721.

1952, three-fifths of total public expenditures were defense-related, while by 1962 this was down to two-fifths (Mosher and Poland 1969, 31).

After World War II, the state and local governments in the United States (as elsewhere in the Western world) gained ground again. In the United States the relative share of state and local public expenditure more than doubled, while that of the federal government increased by less than half. It is interesting that Peters indicates the total share in the GNP of public expenditure to be over 41 percent in 1990, while later figures show a decline to 34 percent in 1993 (see Table 8.6). The general trend appears to be that public expenditure in the United States as a share of the GNP is decreasing. It is, however, much lower than that of most Western European countries in 1993 (Table 8.6).

What is striking about the next table (Table 8.7) is that it shows that five of the six countries started with a more or less comparable share of public expenditure in the GNP, ranging between 27 percent and 31 percent in 1950. Only Sweden was the exception. While in general public expenditure as a percentage of the GNP increases in all countries, it is much higher in Western Europe than in the United States. This again illustrates differences between welfare states.

At the moment, some two-thirds of the U.S. federal budget is spent on social security, medicare, veterans benefits, and so forth. This is *mandatory spending*, which leaves a third for so-called *discretionary spending* (Gordon and Milakovich 1998, 302). This does not mean, however, that the federal government actually has a third of its revenue to play around with. In fact, 95

Table 8.7

Trends in Total Public Expenditures, 1950, 1975, and 1993, as a Percentage of the GNP in Seven Countries

	1950	1975	1993
United States	27.4	36.2	34.4
United Kingdom	30.4	46.1	43.5
Germany	30.8	45.6	50.0
France	28.4	42.4	54.9
Italy	27.8	43.1	56.2
Netherlands	27.0	54.3	55.8
Sweden	37.5	51.0	71.3

Sources: Data for 1950 and 1975 from Flora and Heidenheimer 1990, 310; data for 1993 from Gordon and Milakovich 1998, 335.

percent of the budget is considered uncontrollable because it consists of legally mandated expenditures (the entitlements mentioned above) as well as expenditures that are the consequence of demographic (population growth) and economic developments (inflation, declining growth rate, and increased scarcity). These demographic and economic developments especially are outside government control and help to explain why government in the twentieth century increasingly had to operate on the basis of a prospective and centralized budget.

The trends in public expenditure and public personnel size are comparable. Big government in the United States is relatively recent. Around 1800 the federal government employed some 3,000 people, which number had doubled by 1816 (Van Riper 1958; Ingraham 1995, 18). In 1816 federal employment in terms of percentage of the male working population has been estimated to be 0.7 percent. At the onset of the Civil War, federal employment was about 2.6 percent but rose during the war years to 14 percent of the adult male population. In 1871 it was back down to 0.8 percent. The effect of World War I was not quite as severe as that of the Civil War nor would it last. Federal employment grew from 1.4 percent in 1911 to 8.9 percent in 1918 and quickly decreased again to 1.9 percent by 1922 (Peters 1987, 232). Reliable figures about local government do not go back further than the 1920s. In 1929 the number of state and local employees was 2.5 million, about three times the number of federal government workers. Since then both federal and state and local governments have increased enormously in size (see Table 8.8).

The impact of World War II is clearly visible, even without the military component of the public workforce. Between 1929 and 1990 federal, state,

Table 8.8

Public Civilian Employment 1929–1997 (x 1000)

Year	Federal	State and local	Total	% of Workforce
1929	.580	2,532	3,112	+ 6.9*
1932	.605	2,666	3,271	+ 6.9*
1939	.954	3,090	4,044	+ 7.8*
1945	3,816	3,137	6,953	12–13**
1950	2,117	4,285	6,402	10.9
1960	2,421	6,387	8,808	13.4
1970	2,881	10,147	13,028	16.6
1980	2,876	13,315	16,191	16.0
1990	3,143	14,976	18,119	15.1
1997	2,807***	16,733	19,540	15.1

Sources: The years 1929–45 from Peters 1987, 233; the years 1950–90 from Peters 1993, 32; figure for the year 1997 from *Statistical Abstract of the United States* 1999, table 534.

*The data on percentage of the labor force for the years 1929–39 are indicated as approximate because I have subtracted military personnel from Peters's figures for those years.

**The percentage for 1945 is an estimate. The military contributed more than 12 million employees to the total public workforce. Given that the number of civilian employees was almost 7 million, we may assume that this is about 12–13 percent of the total workforce.

***The figure for federal government employment in 1997 includes civil employees outside the United States.

and local government increased sixfold. Personnel size of state and local government in 1990 was almost five times larger than that of the federal government. As a percentage of the total workforce, public sector employment between 1929 and 1990 doubled. While this is a significant change, it is low when looking at comparable data from Western European countries, ranging in 1981 between a low of 24 percent for Italy and a high of 38 percent for Sweden (Rose 1987, 11). In a comparative perspective, complaints about big government in the United States are relative. However, such comments are not very helpful when they do not take national identities and cultures into consideration. Ever since the beginning of the twentieth century, European countries have opted for far more interventionist governments than in the United States. Nevertheless, despite the American appreciation of individualism and limited government, the size of the U.S. government at all levels is indeed bigger than ever before. Whether it is too big is only a political issue (Neiman 2000). When contract workers and employees of government-dependent organizations are considered, the size of government is even bigger.

Public expenditure and personnel size are fairly visible measures of government size. Data on these are also relatively easy to access. Less visible and more difficult to determine is the size of government in terms of its rules and regulations. In the United States there were three distinct periods of regulatory growth (Neiman 2000, 37–41). Between 1861 and 1932, the federal government elaborated its role in regulating markets and industries (e.g., Interstate Commerce Commission, 1887; Sherman Antitrust Act 1890), and banking (e.g., Federal Reserve System, 1913) and made its first moves into social regulation (e.g., Food and Drug Administration, 1906). The 1932–40 period witnessed further social regulations as well as a variety of regulations to build confidence. In the third period, from 1960 to 1980, social regulation came to dominate. Since the early 1980s, a clear preference for deregulation has existed. Government regulations include both primary and secondary legislation. Primary legislation is the sole prerogative of the legislature, while secondary legislation is enacted by the various departments and agencies upon delegation of Congress. A recent study by Page suggests that more attention should be given to this secondary legislation. In his study of the 28,000 statutory instruments (i.e., secondary legislation) issued in Britain in the 1987–97 period, it becomes clear how important this type of regulation is. By way of comparison: the British Parliament enacts an average of 60 pieces of legislation a year, while the bureaucracies issue an average of 3,000 regulations a year (Page 2001, ix, 14, 186). While primary legislation generally concerns "high politics," it is the "low politics" of secondary regulation that permeates everyday life in all its aspects and "allows the bureaucrat to dominate," involving "officials several ranks below the most senior ones" (Page 2001, 12, 180).

The consequences of growing public sector size and welfare services for organizational structure, for policy and decision making, and for policy implementation are further explored in chapters 10 and 11.

8.5. The Professionalization of the Budget: Mechanisms for Large-Scale Redistribution

In section 8.1, I argued that the welfare state could not have come about had nation and state not merged and had there not subsequently been an imagined community wherein government could legitimately take some of the surplus through direct taxation for purposes of redistribution to the unfortunate. For several reasons, the welfare state has helped to narrow, not close, the gap between government and society. First, in political terms, the transformation of mere national states into consolidated welfare states was possible because of mass democracy. Second, and equally important, was the rise of (middle-class) capitalism, which, from an economic point of view, resulted in an interventionist government, penetrating ever more into the economy. Under seventeenth- and eighteenth-century European mercantilism, the state controlled the economy, but not to the degree that became normal in the twentieth century. Third, from a sociological point of view, state intervention was motivated by the emerging notions of social mobility and improvement, redistributive justice, and equal opportunity.

The consequences of this growing government intervention would be felt at national and subnational levels and would fundamentally change another traditional government function: that of public finance and taxation. In the early modern state, public finance was basically concerned with debt financing. Governments in Europe constantly borrowed money and raised taxes in order to finance their wars. Taxes in labor and in kind became less important than the ever growing indirect taxes (on foodstuffs) and the rather frequent levy of extraordinary taxes. Indirect taxes were the principal source of revenue. Direct taxes, such as the income tax, were not considered in the early modern period, basically because such a tax was not popular among those with the kind of money or property that gave them the right to vote in a census polity. Furthermore, having real estate did not necessarily mean that there was cash lying around. Hence, taxation burdened disproportionately the lower income groups. As a technique, budgeting involved nothing else but retrospective line-item accounting of expenditure. This was not an extremely laborious exercise, but it provided little if any insight into total expenditure since that was seldom totalized. Local governments carried the larger share of public sector expenditures. Local public servants collected some of the indirect taxes, but in many cases they were contracted out to tax farmers against a fee (see, e.g., Webber and Wildavsky 1986, 230, 278, 294). This custom opened many opportunities for abuse. The general features of the public finance and taxation system before and after the 1850s are summarized in Table 8.9.

The change in the public finance and taxation system took place in two main phases. First came a normative change in the eighteenth century when in theory *balance* became an important organizing and universal principle that was quickly related to the principles of efficiency and rationality. This translated into the idea of a balanced budget, which emphasized limited spending, light taxation, the creation of a surplus, a minimum of borrowing, and paying off debts. The creed for nineteenth-century public budgeteers thus included centralization, consolidation, and retrenchment (Webber 1980, 170–172). No longer could every national department enjoy autonomy. Instead they were forced into the same fiscal year, they had to use the same accounting method, and they were prohibited from using money for any other but the designated purpose. This last element was monitored through the post auditing of receipts and of spending (Henry 1999, 271; Webber 1980, 169).

Table 8.9

Public Finance and Taxation in Transition

	Before 1850s	After 1850s
Objective	Debt financing	Balanced budget, deficit spending
Function of budgeting	Retrospective accounting	Prospective budgeting
Type of taxes	Taxes in labor and in kind, and indirect taxes in money	Direct and indirect taxes in money
Organization	Fragmented system of tax collection	Centralized system of tax collection

In the second phase, the basis of taxation changed. In the latter part of the nineteenth century and the early decades of the twentieth century, many of the indirect taxes were abolished, to be replaced by income taxes on personal as well as corporate income. As the decades went by, and especially after World War II, a new type of income tax expanded rapidly: the social insurance taxes. Together the personal and corporate income tax and the social insurance tax function as the main suppliers of revenue for the welfare state. Taxes on property continue to be levied (on real estate, on wealth, on inheritance) but are not so important in terms of volume. Income and property taxes are characteristic for all three welfare regimes since they proportionately burden the various income groups. Ideally, indirect taxes are to be avoided, especially when they are levied on primary goods of consumption (foodstuffs, clothes, etc.). Yet most Western countries had to reintroduce or strengthen the revenue out of sales and value-added taxes. These taxes on expenditure are nowadays as indispensable as the income and property taxes.

From the material provided in this and the previous section, it is clear that the executive power of government increased as government intervened more in industry, in the private economy, and in society at large. As a consequence, budget decisions now had to be considered in terms of their scope and impact as political choices (Wildavsky 1964, 4–5), required enhanced efforts of effective coordination, and became part of the *executive budget* (Gordon and Milakovich 1998, 311). This executive budget was the fruit of the budgetary reforms since 1900. The development in public budgeting since then has been summarized for the United States by Henry, from whom the following overview is taken in brief (1999, 242–268; for the general development, see also

Cozzetto et al. 1995, 14–72, and for the development of municipal budgeting, Rubin 1998, 31–54).

As the starting point of his analysis, Henry has taken the Budget Accounting Act of 1921, which established and consolidated the executive budget, established administrative integration of the budgetary process, and sought to restrict the discretionary powers of the civil service. By this act, the Bureau of the Budget, accountable to the Treasury Department, and the General Accounting Office, accountable to Congress, were created. In this period of *line-item budgeting* (1921–1939), efficiency was the most central feature. In the next period, that of *performance budgeting* (1940–1964), the Bureau of the Budget was transferred to the Executive Office of the President. In its managerial orientation, it was focused not only on inputs (as in the previous period) but also on outputs. Elaborate performance standards and measures were developed, befitting the rationalist mood of that period.

This was followed by a period of experimentation with budgeting techniques that is more or less tied to the tenure of presidents. Under *planning-programming-budgeting* (PPB) (1965–1971), which had started at the Department of Defense in 1961 and is still in use there, political choice was systemized (planning) and deadlines were set (programming). Not only inputs and outputs, but also effects and alternatives were considered important. At the national level, PPB did not last very long, and one of the major problems was that it required too much detail. It is, however, still used by more than a third of the state agencies, cities, and counties (Henry 1999, 250). Under the Ford presidency, the emphasis in budgeting became project management, which sought to increase the participation of organizational members in the process. This approach came to be known as *management by objectives* (MbO), which constituted a return to the managerial orientation of the second phase and was at the same time more flexible than PPB. MbO is still quite popular at the subnational level (Henry 1999, 252). President Carter introduced *zero-base budgeting*, a concept he had successfully worked with as governor of Georgia. This required periodic evaluations of entire programs and was based on a ranking of decisions and an evaluation of the funding necessity. This approach is still very popular at the subnational level (where it is known as sunset legislation). Under the Reagan and Bush administrations (1981–1992), budgeting was focused on cutting expenditure, with the budget targets centralized in the executive and the implementation decentralized to departments and agencies. This has become known as *top-down budgeting*. Its subnational complement is *target-base budgeting,* which is driven by revenue and the need to balance budgets. Balancing the budget and a return to a managerial orientation connect the 1980s and the 1990s. Under the Clinton administration, *budgeting for results* was the creed, but the policy-making style was more participatory and decentralized.

The various changes in budgeting procedures at the federal and the state and local levels are a reflection of the development of the welfare state. When spending in terms of volume and as a percentage of the GNP is low at the federal (mostly defense-related) and at the state and local level (mostly education-related), there is little need for experimenting with budgeting procedures. When, however, after World War II the sheer volume of total public expenditure increased rapidly, and intergovernmental transfers from federal to subnational levels increased rapidly, tighter controls were considered necessary in order to legitimate expenditure of ever scarcer resources.

8.6. Global Welfare: Development Aid and Its Boundaries

What motivated the nationwide redistribution of income in the first half of the twentieth century also drove the emergence of development aid in the decades following World War II. Starting slowly in the 1940s and 1950s, development aid became large-scale after the establishment of the Development Assistance Committee (DAC) of the Organization for Economic Cooperation and Development (OECD) in 1960. The OECD's predecessor was the Organization for European Economic Development Cooperation (OEEC), created in 1948 for the coordination of the European Recovery Program (better known as the Marshall Plan). In the same decade, the World Bank and the International Monetary Fund (IMF) were born. The IMF, created in 1944, sought to improve international monetary cooperation in order to protect a system of fixed exchange rates. The International Bank for Reconstruction and Development (better known as the World Bank) was created in 1946 and designed to help finance the economic development of its member states. From 1949 on, the emphasis of the World Bank shifted to economic development in areas other than Europe. The World Bank and the IMF both serve to channel *multilateral aid.* They function in a way comparable to the treasury of a state. Membership fees and contributions are collected into one pool and redistributed where they are needed. The donors cannot determine the destination for their specific contribution. *Bilateral aid*, on the other hand, is based on a direct relationship between donor and recipient country.

Olav Stokke made a distinction between *realist internationalism,* based on a view in which states pursue national interests and perceive the world as an anarchy, and *humanitarian internationalism,* in which states believe it is the moral obligation of industrial countries to foster social and economic development elsewhere (as summarized in Bivin Raadschelders 1995, 12). Within this second motive Stokke distinguishes between three strands of thought. *Reform internationalism* strives to further equity and social and economic justice. State intervention is considered the best instrument for these objectives.

Liberal internationalism opposes too much state intervention and is based in enlightened self-interest. Finally, *radical internationalism* emphasizes an obligation of solidarity with the poor and the oppressed, to the point which might even result in sacrifice on the part of the donor. Advocates of this approach are strongly in favor of government intervention.

In general, it appears that volume and recipients of bilateral development aid are determined by historical, political, and/or humanitarian motives. Recent analysis of bilateral aid of the seven largest donors showed that American development aid was predominantly driven by security interests (Bivin Raadschelders 1995, 92). The U.S. Official Development Aid (ODA) also showed a tendency to give larger amounts of aid to lower-middle-income countries. This signifies the United States as a *developmentalist* (transfers to lower-middle-income countries). France's aid was driven solely by *postimperial interests,* while English ODA was developmentalist as well as guided by postimperial interests. Japanese and German aid was motivated by the need to *reconstruct relations* with former enemies and former occupied territories. Thus, Japan gave much aid in Asia, while Germany focused on Northern Africa, the Middle East, and, after 1991, central and Eastern European countries and new independent states. Dutch aid displayed an *altruist motive* (i.e., aid to the lower-income countries, especially the least developed) but was directed by postimperial interests. Of all the donors investigated, Sweden was the most altruistic (Bivin Raadschelders 1995, 92, 131, 139).

The two most basic motives for development aid can be tied in with the motives underlying the various possible choices in the international relations and political science debates about the role and position of the state. Given the subject matter of this and the previous chapter, I will limit myself for the moment to briefly explore the formulation of realist internationalism and the realism school. The deeper foundations for humanitarian internationalism and for the welfare state were discussed in chapter 4.

At least since 1648, international relations have been guided by a balance of power politics, further strengthened and institutionalized by more formal patterns of mutual consultation in the nineteenth and twentieth centuries. Foreign policy was driven by the need to protect security interest, which, whenever necessary, could ultimately be protected by means of war. The territorial expansion of the West was accompanied by a dissemination of Western ideologies about state, nation, and government. This was certainly a conscious objective in the "civilization policies" of the colonial powers in the nineteenth century and the early decades of the twentieth (for instance, the French policy of *assimilation* and the Dutch "cultural policy"). What is striking in the development of foreign policy is that territorial expansion became the lesser objective, with Japan, Germany, and the Soviet Union being the last that attempted it on a large scale. The emergence of development aid after World War II made the increased importance of the ideological motive in and for international relations more apparent. The Western world set the conditions under which aid could be considered. Social and economic aid thus also served to advance the Western beliefs in freedom, self-determination, democracy, the market, and so forth. What better way to serve national security interests, and what better way to reinforce one's own belief in particular values, than to slowly reel in non-Western countries into this embrace (Adamolekun 1999; Farazmand 1999). In this respect, Wolin diagnoses the modern foreign policy as one that seeks *Lebensraum* (Wolin 1989, 201). A powerful analogy no doubt, perhaps a bit strong, but the message is brought home. In similar fashion, Mansfield argues that Americans are not content with liberty for themselves, but they have to sell it to the world (Mansfield 1991, 131). While the analyses of both Wolin and Mansfield concern the United States, the more general argument, that of ideological instead of territorial expansion, applies to the foreign policy of most Western countries. The fact that developing countries depend upon the West was not lost on the first president of Ghana, Kwame Nkrumah, who coined the concept of neocolonialism as the situation in which political dependency was replaced by economic dependency. This situation, however, does not have to be all that negative, especially now, given donors' increasing awareness of the need to consider and include indigenous societal, state, and administrative values next to or even instead of Western-based values when determining eligibility for aid.

8.7. Limits to Welfare: Collectivism Off Balance or Social Justice?

It was not long ago that government performed a limited function in society and was mainly reactive to societal change. Among the Western countries, the United States was least equipped to build a welfare state because the Founders never intended their government to be so strong that it could support a welfare state. The following quote captures this point nicely: "If public goals were occasionally to foist themselves on the nation—a gift of the Four Horsemen as it were—they could be gratefully accepted. But war, plague, famine, and death were sometimes events, without the compelling moral power or the permanence to provide more than a temporary, reactive unity" (Barber 1986, 52). The rationale for providing welfare services through public means is the same domestically and internationally: the idea that public authorities are able to take care of those who cannot take care of themselves, and the idea that in doing so public authorities legitimate themselves. The domestic welfare state was under construction between, say, 1880 and 1950. The heyday of the welfare state did not last long: roughly from 1950 to 1975. In the past two and a half decades most Western governments have been making attempts at redefining and recasting the welfare state. In the second period the welfare state bloomed, but under conditions of austerity, most certainly so in Europe. Under the austerity society (the concept from Flora and Heidenheimer 1990, 20), the concept of welfare state was embraced. Now, under the affluent society, it has come under siege. In the U.S. Balanced Budget Act of 1997, major cuts are envisaged in medicare. If nothing is done about current public expenditures, it is said that by the year 2030 federal expenditures as a percentage of the gross domestic product (GDP) will have doubled to 47 percent, that social security and health entitlements will have doubled to 18 percent of the GDP, that the federal debt will rise, that the interest rates will rise, and that the investment levels will decline (Henry 1999, 274). Henry wonders whether the economists are correct when they argue that "democracies are unable to avoid burying future generations in debt due to the need of elected policymakers to be elected and reelected, which they assure by giving voters more and more desired programs, and fewer and fewer taxes with which to pay for them. Eventually this accrued debt crushes some future generation to the point that it overthrows democracy as its form of government" (Henry 1999, 275). Are the budgetary mechanisms that, for instance, Gordon and Milakovich suggest, such as enhancing the productivity and quality of existing programs (1998, 332), enough to prevent the type of scenario sketched by Henry from actually happening? Avoiding such a scenario requires a thorough self-examination by politicians but also by citizens. Citizens can no longer afford to say that their grandchildren are entitled to the same services that they have had. If this is so, they ought to do away with this need for immediate gratification through the consumption of income. Who is willing to calculate to what extent politicians and citizens are now burdening the future through maintaining welfare state services for the present? The need for recasting the welfare state has resulted in enhanced awareness of intergenerational fairness and equity. On this point, Frederickson notes, "The single most interesting thing about the concept of intergenerational social equity is that it is so routinely and commonly practiced in policy making and public administration" (1994, 461). This is reassuring, but some questions remain. Perhaps a vertical moral community exists that makes contemporary generations act on behalf of the generations to come, as Frederickson believes (461). But on what grounds can we require young people now to pay for the retired when there is a serious chance that the young will receive much less upon their own retirement than their parents had? If our government fails to provide welfare, will we rise against it like the seventeenth- and eighteenth-century crowds who protested against excessive taxation? Have we lost the ability to rely on our resourcefulness, as Heilbroner suggests? What kind of civilization are we willing to invest in, not knowing what the returns in the long run will be? If these are difficult questions, they become even more difficult when we consider that welfare is no longer only a domestic issue but has assumed global proportions. It takes political courage and a fair amount of blissful ignorance to restructure the domestic and international welfare policies adequately.

8.8. Concluding Remarks

In this book's framework, the welfare state constitutes a particular balancing act between individualist and collectivist needs that has so far proved to be flexible enough to satisfy supporters at both ends of this continuum. This said, there is no reason to trumpet the success of Western civilization, let alone argue that the liberal free market ideology, representative democracy, and welfare state combined present us with the end of history, as Fukuyama suggests (1991). The welfare state and all that has made it possible is merely a phase in history. It is a fallacy to believe that we have reached the pinnacle of civilization. Assuming that this civilization will continue to be regarded as valuable, it will be preserved, but how and in what configuration will the decades to come unfold? Moving toward the future, we may feel that we are groping around in the dark, for we have had little experience in dealing with a globalizing world and with redefining a welfare state. But we are not totally blind, for from our collective memory and our past experience, we can reconstruct how particular policy choices were made and why they were made so.

Such enhanced understanding is provided through a comparative analysis of the mechanisms that made the welfare state possible. The knowledge about the what, who, how and why of the welfare state can be interpreted in its present context and thus helps to explicate the desired choices for the years to come.

We also need to be somewhat cautious with comparative data. By nature, a comparative study must work with data analyzed under a common denominator that is provided by theory and conceptualizations. Perhaps this is possible at the most concrete level, that of the raw and subsequently analyzed data. Moving into each unique case and into deeper levels of motivation and abstraction, though, we may end up comparing apples and oranges. There is no doubt that comparative studies in general are very useful to policy makers. If anything, comparative research helps them to recognize wherein each country is unique and perhaps even to see what can be learned from others. But what can comparative research mean to the individual citizen?

As valuable as empirically comparative research on the welfare state is, the conclusions do not take into account one's familiarity with and tacit knowledge about the country where one was raised. The most rigorous researchers are not beyond partiality, which is a charge that Goodin et al. need to address. Perhaps the Dutch welfare regime is the best in terms of the measures Goodin et al. selected, and I am sure that the Dutch think so too. I am equally convinced, however, that most of the German or American poor would not choose to live in the Netherlands. Besides the minor language problem, they simply would not feel comfortable in an environment they do not know. Most citizens will accept the values of their own society and government. And those who move to other places (with the exception of young children and teenagers) will never be able to really shed their upbringing, even when they come to recognize and appreciate the values of a different societal and governance system.

PART III

HOW DOES GOVERNMENT OPERATE? THE ORGANIZATIONAL (ACTOR) LEVEL

Changing perceptions of the relation between society and government had a major impact upon the political structuring and the scope of service delivery of modern government. Part I of this book concerns the foundation of government in society and what values underlie contemporary governance and government. The values at the ideational level find their expression at the societal level (part II), in terms of the superstructure of governing (representative democracy and intergovernmental relations) that, in turn, make an expansion of traditional public services (justice, police, defense, taxation) as well as the adoption of new public services (education, health, social insurance, etc.) possible. Parts I and II concern institutions, while parts III and IV concern actors.

In view of the changes described in chapters 2 to 8, it is clear that as a consequence of the changing role and position of government in society, the internal structure and functioning of government had to change as well. I have already discussed one such change of internal functioning when describing the development of public budgeting techniques and procedures. In part III, I focus on the organizational level. While I opened part II with a chapter on democracy as the basic value of Western political structure, I open part III with a chapter on efficiency as the basic value of Western public administrative structures (chapter 9). I will not duplicate what has been said earlier on the concept of efficiency (see chapter 5), but will expand upon that by showing how efficiency requires that at the organizational level a balance is struck between legalist-administrative and managerial demands. In chapter 10, I focus on various organizational structures as they have been developed in the course of this century as a response to the expanding service levels. I also discuss changes in organizational culture and work processes. In chapter 11, I focus on the functioning of government, more specifically on decision making, policy making, implementation, and evaluation.

The topics of both parts III and IV are considered mainstream to the study of public administration. The treatment of these various topics is brief, as befits the nature of this book. I provide references to literature that guides the student to more in-depth studies.

9 EFFICIENCY: GOVERNMENT BETWEEN LEGALIST-ADMINISTRATIVE AND MANAGERIAL VALUES

The important thing for Government is not to do things which individuals are doing already, and to do them a little better or a little worse, but to do those things which at present are not done at all.
—John M. Keynes, 1926

If democracy were to survive it had somehow to add efficiency to its ideals of liberty and equality. It had to bring efficiency out of factory, school, and home, where it was already a popular ideal, and make the nation as a whole an efficient business.
—Dwight Waldo, 1984

While the era of the Atlantic Revolutions laid the groundwork for representative democracy upon which nineteenth-century political thought proceeded, it also gradually became clear that the structure and functioning of government as it had been no longer sufficed. The great social changes brought about by population growth, democratization, industrialization, and urbanization took their toll on a small government with little experience in wide-ranging service delivery. By the end of the nineteenth century, the time had come to put a century of thought about citizen rights, social justice, and welfare to the test of practice. The consequences of this process of social change have been discussed in more depth in chapters 5 to 8. The burden to meet the challenges of these social changes fell upon local government first and higher government levels later. On both sides of the Atlantic Ocean, the ideal of democracy was complemented with and balanced, although not replaced, by the ideal of efficiency.

The focus of efficiency was to improve organizational structures, to develop standardized procedures, and to prevent corruption or biased personal influence of public officeholders not only so that the quantity of public services could be handled better but that their quality would be enhanced. Concrete reform efforts in the United States and Western Europe from 1880 to 1920 included the professionalization of the civil service (developing and standardizing recruitment and selection, training, career patterns, etc.), the formalization of the distinction between political and political executive offices on the one hand and administrative or bureaucratic positions on the other, and a gradual intensification of intergovernmental relations.

In a stereotypical characterization of reforms, the approach in Europe was legalist and administrative, while in America it was seemingly more managerial. Several American practitioners (e.g., Dorman Eaton 1880) and academics (e.g., Woodrow Wilson) traveled to Europe to learn about its administrative traditions and reforms. Upon their return, they adopted and adapted these European ideas to fit the American appreciation of efficiency and managerialism. A business administration perspective received no attention in Europe until after World War II. From that point on, American scholarship increasingly influenced developments in the study of public administration in Europe and the rest of the world.

As already noted above, efficiency balanced but did not triumph over democracy. A recent comparative study among the twenty-nine member states of the Organization for Economic Cooperation and Development (OECD) indicated that the eight most frequently stated core public service management values (in terms of the number of countries stating each value) were impartiality (24 countries), legality (22), integrity (18), transparency (14), efficiency (14), equality (11), responsibility (11), and justice (10) (PUMA 2000, 2; OECD 2000, 32). These figures suggest that the legalist-administrative values are not considered less important than the managerial values.

In this chapter, I first provide a comparative perspective on the balancing of basic societal and democratic values so important to public administration at large with the professional values emphasized in a managerial perspective (section 9.1). The discussion in section 9.1 will further characterize the state and administrative traditions and complement the country categorizations presented in chapters 4 to 6 and 8. Next, I trace the development of administrative thought in the United States with an emphasis on the place that efficiency held (section 9.2). This will provide a foundation for a discussion about the differences between public administration and public management (section 9.3) and between public and private management (section 9.4). The discussion in these two sections will illustrate how important both the legalist-administrative and the managerial perspectives have been in the thinking about government throughout the twentieth century. In this chapter I discuss managerial principles at a generalist level, while in the next two chapters

I provide more detail about specific management functions at the organizational actor level, such as policy and decision making, organizing, coordinating, communicating, planning, implementation, and evaluation. Financial management has been discussed in the context of the societal (institutions) level, while human resource management will be discussed in the context of the individual (actors) level. The content of sections 9.1 to 9.3 will provide a basis for the discussion on the nature of ideas about and practices of government reforms in the next chapter. From sections 9.1 to 9.4 we can glean what kind of qualities a public servant *casu quo* public manager was supposed to have at different times. Hence, leadership will be discussed in this chapter (section 9.5) since it is the only management function that concerns intellectual capacity, rather than organizational structure, particular procedures, roles, and behaviors in professional positions.

9.1. A Comparative Perspective on Legalist-Administrative and Managerial Values

Is it true that reform in Europe emphasized legalist-administrative values much more than managerial values and that reforms in the United States were much more justified on the basis of managerial values? In the Roman-law-oriented countries of continental Europe, reform was, indeed, grounded in extensive legislative effort regarding welfare policies, while in the United States, with its common law tradition, the legislative effort concerned more the procedures and functioning of public organizations. In chapters 3 to 5, some of these legalist-administrative values were discussed. The issue in this chapter is the degree to which they were balanced with managerial values in the course of the twentieth century.

Recently the OECD published a report under the title *Trust in Government: Ethics Measures in OECD Countries* (2000). The central argument was that trust in government would be enhanced if attention were paid to societal and democratic values on the one hand and to professional values on the other. In the view of its authors, social and democratic values are the "traditional" values of government that reflect the fundamental mission of the public service (OECD 2000, 32). The traditional values that were most frequently mentioned by the reporting countries included impartiality, legality, integrity and honesty, equality, justice and fairness, transparency and openness, and responsibility and accountability. These values emerged between the late eighteenth and the late nineteenth century and have become "traditional" to modern government. These societal and democratic values are translated into legalist-administrative values that emphasize uniformity. The OECD authors considered professional values "new" values that articulated the need for a new ethos in the public sector. These "new" values, which are derived from the basic values and which I label *managerial values,* include efficiency, respect for state resources, confidentiality, and competence. They set a new standard for all public services. These values were embraced in theory in the late eighteenth century but came to guide practice especially during the twentieth century (see section 9.3).

In the report, OECD member states provided information on public servants who work in the central, national, or federal levels of government. Deconcentrated agencies were included (OECD 2000, 22). Of both groups of values, I have listed in Table 9.1 those that were mentioned most by the member states, but only included the countries that were compared in chapter 8. I have also included two professional/managerial values that were mentioned much less frequently: "respect for state resources," as expressed through, for example, nondiscrimination of the human resources and nonabuse of public funds, as listed in the U.S. country study (OECD 2000, 319), and "competence." The first was explicitly mentioned by only five member states while the second was regarded important by eight member states.

Although the OECD report provides many data, its analysis is basically limited to the compilation of the various national reports. The data are not evaluated in a theoretical framework for that is not the mission of the OECD. We can, however, interpret the data from Table 9.1 in the context of some of the country categorizations provided in previous chapters, but even without that context we can see some interesting differences. The United States, Sweden, and Germany are countries where both legalist-administrative and managerial values are highly regarded. Without suggesting that France and Italy have little regard for these values, it is on the basis of their self-reporting that we conclude they are at the opposite end of the spectrum. The United Kingdom and the Netherlands occupy the middle ground. How are we to understand these differences?

In terms of the discussion in chapter 4 it is striking to see that the dominant Protestant countries (United States, United Kingdom, Germany, Sweden, and the Netherlands) place substantial emphasis on the societal and democratic values as they are translated into legalist-administrative values. Only three of these countries (United States, Germany, and Sweden) also regard professional or managerial values as very important. In the predominantly Catholic countries, on the other hand, few of the traditional and even fewer professional values appear to be considered as important. Perhaps this distinction can be generalized by the fact that in Protestant countries, externally (i.e., legally) imposed ethics are considered an important check on individual behavior; in the Catholic countries, there is more reliance upon a strongly developed internal sense of right and wrong without, though,

Table 9.1

Public Service Core Values as Stated in Public Documents in OECD Countries

		US	UK	SW	NL	GE	FR	IT
Societal and democratic values	Impartiality	X	X	X	X	X		X
	Legality	X	X	X	X	X		X
	Integrity/honesty	X	X	X	X	X		
	Equality	X		X	X	X		
	Justice/fairness			X		X		
	Transparency/openness	X	X	X				
	Responsibility/accountability		X	X		X	X	
Professional values	Efficiency	X		X				X
	Respect for state resources	X		X				
	Confidentiality	X		X	X	X		
	Competence					X		

Source: OECD 2000, 33.
Legend: US = United States of America; UK = United Kingdom; SW = Sweden; NL = the Netherlands; GE = Germany; FR = France; IT = Italy.

any guarantee that this inherent moral compass is more effective than ethics-as-law.

The discussion about intergovernmental relations and Roman and common law countries in chapters 5 and 6 could provide further explanation. Of the continental European Roman law countries, Germany and Sweden especially emphasize both groups of values. By tradition, the Germans and the Swedes share a strong belief in codifying standards of policy (e.g., legalist-administrative standards) as well as standards for behavior (e.g., managerial values). The Netherlands is much more focused on policy alone, while France and Italy, again, do not seem to place much value in either one of these standards. As countries with a common law origin, both the United States and the United Kingdom consider the societal and democratic values as important, but only the United States appears to embrace managerial values with equal fervor. What this reflects, really, is the division of labor between levels of government. In the United States, the levels of government are very much intertwined, and the federal level, through legislation, judicial review, preemption, and so forth, does set standards for subnational governments. In the United Kingdom, on the other hand, the national level is mainly responsible for preserving the legalist-administrative values. The "governing-from-a-distance" tradition could explain why it is not the national level where the managerial values are emphasized. Since service delivery in Britain is especially organized at the local level, we may expect that managerial values are much more important there. The same argument could be made for France and Italy, where the mesolevels of government are the primary service providers.

Finally, we can consider the OECD self-reported data also in the light of the welfare regimes as discussed in chapter 8. The liberal welfare regime of the United States and the social democratic regime of Sweden place almost equal importance on both groups of values. Of the corporatist welfare regimes, only Germany ranks with the United States and Sweden. In a liberal welfare regime, individual liberty is protected and thus the two groups of values especially emphasize the limits of government intervention. In the social democratic welfare regime, government intervention is considered vital to social stability and welfare and thus both groups of values will be defined in terms of government's scope of authority. In that sense, Germany is much more a social democratic than a corporatist welfare regime. In the more traditional corporatist welfare regime, the formal-legal position of the state is strong (France) or weaker (Italy), but social welfare services depend much more on private initiative and on societal institutions and networks. It is thus that national government may feel less inclined to clearly define what it holds valuable beyond that which is stated in a constitution.

This discussion about the meaning of the data in Table 9.1 is, obviously, very tentative and impressionistic. A systematic and critical analysis of the OECD data requires a book-length study of its own. For the purposes of this book, the data at least provide some extra characterization of various countries and also illustrate the importance of developing a holistic perspective on state and administrative traditions and national policies. A discussion of the American welfare state in terms of social expenditure is incomplete without considering that nation's traditional values. Likewise, a discussion of the importance of efficiency in American administrative thought would be incomplete if attention were not paid to the importance and specific interpretation of democracy.

9.2. The Development of Administrative Thought in the United States

The emergence of the study of public administration in the United States at the end of the nineteenth century was a response both to growing local government activity and to major discontent with corruption. The hope of these reformers in the Progressive Era was focused on a planned and administered society that required the strengthening of both democracy and efficiency (Waldo 1984, 18). The initial reform focus was democracy in terms of less political corruption, less political influence over administrative functions, open access to public office for all on the basis of competitive examinations, and so forth. By the early twentieth century, the demand for more efficiency rapidly surfaced. When discussing the development of administrative thought in the United States, I first look at the demand for more democracy and then at the demand for efficiency.

The desire to strengthen democracy almost inevitably lead to attention for administrative law and comparative administration. Indeed, the focus of the American Political Science Association in the early years included more attention to public administration than to political science, and that is why the study of American public administration initially leaned quite a bit on European scholarship (Martin 1987 and 1988; Miewald 1984 and 1994). The early scholars of public administration were basically interested in three types of comparison: first, the conceptual comparison and definition of *politics* and *administration*; second, a practical comparison of the *public* and the *private sector;* and, third, a *cross-national comparison,* equally practical and focused on looking for new methods, techniques, and so forth.

Regarding the first distinction, Woodrow Wilson and Frank Goodnow are often mentioned as the two authors who established this dichotomized thinking about American government. However, Woodrow Wilson's central concern is not so much how to distinguish politics from administration as how to adopt principles of organization, as used in the private sector, so as to enhance the quality of public services. Wilson expresses a deep-felt concern for the linkage between the constitutional foundation of a society (in terms of my framework, the ideational level) and the day-to-day operation of government (in terms of my framework; the organizational and individual actor levels). In his own words:

> The study of administration, philosophically viewed, is closely connected with the study of the proper distribution of constitutional authority. To be efficient it must discover the simplest arrangements by which responsibility can be unmistakably fixed upon officials; the best way of dividing authority without hampering it, and responsibility without obscuring it. . . . If administrative study can discover the best principles upon which to base such distributions, it will have done constitutional study an invaluable service. (Wilson 1992, 12)

Two things are striking about this remark. The first is that in Wilson's view, a separation of politics and administration is a means, not an end, toward strengthening the constitutional foundations of American government. Indeed, his line of reasoning indicates deep concern about the legitimacy of American government in practice. The second is that Wilson's principles refer to the distribution of authority, and not only to the way in which day-to-day actions are carried out. Efficiency, as it came to be defined in the course of the twentieth century, could not have been further from his mind. Wilson recognizes the moral importance of separating politics from administration, but later in his article this demarcation serves a practical purpose as well:

> Let it be noted that it is the distinction, already drawn, between administration and politics, which makes the comparative method so safe in the field of administration. When we study the administrative systems of France and Germany, knowing that we are not in search of *political* principles, we need not care a peppercorn for the constitutional or political reasons which Frenchmen or Germans give for their practices . . . if I see a monarchist dyed in the wool managing a public bureau well, I can learn his business methods without changing one of my republican spots. (15–16)

It is interesting to see the degree to which Wilson compartmentalizes politics and administration. Politics is concerned with the protection and advancement of constitutional and societal values, while administration merely involves the application of value-free techniques and procedures. It is in this respect that Wilson appears to be very much concerned with efficiency and it is clear how much his understanding of it is the product of American culture and history. With regard to the political side of the equation, he is very sensitive to American culture and history. In his words: "Our own politics must be the touchstone for all theories" (16).

In a way, in Wilson's article we can see what would become characteristic for the study of public administration throughout the twentieth century: cultural (including political) traditions and practices are compared out of curiosity, while techniques, reform styles, management models, and so forth are compared for practical reasons, in the hope of deriving useful lessons for Americans. The comparative study of the cultural and historical context of American public administration is focused at the most abstract (constitutional) and intermediate concrete (decision making) levels, and is not particularly dominant in the study of public administration (Raadschelders 2000b). Public administration has been much more focused on the most concrete (managerial) level of analysis, which involves the (comparative) study of techniques, reform styles, and management models.

Combined, the forces of the industrial and corporate revolution and the advent of the business civilization fueled the rise of scientific management (more efficient production in factories), efficient organization (in the corporate sector; Wren 1972), and "benevolent feudalism" in business and politics (Waldo 1984, 9; Peters 1990, 8, 143–145). It is well known how efficiency quickly became a concept as important as democracy, and it is in this sense that American scholars started to develop their own curriculum of public administration, which, in the second half of the twentieth century, would be extremely influential in the public administration discourse in Europe and the rest of the world. The *scientific management* movement and the various ideas about applying the private sector experience to government found their culmination in the *administrative science* as envisaged by Luther Gulick:

> "should" is a word political scientists should not use in scientific discussion! In the science of administration, whether public or private, the basic "good" is efficiency. The fundamental objective of the science of administration is the accomplishment of the work in hand with the least expenditure of man-power and materials. Efficiency is thus the axiom number one in the value scale of administration. (Gulick 1967, 5)

The study of public administration in the 1930s had been stripped of its normative nature and focused entirely on the positivist values of a scientific observation of facts and the deduction of logical consequences from these facts. Policy making was based on planning and principles of administration, the latter defined in terms of management functions. The 1930s was the age of the *scientific man*, and the hope for a *science of public administration* would continue to influence (or haunt) the study up to this day, especially in organization studies and in the quantitative and managerial approaches.

The countercurrent came fairly quick, though. Simon's (1946) attack of the proverbs of administration in the late 1940s will be discussed in the next chapter, but here it is important to note that he pointed out that administrative and managerial principles were more normative than some would like to admit. Waldo argued the same in his *The Administrative State* (1984), showing that administrative thought was embedded in the political theory of the contemporary state. Dahl, expressing the same sentiments, pointed to both the individual and the societal context of administration:

> It is often implied that "principles of public administration" have a universal validity independent not only of moral and political ends, but of the frequently nonconformist personality of the individual, and the social and cultural setting as well. (Dahl 1947, 1)

Dahl distinguished three problems in the study of public administration. First, the study appeared to lack an *appreciation of cultural and historical context*. In his view, the individual and social context were nationally defined and of a distinct historical nature. Thus, one could argue that there was a study of public administration of the United States, Great Britain, Germany, Japan, and so forth, rather than a study of public administration that transcended the national boundaries. At the same time, the national features could become really clear only in a comparative perspective. The comparative perspective, so strong before World War I but then dwindling, was back on the rise after

World War II (Heady 1996 and 1998; Riggs 1964 and 1998) as part of the larger development toward increased American economic, military, and political involvement in various parts of the globe. This advent of the *Pax Americana* also placed renewed pressure upon the study of public administration to come up with the kind of usable knowledge that would solve domestic as well as international problems.

The managerial approach to study and field would continue to thrive, but it ran the risk of forgetting *the human factor,* which was Dahl's second problem (for more, see section 9.5). The third problem (actually the first in his article), one that increasingly bothered scholars, is that the managerial approach tended to downplay the *normative nature of choices made in the administrative state.* The advent of attention to state and administrative law, ethics, and even theology in the past two decades strongly indicates that normative issues are now receiving more attention than ever since World War I.

9.3. Public Administration and Public Management

In the past two decades, it has once again become fashionable to consider public administration from a managerial perspective in which public organizations are not viewed as different from private organizations. In the managerial perspective, the challenges to and solutions for problems of organizational structure are the same, and higher-level civil servants are considered comparable to CEOs of big private corporations. In a variety of public administration texts, public management is defined in terms of its functions, more or less following Gulick's (1937) classic distinction between the functions of planning, organizing, staffing, directing, coordinating, reporting, and budgeting (POSDCORB). When Bozeman, for instance, defines public administration as a "quasi-academic, quasi-professional, defined-by-practice set of activities," he lists the routines of public administration as personnel management, financial management, the management of organizational structure and operations, and the management of public policy (Bozeman 1979, 7, 14–21). In parts III and IV of his book, he discusses these in detail, including attention to leadership, information and communication, systems analysis, and program evaluation. A more or less comparable listing is provided by Starling, who distinguishes between five (program) management functions: planning, decision making, organizing, leading, and implementation and evaluation (Starling 1998, 23). Henry provides a generic definition of public management:

> the development or application of methodical and systematic techniques, often employing comparison, quantification, and measurement, that are designed to make the operations of public organizations more efficient, effective, and, increasingly, responsive. (1999, 155)

The chapters in his book on public management focus on the systems approach, program evaluation, the public budget, and human resource management. At the conceptual level, Henry's definition of public management provides the unity that cannot come from a definition based on a listing of concrete management functions. However, such conceptual unity is limited as well, for the definition of public management also varies with disciplinary angle.

Public management studies find their origin in the early 1970s (Kettl and Milward 1996, 4). First, Pressman and Wildavsky's 1973 study shifted the attention from organizational structure and processes to the implementation and performance of public programs (1984 [1973]). Second, implementation studies increasingly adopted an interdisciplinary focus, drawing upon literature from, for instance, political science, sociology, economics, and psychology. As a consequence, the definition of public management has come to vary with disciplinary angle. Political scientists will have an eye for decision making, especially at the political-administrative summit. Economists look at the impact of administrative rules upon organizational design and efficiency. Psychologists have greatly contributed to knowledge about the "micro-dynamics of macro structure," including attention to organizational memory and previous experience, motivation, and the blending of cognitive and emotional issues. Finally, sociologists have looked at the role and position of the public sector in society in terms of how its services are valued by members of society (see various authors in Kettl and Milward 1996, 60, 85, 112, 137). The definition of public management also varies with the dominant underlying type of (mix of) organizational culture(s). Analyzing the nature of public management from the four perspectives (fatalism, individualism, hierarchy, and egalitarianism) of cultural theory, Hood concludes that public management is not converging toward one paradigm and that plural paradigms are desirable since no style of organization is without weaknesses (Hood 1998, 220).

Most public administrationists agree that public management is part of public administration and that it is especially concerned with the day-to-day practice of governing, but the study has not provided a theory and a philosophy of public management in a democracy, as was recently suggested (Moore 1997, 5). In my view, such a theory and philosophy should consider public management functions as an integral part of public administration and hence as something that is embedded in deeper levels of understanding. Public management and public management functions in such a theory are regarded as expressions of societal and ideational values.

The paired concepts of democracy and efficiency are central to the study of public administration. The efficiency aspect of public administration has traditionally focused attention on organizational structures and coordination challenges. In chapter 5 I already mentioned how the demand for efficiency was heard loud and clear at the time that the American Constitution was drawn up. One could say that attention to the efficiency element of the classical balance with democracy was submerged for most of the nineteenth century. De Tocqueville did not even pay attention to it. Since the end of the nineteenth century, the efficiency issue was back, never to submerge again, because democracy—as Waldo characterized the state of mind in the early twentieth century among scholars and practitioners—could survive only if efficiency was provided for as well (Waldo 1984, 13). Efficiency was a strong if not leading value in the development of the study in the early part of the century, and it was complemented by some consideration for normative issues and comparative research after World War II. The attention to efficiency has apparently been stronger than ever in the past fifteen to twenty years, but it may come with a price. In the eyes of Jan-Erik Lane (1994), there is a crisis in public administration because of the increased domination of the management approach. Lane contrasts the administrative state with the management state.

The public administration approach is grounded in a notion of *rechtsstaat.* This approach emphasizes a public sector that protects the public against corruption and abuse of power; that enhances the predictability of public action by means of bureaucracy and an explicit rule structure; that is formal in its dealing with individuals (i.e., in terms of fairness and equity); that is formal in its development of policy, (i.e., following agreed procedures); that is open and accessible to all; that voices complaint rather than uses dissatisfaction as a justification for exit; and that encourages its officeholders to perceive their job as a vocation and to believe that they serve the public interest (Table 9.2).

Lane's contrast of the public administration approach with the public management approach brings a sharp focus, or edge, to what he believes the discussion to be: should legalist-administrative or should managerial concerns drive the public sector? In reality, both approaches are relevant for understanding government. Lane argues that the field and the study of public administration are presently leaning too much to the public management approach. The most radical of management models in his view is that of the *internal market,* where public organizations are perceived as production units that compete with other production units and where there is an interaction in the public sector between a *board of purchases* (demand) and a *board for production* (supply). Internal markets allegedly enhance efficiency of public resource allocation and thus guarantee Pareto-efficient outcomes (Lane 1994, 149).

While Lane mentions the existence of several managerial models, he discusses only the model of the internal market. This model is one of the four governance models that Guy Peters explores as potential avenues for the future of governance (Table 9.3).

Table 9.2

Public Administration Versus Public Management

Public administration approach	Public management approach
Rules	Objectives
Due process	Efficiency
Anticipation	Adaptation
Responsibility	Direction
Formalism: case	Innovation
Openness	Secrecy
Complaint: voice	Exit
Legality	Effectiveness
Vocation	Self-interest
Public interest	Profit

Source: Lane 1994, 144. Reprinted with permission from Jan-Erik Lane and editors.

Table 9.3

Major Features of Emerging Models of Governance

	Market government	Participative government	Flexible government	Deregulated government
Principal diagnosis of problem	Monopoly	Hierarchy	Permanence	Internal regulation
Desired organizational structure	Decentralization	Flatter organizations	"Virtual organizations"	No particular recommendation
Financial and human resource management	Pay for performance; private sector techniques	Total quality management teams	Managing temporary personnel	Greater managerial freedom
Role of civil service in policy making; role of private sector	Internal markets; market incentives	Consultation; negotiation	Experimentation	Entrepreneurial government
Public interest; criterion of good governance	Low cost	Involvement; consultation	Low cost; coordination	Creativity; activism

Source: Reprinted from B. Guy Peters, *The Future of Governing: Four Emerging Models* (Lawrence: University Press of Kansas, 1996), p. 19. Copyright © 1996 by University Press of Kansas (www.kansaspress.ku.edu). Used by permission of the publisher.

What Peters calls the "principal diagnosis of the problem" is often based on the general, vague feelings and perceptions of citizens (Peters 1996, 18). Thus, in his *market model* of governance, monopoly refers to the perception that government controls public policy too much, while it should allow for more competition with other (private) actors. The *participative model* highlights the perception that there is too much emphasis on hierarchy in governance. The top-down, if not paternalistic, nature of governance should be balanced with more interaction between policy makers and citizens. In the *flexible model,* the perceived permanence of government structures stands in the way of effectiveness and efficiency, and governance should be served with more flexibility. Finally, in the *deregulated model*, internal regulation refers to the perception that there is too much emphasis on rule-boundedness and on rules that provide unnecessary detail. As Peters discusses these four models as alternatives, he also emphasizes that they are not mutually exclusive. A case for reform would probably not be served by selecting one of these models. In Peters's words:

> It may well be that for the provision of certain marketable services the market models are adequate and desirable, but that same model would be totally inappropriate for many social services, for example, education. Likewise, the participatory model would be well suited for urban planning or environmental issues but would produce difficulties for criminal justice programs. The flexible model probably would work well for complex issues such as the drug problem and also for transient concerns such as disaster relief. (1996, 132–133)

What Peters's discussion brings out is that a legalist-administrative approach to government is in and of itself insufficient because it deals with different policies and concerns on a uniform basis and only with regard to proper procedures. A managerial approach, on the other hand, acknowledges the differences between various policy areas and thus implicitly embraces a more bottom-up approach to governance. We can take this comparison one step further. In a legalist-administrative perspective, a generic theory of public management is possible and would focus on managerial functions at a very abstract level. In a managerial perspective, there are multiple theories of public management, based on the experiences and practices of specific policy areas.

In terms of organization and coordination, three out of the four models consider avenues of reform within public organizations, regarding specifically the managerial level of government. Only the participative model takes citizen involvement explicitly into account. As is common in the study of public administration, Peters implicitly argues that the best chances of reform are those that are pursued within the organizational structures of government itself. This acknowledges that government can impose reform only upon itself and thus lead by example. It cannot, and should not, impose reforms on the private sector or society at large. At the same time, though, the awareness is increasing that government reforms with an eye for both democracy and efficiency are less successful when not complemented by efforts to recast the relation between government and the private sector and between government and the citizenry (see, for more, section 9.5). Reforms relevant to and peculiar to the public sector, however, may not be useful to the private sector. Conversely, managerial reforms in the private sector may not be entirely or at all relevant to the public sector.

9.4. Public and Private Administration

When Socrates argues that private affairs differ from public concerns only in magnitude, he specifically states that those who know how to properly conduct their private affairs are most likely able to do the same with public concerns (Shafritz and Ott 1996, 39). Socrates is clearly an early representative of the notion that public and private affairs do not differ at the level of individual conduct. When we apply his notion of magnitude at the collective level, that of institutions and organizations as a whole, two radically different conclusions can be drawn. One conclusion is that there is no difference between the public and the private realms. In both realms efficiency is considered important, and the challenge for the public sector is to incorporate the values of factory, school, and home (Waldo 1984, 13) into the business of government. The other conclusion is that efficiency in the public sector does not end with profit-for-the-company in monetary terms but with profit in terms of societal benefit. And the nature of these benefits, as Waldo convincingly argues, means that efficiency can be measured only in terms of other values and is therefore not an end in itself. An "objective" interpretation of efficiency is possible only in a normative framework (Waldo 1984, 193–194). Such a normative framework would include a set of explicit valuations that enables us to determine whether or not a particular problem requires a public or a private solution. In striving for efficiency, the adoption of managerial styles from the private sector, most of all from business administration, has found a willing audience at the highest levels of government. For example, the reinventing government movement attempted to make a case that the study of public administration had always been fashioned after the radiant example of business (Osborne and Gaebler 1992; Gore 1993, 9). In this line of argument, the legal and political considerations so characteristic of the early study were conveniently swept under the rug. Neither the practitioner nor the academic community has accepted the idea that business led the way, and the response to the various proposals made by Osborne and Gaebler has not been favorable and they were generally found to lack historical understanding (e.g., Goodsell 1993; Green and Hubbell 1996; Williams 2000). In reality, the public and the private sectors together developed and explicated valuations, with the public sector leading the way regarding the societal and democratic values and the private sector leading the way with respect to managerial values.

More challenging than demarcating the public and the private sectors is mapping and understanding the degree to which both have become interdependent. At the turn of the last century, many services initially provided in the private domain were incorporated in the public domain—if not in terms of total service delivery, then certainly in terms of regulation and supervision. With respect to more recent times, Wolin points out several areas in which social problems have become an interest for the private domain. These areas are no longer limited to hospitals, welfare services, and education, but have also come to include services that had long been strictly public, such as prisons (Wolin 1989, 26). If ever there was a clear separation between the public and the private sphere (a nostalgic past?), such is no longer the case.

There are thus shades and degrees of publicness along a continuum of which the pure public and the pure private sectors are only the extremes. In a classic article, Allison outlines how public managers differ from their private counterparts (1982). The time horizon of public managers is short because it is determined by the political agenda. The length of tenure of public managers is shorter. Both of these observations especially concern the elected and appointed political officials. They do not refer to the members of the permanent civil service. Political-administrative relations do pose a particular constraint upon public managers quite unlike that which is normal in the private sector (see also Cooper 1998, about the differences on the ethical level). In addition, public managers have no clear standards for performance measurement. Their goals are not as clear-cut as in the private sector and often the results cannot be defined in terms of monetary profit. Public policy has to serve both equity and efficiency; its process is more open and subject to legislative and judicial scrutiny. Also, public managers have to rely on mediation rather than direction, have to pay tribute to many superiors, and are closely followed by the members of the press. In Allison's overview, we recognize several of the concepts presented by Lane.

There are organizations that are clearly either public or private, but there are also organizations that operate between these two extremes; Elinor Ostrom's (1990) common pool resources (CPRs) are a perfect example. Rainey (1997, 68) refined the public-private distinction, suggesting degrees of publicness varying with funding and ownership. When funding and ownership are both located in one hand, we have a case of pure public or pure private

Table 9.4

Three Sets of Core Values in Public Management

	Sigma-type values (keep it lean and purposeful)	Theta-type values (keep it honest and fair)	Lambda-type values (keep it robust and resilient)
Standard of success	Frugality	Rectitude	Resilience
Standard of failure	Waste	Malversation	Catastrophe
Currency of success and failure	Money and time	Trust and entitlements	Security and survival
Control emphasis	Output	Process	Input/process

Source: Reprinted from Christopher Hood, "A Public Management for All Seasons?" *Public Administration* 69, no. 1 (1991): 11. Reprinted with permission from Basil Blackwell Ltd.

bodies. Police and defense are examples of policy areas in which means and ownership are generally public. In any purely private organization, on the other hand, funding and ownership are entirely in the market. There are, however, organizations that largely depend upon government contracts (e.g., defense industry) and the funding is public but the ownership is private. There are also organizations whose means are private but whose ownership is publicly controlled. Such is the case with, for instance, private prisons. The economic authority to make decisions about costs and benefits thus increases or decreases with the degree to which the political authority decreases or increases. In comparison to other countries, the United States has relied upon private or semiprivate organizations to a much larger degree than other Western countries (McGraw 1992).

In an article as classic by now as Allison's, Christopher Hood outlined what he believed to be the core values of public management (1991). His sigma-type values clearly correspond with hard-core managerialism, the theta-type values display more of a public administration angle, while the lambda-type values seem to represent a mix of both approaches (Table 9.4).

The managerial values are clearly visible in, for instance, the concepts of *frugality* (the matching of resources with tasks for given goals) and *waste* (muddle, confusion, inefficiency) and considerations of *money and time* (resource costs of producers and consumers). Traditional public administration concerns are relevant to the second set of values, that of *rectitude* (achievement of fairness, mutuality, proper discharge of duties), *malversation* (unfairness, bias, abuse of office), and *trust and entitlements* (consent, legitimacy, due process, political entitlements). In the third column, administrative and managerial values seem to have merged in view of the emphasis on *resilience* (achievement of reliability, adaptivity, robustness), *catastrophe* (risk, break-down, collapse), and *security and survival* (confidence, life and limb).

Hood's values provide the normative type of framework Waldo advocates, but they do not yet outline when and why a particular task or service should be provided within the public sphere. It is government that has the responsibility of making a case for publicness, and it should abstain from public intervention if it cannot do so convincingly. Subsidiarity seems to be at play here. Preference for market solutions rests on a deep respect for the market's power, on the idea that the private sector is more susceptible to individual initiative, and even on the conviction that private institutions are an important bulwark of freedom against the power of government (Moore 1997, 43). These motives help explain the surge of privatizations in the Western world. However, privatization is not only a limitation of government intervention; it could represent the end of the public discussion about the use of power, about the ends to which power is used, and about the question of who can ultimately be held responsible (Wolin 1989, 182).

9.5. No Shortcut to Quality: Public Leadership Beyond Tricks

Such a balancing between democracy and efficiency places public managers in a most complex situation. They have to be sensitive not only to the democratic context in which they operate but also to the demands for efficiency placed upon them. Indeed, if government would be driven primarily by profit, then public managers should make larger salaries than their counterparts in the private sector in view of their national responsibilities. This responsibility for society as a whole stimulated the research on what constitutes excellence in the public sector. The literature on excellent managers has mushroomed since Peters and Waterman concluded that managers in excellent companies display an unusual ability to resolve paradox and to translate conflicts and tensions successfully into excitement, high commitment, and superior performance (Peters and Waterman 1982; Quinn 1988, 27). How does the poor bureaucrat compare to that? Does not the democratic context balanced with demands for efficiency require an uncanny ability to resolve paradox? Perhaps public managers have to be more excellent because their performance cannot be measured by something as simple as profit. Instead, it is measured in terms of the much more complex and ambiguous public values.

Public values have entered the managerial vocabulary, perhaps upon the conviction that it is better to include than to oppose. Moore provides us with an indication of what is required of public managers. While the integrative role he sees for public managers is not at all different from what Self calls *administrative (or intellectual) appraisal* (1979, 192) or from what Waldo calls the *normative framework of efficiency* (1984, 194), Moore's managerial background actually helps him to outline what it is that needs to be integrated. He starts by saying that

> society needs value-seeking imaginations (and associated technical skills) from the public sector executives no less than from its private sector managers. (1997, 21)

He then proceeds by describing what it is that successful public managers are able to integrate (22, 71). First, the public manager should consider *substantive values*, which involve a judgment of what could be valuable and whether or not the organization is actually able to produce such value. Second, the public manager should be able to develop *a diagnosis of political expectations*, paying attention to the legitimacy and to the political sustainability of what is being proposed. Public organizations should attract both the authority and the money from the political sphere to which they are accountable. Finally, it is the specific responsibility of the public manager to *calculate what is operationally and administratively feasible*. Faithful to managerialism, Moore calls this the strategic triangle, but it is clear that much more is involved than mere cost-benefit analysis or some flaky reform of an organizational structure.

The values now considered important to public sector performance include attention not only to the organizational level but also to human behavior, which was one of the problems highlighted by Dahl (1997) more than fifty years ago. Attention to human behavior is not quite new to the study of public administration. McGregor's theories X and Y are based on fundamentally different views of human nature, with theory X emphasizing management by direction through high degrees of organizational control and theory Y relying on flexible management, creativity, and human needs (McGregor 1960). Management-by-objectives (MbO) is illustrative of a theory Y approach. The one element that is nowadays especially emphasized is trust. Scientific management and McGregor's theory X are low on trust (Carnevale 1995, 36, 40). Theories of collective action, the tragedy of the commons, and the prisoner's dilemma game are equally illustrative of low trust (Hardin 1968; Olson 1965). Conversely, Elinor Ostrom's description of successful CPRs suggests that high levels of trust are required for proper functioning (1990).

No one will deny that trust is a healthy and important element for any organization, but arguing that the bureaucratic model served its purposes in early industrialization and is inherently unfriendly to trust because it is impersonal and formalistic, and denies the value of social capital as Carnevale (1995, 13–14, 29) and Hummel (1977) argue is going too far if unsubstantiated by empirical research. One could just as well argue that bureaucracy generates trust because citizens can expect unbiased treatment. If anything, bureaucracy has become increasingly necessary because the number and range of public services have exploded since early industrialization, while at the same time a greater variety of citizens have come to express their own interpretation of how democracy and efficiency should be balanced and valued. The large demand of society upon government was met with the *adequate response* of bureaucratization. How else could both equity and frugality have been served? Thus Crozier's *vicious circle of bureaucratization* (1964) is not merely about new rules to affirm and strengthen existing rules, it is also an expression of bureaucracies' response to more varied demand for services.

There is yet another angle that needs to be considered when trust is concerned. While some individuals will welcome increased responsibility and increased expectations of creativity, others may simply follow the leader. Some people like responsibility and the burden and blame that may come with it, while others prefer less responsibility. Keeping this in mind, the public manager or leader should not only display vision, capabilities of intellectual appraisal, and general communicative skills, but should also be flexible enough to accept that some subordinates want and can live up to challenges, whereas others merely like clear directions. An excellent public manager leads the leaders as well as the followers. Those who preach how healthy constant change is to organizations tend to gloss over the fact that organizations are populated not only with innovative and flexible employees but also with those who need security and predictability. Advocates of change are also, ultimately, supporting a one-best-way: that of change. They view and embrace change as opportunity rather than as a potential source for unrest and instability.

9.6. Concluding Remarks

Public administration and public management cannot and should not be separated. The managerial literature about excellence appears to provide a shortcut to quality. Nothing could be more one-sided or deceiving than this. Pursuing quality and excellence is hard work and is gradually acquired rather than quickly learned in a high-priced seminar.

One cannot learn managerial tricks without considering what legitimates them. In this chapter, I looked at managerial values as they are embedded in legalist-administrative values. In terms of my framework, the managerial values at the organizational (actor) level are an expression of the institutional values at the ideational and societal level. Public administration as a study cannot disregard the fact that conceptualizations of managerial values emanate from deeper levels of understanding. The practice of government cannot ignore these deeper levels either, for they ultimately legitimate government action.

The juridical perspective emphasizes uniformity of values and rules, while the sociological perspective highlights the contextual nature of public management. In a collectivist perspective, public management functions are regarded at a very generic and abstract level, resulting in a list with principles and activities that apply to all organizations. Personnel management or budgeting are management functions relevant to every organization. From a more individualist perspective, the way public management functions are exercised may vary with policy and with organization. Thus, personnel policy in the military branch may differ from that in social security or public health agencies. Also, public management functions can be understood at different levels of abstraction. We can look at levels of reform (from the abstract level of civil society to the most concrete level of administration), at the organization of governance at different levels (from the abstract institutional to the most concrete primary work level), and at levels of managerial values. Finally, I believe that the historical perspective provides a more embedded understanding of the contemporary challenges of public management. Obviously, government and its public management functions are highly bound by societal problems in a specific time and context. That may amount to time- and context-specific theories of public management. The historical perspective is helpful for seeing the continuity as well as the change in thinking about public management. The most important conclusion, though, has to be that public management is part of the study of public administration, for only then can public management thought escape being regarded as a manager's tool kit.

10 ORGANIZATIONAL STRUCTURE, CULTURE, CHANGE, AND REFORM

What will the future organization be like? The question has particular pertinence for young people who are moving out of the colleges and have a lifetime of contact with organizations ahead of them.
—John Pfiffner and Frank Sherwood, 1960

Decision making in highly organized settings is characteristic for contemporary society, but it is only in the past few decades that earlier concerns with the consequences of the organizational revolution have subsided. The decline of individualism was feared by Nietzsche (late nineteenth century) and by Ayn Rand (1930s–1960s). Organization literature of the 1950s and 1960s paid equally serious attention to the battle of the individual against the organization. In his very popular (1956) book William Whyte, who was editor of *Fortune* at that time, described the *organization man* as a noncreative puppet who depended upon supervisors. He met with opposition from Lloyd Warner, a social research professor from Michigan State, who argued that the *autonomous man* and organization were not at all at odds with each other. At the end of his Ford Distinguished Lecture Series, Warner described what was happening in society:

> One great society is now in being. The great corporations grow and expand. Big government extends itself enormously. Across the nation, primary, face-to-face interaction grows as the national community enters maturity; the future invades today, and each tomorrow advances the time of its arrival. Local communities are still important and still necessary parts of our social life, but instead of having their own autonomy, they are integral parts of the larger American—not to say world—social system. (Warner 1962, 63)

This quotation is interesting because Warner recognizes that local communities no longer operate in isolation, and it also shows an early recognition of globalization. I disagree, however, with the observation that primary, face-to-face interaction is growing across the nation. Interaction has grown, but as the indirect interaction of the imagined communities through the various interest groups. Society increasingly relies on indirect, written, and standardized types of interaction (formal meetings, faxes, teleconferences, e-mail, etc.). Increased *indirect* interaction between various communities has raised the awareness of differences in the quantity and quality of public services. Together with a declining number of collective services provided by private associations, the demand for more public services means that nowadays, public officeholders have to juggle more varying demands than any of their predecessors. As a consequence, much attention has been given to the improvement of the organizational structure and functioning of the public sector. Through reforms of organizational structure and through the standardization of procedures, public officeholders attempt to make sure that this juggling proceeds in a legitimate manner.

In this chapter, I discuss the development of organizational theory in the twentieth century in relation to actual developments in the structure and culture of public organizations. During the first half of the twentieth century, organizational theory was focused on organizational structure itself. The classic bureaucratic line-staff model initially dominated, but after World War II, a variety of other organizational structures were developed (section 10.1). Since the 1950s, organizational change increasingly came to be regarded as a response to environmental pressures, and much more attention was given to the evolution and change of organizations as a response to interaction with the environment (section 10.2). In the past two decades, the increased effort to restructure organizations has also raised awareness of the importance of organizational culture and organizational philosophy (section 10.3). Organizational change may concern organizational structures at large or may involve organizational subunits. In this chapter, I only focus on the reform styles at large (section 10.4). Some of these reforms regard the division of labor between tiers of government, and so theory and practice of some of the reforms in intergovernmental relations will be discussed in the context of centralization, decentration, and decentralization (section 10.5). Other reforms regard efforts to recast existing detailed regulations into more general rules (deregulation), efforts to establish a more flexible bureaucracy (debureaucratization), and efforts to recast the division of labor between the public and the private sector (privatization) (section 10.6). A major consequence of the continuous restructuring of organizations is that information and communication flows have changed. In this chapter, I briefly discuss information and communication in the organizational theory context (section 10.7).

At the opening of the twenty-first century, it seems as if the fear that individuals might be absorbed by organizations, as Nietzsche, Rand, and Whyte believed, no longer exists. In the more recent literature, one will not find fear about organizational control, centralization of power in large organizations, and organizational society. The literature in the field of human resource management is more than politely appreciative of the inherent tension between the pursuit of organizational goals and the respect for the employer's needs. Literature in the field of organizational theory takes horizontal, flatter organizations as seriously as the hierarchical structures of old. Everywhere, intergovernmental relations are cast in different, much less hierarchical molds. And yet the organizational society Presthus described in the early 1960s has not disappeared (Presthus 1978). If anything, society and government have become even more organized.

10.1. The Structure of Public Organizations

Organizations are characterized by their *distribution of authority* according to a *dominant philosophy of society.* Most attention in organization literature is devoted to the variations in the distribution of authority. Most organization theory in the early part of the twentieth century was concerned with determining the best way to organize. But in the second half of that century, it became increasingly clear that organizational structure may well vary based upon a given set of functions in a given environment.

The most dominant type of organization in contemporary society is bureaucracy; that characterizes not only large but also smaller and small organizations. All of the definitions of the concept of bureaucracy can be reduced to two, which really represent two sides of the same coin. One side refers to twelve characteristics of functionaries (for these, see chapter 13), while the other side includes eight characteristics of the organizational structure and functioning. All twenty characteristics together form the *idealtype* of bureaucracy. Weber distinguished eight characteristics of bureaucracy as organization (*legal-rationale Herrschaft*) (Table 10.1).

An idealtype is a theoretical tool that allows comparison with reality. In more abstract terms, an idealtype is a situation developed to its logical extremes. If all of the twenty characteristics of bureaucracy were fully developed, then that would constitute the perfect bureaucracy. In reality, however, such is not possible. The forces of politics and interest groups, even though these too are bureaucratized in terms of their functioning, are still and always will be strong enough to counteract full bureaucratization. What is more, the checks and balances established in most Western countries guarantee that bureaucracy will never come even close to full realization. Some of the stereotypes about government concern the organizational aspects of the bureaucracy concept: impersonal and cold application of rules, red tape, and so forth. In terms of organizational theory, bureaucracy has sometimes been presented as a *fourth*

Table 10.1

Eight Dimensions of Bureaucracy as Organization

1. Continuous administrative activity
2. Formal rules and procedures
3. Clear and specialized offices
4. Hierarchical organization of offices
5. Use of written documents
6. Adequate supply of means (desk, paper, office, etc.)
7. Nonownership of office (separation of office from officeholder)
8. Procedures of rational discipline and control

Source: After Van Braam 1986; Raadschelders and Rutgers 1996, 92.

power, next to the three distinguished by Montesquieu (the *trias politica* of legislative, executive, judiciary). Placing bureaucracy in that list disregards the fact that each of these three powers is supported by bureaucracies.

In the classic bureaucratic organization, the *line-staff model* (see Figure 10.1), the line represents the hierarchy of authority in relation to the external goals of the organization. Staff units are those that help the organization to function properly. Staff functions are internal to the organization and include, for instance, secretarial units, the cleaning department, personnel services, the company restaurant, research and development units, and so forth.

In this model, lines of authority are determined by *unity of command* so that every subordinate has one supervisor. The lines of communication can be very long, especially in large organizations. Staff units are added as soon as organizational complexity increases. These staff units have no formal line authority but informally they do influence the work of the line (e.g., personnel units, research and development units). A major challenge in any organization of some size is the *span of control*, which is the number of people a manager can effectively supervise. In the early 1940s, Urwick concluded that the optimal span was between four and six, but he later modified that to a top management span of four people and for others a span of eight to twelve subordinates. In 1957, Davis distinguished between an *executive span* of three to nine and an *operative span* of ten to thirty (*The Fundamentals of Top Management*). These varying numbers for spans of control suggest that there is no ideal span of control. It has been reported that in 1985, the American president had a span of control of 128, while industrial organizations can work with 70. In the 1950s, the Bank of America in California functioned with a span of control of 600 (i.e., each of the local branches report-

Figure 10.1 **The Line-Staff Model: Any Classic Bureaucracy**

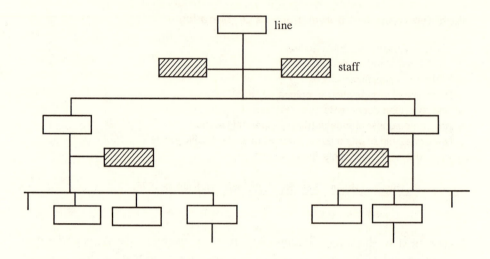

ing directly to the San Francisco headquarters) (Heffron 1982, 38; Pfiffner and Sherwood 1960, 161).

Span of control is not just determined by an individual's supervisory capabilities. First, span of control is influenced by characteristics of organizational structure and operating philosophy. We can think here of the number of hierarchical levels in an organization (e.g., the higher the span of control, the flatter an organization), of managerial philosophy and culture (e.g., McGregor's theory X and Y), of size of the organization (e.g., the smaller an organization, the more chance for interpersonal contact), and of mutual adjustment (e.g., the greater the degree of goal alignment and goal consensus between hierarchical levels, the larger the span of control can be). Second, span of control is determined by the nature of the job. Aspects to consider are whether the job is repetitive or challenging (if repetitive, a larger span of control is possible), to what degree work processes are standardized (if standardized, a larger span is possible), what monitoring systems exist (if automatic, for instance with accounting, then a higher span is possible), geographic location (when manager and subordinates work in the same building, a higher span is possible), and safety or danger of position (in a high-risk job, a smaller span is desirable). Finally, span of control is determined by characteristics of employees. Are they independent, creative, and driven (the so-called *knowledge workers*) or do they need guidance? (Robbins 1980, 198–203).

To illustrate classic line-staff organizations, public administration literature often discusses a few federal government departments. It has often been said that since the seventeenth century, governmental organizations have been fashioned after the organizational structures of the military. However, both civil and military organizations in the public sector took the organizational structure of the Roman Catholic church as their model, which in turn had copied from the administrative practices of the Roman Empire (Miller 1983; Strayer 1975). Instead of looking at some public organizations to illustrate and discuss the line-staff model, here I concentrate on different organizational structures of various churches. Doing so will also illustrate that particular religious or secular ideas can have very practical consequences, in this case for the structure of public and of private organizations.

The Roman Catholic church is an example of a line-staff organization and is particularly instructive in the context of this book because it functions upon the existence of a universal authority (i.e., unity of command). For such a large organization, the organizational structure of the Roman Catholic church is surprisingly simple; it consists of two intertwined hierarchies (Figure 10.2).

The *pastoral hierarchy* serves the flock and is the perfect example of a flat organization because it consists of three levels: the church at large with the pope as its pastoral head, the bishopric and the bishop, and the parish and the parish priest. The functionaries at these three levels also perform managerial functions. The *managerial hierarchy* has two extra layers. Between pope and bishop, cardinals and/or archbishops coordinate several bishoprics. In small countries, there is generally one cardinal or archbishop, while in large countries there are several. Between bishop and parish priests, the deans coordinate the work of various parishes. Cardinals or archbishops and deans also have their own parish, and their function in the pastoral hierarchy is no different from that of a parish priest. While the managerial hierarchy thus consists of five tiers, the pastoral hierarchy consists only of three. The priest reports annually to the bishop, and the bishop reports every five years to the pope in a visit to Rome (the *ad limina* visit). Officeholders are appointed by a higher hierarchical level (in the case of priests, deans, bishops, archbishops, and cardinals) or by peers (in the case of the pope by the College of Cardinals) upon divine inspiration (represented by the cloud in Figure 10.2). At each of the pastoral and managerial levels, committees and departments provide staff functions.

Protestant churches have a very different and much less hierarchical organizational structure. The organizational hierarchy of some of the Protestant denominations still maintains elements reminiscent of their roots in the Roman Catholic church. This is especially the case in the Anglican and the Methodist churches. Others are more grounded in the local self-governance models that were embraced in the northern European and North American territories. The Anglican church is closest to its Roman Catholic roots in terms of centralized establishment of rituals and appointments. In terms of hierarchy, it is different since the highest authority is invested in the head of state (i.e., for

Figure 10.2 **The Line-Staff Model Under Universal Authority: The Roman Catholic Church**

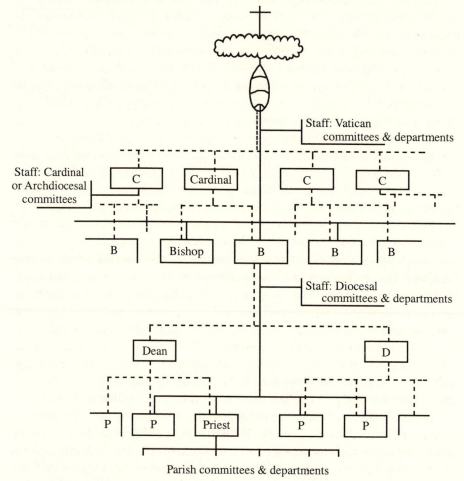

pastoral hierarchy ——————
managerial hierarchy - - - - - - - -

the Anglican church in England, this is the monarch). The highest spiritual authority is that of the archbishop of Canterbury. The organizational structure of the Methodist church has elements of the Roman Catholic and Anglican churches as well as of the self-governing Protestant denominations. The highest line authority in the Methodist church is the bishop, who recruits and selects the local ministers irrespective of approval of the congregation. The bishop is also instrumental in defining policy but is constrained by a college of peers. There is no formal higher authority. In both the Anglican and Methodist organizational structures, the British tradition of governing-at-a-distance is visible.

Most of the other Protestant churches operate as functional organizations wherein the key officeholder (minister, reverend, etc.) is supervised by the congregation as well as by a body of peers. They are models of local self-governance. The minister is selected according to a standardized procedure of recruitment and selection directly by the members of the congregation (as with Baptists, Lutherans, Presbyterians, and Quakers). Policy or mission is also set directly by the membership of the congregation (as with, e.g., Quakers) or indirectly through a council of elders (as with, e.g., Presbyterians). There is no hierarchical level above the local level with respect to ministerial appointment, but there is some authority exerted through a regional and/or national synod or convention to establish some degree of uniformity of policy.

Where the Roman Catholic church copied the centralized and hierarchical organizational structures of the Roman Empire, the Protestant denominations that broke away most from that model adopted an organizational structure of local self-governance characteristic of the independent Germanic tribes.

Like the line-staff model, the *functional organization* (see Figure 10.3) was developed before World War II by the father of scientific management, Frederick Taylor (Pfiffner and Sherwood 1960, 184). In the functional organization, there are upper management central units for such staff functions as personnel, finance, planning, and research and development. Each line unit, however, also has these staff functions. Hence, someone working for the personnel section in one production unit is accountable not only to the immediate line supervisor, but also to the central personnel manager. The advantage is that line managers are more directly supported by staff functions. The disadvantage, obviously, is that the unity of command is challenged.

The line-staff and functional organizations were considered favorably in the days of scientific management. Both the line-staff and functional models dominated organizational theory well into World War II. Immediately prior to the war, the improvement of existing organizational structures was pursued by attempting to identify characteristic principles and processes of organization. The most famous of these are the four principles of organization (place or geography, process, goal, clientele) and the seven functions of management (planning, organizing, staffing, directing, coordinating, reporting, budgeting: POSDCORB) as identified by Luther Gulick. Between Taylor (1910s) and Gulick (1930s), the focus on public organizations had been limited to scientific management of the work floor and to the administrative management of the organization at large. There was little if any distinction made between public and private organizations.

The attack upon these generic approaches to organizations came from the (economic) decision-making theory corner and from the avenues of political theory (e.g., Robert Dahl, Dwight Waldo). Simon (1946) called Gulick's prin-

Figure 10.3 **The Functional Organization**

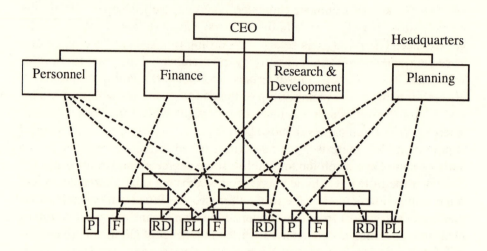

ciples proverbs, and he, Dahl (1947), and Waldo (1984) pointed to the assumed rigidity of organizations as portrayed in classic organization theory and to the importance of values. The emergence of more flexible organizational models in the postwar era broke through the rigidity of the classic models. The *project organization* (Figure 10.4) is designed to serve an ad hoc, specific task for a defined period of time. Its members belong to a standing organization but are temporarily loaned to the project organization. In the *matrix organization* each subordinate has a functional and a project supervisor, so that this model is a combination of the functional and the project organization.

Other types of organizational structures have been developed, but I have mentioned only those that are most frequently used. In all of these different types of structures, there is some degree of hierarchy.

One type of organizational structure that merits special attention is the *collegial organization,* since it was often used in early modern times and still exists—although in a restricted fashion. A collegial organization is characterized by the sharing of authority rather than by a hierarchy of authority. In a collegial organization, the members participate on the basis of equality and they do not belong to another standing organization (as in the project organization). In fact, they are members (for life or for a specified term of office) of the collegial organization. Presently, in public organizations, the best examples are the legislative bodies at national, state, and local levels (in the United States: U.S. Congress, state legislatures, local councils); the college of judges in the judiciary system (the U.S. Supreme Court, any other type of court with more than one judge); the executive bodies at national, state, and local levels (e.g., the president's cabinet); and the boards of special-purpose governments,

Figure 10.4 **The Project Organization**

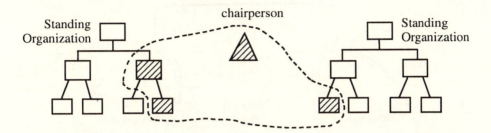

such as school boards in the United States. In private organizations, any executive board, such as a church council or a board of commissioners, would serve as example. Since the second half of the nineteenth century, the collegial organization has been the standard model only for the (political) top of public organizations. Before that time, collegial organization was also characteristic for the middle management levels in public organizations.

In addition to designing organizational structures to improve performance, scholars have also developed analytical models aimed at outlining the basic configuration of organizations irrespective of their specific structure. Mintzberg's work in this area is an example (1979 and 1983a). Based upon the five elements he distinguished in an organizational structure (Figure 10.5), Mintzberg identified six basic organizational configurations or patterns: the simple structure (e.g., small businesses), the machine bureaucracy (principal author: Taylor), the professional bureaucracy or garbage can model (Cohen, March, and Olsen 1972), the divisionalized structure (e.g., multinational corporations), the adhocracy (e.g., consulting firms), and the missionary organization (e.g., Roman Catholic church, Greenpeace). These patterns reflect the age and size of the organization, the technical system, the external power relations, and the dominant organizational theory. The survival of organizations depends upon their adaptive capacity in changing environments (e.g., the approaches of contingency theory and of the population ecology model) and upon the internal coherence of the various characteristics of the organization.

What makes Mintzberg's work especially appealing to public administrators is that he gradually moved from a focus on individual organizations in his early work to power (1983b) and to strategic decision making and planning and the role of norms and values in those organizational processes as they originate in society (1994).

In the second half of the twentieth century, the organizational environment became increasingly important for understanding the development of organizations. The first subject that attracted attention was the influence of the environment at large upon the organization. Classic organization theory, after all,

Figure 10.5   **The Elements of Organizational Structure**

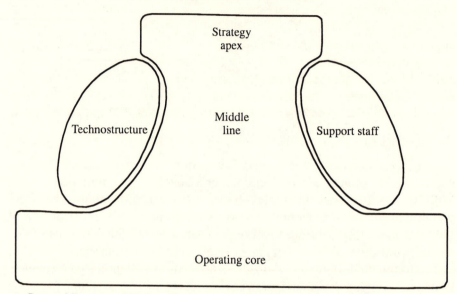

Source: Mintzberg 1979. Reprinted by permission of Pearson Education, Inc., Upper Saddle River, NJ.

was based upon the assumption that the best way to organize could be discovered. Organizations were increasingly seen as organisms that interacted with and were influenced by their environment. The focus on organizational philosophy and culture is more recent—and quickly becoming a subject that few organization and management theorists can afford to avoid (section 10.3). Amidst all of these changes of focus, however, it is almost paradoxical that the composite force of environmental pressures appears to continue to support bureaucracy as the dominant form of public and of private organizations.

10.2.   Organizational Evolution, Change, and the Environment

In the past 120 years or so, organization theory has come full circle. In the earliest decades of public administration, the dominant approach to the study of state and government was that of organic theory. This was abandoned in the early twentieth century in favor of a focus on the internal structure of organizations. After World War II, attention to the impact of the environment upon organizations increased, and now it appears we once again promote a more organic, holistic approach to organizations.

In the nineteenth century, organic theory dominated the analysis of government and thus of organizations. Interestingly, in this approach, government and its public organizations were considered in interaction with the environment. In 1860, Duganne described the development of society in terms of a life cycle: from infancy (or spring-time), youth (or summer-time), prime (or autumn-time), to maturity (or winter-time) (Duganne 1860, 11). The organization of government and the body politic is the outcome of a bottom-up process determined by an ever increasing sense of togetherness. In much the same fashion, Wilson described the development of the state and its government: "Government is merely the executive organ of society" (1892, 598). Almost twenty-five years later, he said during one of his campaign speeches,

> government is not a machine, but a living thing. It falls not under the theory of the universe, but under the theory of organic life. It is accountable to Darwin, not to Newton. (1913, 47)

With the emergence of scientific management theory, the organic approach was dropped in favor of a more detailed analysis of the internal structure and functioning of organizations. Furthermore, and as a consequence of the politics-administration dichotomy, the focus of organization theory was on the facts of administration. It was believed that organizations operated on the basis of laws about to be discovered. Taylor's time and motion studies are a good example, as are Gulick's administrative management functions expressed in the acronym POSDCORB and his organizational principles of client, process, goal, and area. Theirs was a rather mechanistic approach to organization theory. Organizations were regarded as closed systems in which the functioning of the organization was conceptualized as analogous to blood circulation.

After World War II, the open systems approach to organization theory rose to prominence in two different ways. First, there was a revival of organic or evolutionary theory, which views the origins and development of the organization as a product of the environment it serves. Second, the open systems approach generated substantial research into the relation between various attributes of organizations (such as size, vertical and horizontal differentiation, technology) in relation to the environment. The traditional open systems approach emphasizes that an organization is influenced by the environment. A less traditional view is that organizations may shift from being relatively closed to being more open when a situation so demands. The application of open systems theory to the study of organizations was advanced by Katz and Kahn and by Thompson. Early in their study, Katz and Kahn argue,

> Social organizations are flagrantly open systems in that the input of energies and the conversion of output into further energic input consist of transactions between the organization and its environment. (Katz and Kahn 1966, 16–17)

They emphasize that open systems theory is not to be considered a theory in the strict sense but rather a metatheoretical framework that would be helpful in describing the actual functioning of organizations (452). What is more, they also look at the influence of (groups of) individuals in organizations, thus including the human relations and behavioralist perspectives.

Following Parsons's distinction between three levels of responsibility in organizations—that is, the technical, managerial, and institutional levels—Thompson argues that classic organizational theory was mainly focused on the technical level and looked at establishing strategies for certainty. He considers the closed systems approach most relevant at that level. The managerial level serves to mediate between the technical and the institutional levels. At the institutional level, the organization deals with the influence of the environment and it is at that level that strategies for uncertainty control are developed and that an open systems approach is most useful (Thompson 1967). This approach has been mentioned again recently by Frederickson (1999, 5–6), who distinguished between an *institutional level* (stable formal and informal rules, boundaries, procedures, regime values, type of authority), an *organizational or managerial level* (all the public organizations, NGOs, and so forth), and the *technical or primary work level* of government (discretion, implementation, performance measurement, etc.).

The first, fairly small, strand of literature that developed from the open systems perspective was that of organizational life cycle theories reminiscent of the organic approach at the turn of the last century. Thus, Downs describes the evolution of organizations in terms of birth, youth, maturity, and old age, and he linked each of these with particular personality types (Downs 1967, 5–23). Organizations are born in response to a particular need. Young organizations grow fast to ensure survival and are dominated by *zealots* or *entrepreneurs* who favor a particular program or policy. New organizations and, especially, new organizational forms have a higher chance of death than older (forms of) organizations. Arthur Stinchcombe referred to this as the *liability of newness,* underlining the inherently conservative nature of society (Hall 1977, 316–317). Growth is vital to young organizations because it proves that they provide a needed service. The growing organization is an ideal environment for *climbers* since there is ample opportunity to advance personal mobility. Once an organization reaches maturity, the *conservers* among the managers take over. They are mostly interested in stabilizing the organization's activity. This is achieved, for instance, through standardization and formalization, so older organizations tend to be more rigid. The mature organization can provide room for *advocates,* who have an eye for comprehensive policy programs, and *statesmen,* who look at the general interest at large. In old age, organizations may experience decline or revival. In the first case, the organization is ultimately dissolved. In a revival scenario, the conservers are forced out and replaced by another batch of zealots and/or climbers. In this context, it is interesting that Downs remarks that few organizations such as bureaus have managed to survive over a very long period of time. The example he mentions is that of the bureaus in the Roman Empire (1967, 23). Indeed, they disappeared but only in terms of the functions they served. As an administrative arrangement, the habit of organizing by bureaus was adopted by the Catholic Church, which, from the tenth century onward, was instrumental in disseminating that practice to secular governments.

The organizational life cycle theory is slightly problematic since we really cannot assume that organizations behave and develop in a manner comparable to human beings. With that in mind, Greiner's model is more useful because it takes management styles and management problems as point of departure (1972, 40). His five evolutionary phases of growth are creativity, direction, delegation, coordination, and collaboration. Each of these five phases is followed by a management crisis or problem: the crisis of leadership, of autonomy, of control, and of red tape; Greiner himself places a question mark at the fifth phase in his model (41) but elaborates a few pages later that the next crisis would be one that involved

> psychological saturation of employees who grow emotionally and physically exhausted by the intensity of teamwork and the heavy pressure for innovative solutions. (1972, 44)

Greiner's expectation that organizations might see the development of a *habit structure*, for the day-to-day activities, and of a *reflective structure*, for stimulating perspective and personal enrichment, has become reality. In the 1980s and 1990s, the study of organizational life cycles and organizational change and development expanded rapidly (for an overview, see Rainey 1997, 318–340).

The second body of research that open systems theory helped generate is much larger and can be divided into two main subgroups. The first subgroup includes scholars who investigated degrees to which various organizational properties were related. In part, this was an effort to test the coherence and consistency of Weber's idealtype, and it focused on determining empirical relationships between size, organizational differentiation, technology, and so forth. One of the major debates, from the late 1960s to the late 1980s, concerned whether organizational size is an element of the organization's environment (as the Aston group researchers argued; see also Blau and Schoenherr 1971) or is a structural property of the organization (for an early review of the Aston group, see Aldrich 1972; for summary of this debate and testing of the two arguments, see Raadschelders 1997b, 420, 423–429). These types of studies, however important to the study of government, were mainly conducted in the realm of organizational sociology.

The second subgroup, discussed at much more length in public administration literature, consists of researchers who investigated the fit between organizational structure at large and the environment at large, and they assumed that there was a best way to organize for each type of environment (Lawrence and Lorsch 1967, 3). Thus, mechanistic or management systems are bureaucratic and fit best in a stable environment. Organic systems, on the other hand, serve best in a rapidly changing and dynamic environment (Burns and Stalker 1961, 119–123). Four years later, Emery and Trist developed a taxonomy of environments. Varying from very stable to highly unstable, this causal texture of the environment determined what degree of rigidity or flexibility was expected of an organization (Emery and Trist 1965, 22; see Aldrich 1979, 71 for a visual presentation of their theory). In his study, Thompson presented a simple four-cell typology distinguishing between homogeneous versus heterogeneous and between stable versus shifting environments (1967, 70–73). Lawrence and Lorsch (1967, 23–54) also distinguished four types of environment (low and high diversity with no or much dynamic). Some years later, Jurkovich argued that these and other representations of the environment were too simplified and proposed a typology that resulted in sixty-four different types of environment (Jurkovich 1974). The influence of the environment upon the organization was, in the view of Lawrence and Lorsch, most visible in the balancing between the needs for differentiation (segmentation into separate units) and integration (the challenge of coordinating more or less autonomous units) (1967, 8). They concluded that the more complex, turbulent, and differentiated the external environment, the greater the degree of organizational differentiation. A few years later, Lawrence and Lorsch gave this body of literature its name:

> Basically, this approach seems to be leading to the development of a *"contingency" theory of organization* with the appropriate internal states and processes of the organization contingent upon external requirements and member needs. (emphasis added; 1970, 1, see also Kast and Rosenzweig 1996, 311)

Contingency theory met with criticism, but the adaptation perspective continues to be important today. Where Downs argues that "private bureaus do not usually outlive the cultures that spawn them," mentioning churches and universities as the heartiest species, one could also argue that both these types of organizations have been highly successful in adapting to a changing environment as well as actually adapting the environment to their organizational needs. In a sense, an organization selects and shapes an environment.

This notion of selection provided the foundation to the strongest critique of contingency theory. The population ecology theory of organizations centered on the idea that organizations are somehow selected by their environments.

Hannan and Freeman argue that the contingency theories, especially in management studies, subscribe to the

> *adaptation perspective.* According to the adaptation perspective, subunits of the organization, usually managers or dominant coalitions, scan the relevant environment for opportunities and threats, formulate strategic responses, and adjust organizational structure appropriately. (Hannan and Freeman 1978, 132)

They argue, instead, that adaptation has to be regarded as a function of selection (142). As a consequence, they pay far more attention to the environmental capacity for supporting forms of organization, to the rate at which a population (or organization) grows or declines in response to environmental change, and to the fact of multiple, rather than single, dynamic environments (145).

In the *population ecology model*, the environment may very well impose goals upon an organization. The response of the higher leadership in an organization may therefore be a source of change, but its effectiveness is dependent upon context. Aldrich pulled the contingency and population ecology theories together in an analysis of sources of organizational change and argued that interorganizational networks and social and cultural factors at large are far more influential. Network theory has gained importance in the study of public administration in the 1980s and 1990s both with respect to organizational theory as well as to policy networks (for a brief overview, see Rainey 1997, 117–118, 140–141). Aldrich was also among the first authors in organizational theory to explicitly recognize that social and cultural change had profound impact upon organizations and that "innovations have failed when introduced into societies with non-supportive cultural and institutional traditions" (Aldrich 1979, 22).

10.3.   Organizational Philosophy and Organizational Culture

The notion of congruence between societal culture and organization is highlighted by attention to organizational adaptation to changing environments or to selection of organizations by the environment. The various organizational structures, however, not only reveal a particular distribution of authority and style of responsiveness, but—and consequentially—are based in a dominant philosophy about and culture of society. In this section, I first discuss general societal philosophies of organizations and then organizational culture at large.

The element of the underlying societal philosophy of organizations is not often discussed in organizational theory or public administration, but more so (though not that much more) in political theory. De Geus's contribution to organizational theory is instructive for its distinction between three conceptions or traditions in the political philosophy about organizations (the following discussion is based on De Geus 1989, 232–238). In the *rational conception*, the various parts of the organization are ruled from the top. Hierarchy, discipline, and rationality dominate organizational theory. Plato, for instance, considers the best decision maker to be a king-philosopher, a person with the necessary wisdom, experience, and restraint to guarantee policies beneficial to all, operating in a centrally guided authority system where subjects faithfully carry out commands. Thomas Hobbes also favors a centralized authority where the organization functions as a mechanized unity upon the principles of obedience and duty. And then, finally, Max Weber presents organization (i.e., bureaucracy) as solidified spirit (his phrase: *geronnener Geist*) run by the manager as a machine.

The *integrated conception* takes a more horizontal approach. The literature in this tradition emphasizes processes of deliberation, participation, and majority ruling, all aimed at the best possible integration of desires and wills. Aristotle's organizational theory is based on equal relations, individual freedom, and participation (even though limited). He believes the organization should function as an association of the polis, of the political community. In the political community, people associate for the achievement of a common goal. In the same fashion, John Locke advocates that organizations operate on the basis of consent and trust. Public organizations should strive to meet the public will. Another exponent of this tradition is Jean-Jacques Rousseau, who argues that public organizations should be obedient to and should serve the general will of the people.

In the *libertarian conception,* the individual actor (as person or as, for instance, a local government) is the central, self-regulating, and decentralized unit. Voluntary federation with other comparable subunits is possible. In this conception, organizing is nothing more and nothing less but the structuring of freedom to assure full independence of the individual actor. Advocates of this approach include the classical anarchists Bakunin and Kropotkin. Examples in the real world are abundant. Most of the Protestant denominations in the United States operate on the basis of a libertarian conception of organization that goes back to Luther's and Calvin's preference for local units for worship and synods to coordinate and settle theological disputes. Local government in the New England towns up to the early twentieth century also operated according to this principle of self-governance. Representative thinkers in the libertarian conception in the United States are the early Progressivists, Mary Parker Follett, and, more recently, Vincent Ostrom.

More common to recent public administration and organizational theory is the attention to organizational culture. A first approach to analyzing organizational culture is through the distinction between technical, managerial, and institutional levels of organizations mentioned earlier (section 10.2); it is the institutional level where values and thus culture resides. A second angle, grounded in contingency and population ecology models, is the analysis of a particular organizational culture as it is embedded in a more encompassing societal culture. Thus, Schein (1980, 1993) distinguishes between three levels of organizational culture. The *artifacts* are the most visible and include physical setting, archives, organizational charts, and collective memory. The *patterns of behavior* are still fairly visible and are rooted in beliefs, values, and ideologies. The *underlying basic assumptions* emanate from culture at large and are generally taken for granted. With Schein's distinctions in mind, it appears that much of the thinking about organizational structure focused on the organizational and technical levels. The institutional level, which I call societal philosophy of organization, has been discussed briefly above.

Building upon the work of Schein and of Ott (1989), Van Wart proposes to distinguish between four levels of culture. The value levels include the *basic assumptions* level (the least visible aspect of culture: the implicit understanding of how the world operates, of human nature, etc.) and the *beliefs* level (the explicit values about how the world does and should operate: hence, rationales, justifications, codes). The more tangible levels of culture include a *patterns of action* level (norms, rules, habits, rites, etc., that determine behavior) and the *artifacts and actions* level (most visible level of culture: art, technology, language, individual action, etc.) (Van Wart 1998, 167–170). Both Schein and Van Wart underline the importance of understanding culture as a complex phenomenon of which the most visible expressions are embedded in deeper levels.

The more visible technical and managerial levels have attracted the most attention in the study of public administration. Much of that literature, however, is focused on leadership and cultural reform of the internal organization and emphasizes the importance of flexible supervisor-subordinate relations and flexible organizational structures (for very useful summaries of this body of literature, see Shafritz and Ott 1996, 485–493, and Rainey 1997, 259–293). In the context of this chapter, it makes sense to look at the core values of organizations because they are a reflection of values held in society at large.

The work of the Dutch sociologist Hofstede is especially relevant since it has greatly contributed to the identification of cultural values in work environments. His work is empirical and comparative, based on two initial surveys (conducted in 1968 and 1972) with a total of 116,000 questionnaires. His first major study based on both surveys focuses on organizational cultures in various branches of IBM across the globe (1980). In the second major study (1997), he outlines the relevance of three dimensions of societal culture (i.e., the culture in family, school, and workplace) for the understanding of the state and thus of public organizations. We will discuss these dimensions in some detail because they are helpful in further identifying the cultural foundations of governance and government.

In countries characterized by *small power distance,* subordinates are less dependent upon their bosses. The preferred relationship is one of consultation and interdependence. Examples of such countries are found in northwestern Europe and North America. In the developing world, the power distance in organizations is much greater (Hofstede 1997, 26–29). In small power distance societies, power is based on formal position and expertise rather than on family, friends, and charisma. They also tend to have pluralist government structures instead of autocratic or oligarchic governments (43).

Hofstede's second dimension is that of *collectivist versus individualist societies.* In individualist societies, organizations tend to pay more attention to task than to personal relationships, while this is reversed in collectivist societies. Northwestern European and North American countries score high on the individualism dimension (52–54). In individualist societies, state and government play a restrained role in the economic system, political power is exercised by voters, there is freedom of the press, there is a pursuit of equality before the law, and so forth (73). It is in this type of society that economics as a discipline was founded upon the idea that the pursuit of individual self-interest would lead to maximum wealth of nations through an "invisible hand" (Hofstede 1997, 71).

Hofstede's third dimension differentiates societies according to the degree to which they have clearly distinct gender roles. In *masculine* societies, men are supposed to be assertive, tough, and focused on material success, while in *feminine* societies, the social gender roles overlap. With respect to this dimension, the United States ranks among the masculine countries (although not nearly as high as, for instance, Japan, Austria, and Venezuela), while the Scandinavian countries and the Netherlands rank highest on femininity (Hofstede 1997, 82–84). It will come as no surprise that governments in masculine societies favor individual performance. They also appear to spend less on development aid and spend relatively more on defense. Also, the number of women in elected political positions is smaller than in feminine societies. The latter emphasize welfare policies, spend relatively large amounts of money on development aid, and pay more attention for, to instance, environmental policy (Hofstede 1997, 103).

Hofstede's final dimension concerns the degree of *uncertainty avoidance.* In countries that score high on uncertainty avoidance, such as Greece, Portugal, and Guatemala, there is an emotional need for precision, punctuality, and written and unwritten rules. Uncertainty is regarded as a threat rather than as a fact of life or even an opportunity, as is the case in countries with weak uncertainty avoidance (Hofstede 1997, 123–125). Northwestern European and

North American countries score low on uncertainty avoidance, as do several of the former British colonies or current dominions (Canada, Hong Kong, India, Malaysia, and New Zealand). In terms of traditions of governance and government, cultures with strong uncertainty avoidance tend to have a more intolerant attitude toward varying political and religious ideologies. Also, citizens are more repressed, attitudes toward the young are more negative, and there is a tendency toward grand theories of societal development. Grand theories in philosophy and science are more quickly conceived in high uncertainty avoidance cultures; Hofstede mentions Germany and France as examples. In contrast, weak avoidance cultures are much more tolerant toward religious and political variation and have a more positive attitude toward youth. With respect to philosophy and science, the low avoidance cultures have produced great empiricists (such as Newton, Linnaeus, and Darwin) who theorize on the basis of induction (Hofstede 1997, 133).

Of these four dimensions, Hofstede argues that power distance and uncertainty avoidance are especially relevant to thinking about organizations. The American business professor Stevens characterizes some Western organizational cultures that also happen to have had major influence upon organizational theory (Hofstede 1997, 140–143). The organization model in France, according to Stevens's characterization, is a *pyramid of people* with a general manager at the top and with each subordinate level at a proper place. Conflict is resolved through managerial intervention. Henri Fayol's emphasis upon unity of command as an organizational principle thus has a clear cultural basis (1987). In Hofstede's analysis, this model is illustrative of a culture with a large power distance and with strong uncertainty avoidance. Stevens argues that Germans see the organization as a *well-oiled machine* where management intervention should be limited to exceptions and daily problems ought to be settled by rules as much as possible. In this model we can recognize Weber's emphasis upon the importance of rules in organizations. In Hofstede's analysis, rule-boundedness is characteristic for a country with small power distance and high uncertainty avoidance. In Stevens's view, British culture looks upon organizations as a *village market* where neither hierarchy nor rules determine what happens. Instead, the demands of the situation provide guidance to managers. In the United States, we see this type of reasoning in the work of Mary Parker Follett (Follett 1920; Fry 1989, 98–120). We also see it in the work of Frederick Taylor (1996), who was interested not in authority or rules, but in the most efficient production methods. Also, there is more reliance on expertise. In Hofstede's framework, reliance on expertise is illustrative of countries with small power distances and weak uncertainty avoidance. Hofstede also attempts to show how his work is relevant to organizational theorists. He links Mintzberg's five different parts of organizations (strategic apex, middle line, operating core, support staff, and technostructure; see Figure 10.5), five different coordination mechanisms (mutual adjustment, direct supervision, standardization of skills, standardization of work processes, and standardization of outputs), and five typical organizational configurations (adhocracy, simple structure, professional bureaucracy, full bureaucracy, and divisionalized form) to his dimensions of uncertainty avoidance and power distance for five different countries (China, France, Germany, Great Britain, and the United States). By way of example, Great Britain is then characterized by low uncertainty avoidance, low power distance, adhocracy, mutual adjustment, and support staff. France, on the other hand, is characterized by high uncertainty avoidance, high power distance, full bureaucracy, standardization of work processes, and technostructure. The United States occupies the middle, with a divisionalized form, standardization of outputs, and middle line (Hofstede 1997, 152).

Hofstede's 1997 study contains an extra dimension, Confucian dynamism, which is relevant to Asian and African countries. This dimension refers to a long-term orientation in life in contrast to the short-term orientations and need for immediate gratification in Western culture. In a Confucian culture, behavior is virtuous when one works hard, is patient, displays perseverance, and does not spend more money than necessary. The organizational prototype or model fitting that culture is the *family* (Hofstede 1997, 164–165, 171).We can assume that this is an extended family understood not only in terms of a blood or marriage relationship but also in terms of *organizational family*. The American concept of *church family* is somewhat comparable. Hofstede discusses certain (Protestant?) elements of Confucianism and disregards its (Catholic?) inclination to strive for moral perfection (e.g., Dror 2001, 13) through rote memorization of "traditional" values (Mooney 2002, 51). The Confucian culture can especially be found in Southeast Asian, Arabic, and Mediterranean countries. In a study written to help American business people understand their French and German counterparts, Hall and Hall define *high-context cultures* as those where people, and thus managers, place much emphasis on extensive informal networks and trust, where there is a relaxed view of time, and where punctuality is not very important. In *low-context cultures,* on the other hand, managers operate on the basis of explicit, clear, written forms of communication, economize their time, and mind being interrupted (Hall and Hall 1990, 6–7; also Leeds, Kirkbride, and Duncan 1994, 12–13).

It is important to recognize that societal and organizational cultures and values are as much subject to change as anything. Hofstede's work spawned many studies. A recent study showed that value structures are not static. In a survey conducted twenty years after Hofstede's initial survey, Fernandez et al. (1997) found significant shifts. The United States had moved from being a weak to a strong uncertainty avoidance country, and Germany and the United States had moved from being masculine to being more feminine. At the same time, however, rankings for power distance and individualism had not changed much. External environmental changes account for these shifts, especially changes in the domestic economy, changes in how a population perceives the economy's strength, and changes in what people desire government to do. These environmental pressures have not only changed public organizational culture in the past two decades. Indeed, the reforms in and of government since the 1880s have had lasting impact on the structure and functioning of government.

10.4. Government Reform in the United States, 1880s–1990s: Types, Motives, and Timing

Above, I argued that public sector reform in the past century has had a tendency to be focused on the managerial and technical levels and predominantly focused on efficiency. This tendency goes back to the reform motives of the Progressive Era. It is useful to adopt a cross-time perspective, for that will demonstrate how much government reform as a planned, continuous, large-scale effort is the normal situation (but see Chandler 1977; and Nelson 1982). Domestic environmental changes do not allow for a protracted status quo period in governmental structure and functioning.

The nature and direction of reform can be characterized by looking at its territorial and functional dimensions. In terms of direction, a reform can be limited to one government level (horizontal direction) or may include a reshuffling of responsibilities between tiers of government (vertical direction). In terms of their nature, reforms can be territorial, functional, or a combination of these. Amalgamation and regionalization are examples of territorial, horizontal reform. Examples of functional horizontal reforms are departmentalization, (de)bureaucratization, and civil service reform. (De)centralization and (de)concentration are two examples of territorial vertical reforms, while changes in planning structures or central-local financial relations are examples of functional vertical reforms. These types of reforms concern government at the managerial and technical levels only. Since these reforms are focused on changing the internal structure and functioning of government, they reflect a change of government's role and position in society. Changes in the institutional or constitutional level are reactive to changes at the technical and managerial levels, but they generally do not significantly change the existing constitutional framework.

In the United States, as everywhere else, government reform has been a function of increased demand of the public at large for more public services.

The development and change of public bureaucracy in the United States have been characterized in terms of *gradualism* (it did not happen overnight), *experimentalism* (developing different types of bureaucratic organizations), *majoritarianism* (public demand), and *complexity* (in terms of size and organizational differentiation) (Stillman 1992, 71). These four features are just as characteristic of the development of government in other Western countries. The following description is based on Stillman's account (1992, 50–74, unless stated otherwise) and is by and large illustrative of comparable developments throughout the Western world. Obviously, when descending into detail there are differences between countries, but the general response to such environmental changes as industrialization, urbanization, demographic growth, and so forth was *grosso modo* very similar.

I will not discuss the expansion of public policy from a few core areas in the late eighteenth century to a wide range of areas in the late twentieth century in great detail. Some of that has already been outlined in chapter 8. In this chapter, I look at the consequences of these societal developments for the internal structure and functioning of government. I do so by discussing changes in organizational structure, in jurisdictional structure, in administrative procedures, and in the preparation and management of reform.

Reforms of Organizational Structure

The organizational structure of the U.S. government at the time of independence was quite simple. Government at the local level was very small and generally based on voluntary effort and civic duty. At the federal level, four departments (State, War, Treasury, and Postal Services; Navy split off from War to become a separate department in 1798) and one office (that of the attorney general) were created. In response to the westward expansion, the Department of the Interior was created in 1849 to facilitate domestic growth and national development. A real surge of departmentation (i.e., the creation of a new department) and reorganization (of an existing department) occurred during and immediately following the Civil War. The Department of Agriculture was established in 1862 with special responsibilities for overseeing the execution of the Morrill Act (land grants to agricultural colleges in Western states) and the Homestead Act (opening public land to homesteaders), which had passed Congress in the same year. This department was headed by a commission and acquired cabinet status in 1889. Other reforms concerned reorganizations, including expansion, of existing departments. In 1870, the Office of the Attorney General was elevated to cabinet status through the creation of the Department of Justice. In 1866, the Freedman's Bureau was added to the War Department to help former slaves. The Controller of the Currency (1863), the Secret Service (1865), and the Internal Revenue Service (1866) were established within the Treasury.

Since the late nineteenth century, two other types of public organizations have emerged. *Regulatory agencies* and *commissions* have been created to oversee and regulate private corporate trusts, basically to curtail the enormous political influence these trusts had acquired on the basis of their sheer financial and economic power. The government's response to public demand (for instance, from individual farmers and small businesses) was twofold. First, through legislation, such as the Sherman Anti-Trust Act of 1890, government hoped to break up the large trusts. Second, government created regulatory commissions to supervise private enterprise. The first of these was the Interstate Commerce Commission of 1887, which supervised railroad development. The second type was the *government corporation,* an organizational device designed to quickly develop new programs and policies in areas such as roads, schools, and public utilities. The first government corporation was the one that operated the Panama Canal, but the most well known is probably the Tennessee Valley Authority (TVA) of 1933. Since the early twentieth century, a variety of regulatory commissions and agencies and more than a hundred government corporations have been created. Currently, there are sixty regulatory commissions and corporations (Cann 1995, 12–13) with almost a million employees.

Especially during the New Deal period, a variety of new agencies was created in the effort to battle the economic depression. The TVA has already been mentioned. Equally important were, for instance, the Civilian Conservation Corps (1933), the Federal Emergency Relief Administration (1933), the Works Progress Administration (1935), and the Federal Security Agency (1939). With the exception of the creation of the Department of Commerce and Labor (1903; split into two in 1913), departmentation was not the favored reform type between the Civil War and World War II. After 1945, however, departmentation again became popular, a testimony to the expansion of the American welfare state. In 1949, the Departments of War and Navy were amalgamated into the Department of Defense. The first new department was the Department of Health, Education and Welfare (1953), which split in 1979 into the Department of Health and Human Services and the Department of Education. Other new departments were those of Housing and Urban Development (1965), Transportation (1966), Energy (1977), and Veterans Affairs' (1989) (Shafritz 1988, 166; Bosso, Portz, and Tolley 2000, 437). On a side note, in Western Europe, health and housing departments had been established before or shortly after World War I.

By way of summary, it is through the reorganization of structure that government has served three categories of functions (the distinction after Bosso,

Portz, and Tolley 2000, 434–441). The first group of functions is *basic services* in areas such as foreign policy and defense, taxation, justice and police, mail, education, housing, and health. These benefit the population as a whole. A second group of functions is focused on specific target groups, such as farmers (e.g., Department of Agriculture, 1862), private entrepreneurs (e.g., Department of Commerce, 1913), employees (e.g., Department of Labor, 1913), and veterans (Department of Veterans' Affairs in 1989). The third group of functions are the *regulatory policies* that do not provide a service but supervise private corporate and individual activity in a particular area. These include economic and financial regulations ever since 1887 (e.g., the Federal Reserve System, 1913; the National Labor Relations Board, 1935), safety regulations (e.g., the Occupational Safety and Health Administration, 1970), and environmental regulations (e.g., the Environmental Protection Agency, 1970).

Reforms in Jurisdictional Structure

The reorganizations in the public sector described above can also be regarded as changes in the jurisdictional structure. Departments, regulatory agencies, and government corporations hold jurisdiction over a specific policy area. While we have discussed only the federal government, similar developments occurred at the state and local levels (e.g., Garnett 1980). The growth of government services at all levels of government also had major consequences for the relations between levels of government. At the local level, the jurisdictional boundaries changed most in the twentieth century. In the effort to improve the local economies of scale, widespread amalgamation and annexation occurred in the general-purpose governments and more specifically in the urban areas. This resulted in a proliferation of local government departments. It was accompanied by an enormous growth of specific purpose governments at the local level (Burns 1994). This development is parallel to the establishment of agencies and corporations at the federal level.

The emergence of the administrative state since the late nineteenth century also resulted in a strengthening of the ties between the local, state, and federal levels of government. As far back as the mid-nineteenth century, federal government had supported local and regional development, but it has only been since the Great Depression of the 1930s that a system of intergovernmental relations was established that involved three types of intertwinement. First, there are the *financial relations,* such as through the allocation of block and specific grants. Second, there are the *cooperative relations* between levels of government for the planning and implementation of policy. Third, there are the *regulatory relations,* such as those where federal legislation and regulation have consequences for the state and local levels. The importance of intergovernmental relations was underlined by the creation of the Advisory Commission on Intergovernmental Relations in 1959 (abolished in 1996).

Reforms in Administrative Procedures

The twentieth century has also witnessed a great variety of reforms in administrative procedures. Reforms in the fields of personnel and budget occurred almost simultaneously at local, state, and federal levels. At the federal level, the Civil Service Reform Act of 1883 (also known as the Pendleton Act), the Retirement Act of 1920, and the Job Classification Act of 1923 are landmarks in the development of the civil service. The Budget and Accounting Act of 1921, which created the Bureau of the Budget (since 1970, the Office of Management and Budget), is of equal importance with respect to the federal budget. The 1939 Reorganization Act established the Executive Office of the President (EOP), which, from then on, would include the Bureau of the Budget. The Administrative Procedure Act of 1946 heralded an effort to standardize administrative practices across federal agencies.

Several federal laws and regulations since World War II have had immediate consequences for subnational government. By executive orders, President Kennedy established affirmative action (1961) and allowed unionization of federal employees (1962). The Civil Rights Act of 1964 was instrumental in establishing equal employment opportunity. Since then this act has provided the basis for an array of acts and regulations in the field of personnel management.

Reforms in the Preparation and Management of Encompassing Reform

A final feature of government reform in the twentieth century is that it has become more encompassing and increasingly pursued on the basis of the work of special advisory commissions. These commissions have been specifically instrumental in changing the executive branch of the federal government (the following is based on Cozzetto, Pedeliski, and Tipple 1996, 32). Among the earliest are the Keep Commission (1905–1909), which advised on personnel and information management and contracting out; the President's Commission on Economy and Efficiency (1910–1913), which advocated a national executive budget; and the Joint Committee on Reorganization (1921–1924), which explored methods to redistribute executive functions. Among the better known of these commissions are the President's Committee on Administrative Management (1936–1937, also known as the

Brownlow Commission), which served as the basis for strengthening the executive powers of the presidency; the First and Second Hoover Commissions (1947–1949, 1953–1955), which, first, advised on ways to expand the managerial capacity of the EOP and, second, recommended the curtailing and abolishment of federal government activities that competed with private enterprise; the Ash Council (1969–1971), which called for the amalgamation of government departments into four super departments; the Grace Commission (1982–1984) which surveyed inefficiencies in federal government; the Volcker Commission (1987–1989), which recommended a revitalization of the civil service; and the National Performance Review (1993–2000), which aimed at a reinvention of federal government.

As I remarked at the opening of this section, most Western governments have experienced the same types of reforms. It is useless to provide a list of publications that would substantiate this statement because such a list would be huge. Reforms in organizational structures, jurisdictional structures, and administrative procedures have been reported for most Western countries. Likewise, other government reforms, in Austria, France, Germany, Great Britain, the Netherlands, and Spain (Raadschelders and Toonen, 1999, 48–49), have been pursued through special commissions and have also become more encompassing in that they increasingly target the structure and functioning of government as a whole.

How has this century of reform affected the organizational culture in the public sector? To date, there is no general study available in which this question has been addressed. No doubt, studies of the development of various government departments and agencies provide a useful starting point for such a study. At the moment, we can only say that increased government intervention in terms of direct service delivery and in terms of regulation has resulted in a bureaucratization of government. This bureaucratization is expressed not only in the proliferation of organizational units (departments, agencies, but also intraorganizational differentiation), but also in the vast standardization of structure and functioning within and between levels of government. As a consequence, bureaucracy in the eyes of the citizens comes across as inaccessible, coldhearted, and impersonal. The activities of those who work in public organizations have increasingly been subjected to formal, written rules and regulations. Thus, the small-scale, personal government of a century ago has given way to the large-scale, impersonal government of today. In terms of government-society relations and of intergovernmental relations, this has resulted in a call for debureaucratization, deregulation, decentralization, privatization, and so forth. With respect to the internal structure and functioning of government, reforms have especially been pursued in the area of manager-subordinate relations.

10.5. Government Reform in the World, 1980s–1990s: Globalization and Localization

Reform of the public sector has been widespread in the postwar decades, and it has compelled government to look across national boundaries for new ideas and for different applications. Indeed, as Peters remarked, there is no shortage of ideas. Rather, there are too many ideas and a lack of systematic thinking about what is applicable in what situations and about the compatibility of ideas (Peters 1996, 128).

Attention to the collective and constitutional levels of public sector reform cannot but include a focus on participating actors (i.e., the political-administrative system, including all participants) as well as on the foundations of civil society since the concept of the *public sector* includes not only government itself, but all institutions, organizations, and associations that are somehow or other involved in tending to public issues.

It is revealing that the triumph of the managerial approach is accompanied by a growing awareness of truly collective concerns, of participatory democracy and of civil society. To reverse the argument that government usually steps in when the market fails, it is no longer obvious that in case of public failure, the market should step in. Added to this, a case can also easily be made that in case of market failure, government should step in, especially when societal values at large are at stake. Here, too, Keynes's observation that government should do those things that are not done by others is relevant. Environmental policy provides an excellent example. Although the public at large increasingly expressed concern for the environment, it was government that addressed that concern through legislation and thus set the example. Both participatory democracy and civil society inevitably draw attention to the role of individual citizens in public policy making and implementation and the role of associations of whatever kind between state and market. Thus it appears that attention is no longer limited to government reform only, but is increasingly concerned with a recasting of the relation between citizen and government (e.g., one-stop-shop, citizen's charters, work-welfare programs).

This has opened up the debate about the proper balance between individual and collective responsibility: what are our current, shared values? That individualism and collectivism are at the root of the discussion is clear from all that has been said about the future of the welfare state. There is, however, little experience with reorganizing a welfare state. And how could there be? The appeal to civil society and the development of, for instance, work-welfare programs are hesitant attempts to establish a different division of labor between government and society. Some of the government-citizen reforms focus on the direct, face-to-face interaction with individual citizens in localized communities (neighborhood councils). But most of these types of reform are concerned with the rather abstract society level and are pursued in a more indirect, dispersed manner. Some have direct impact upon the individual, such as one-stop-shop offices. More frequently, however, reforms seek to influence the collective level. Good examples are the citizen charters, but they are too general and too romantic to serve any real purpose. The alternative of privatization involves the total transfer of authority to the private sector. Another avenue is the separation of policy making from execution, where policy making remains within the public realm (political authority) and the execution may be left to the private sector (e.g., contracting out). This type of separation suggests that public direction is clear enough for private execution to be followed to the letter. That a policy implementation gap exists or even that goal displacement may occur is a possibility that is not considered or viewed only as a remote chance at best. In view of Rainey's degrees of publicness, we cannot really satisfactorily draw a line between public and private, and so that organizational option to the solution of social problems is closed. Equally simplistic is the idea that policy making and execution can be separated, and so that avenue is closed as well. This leaves the mixed solution that can only work if the issue of democratic control is settled. As seductive as the promises of managerialism are, they leave little concern for the human being if not balanced by the value of democracy as a principle equally important to the shaping of governments' role in society.

It appears that widespread government reforms have been fueled by the Anglo-Saxon countries. Kettl recently distinguished between two broad models, the Westminster- and the reinvention-style reforms (2000a). The *Westminster-style reforms* originated in New Zealand in the early 1980s and were quickly adopted by the British government under Prime Minister Thatcher. They involved widespread privatization, the introduction of market incentives, a focus on output budgeting, and attention to customer services (Kettl 2000a, 8–12, 42). The American *reinvention-style reforms,* which followed about a decade later, involved downsizing (especially at the federal level, cutting middle management), performance management (e.g., the Government Performance and Results Act of 1993), widespread decentralization, and increased attention to customer services (Kettl 2000a, 19–27, 41).

There is little doubt that these reforms have occurred in other parts of the world. In Western countries they occurred simultaneously from the early 1980s onward. If there was spillover from the Anglo-Saxon style reforms in continental Europe, it was a function of copying behavior on a voluntary basis. Many Western countries are faced with the challenge of reforming the welfare state and establishing a different public-private mix in the production of collective services. In the non-Western world, however, spillover has been a function of unilateral dependency. Increasingly, Western countries and international actors such as the International Monetary Fund (IMF) and World Bank more or less demand Western-styled reform programs as a condition for loans and development aid (Adamolekun 1999; Farazmand 1999). It does not appear that Western donors have taken Aldrich's observation to heart, that "innovations have failed when introduced into societies with non-supportive cultural and institutional traditions" (Aldrich 1979, 22).

It has been argued that the fact of worldwide reform is an expression of globalization, but this statement needs to be qualified. It is true that in economy and trade, there has been growing interdependence. It is equally true that the information revolution has brought governments and people closer together. Globalization defined as intertwinement is especially relevant at the technical and managerial levels, and some convergence can be seen with regard to the language of reform. As far as the institutional level is concerned, globalization defined as homogenization is much less an issue. In the words of Hofstede:

> A worldwide homogenization of mental programs about power and dependence, independence, and interdependence under the influence of a presumed cultural melting-pot process, is still very far away, if it will ever happen. (1997, 47)

Thus the globalization of economy and of information flows is accompanied by enhanced awareness of cultural distinctness, and so the concept of globalization then becomes much less clear-cut than many realize.

10.6. Decentration in Various Guises: Recent Trends

The larger an organization becomes, the more it requires a delicate balancing between specialization and the parceling out of tasks and authority on the one hand and maintaining some degree of integration and coordination on the other. There is not one best way to do this. An organization of some size experiences both centrifugal and centripetal forces. Centrifugal forces, which Mintzberg labels as the *pull to balkanize* (Mintzberg 1979, 302), will be found among the specialists and immediately below the top of an organization. At the top, the need to maintain adequate control, the *pull to centralize*, dominates. In his attempt to identify the laws and regularities of bureaucracies' functioning, Downs formulates three laws that concern the consequences of increased organizational size (Downs 1967, 271). The *Law of Imperfect Control* refers to the fact that no individual or collegial board can fully control the behavior of large organizations. The *Law of Decreasing Coordination* hypothesizes that as organizations grow larger, their coordination worsens. And finally, the *Law of Diminishing Control* suggests that as organizations grow larger, the control of the top over its actions becomes weaker. While certainly relevant to organizations and provocative in their content, these are not laws in a natural science sense. At best, they are hypotheses that can be (and have been) tested. The central problem here, of course, is the size of the organization. In Downs's formulation, only a continuum from smaller to ever larger size is stated, while implicitly the issue of the proper or optimum size is suggested. Some scholars believe that such an optimum exists for every type of organization (e.g., Boulding 1953, 78), while others argue that the very concept of optimum size would require an objective yardstick (Pfiffner and Sherwood 1960, 445). Such a yardstick, however, does not exist. Instead, people generally do not agree about what is considered big, too big, or too small. The problem that increased organizational size raises is that of balancing the need for functional specialization and organizational differentiation, on the one hand, and integration and increased coordination on the other. These managerial concerns and challenges cannot be solved in a technocratic manner through the application of some type of administrative reform. Instead, they generally require reflection about the concentration and dispersion of authority.

In the context of organizational theory, the concentration and dispersion of authority concerns the balancing of decentralization and centralization. These can be defined as static concepts, in which case they refer to an existing and a desired situation. This static approach emphasizes the legalist aspect of (de)centralization. If defined as dynamic concepts, emphasizing the sociological aspects, they point to the constant balancing of the two forces. Usually some degree of centralization is a fact, while more decentralization is a desire (Figure 10.6).

Decentralization (or, in the United States and England, devolution) involves the transfer of tasks *and* authority from a higher to a lower level of government. *Deconcentration* (or field administration) only involves the transfer of tasks to smaller geographical units, dispersed across the territory. The Internal Revenue Service in the United States, for instance, has branches across the country while the ultimate decision-making authority continues to rest with the federal Department of the Treasury. Intraorganizational decentralization would, for instance, include the replacement of one central personnel department (or any other staff unit, for that matter) that serves the entire organization by a system of personnel units for every major line unit.

The question whether more centralization or more decentralization is required, is—like most questions about organizations—not one that can be addressed a priori in objective zero-sum terms. In reminiscence of Simon, measures of centralization and of decentralization need to be determined (Smith 1985, 83–91). Next, a threshold has to be defined. When is there too much

Figure 10.6   **Statics and Dynamics of Processes of Task and Authority Distribution or the Balancing of Centralization and Decentralization**

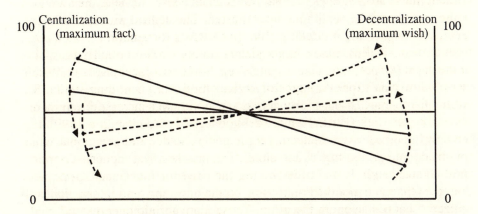

centralization? Finally, who is involved in determining where that threshold lies? When a consensus is achieved about these three issues (reliable indicators/measures, the threshold, who decides), another major challenge is determining what resources will accompany the transfer of tasks and authority. As with the first three problems, resource decisions are highly political matters that involve the explication of values more than anything else. Generally, processes of decentralization between tiers of government and between levels in organizations are used as budget-cutting procedures. Seldom does the lower level receive the same amount of money the higher level had when responsible for a particular service.

Decentralization is a type of reform where the national/federal level of government transfers tasks, authority, and (hopefully sufficient) financial resources to lower-level governments. Public sector tasks have also been partially or entirely off-loaded to semigovernmental or private partners. What connects decentralization with other types of off-loading is *decentration.* By definition, decentralization can only involve public partners. Contracting-out and "agencyfication" may involve public or private partners. Privatization, by definition, only involves private partners. In the United States, contracting-out and privatization efforts are based in the belief that reliance on nongovernmental contractors and private companies reduces costs and improves results, while in England and New Zealand, they are based in the belief that government sets policy and that execution can be left to other partners (Kettl 2000a, 39). Kettl points out that evidence of savings does not necessarily mean that contractors or private suppliers provide the same quality service nor does it mean that they have a focus on fairness and equality.

Contracting-out, which has been popular in most Western countries, involves an expansion of partnerships between governmental actors as well as between governments and private actors. Privatization has not been as important in the United States as in Europe, simply because there were never as many public enterprises as in Europe. In Europe, on the other hand, there was a privatization craze as Wright calls it (1995, 3). Wright makes a distinction between timid (Greece and Sweden), middle-range (Belgium, Italy, the Netherlands, and Spain), and radical (France, Germany, Great Britain, and Portugal) privatizers (Wright 1994). Paul Van Riper outlines the motives for government intervention and warns that contracting-out and privatization may very well increase government's role in monitoring contracts while raising issues of accountability (1999). It is equally important to remember that the municipalization and/or nationalization of private enterprises (such as gas, electricity, water supply, telephone, and transport companies) in late nineteenth- and early twentieth-century Europe were based on the same motives (innovation, cost cutting, service accessibility to all citizens) that now support contracting-out and privatization arguments.

Many decentration efforts involve debureaucratization and deregulation. While these concepts are not synonymous, both define efforts to make government functioning more flexible. Debureaucratization, which has permeated government at all levels, concerns attempts to simplify administrative routines and procedures. It also involves programs to reduce transaction costs and to make government more transparent for the citizenry. In the United States (Ingraham 1999, 180) as elsewhere, debureaucratization efforts include simplified classification and compensation procedures for civil servants, increased emphasis on teamwork, increased partnership between public organizations and private citizens as members of civic associations, and partnerships between public and private providers of collective services.

Deregulation specifically refers to the reduction of government regulations. Again, this is a widespread reform and not only limited to Western countries (Kettl 2000a, 47). Some deregulation measures concern personnel and organizational structures. Others are focused on managerial practices, such as in the area of procurement. Initially, in the early 1980s, deregulation referred particularly to the reform of intergovernmental relations, which was a response to the demand for more administrative decentralization in the 1970s. It simultaneously involved (re)regulation at the subnational level. From the late 1980s on, however, deregulation has primarily been defined in terms of establishing market-type mechanisms (MTMs) for the provision and production of public services. As with privatization, it is probably too early to tell whether deregulation has actually been successful in creating MTMs for services that are less costly than former publicly provided services. But there are signs that the results are mixed, to say the least, and the recent problems of the state of California with its energy supply are just one illustration.

10.7. The Structuring of Communication and Information

The reforms discussed in sections 10.5 and 10.6 do not all influence the structure and functioning of public organizations to the same degree. What has influenced government at large is the structuring of communication processes and of information. I will not dwell in detail upon the hardware of the technological revolution. Instead, I first discuss the standardization of communication and then the mechanisms of information collection and distribution.

According to Simon and his coauthors Smithburg and Thompson (1964), the communication process was the vehicle upon which processes of coordination and compromise were possible, and it has become a major topic of interest in recent public administration (e.g., Garnett and Kouzmin 1997). Blockage of communication, so Simon, Smithburg, and Thompson reason, was also a central problem for public administration and could occur at any time in the communication process.

They distinguish between seven interrelated blockages or barriers, some of which are institutional and others psychological in nature (Simon, Smithburg, and Thompson 1964, 229–243). The *barrier of language* refers to the existence of different vocabularies. Understanding what someone is saying depends on familiarity with the words or jargon used. People also have varying *frames of references*. The message sent may be understood differently by the receiver, simply because the receiver regards other elements of the message as more important. *Status distance* especially operates vertically in an organization. Subordinates will gloss over mistakes and present favorable information to superiors. Superiors do not like to be bothered with the day-to-day concerns of the lower levels and at the same time may not wish to express their ignorance of what happens on the work floor, so they thus gloss over their own limitations. Related to the status distance barrier is the inborn need of *self-protection.* Individuals will not quickly transmit unfavorable information. *Geographical distance* has not become any less of a problem than it was at the time Simon, Smithburg, and Thompson wrote their study. Even though the technological capabilities have increased enormously in the past five decades, there is still no substitute for face-to-face interaction. In terms of technology, of course, there are, it appears, no limits to the amounts of information that can be processed every day. In this sense, geographical distance has become less important. What technology cannot solve, however, is the fact that because of geographical distance, various local branches of the same organization (for instance, the IRS) can move into directions that differ from the official policies and guidelines of the central organization. The *pressure of work* can prevent messages from being processed. And finally *censorship* of information and communication is a method invoked, for instance, when national security is believed to be at stake.

With respect to communication, much attention in the literature has been focused on the consequences of technological advancement for the decision-making process and for the psychology of communication processes. Less attention has been given to the rule-bound nature of communication in policy- and decision-making processes. Policy and decision makers have meetings and conferences at which they negotiate and bargain. All of these processes have been increasingly embedded in rules of personal conduct as well as rules of procedure. The proliferation and refinement of rules illustrate the rationalization process Max Weber analyzed as well as the civilizing process in Western society from the age of Charlemagne (768–814 C.E.) onward (Elias 1982; see also Van Vree 1994, 287–290). With respect to the Western world, since more than 1,000 years ago, meetings have become increasingly regulated, starting with the need to keep minutes and register decisions. In the early modern period (say, from 1500 to 1795), fixed meeting times and places, a division of labor (the chairperson, etc.), voting rights and vetoes, rules concerning presence and absence (with the appropriate rewards or penalties), arrangements for opening and closing and for speech time were established. From the early nineteenth century on, the do's and don'ts in formal meetings were elaborated in great detail. This formalization of meetings was a response to the growing number of meetings and testifies to the growing interdependencies between people and their private and public organizations. In general, one can say that the more complex society and government become, and the more each individual expects from the other, the more procedures tend to overshadow the substance of policy making.

There is no better illustration of the formalization of codes of conduct and proper procedure in public meetings than when a manual is published to replace on-the-job training. Among the earliest of such manuals is *Jefferson's Manual,* published in 1823 and intended to regulate the meetings of the U.S. Senate. Shortly after its publication, this manual was accepted as the official rule of order. It fitted quite well with the American appreciation of meetings. In the observation of de Tocqueville:

> The cares of politics engross a prominent place in the occupations of a citizen in the United States; and almost the only pleasure which an American knows is to take a part in the government, and to discuss its measures. . . . An American cannot converse, but he can discuss; and his talk falls into a dissertation. He speaks to you as if he was addressing a meeting; and if he should chance to become warm in the discussion, he will say "Gentleman" to the person with whom he is conversing. (1984, 109)

Not so long ago, a heated discussion could end in a fistfight or duel. But from the early nineteenth century on, the code of conduct demanded some measure of restraint. As technology became more advanced, the need for more formalization of meetings increased. Throughout the twentieth century, manuals have been published on how to conduct meetings, thus testifying to increasing professionalization. In the first half of the last century, these manuals were juridical by nature and focused on formal, parliamentary procedures. From the 1940s onward, attention increasingly centered on the social and psychological side of meetings. Both the juridical and the social and psychological elements of meetings have resulted in the development of training methods, especially in the United States. The United States is also the country where almost half of the meeting manuals have been published: Van Vree counted some 800 titles, of which 380 were by American authors, 100 by English, 170 by German, 120 by Dutch (of which several were translated from American sources), and 50 by French authors (1994, 233).

Communicating information in whatever manner is central to the fulfillment of the needs of individuals and people. Communication is what binds members of organizations to each other and to their relevant publics. But even if the barriers of communication have all been conquered, there is no guarantee that the policy decided upon will be implemented in the desired manner. While this issue will be pursued in the next chapter, it should be pointed out that, in Heffron's words, organization theory still suffers from conflicts that remain unsolved. Should the focus be on formal or informal structure? Is the proper approach rationalism or humanism? Should organizational goals emphasize efficiency and effectiveness or equity and democracy? Should the organization have a sense of responsibility for the personal and professional development and satisfaction of the employee or not? (Heffron 1982, 8). In line with the argument in this chapter, I argue that such a dichotomous presentation of problems may be attractive for analytical reasons but it obscures the fact that, in reality, a balancing of extremes rather than a choice between extremes characterizes the structure and functioning of organizations.

Not only has the communication process become more formalized but the amount of information digested daily through specialized channels has increased exponentially in the past few decades, placing a heavier burden upon those responsible for coordinating policy. The mechanism of the collection and dissemination of information about social reality has become simpler, courtesy of the introduction of the computer and of globalization. Kettl recently argued that the development of fast communication systems is at the core of globalization and that this has transformed the system of governance fundamentally. In his words:

Widely accessible and affordable technology has broken governments' monopoly on the collection and management of large amounts of information and deprived governments of the deference they enjoyed because of it. (2000b, 491)

He also claims that globalization has helped to homogenize cultures, for instance, through the expanded use of the English language as the *lingua franca* of the world (2000b, 492). I do not believe that cultures homogenize. No doubt, language is an important aspect of culture, but the use of English as the international language does not necessarily change the way in which an organization functions. The speed of communication and the mechanism used do have serious consequences.

The most visible consequence of the computer upon public and private organizations at large is that it has strengthened and confirmed the dominating organizational structure of bureaucracy. What bureaucracies and computers have in common, so Fraser argues, is that they must work reliably by fixed laws and without ambiguity. Computers also contribute to a homogenization of thought, simply by virtue of the type of information that can be stored: facts and figures rather than inferences, interpretations, analyses, multidisciplinary insights, and so forth (Fraser 1987, 327). A second consequence is that electronic information exchange is the latest in a series of inventions that have rapidly shortened the *width of the social present,* to use Fraser's term, which he defined as "the time necessary to make people take concerted action" (196). He describes how a Norwegian living in Philadelphia at the end of the eighteenth century and writing to his relatives in Bergen, Norway, would have to wait forty days for his letter to get there and another forty days for a reply. Hence, the width of the social present for him was eighty days. A series of inventions since then has decreased the width of the social present (and, of course, also changed office administration). The telegraph (invented in 1844) and telephone (end of the nineteenth century) have accelerated communication. The use of the steel pen (since the 1830s), the typewriter, and stenography (since the mid-nineteenth century) accelerated the speed with which information could be recorded. Around 1890 in the United States the invention of the punch card, linking paper and electricity, served the documentation of standard information. The invention of stencil and carbon paper around 1900 made handwritten copying of texts obsolete. Combining the properties of electricity and photography resulted in the invention of the copy machine in 1938. This was followed by the introduction of the computer in 1944 and electronic mail and fax machines in the 1970s. Each of these technologies has accelerated the exchange of information. What does this mean for the width of the social present? Basically, it has shrunk to a matter of seconds, and *waiting time,* the period of time that people are prepared to wait for a response, has shrunk as much. The major consequences of this declining of waiting time for the content and focus of policy and decision making will be explored in the next chapter.

Meanwhile, there is a third consequence of the use of computers and that concerns the technical challenge. Technological innovations succeed one another rapidly. It appears that electronic information stored with hardware and software in the 1970s is not very accessible—if at all—with newer technology. The National Archives may have to maintain operating hardware and software of different periods, so that information will not get lost. The challenge of dealing with the fragility of electronically stored information is equal for all Western governments, but might be more of a challenge to American government. As de Tocqueville observes,

> the acts of society in America often leave less trace than the actions of a simple family. . . . The only historical monuments of the United States are newspapers. . . . In fifty years it will be more difficult to gather authentic documents on the details of the social existence of Americans of our day than on the administration of the French in the Middle Ages. (de Tocqueville 2000, 198)

In Europe, most of the important government documents are stored electronically as well as in hard copy. Americans have less of a tradition of documenting and storing public action (with the exception of officeholders at the top of organizations) and thus preserving collective memory. This, too, is something that will be further explored in the next chapter.

10.8.   Concluding Remarks

Organizations have no basis for existence if they do not serve a particular objective. In this chapter, I described different organizational structures as they developed in the course of the twentieth century in response to significant environmental changes. I also discussed various ways in which organizational culture can be analyzed and how organizational culture has changed, in terms of bureaucratization (standardization, formalization, and so forth). The discussion in this chapter again demonstrates the importance of analyzing organizations as dynamic phenomena whose internal structure and functioning are embedded within an organization (the technical, managerial, and institutional levels) and in a larger organizational and societal environment. The development and growth of public bureaucracies at large, and their degrees of internal vertical and horizontal differentiation, are mainly a function of public demand and have fueled organizational reforms since the 1880s. The attention to the relation between organizational objective (efficiency) and organizational functioning (including an appreciation of supervisor-subordinate relations) is mainly a function of intraorganizational culture and has been a focus for reform only since the 1950s. With increased pressure from the public at large for better government that costs less, Greiner's observation (1972, 44) that intensity of teamwork and heavy pressure for innovative solutions would emotionally and physically exhaust employees has thus become true today.

In the Western world, public demand appears to fluctuate. Between the 1820s and the 1880s, the public called for a restricted government. In the 1880 to 1970 period, policy makers responded to a demand for a more efficient as well as a more interventionist government. In the three most recent decades, it appears that once again a more restricted government is desired. However, one thing that public organizations cannot do as easily as private organizations is abolish responsibilities they took upon themselves in earlier days. Fortunately, the rule of law prevents whimsical government and that may very well be the reason why a return to the days of small government is virtually impossible.

11 THE FUNCTIONING OF GOVERNMENT

"Representative government must not only represent, it must also govern" [has the] clear implication that representativeness comes at the expense of effective government.
—Arend Lijphart, 1999, quoting Samuel Beer

A great part of that order which reigns among mankind is not the effect of government.
—Thomas Paine

The quality of decision making is determined more by the intelligence, imagination, and knowledge of the policy advisor, than by formal decision making instruments.
—Graeme Donald Snook, 1993

Policy and decision making are crucial to understanding governance and government in the Western world, yet they are such commonplace notions that the question of when a policy—as it is understood today—was first designed is hardly ever raised. We should distinguish between international or foreign and domestic policy. Foreign policy has been conducted throughout the ages with one objective in mind: to protect and, if possible, to expand the integrity and the interests of a sovereignty. In this sense, foreign policy is international politics. For millennia, the ruler's domestic concerns were solely the maintenance of public order and safety and the ways and means to raise revenue.

It is only in the past two centuries that governments at large have turned their attention to domestic policy and have been forced to make it as important, if not more important, than international politics. The foundation of this domestic attention was based on ideas about freedom, liberty, and fraternity and about the value of the individual's life, liberty, and property. What forced the governments' attention to domestic policy was the sudden and very visible impact of the simultaneously occurring forces of population growth, industrialization, and urbanization. Wedged between the international politics of national sovereignty and the political theory of domestic welfare (*eudaimonia*), the nation-state emerged as the protector of international and of domestic concerns.

Governments at large, but especially local (urban) governments, faced the need to address the social consequences of economic growth. Modern policy and decision making found their origins in the need for urban planning, better housing, water supply, electricity, and so forth. Increasingly, domestic policy was supported by statistical data supplied by national governments. Policy making in the modern world was increasingly based on aggregate data of the demographic, economic, and social trends in an area. These data provided a foundation for *prospective* policy making, which distinguished between an existing and a desired state or standard of living and thus made policy making increasingly future- as well as input-oriented.

In this chapter, I focus on the functioning of government, and specifically on the processes that are involved in translating societal demand into public action. I first discuss the public policy-making process (section 11.1) and models of decision making (section 11.2). Next, attention will be paid to the planning and management of implementation (section 11.3) and the variety and use of policy instruments (section 11.4). Increasingly, public policy is evaluated in terms of efficiency and effectiveness. Government performance is assessed through policy evaluation, and we can see that performance is generally evaluated in a short-term perspective (section 11.5). In sections 11.1 to 11.5, these processes of policy making up to policy evaluation are presented in the manner in which they have been conceptualized in the Western world. While there is much case literature on each of these topics, there is generally a feeling that theory development is lagging behind (section 11.6). This is partially a consequence of the type of information that is considered objective and thus believed to legitimate policy making as well as considered useful for research (section 11.7).

There is, however, another explanation for our limited understanding of policy processes that is related to the cultural characteristics of Western government and society. How are policy processes conceptualized? Why are they conceptualized in a particular way? What does that mean for the understanding of Western government and, for instance, for the relevance and applicability of Western reform efforts in other parts of the world (section 11.8)? In the concluding section, I argue that managerialism based on aggregate data is a trap that does not enhance but severely limits the wisdom of public policy making.

11.1. Societal Concerns, Political Agendas, and Public Policy Making

There is a substantial body of literature focused on the *content* or *substance of public policy* that analyzes and sometimes evaluates policy in terms of objectives and impact on society. This type of literature is concerned with political

Table 11.1

The Interplay of Social and Bureaucratic Engineering

	Bureaucratic engineering	
Social engineering	High	Low
High	Substance and process	Substance
Low	Process	Neither substance nor process

value choices and thus with *social engineering* and is mostly pursued within political science (Henry 1999, 347). Since the content of public policy has been discussed in chapters 6 to 8, I will focus in this chapter on a second body of literature that is more identified as part of the study of public administration and concerns the *process of public policy making* as it unfolds from the stages of problem identification to implementation and evaluation. This literature focuses on how to structure functioning or process and thus can be said to regard *bureaucratic engineering.*

When public policy is both an expression of social and of bureaucratic engineering, hence when the public at large, interest groups, politicians, and civil servants recognize the urgency of a policy, attention is paid to both the content or substance as well as the process of policy making and implementation (e.g., Birkland 2001). When policy making is mainly an expression of social engineering, thus involving high political interest, it is focused more on substance and less on process. Public policy in this case is potentially focused on change rather than continuity and requires citizen involvement in its design. However, such a policy might be less successful for lack of bureaucratic interest. If, on the other hand, a particular public policy is illustrative of bureaucratic engineering, hence focused on (improving) process, the emphasis is much more on continuity and may require citizen involvement only when evaluating existing policy. In this case, continuity triumphs over change and less substantive policy changes can be expected (Table 11.1).

When public concerns fail to attract the attention of political and bureaucratic officeholders and thus do not result in efforts of social and bureaucratic engineering, neither substance nor process of existing policy will be subject to scrutiny. To understand this, we need to explore why some problems and issues attract political and/or bureaucratic attention and others do not. Various authors have addressed this issue. I will discuss several of them in terms of their emphasis on substance, on process, or on both.

Upon what grounds is it decided that a societal concern requires public decision making? It can be assumed that there is some type of process that determines what issues arrive at the public policy-making stage. The rational process would be one where political representatives listen to their constituencies, sit around the table, compile a list of public concerns, and subsequently rank them on the basis of carefully developed criteria. Reality is quite different, however. In literature, various explanations are offered as to why some issues make it to the public policy-making stage. They all provide insight into the process and are complementary rather than mutually exclusive.

Schattschneider reasons that people will find it easier to get political attention for their problem once they combine forces and organize, since organization is the *mobilization of bias in preparation for action* (Schattschneider 1990, 245). Upon Schattschneider's analysis we could assume that it is the interest of a cross section of the public that organizes and searches for support. Ideally, in his analysis, the mobilization of bias is the consequence of a public concern. In reality, however, it is not, because a closer look at the pressure system reveals a business or upper-class bias (246–248). In Schattschneider's analysis, public policy is explained in terms of the people involved, more specifically a small group that includes, in addition to those mentioned above, the top political and bureaucratic decision makers. In his analysis, the policy-making process is dominated by certain elites, and if the process is biased, therefore, the substance of policy must also be biased.

Kingdon, on the other hand, provides a more situational explanation for the surfacing of societal problems into the public agenda. He claims that if the three streams of *problem urgency* (the public's attention, the immediate impact of a problem), *policy expertise* (new scientific knowledge, accumulation of ideas, input of interest groups, etc.), and *political situation* (national mood, pressure of interest groups, upcoming elections, balance of power, etc.) are just right, then a *policy window* may open through which a societal concern makes it into the political agenda and subsequently becomes an issue of public policy (1984, 174–179). If these three streams do not meet, there is no way that an issue can attract even the smallest amount of official attention. Kingdon's analysis appears to focus on the substance of policy. Substance cannot be driven by process since no one can predict when the three "streams" will meet. While Kingdon does address the predictive qualities of his model (see below), the policy processes he refers to are basically focused on incremental rather than fundamental change.

Kingdon's image is powerful but its usefulness mainly concerns incremental policy making. He argues that policy·windows open up with fairly great predictability. When a particular program is about to expire, it must be reauthorized, and that provides a window of opportunity. The budget cycle is another example since policy makers and budgeteers can predict the moment when they can best intervene. Scheduled reports and memos—for instance, for evaluating a program—provide a third type of window. Budgets, the distribution of resources, and public acceptance of policy all structure the policy-making system in predictable ways. Policy windows open up not only in such foreseeable events, but even in larger cycles such as the reform cycles in American politics. Ever since President Theodore Roosevelt's reforms, there have been reform surges every fifteen to twenty years (Kingdon 1984, 195–199). Kingdon acknowledges some degree of unpredictability, which can make it sometimes difficult to use his model as a prospective tool (216).

His model is not useful for predicting major political and policy changes, since their impact can only be recognized in retrospect. As far as we can tell, the major political and policy decisions in the twentieth century were not based upon extensive analysis of a problem and a well-calculated solution and design, but were rather leaps in the dark that—fortunately—worked out well. The New Deal policies that formed the foundation for the American welfare state are just one example. Kingdon's analysis is also somewhat limited since he pays little or no attention to what happens after a social problem has been recognized as a public policy challenge that requires action. He does recognize that once a problem is on the agenda, various constraints stand in the way toward solution. These include, for instance, scarce resources, rules of procedure, precedent, customary decision-making modes, and interpretation (Kingdon 1984, 217–218). It is intriguing that his observations about constraints do not include a discussion of the groundbreaking study by Bachrach and Baratz, who argue that the primary method for sustaining the mobilization of bias (i.e., limiting policy and decision making to a small group) is nondecisions (1970, 44). They outline that for any public policy to be successful, four barriers have to be overcome. The first is the values, beliefs, and myths that the dominant portion of the population embraces; those with high status and in harmony with community values have more clout. The second barrier is procedures and institutions, which, in the highly organized Western society, is a significant barrier. Bachrach and Baratz were among the first to recognize that the shaping of policy continues in implementation (see section 11.3 below), and this constitutes a third barrier. The final barrier is administrative interpretation (55–61). Hence, Bachrach and Baratz implicitly recognize the influence of administrative culture and tradition.

In all fairness, Kingdon's analysis does not leave out the actors since he argues that the governmental agenda (the list of subjects getting the attention of people in and around government) is set by the problem (citizens) and the political stream (politicians), while the selection of alternative solutions to the problem is generated in the policy stream (bureaucrats) (1984, 4, 204). Thus, in Kingdon's view, the public (the people, an interest group, the media) and politics take the initiative, and policy follows. This fits nicely with the politics-administration dichotomy, dominant in the thinking about public policy making well into the 1950s. Since then, bureaucracies have been recognized as a power in their own standing that plays a role both at the input and at the output side of the policy-making process.

In contrast to Schattschneider and Kingdon, in the early 1960s Lowi embraced the view that policies—being issue arenas—determine politics (Lowi 1990). While this view has met with considerable criticism (for a summary, see Parsons 1995, 132–133; Meier 2000, 69–101), Lowi's classification of initially three and later four types of government functions or policies still stands. *Distributive policies* concern decisions without the necessity to consider limited resources. The impact of this decision is specific and individual (i.e., focused on a particular group) and really does not amount to a policy at all, and if so only by accumulation. Lowi suggests that patronage is the proper synonym for this type of policy. Those who are favored and those who are deprived may never meet. *Regulatory policies* also have specific and individual impact, but here a choice is made between the favored and the deprived that is visible to all. It involves broad categories of individuals. Unlike distributive policy, a regulatory policy cannot be disaggregated to private individuals or a single firm because it is a general rule that determines action. Much larger categories of people, such as social classes, are the targets of *redistributive policies*. These do not concern the use of property (as in distributive policy) or the equal treatment of people (as in regulatory policy), but the property itself and equal possession. Welfare state programs and proportional taxation systems provide the best examples (Lowi 1990, 513). Finally, *constituent policies* are concerned with the creation, reorganization, and reform of institutions (Lowi 1972).

Naturally other typologies are conceivable, and what makes any of them interesting is how they relate to a particular type of society and what organizational form they require. To use Lowi's typology as example, the distributive policy arena assumes a society in which various groups are not highly interactive, where the degree of organization for public interest is fairly low, where government is fairly small, and where public organizations are not highly differentiated internally nor from other social organizations. A regulatory policy arena requires higher levels of organization and coordination, both in society (interest groups) and in government. Any redistributive policy arena assumes large interdependencies both between various societal groups and between societal groups and governmental organizations. In this case, we will find high degrees of intra- and interorganizational differentiation, in terms of sheer size, in terms of number of organizational levels and units, in terms of the variety of interests served, and in terms of integrative and coordinative mechanisms to counter the centrifugal forces of differentiation and decentralization. It is tempting to suggest a chronology or periodization in which, as far as the United States is concerned, the distributive phase (nineteenth century) was followed by a regulatory phase (say, 1880s–1970s), which in turn was followed by the redistributive phase (since the 1930s). Lowi's 1964 article suggests this, but not explicitly. While such a chronology can be considered, it is clear that these types of policies did not so much succeed one another as that they have come to coexist.

In fact, Lowi's typology can be and has been used to characterize different contemporary policies and suggest the type of organization that is best suited to deal with them. A distributive policy requires only a simple line-staff or even a collegial organization. It is the most common type of federal action: examples are the national parks, health research, crop insurance, and urban grants (Meier 2000, 88). Regulatory policies are focused on constraining individual choice and on keeping behavior within acceptable boundaries. Examples are the legal restrictions of criminal activity, the regulation of business (e.g., product quality, monopoly, price regulation), the limitation of access to public goods (e.g., water, air, communications), and public health and safety (Meier 2000, 70–72). Some of this regulatory activity can be conducted in single organizations, such as the regulatory agencies. However, in line with the notions of *policy subsystem* (Sabatier and Jenkins-Smith 1993, 17) and of *policy community* (Majone 1989, 161), many areas of regulatory policy require the coordination of policy in cooperation between various organizations. While the various bureaucracies involved may be structured according to the classic line-staff structure, their functioning is determined by a network that includes all levels of government. Redistributive policies tax a group of people in order to provide benefits for others. The five main areas of redistributive policy are income stabilization (e.g., the Social Security Administration), welfare, health care, housing, and income distribution (Meier 2000, 81). This type of policy requires not only vast bureaucracies, but also that these bureaucracies consciously act within a network of organizations and interest groups. Finally, constituent policies benefit government in general or the country as a whole (e.g., national security and foreign affairs, the Office of Personnel Management, the Secret Service, the U.S. Mint) (Meier 2000, 96).

Using Lowi's typology in combination with the insights of Majone and Sabatier and Jenkins-Smith, it can be assumed that different types of policies involve different processes. Yet the process of public policy making itself is often presented as a chronology or a stage model of steps taken in a particular sequence. The most general model, not specifically connected with an author, comprises the stages listed in Table 11.2.

Since World War II, several such stage models have been developed (Parsons 1995, 78–79). The advantages are clear. Stage models break complexity down into manageable portions and can actually be used as analytical tools

Table 11.2

Stages of Policy Making

Problem: any kind of problem, not yet defined
a. Problem definition: pinpointing the problem
b. Identification of alternative solutions: developing several options to solve the problem
c. Evaluation of options: ranking alternative solutions according to problem-solving capability
d. Selection of policy option: the decision-making process
e. Implementation of the policy: the actual execution of the policy and the decision(s) made
f. Evaluation of the policy: determining whether the policy goals have been reached adequately in terms of both their effectiveness and efficiency and democracy

Source: After Parsons 1995, 77.

(e.g., Hogwood and Gunn 1989). Also, the stage models are interested in the impact of policy and do not stop at the institutional output (Sabatier and Jenkins-Smith 1993, 2).

The drawbacks are equally clear. First, no real-life policy-making process takes such neatly organized steps. If anything, several steps are taken simultaneously, steps are retraced, steps are overlooked, and so forth. A good example of this line of reasoning is the currently popular model of Bryson (1995), who argues, almost as if he is surprised, that real-life policy processes are much less sequential than is assumed in literature. Second, a stage model of public policy making suggests a degree of rationality that is overrated. Third, a stage model serves analytical clarity and has prescriptive pretensions rather than being descriptive and enlightening by nature. And, finally, it presents policy making as a legalistic and top-down process in which substance is determined by politics and process by administrators (Sabatier and Jenkins-Smith 1993, 3–4).

For analytical purposes, policy making can be defined as a process that precedes the moment of decision, which in turn separates policy making from implementation. At the same time, policy making in reality encompasses all activities from problem recognition to policy evaluation. The discussion in sections 11.1 to 11.5 break the policy process down into digestible portions. But it is clear that this analytical separation of various phases in the policy process really simplifies what happens in reality. Sabatier and Jenkins-Smith criticize not only the stages heuristic but also the traditional political science approach, whose focus on individual interests and values, on organizational rules and procedures, and on the broader socioeconomic environment is, in their view, equally limited. Both approaches underestimate the degree to which all levels of government are involved in the policy process, and both neglect the role of ideas in policy evolution (Sabatier and Jenkins-Smith 1993, 15). Majone had earlier reasoned along comparable lines. The stages heuristic is too technocratic and rooted in what he called *decisionism,* which implies a unitary decision maker and/or group that acts as a unit (1989, 15). Majone and Sabatier and Jenkins-Smith advance the notion that policy development is really a layered phenomenon. Majone argues that policy development requires the distinction between a *policy core,* which is relatively rigid and stable, and a *periphery,* which is more flexible (Majone 1989, 150–151). Sabatier and Jenkins-Smith add a layer to that when they argue that the *policy core* (which comprises the fundamental policy positions regarding the basic strategies for achieving core values) determines the so-called *secondary aspects* (instrumental decisions and information searches necessary for implementation) that, in turn, are grounded in a *deep core* (which includes fundamental normative and ontological axioms) (30–31, 221). In both of these studies, substance and process appear to evolve hand in hand, and the only way that their evolution or development can be understood is through the inclusion of values and cultural differences in the analysis (Stone 2002).

11.2. Models and Theoretical Perspectives of Public Decision Making

Decision making has attracted the attention of scholars from a variety of social sciences, such as public administration, management studies, political science, organizational theory, (social) psychology, (organizational) sociology, and (macro-)economics. While policy making is clearly different from decision making, it is intriguing to see to what degree policy making has been analyzed as if it is a decision process. A decision process, however, merely looks at outcomes, rather than at the processes that generate those outcomes. Decision-making analysis focuses on a choice moment, whereas policy making encompasses a far larger subject (Majone 1989, 16). Parsons (1995, 247–248) categorizes the various decision-making theories into five groups. The *rationality group* looks at the decision-making process itself; these are the models generally discussed in the context of decision-making theory in the study of public administration. I will discuss these at some length before briefly discussing the other four groups of theories (unless stated otherwise, the following section is based on Parsons 1995, 271–306).

In this section, I first focus on the economic theories of rational decision making and the criticism that these theories have met. True rational decision making assumes that the decision maker has a complete grasp of the problem, can collect all necessary information, is able to identify the complete set of alternative solutions, and is able to select the best possible solution. Given the emphasis on completeness and the best solution, the model is known as the *rational-comprehensive model.* In terms of the type of decision maker, this model is also referred to as the *economic man model;* it presupposes individuals who are calculating, driven by self-interest, and out to *maximize* their result. In this economic model of decision making, values and facts are clearly demarcated.

It is this very distinction that made Herbert Simon criticize the economic man model and led him to develop an alternative model. The reality of decision making is quite different, if only because the information storage and processing capabilities of human beings are limited, to say the least. Simon's decision maker is an *administrative man* whose reflections are characterized by *bounded rationality* and whose actions are aimed at *satisficing* rather than *maximizing*. Administrative man cannot collect all information and consider all alternatives; thus, he cannot necessarily make the best choice. Administrative man only selects those alternatives that are logical and relevant to an existing situation (1957). It is here, in the logic of the situation, that we come to full understanding of Kingdon's analysis, for instance, or of Follett's notions of organization by association. Of all the models that have questioned the realism of the economic man model, Simon's is the most rational-comprehensive. In a 1958 article, he argued that wisdom, when applied to public administration, had not seen much progress since Aristotle but that in several fields of human knowledge progress had been made once the scientific method was applied. Simon did not so much have physics in mind, but biology and medicine (1961, 90). For the scientific method to be successfully applied, it was of utmost importance that decision makers realize that facts can be determined only after objectives have been set. However, rational processes do not necessarily beget rational outcomes:

> The process of validating a factual proposition is quite distinct from the process of validating a value judgment. The former is validated by its agreement with the facts, the latter by human fiat. (Simon 1957, 56)

In Simon's view, we should look seriously at judgment (51). In Majone's terms, the evidence of the facts is too infrequently questioned in terms of their valued content. More attention should be given to argumentation (i.e., Simon's judgment), which starts with values and opinions (Majone 1989, 2, 22). In Simon's view, objectives and values cannot be separated, as is clear when he and two coauthors reflect upon the difficulties of measuring efficiency. The first step for any decision maker is to define a set of values or objectives that will be used when the policy is evaluated. The second step is to see if there is more than one value or objective. If so, a decision needs to be made about how they are to be weighed. The third step involves an attempt to agree on value(s) and objective(s) (Simon, Smithburg, and Thompson 1964, 504–505). It is interesting that, despite the force of Simon's argument, several of the budgetary models developed in the 1950s, 1960s, and 1970s (e.g., PPBS, zero–base budgeting) grew out of the economic man model rather than from Simon's administrative man model. These budget models targeted the managerial level and thus showed preference for objective and neutral decision-making processes, the content of which is seemingly easier to justify to taxpayers than subjective selection of values. To include the notion of subjectivity at that level would have left little of the desire for objectivity.

Where Simon's decision-making model represents the most rational-comprehensive side of administrative man, Charles Lindblom's *incremental model* moves to the other side of the continuum, positing that decision making is a noncomprehensive process of successive and limited comparisons (1978). Lindblom's very concise comparison of both approaches has often been reprinted (Table 11.3).

Later, in the attempt to strengthen his initial argument, Lindblom reasoned that analytical policy making could only be limited (and constrained by politics) because people know it to be fallible, it can never resolve conflicts of values and interests completely, it is too slow and costly, and it is inconclusive about which problem to tackle (Lindblom 1980, 19–25). Lindblom's model provided the foundation for a more realistic analysis of budgeting that his student Aaron Wildavsky provided in *The Politics of the Budgetary Process* (1964). The title is intriguing because it indicates that values (i.e., politics and process) rather than facts (i.e., substance) determine budgetary decisions, a message also conveyed in the titles of two of Guy Peters's books (1989 and 1991).

Simon and Lindblom represent the two extremes of a continuum concerning decision-making processes. Any modeling since theirs occupies a position somewhere in between. Dror believes that Lindblom's model is more realistic than Simon's but that it also is unsatisfactory. Dror argues that the incremental model assumes that the result of existing policies and processes is satisfactory and that there is a high degree of continuity in the nature of the problem and in the available means for solving the problem (cf. Kingdon's assumption about the predictive quality of his "streams"). Thus in Dror's reading of Lindblom's model, a high degree of social stability is assumed. Dror claims that his *normative-optimum model* enhances rationalization, uses extrarational elements given the lack of complete rationality, and improves the quality of extrarational input via sensitivity sessions and brainstorming (1978, 77–78). It appears that on the continuum of decision-making models, Dror is closer to Simon than to Lindblom. Amitai Etzioni develops a middle

Table 11.3

The Rational-Comprehensive and the Incremental Decision-Making Approaches

Rational-comprehensive (root)	Successive limited comparisons (branch)
1a. Clarification of values or objectives distinct from and usually prerequisite to empirical analysis of alternative policies	1b. Selection of value goals and empirical analysis of the needed action are not distinct from one another but are closely intertwined
2a. Policy formulation is therefore approached through means-ends analysis: first the ends are isolated, then the means to achieve them are sought	2b. Since means and ends are not distinct, means-ends analysis is often inappropriate or limited
3a. The test of a good policy is that it can be shown to be the most appropriate means to desired ends	3b. The test of a good policy is typically that various analysts find themselves directly agreeing on a policy (without their agreeing that it is the most appropriate means to an agreed objective)
4a. Analysis is comprehensive; every important relevant factor is taken into account	4b. Analysis is drastically limited: (i) Important possible outcomes are neglected (ii) Important alternative potential policies are neglected (iii) Important affected values are neglected
5a. Theory is often heavily relied upon	5b. A succession of comparisons greatly reduces or eliminates reliance on theory

Source: From Charles E. Lindblom. 1978. "The Science of 'Muddling Through.'" In *Approaches to the Study of Public Administration,* ed. R.S.G. Brown, 66–76. Milton Keyes: Open University Press. Reprinted with permission from Basil Blackwell Publishing.

way between Simon and Lindblom with his *mixed-scanning model,* which distinguishes between *contextuating decisions,* which outline the basic directions of policy (i.e., substance), and *bit-by-bit decisions* or incremental steps (i.e., process), which prepare for or follow a contextuating decision.

The core objective of these models is to establish some degree of rationality, and Simon's model is closest to that ideal (later also as coauthor with James March, 1958). Dror, Etzioni, and Lindblom are all further removed from Simon. Wildavsky speaks of *irrational policy analysis,* arguing that most common-sense researchers would agree that decision making is not very rational. It is very difficult to determine empirically the degree to which decision-making processes are determined by rule of thumb, perception (definition) of the situation, bias, emotion, the need for quick results, groupthink, stress, organizational culture and history, the informal role and position of decision makers, and the physical looks (face, clothing) and expressions (determination, doubt) of decision makers. These four models of Simon, Dror, Etzioni, and Lindblom seem to be helpful in analyzing more or less standard line-staff organizations whose lines of authority are fairly unambiguous. Also, these four models focus the analysis on the organizational rather than on the individual level. Lindblom's model addresses the individual level through the inclusion of the concept of partisan analysis (1980). Another approach that explicitly includes the notion that at the individual level one has to work with conflicting groups of individuals has been developed by Cohen, March, and Olsen in an article (1972; see also Perrow 1979) in which they describe organized anarchy as the *garbage can model* of decision making. Characteristic of this type of decision making is that policies and goals are often vague and, when clear, often conflicting, that the members of the organization have little knowledge of the overall work of the organization, and that decision making is erratic. This model is a good fit for *professional organizations* where individuals at the decision-making level are highly educated, opinionated, and independent—for example, the doctors in a large hospital or the faculty at a university versus the equally highly educated or experienced administrators.

So far I have only discussed decision-making models in themselves, but these can be linked to the issue raised in section 11.1 of why certain concerns never reach the public decision-making agenda. In Schattschneider's terminology, when the *mobilization of bias* leans toward a particular group, it can be assumed that this group is also able to influence what issues may and what issues may not enter the public decision-making arena. Bachrach and Baratz develop this line of thinking into their *model of nondecisions* (1962, 1963, 1970). The latter model also suggests that when implementation is absorbed into planning and design, it implicitly embraces teleological or means-ends theories, and

> leaves out the detours, the blind alleys, the discarded hypotheses, the constraints tightened and loosened, the lumpy stuff of life in favor of a predigested formula consisting of a ranking of objectives, a considering of alternatives, and a criterion that chooses among them. (Pressman and Wildavsky 1984, 165)

This model of nondecisions fits into the first of Parsons's four other groups of theories, which are not, however, concerned with the decision-making process itself but rather with the actors involved. The *power group* is focused on the power structures (concentrated or fragmented) and the sources of power (economic power, organized interest, professionalism, and technocracy) that determine decisions (Parsons 1995, 248–270). The study by Bachrach and Baratz is particularly instructive in its recognition that power is often used as a generic concept that, however, encompasses other relational concepts that really ought to be considered different from power (e.g., authority, manipulation, and force) (1970, 30–32).

The *public choice group* departs from the assumption that decision making is based on bureaucrats and technocrats seeking to enhance their influence (Parsons 1995, 306–323). This line of inquiry was opened by Buchanan and Tullock, who express their belief that "the 'good' political society [is one that] should resemble that held by the philosophers of the Enlightenment" (1962, 306). In their analysis of the interplay of politics and organized interest, they imagine

> a government that undertakes only those activities which provide *general* benefits to all individuals and groups and which are financed from *general* tax revenues. Under these conditions there would be relatively little incentive for particular groups of individuals to organize themselves into associations designed specifically to secure special advantages through governmental action. (287)

Buchanan and Tullock acknowledge the limitations of their assumption of a *pluralist equilibrium* when they suggest that the logical model would be refuted if there were observable cases of a single group giving up special privilege legislation and of a single group requesting special legislation or executive action (300). In the latter case, they recognize the possibility that the political system provides opportunity for specific individuals and groups to impose external costs upon others (304; cf. Lowi's distributive and redistributive policies). Their analysis provided the foundation for studies of bureaucratic self-serving behavior (e.g., Downs 1967; Niskanen 1971, 1973) that, in turn, inspired the "new right" in Britain and the United States in the 1980s to pursue more conservative policies and a smaller government. That the public choice approach has its limitations is forcefully argued by Dunleavy (1991).

The *institutional group* looks at how decisions are embedded in and are processed by institutions, which, in terms of our analysis, is a demonstration of process following structure and substance. Parsons distinguished between three strands of literature, those studying sociological, economic, and political institutionalism (1995, 323–336). Recently, Peters has provided a more elaborate categorization of eight general institutionalisms, each with subgroups, that emphasizes even more the heterogeneous nature of this body of literature. The *new institutionalism,* the generic label for all the various strands of the past thirty years has its roots in the *old institutionalism* of the 1950s. The latter's approach was legalist, structuralist, holistic (in the sense of perceiving social phenomena as embedded as well as adopting a comparative perspective), historical, and normative (Peters 1999, 6–9). The comparative state-making literature of the 1950s and 1960s is an example (Eisenstadt 1963a; Parsons 1966; Wittfogel 1957), as is the more recent study of the history of government by Finer (1997). Many of the interests of old institutionalism are visible in contemporary *historical institutionalism,* of which Archer (1979), Immergut (1992), Skocpol (1992), and Thelen and Steinmo (1992) are examples. The "old" interests are also visible in *normative institutionalism,* which is mainly concerned with the role of norms and values in organizations and decision making (Peters 1999, 24) and of which the work of March and Olsen (1982, 1989) is an example. *Empirical institutionalism,* for instance, is interested in determining the impact of presidential versus parliamentary institutions (Peters 1999, 95) and of majoritarian versus consensus democracies. Lijphart's work (1984, 1999) is an example of this. *Sociological institutionalism* has roots that go back to the work of, for instance, Durkheim, Parsons, and Eisenstadt (Peters 1999, 99–101). Studies in the population ecology of organizations also belong to this genre. Much attention in the 1980s was paid to the role and influence of interest groups and of corporatism in decision making. Peters labeled this as *societal institutionalism.* From the 1970s on, the *rational choice approach* gained prominence, especially in political science. This approach, in which institutions are defined as sets of rules, includes such wide-ranging studies as those of Kenneth Arrow (see Alt, Levi, and Ostrom 1999), North (1990), Ostrom (1990), and of principal-agent theory. Finally, *international institutionalism* is especially concerned with regime theory (Peters 1999, 129).

The final batch of theories Parsons discusses is the *informational and psychological group,* which is focused on how decisions are influenced by the psychology of individual decision makers and by group psychology and groupthink (Parsons 1995, 336–380). Lasswell's work on decision makers is among the earliest studies in this tradition (1930, 1948), while Janis's study on groupthink is of more recent origin (1972; see also 't Hart 1990). Much of the decision-making literature is written by academics. In this psychological group, the work of Vickers (1965) is relevant since he draws upon his experiences as a practitioner, which taught him that

> the real world is an endless dynamic flux, that all goals are transient, that equilibrium is a figment, even though a useful one, and that our images of facts and of

evaluations are inextricably mixed and are formed in an interactive learning process which he calls "appreciation" (from Kenneth Boulding's foreword to the 1983 edition of Vickers's study, as quoted in Parsons 1995, 359; see Vickers 1965)

Vickers thus provides a nice counterpoint to the logical analysis of Buchanan and Tullock. In Vickers's opinion, policy making requires *appreciation*, which is a combination of *reality judgments* of the state of the system (both internally and in its external relations), of *value judgments* about the significance of certain facts, and of *instrumental judgments* regarding innovations and policy instruments already in place (Vickers, as reprinted in Brown 1978, 86, 88). In view of his practitioner background, Vickers argues that policy and decision making are not rational processes but instead require the art of judgment (cf. Majone 1989). He firmly believes that incremental decision making is inevitable (cf. Lindblom), although recognizing that more drastic action is sometimes needed (cf. Etzioni's contextuating decisions) (Brown 1978, 18).

Of these four models that focus on actors, it is the institutional group that points the attention once again to organizations. Understanding decision making in the organizational arena is greatly enhanced when decision making is analyzed in the elegant framework of the three levels of rules or choice (Kiser and Ostrom 1982). At the *constitutional level,* rules are developed and choices made with regard to the foundation of governance (constitutional document; societal values as reflected in codified texts, etc.). At the *collective level,* rules are developed and choices are made concerning policy and decision-making processes (who decides about what; voting procedures, etc.). And, finally, at the *operational level,* there are rules and choices that guide our day-to-day activities. This model clarifies the orientation shift in the study (i.e., academia) and the field of public administration (i.e., government). While the development of the study is usually presented as moving from scientific management, to administrative management, to human resource approaches, to planning, to implementation studies, and so forth, this type of presentation not only obscures the embedded nature of decision making, but it also assumes that the substance and process of policy and decision making can be separated.

The scientific and administrative management approaches basically define bureaucracy as an administrative extension of politics. The *scientific management* approach of the opening decades of the twentieth century was based on a quantification of activities in production processes, the analysis of which helped determine how to specialize and standardize. In the *administrative management* focus of the 1930s, these scientific and bureaucratic principles were specifically applied to public administration. Gulick advocated that organizational efficiency would be enhanced if the organizational structure was based on clear principles. He also argued that the managerial activities involved to produce services could be clearly defined (POSDCORB).

In terms of the Kiser and Ostrom model, it appears that in the prewar period the study of public administration was mainly focused on the operational level of analysis. Implementation was a nonissue, because properly applied principles of organizational structure and processes would guarantee adequate execution or implementation. The collective level was of interest to the emerging political science discipline, while the constitutional level was the playground of the law student. In an article about the proverbs of administration, originally published in 1946, Simon suggested that the prewar public administration was more concerned with how government should operate rather than with analyzing why and how it operated (Simon 1969).

The managerial perspective did not disappear but was supplemented with the idea that attention to policy and decision making would be necessary if the study of public administration was to provide a more realistic analysis and explanation of government. Policy and decision making and the rules and procedures according to which these processes develop are illustrative of attention to the collective level of analysis. The emerging attention to implementation in the 1960s and 1970s indicated that the interdependence between the collective and the operational levels of analysis was recognized. Without this notion of interdependence, an implementation gap cannot be perceived, let alone explained. Equally, the interest in policy instruments, for performance, and for evaluation highlights the importance attached to the link between the collective and operational levels of governance.

11.3.   The Planning and Management of Implementation

A notion of social engineering and planning is as necessary a condition for distributive policies as are, for instance, direct taxation and equality before the law. Public administration frequently adopts images or concepts from the biological sciences. It has also adopted the term "planning," which comes from architecture. In the architectural and building trade, planning refers to floor plans as well as the determination of a particular sequence of activities. Thus the foundations are laid before the structure is erected; the walls cannot be built before the basic structure is finished. Planning is also often used in the context of urban and metropolitan development. In the study of public administration, the definition of planning has changed significantly in the course of the last century, as Henry's (1999, 436–438) five phases of intergovernmental planning in the United States demonstrates (Table 11.4).

In the earlier phases, the more restricted definition concerned with urban and metropolitan issues is relevant, whereas in the later phases planning also comes to include economic development and, ultimately, social engineering. As in the building trade, the planning concept in public administration

Table 11.4

Phases in Intergovernmental Planning

1. Metropolitan regionalism, 1900–1930: emergence of metropolitan planning commissions, governance in monocentric regions, attempts at expanding the power of central cities over suburbs
2. National planning, 1930–1950: regionalism, marble cake federalism, creation of National Planning Board (NPB)
3. Substate regionalism, 1950–1980: preservation of central cities in decline, the NPB abolished and regional councils created
4. Green planning, 1970–1990: increased influence of environmental legislation
5. Cooperation compounded, 1990–present: development of cooperative public, private, and nonprofit partnerships to promote regional growth and economic development

Source: After Henry 1999, 434–436.

assumes that activities are sequential by necessity. What is added to the definition of planning in the public sector is the notion of *social engineering* or reengineering. In the early twentieth century, authors such as Herbert Croly (1965) and Walter Lippmann (1961) argued that a more conscious ordering of American life was needed. In the words of Karl:

> While use of the term "planning" was still confined largely to the urban geographers, the concept itself was clearly in the wind. (Karl 1983, 23)

In the context of society, the definition of planning very much includes the assumption of an interventionist government that takes the lead in the engineering of society, the economy, and so forth. Planning in the sense of social engineering was not new to post–World War I governments, for in the United States it had been practiced ever since the Northwest Ordinance (1787) determined that statehood could be advanced and acquired only when a system of public education was established. Practitioners in the United States recognized the importance of planning and performance since the early 1920s, but it really took off from the 1930s onward. The second New Deal of the 1930s is an example of social engineering, as are the Marshall Plan (1940s), the Fair Deal (Eisenhower), the New Frontier, and the Great Society (Johnson). They all required planning. At the other side of the Atlantic, in the 1920s and 1930s, European governments and so-called social partners (labor unions, employer associations) conferred about the most adequate way in which to develop and organize social-economic policy. The experience of World War I had accelerated the need for creating a relationship between government and the social partners. No single institution or organization could rebuild European society. Planning came to the forefront as a consequence of this continuous discussion and bargaining between government, labor unions, and employer associations. There was a strong belief that planning could direct social and economic life and thus shape the future.

Planning is an element in the policy-making process and is also a policy instrument. The distinction is quite significant. In the conception of *planning as policy making,* planning is part of the policy- and decision-making process and concerns substance. In the conception of *planning as policy instrument,* it is part of the implementation and thus more concerned with the process. The three levels of planning suggested by Jantsch (1969) appear to combine these two approaches. *Normative planning* involves the outlining of long-term and general policy objectives (hence: substance). This is reminiscent of Etzioni's contextuating decisions. *Strategic planning,* which concentrates on the middle range, aims to develop concrete goals and strategies in the framework set in the normative planning phase. The strategic management phase is vital because it provides the link between the long-term desires and needs and the short-term programming of concrete activities conducted in the phase of *operational planning* or process. This operational planning has the characteristics of Etzioni's bit-by-bit decisions.

It often appears that planning is concerned with operational decisions. Taking Jantsch's triad and, for instance, Vickers's ideas, we see how planning is also concerned with explicating the underlying motives (i.e., values) for particular policies. Normative planning has to identify the long-term values or objectives that will legitimate the choices made at the strategic and operational levels. It is rational to include a normative phase as part of the decision-making process, but setting the norms itself is a political act.

Planning also has major consequences for the structure and functioning of the state and administrative system. In his comparative study of government planning in four Western European countries, Dekker (1989) identified six such consequences. First, planning *changes the relation between government and society* because it generally involves the inclusion of interest groups in policy- and decision-making processes and requires that their representatives are members of consultative and advisory bodies. Illustrative are the so-called government-sponsored enterprises in the United States (e.g., the 1916 Farm Credit System, the 1972 Student Loan Marketing Association, and the Federal Agricultural Mortgage Association), of which six were chartered by government between 1916 and 1988 (DeMarco and Rist 1998). Second, the *use of scientific knowledge in policy making* has increased, and planning is increasingly based on the collection of data for the development of future scenarios or forecasts (see, for instance, Hogwood and Gunn 1989, 128–149, but also sections 11.7 and 11.8 below). Third, the *increased need of policy coordination* involves both vertical planning (coordination between federal, state, and local levels of government in one policy area) as well as horizontal planning (coordination between policies at one level of government) in order to avoid too much overlap. Fourth, *planning may threaten parliamentary democracy:* is it still possible for representative political institutions to wield adequate control over policy making when so many bureaucracies and interest groups are involved? Fifth, there is the *emergence of multilevel planning,* which, related to the third consequence, emphasizes the need for central and integrative planning so that sectoral desires, decentralization, planning needs, and the need for control are satisfied. Illustrative here is the emergence of *picket-fence federalism* in the United States (e.g., Peters 1993, 19). The last consequence concerns the possibility that planning develops *a dynamic of its own,* that it becomes an end in itself rather than a means to an end. Planning may be less connected to a particular policy and increasingly connected to a set of independent research and development activities.

As noted above, planning is also regarded as an instrument and is thus part of the policy implementation process. The subject of policy implementation did not receive much attention until the 1970s. All of the Western literature on scientific and administrative management and on policy- and decision-making analysis is illustrative of a focus on the input side of the policy process (Grindle 1980, 15). In this approach, policy and decision making are considered from a top-down perspective in which implementation is only the administrative consequence of political action. In addition to the classical authors in this perspective (Taylor, Fayol, Gulick), we should also draw attention to Elmore's approach (1982). He argues that much policy and decision making, and thus planning, are based on *forward mapping,* a top-down approach that emphasizes synoptic analysis and direction. He advocates that more attention ought to be given instead to *backward mapping,* a bottom-up approach that is more incremental by nature and starts with outlining specific behavior at the lowest level in the organization. In backward mapping, the emphasis is on negotiation. One could also say that in forward mapping, a general policy is deduced from and ideally based on general societal values, thus progressing from general objectives to ever more concrete objectives. Backward mapping approaches policy making from a more inductive angle, building up a policy from the most concrete elements (concrete desires, as well as available financial and human resources) up to more general elements. While Elmore draws attention to a bottom-up perspective, his conceptualization of backward mapping is still grounded in an input perspective to policy making.

The insights of Jantsch and of Elmore can be combined with Simon's distinction between *mediate goals* and *final ends* (1957, 5, 63), and together they serve as a stepping stone for Kuypers's three-level policy analysis (1980). He distinguishes *ultimate goals, intermediate goals* that are steps toward the ultimate goals, and the *instruments in the strict sense.* In his view, policy making and planning can be mapped as a *goal-tree* in which both travel upward and downward between the pure instruments and the ultimate, pure goals.

Decision making, policy making, and planning do not guarantee proper implementation. Bachrach and Baratz note that the shaping of policy continues during the implementation process (1970, 61), and there is no reason to assume that the content of policy does not change in the process. In the literature one can find two conceptions that capture policy change during implementation. An *implementation gap* occurs when the realized outcome is less than what was initially desired by politicians and planned for by administrators. This may be the consequence of a variety of factors, such as unclear goals, vague priorities, lack of resources, inconsistencies, lack of information and bad communication, lack of support, and problems of coordination and organizational fragmentation (cf. Kingdon; Bachrach and Baratz). These factors may also result in *goal displacement,* which occurs when the objectives actually implemented differ entirely from how they were initially defined (Mayntz 1978, 217). Implementation gap and goal displacement draw the attention to the *street-level bureaucrats,* as Lipsky called them (1980). Street-level bureaucrats, from police officers and nurses to social workers and judges, change and actually make policy. In organizational terms, the phenomenon of street-level bureaucracy is relevant to the so-called *centralization paradox,* which holds that the more centralized a government is, the more it must rely on subnational governments for proper implementation of the national policies. In other words, the larger an organization is, the more the top will have to trust the grassroots level for proper implementation (Downs 1967). Implementation studies often emphasize managerial aspects of governance, seeking ways to improve implementation and avoid goal displacement.

Implementation studies appear in a particular type of governance system. The attention to implementation studies emerged in the days when many collective policies and services were developed through and provided within the public sector or through coproduction and public-private partnership. The more government assumes responsibility for the entire production column, from the basic policy and decision making to the detailed implementation, the more attention implementation itself receives. On the other hand, a decline of implementation studies might be expected (including those on policy evaluation, policy instruments, and so forth) in a time that efforts are made to restrain government intervention and streamline service delivery in terms of efficiency and effectiveness on the basis of a managerial approach to government. Although in the past ten to fifteen years deregulation, debureaucratization, downsizing, and organizational reform have indicated a more managerial approach to government—at least to a government that embraces public management values more than the traditional administrative values—the attention to implementation studies as such has not dwindled. In fact, the contrary is the case. The more government and society are intertwined, the more implementation studies are needed to explore how and why particular policies succeed or fail in particular public, private, and public-private settings.

11.4.   Policy Instruments: State Philosophy and Objective Choice

Underneath the policy choices, there is an implicit or explicit philosophy about the role of the decision maker as well as about the role of the state or government in society. With respect to the decision maker, a distinction can be made between two approaches. In the first approach, the decision maker is the king-philosopher who has the experience and the wisdom to decide what is best for society. In the second perspective, all individuals own society, and decision making rests upon the subjective appreciation of the individual's wishes.

With respect to government, one could emphasize a restrained role in which government limits its activity as much as possible to the protection of the territory against outside aggressors (military) and to the maintenance of public order and safety inside the territory (police and justice). Public intervention outside these areas is justified only if all other possible solutions (i.e., market, societal association) to societal problems have failed. Problem solving should be left to the market as long as possible (nightwatch state). A completely opposite approach is one in which government assumes responsibility for many, if not all, collective services because every citizen is considered to have the right to a defined minimum level of services (welfare state). It has been argued that the classical *market versus state dichotomy* is too simple and cannot adequately capture the variety of options that have been tried in response to collective problems. There are, for instance, the *common-pool resource management systems* that operate between state and market. Furthermore, market mechanisms are not the only manifestation of government pursuing a noninterventionist role.

Expanding from a typology of policy choices developed by Anderson (1977), Vedung distinguishes three types of nonintervention and three types of intervention. Nonintervention includes reliance on *market mechanisms*, on *civil society,* and on the *household* (Vedung 1998, 23–24). The household represents perhaps the oldest type of service delivery system. The household is defined as an extended family of children, parents, and grandparents living together. The senior members look after the children while the parents provide labor. In an extended family, many services (health care, education, etc.) are possible that cannot be provided in a society where the nuclear family is the prime social unit. If the extended family is unable to provide particular services, civil society may step in. Civil society is a concept that draws attention to voluntary association and participation in societal organizations (e.g., the church, the trade and craft guilds in the Middle Ages). Today, the concept of civil society is brought to the forefront amid an atmosphere of favoring market mechanisms over interventionist government. It is almost as if the notion of civil society is used to compensate for the harshness of a purely market-oriented society. At best, civil society represents an interesting and compelling philosophy about the relation between individual, society, and government. At worst, civil society is merely used as a phrase cloaking individualistic approaches to democracy. In Western society, the nuclear family has replaced the extended family, and the responsibility for collective services has shifted from the household and from civil society to the public sector. With respect to intervention, Anderson distinguishes between *structured options, biased options,* and *regulation.* In the case of structured options, government establishes public programs and leaves their use to individual discretion. Biased options guide the individual in a particular direction through a system of positive and negative sanctions. The most interventionist type is regulation, determining what the individual is allowed to do and forbidden to do (Vedung 1998, 23–24).

A variety of policy instruments are available to fit government intervention, but it is important to realize that a particular type of organization is not related to a particular type of policy instrument. In reality, organization and instruments can be packaged in just about any conceivable combination (Bemelmans-Videc and Vedung 1998, 257–268). In contemporary literature, policy instruments are often categorized on the basis of their content. This may result in such large laundry lists as those, for instance, by Kirschen (1964) (as reprinted in Vedung 1998, 53–55) and by Osborne and Gaebler (1992, 31). The understanding of the operational choices that government faces is enlarged when we focus on categorizing the authoritative force instead of the content of policy instruments. Drawing upon various sources in the literature, Vedung (1998, 30) and Bemelmans-Videc and Vedung (1998, 250) propose a threefold distinction of policy instruments. *Regulatory instruments* are highly coercive and are sanctioned by negative or affirmative measures. Regulatory instruments include regulatory programs, but also metaregulation, by which government regulates its own regulation. The metaphor sometimes used is that of the *stick.* In the case of *economic instruments,* the emphasis is on affirmative or negative measures with respect to material resources. Affirmative, positive measures include subsidies, grants, contracting-out, and so forth, while taxes, fees, and tolls are examples of negative measures. This group of policy instruments is characterized by the *carrot* metaphor. The *information instruments* are brought to battle if government seeks to persuade its citizenry in a particular direction on the basis of reasoned argument. This is sometimes referred to as the *sermon* or moral suasion (Peters 1993, 9).

Laundry lists of policy instruments may convey a sense of completeness, while at the same time containing very different types of instruments and processes as well as obscuring the value-laden nature of substance. In comparison to the three categories mentioned above, Osborne and Gaebler's list of thirty-six delivery systems is nothing more but a basket in which rather generic types of instruments, such as information and monitoring and investigation, are thrown together with such well-defined instruments as grants, franchising, vouchers, and so forth. Osborne and Gaebler's list leans heavily toward the economic instruments, showing a bias toward a managerial interpretation of the role of government.

11.5. Short- and Long-Term Perspectives on Government Performance

There is little, if anything, in society in which government is not actively involved, either through direct service delivery or through regulation of services and behavior. The growth of the public workforce testifies to a growth of public services, while the changes in the number of local government units indicates a search for the optimal local unit size. The quantitative growth of public services is, we assume, a consequence of external demand rather than of internal machinations by bureaucrats with a lust for power and an inflated sense of self-importance. The size of government, whether measured by number of jurisdictions or personnel size, can be taken as a sign of its responsiveness to public demand and thus concerns the quantity of public services, but it can also be considered a consequence of political motives of certain groups to keep others away from their resources. The literature on motives for boundary change of local governments is instructive in this respect (Burns 1994). Whether or not the quality of public services has improved accordingly is the subject of research into the performance of government.

Performance can be analyzed as part of a policy evaluation, based on such "hard" approaches as cost-benefit analysis or design science (Miller 1984). Performance can also be evaluated according to the softer approach of citizen appreciation for government services. Another way of understanding performance is by looking at so-called planning disasters or policy failures. Attention to this method has increased with the growth of government. This is a consequence not just of substantive failures in public service delivery, but also of social expectations and political ideology (Bovens and 't Hart 1996, 146). With respect to political ideology, Bovens and 't Hart argue that public dissatisfaction with bureaucracy and public service delivery is reinforced by the campaign promises and rhetoric of politicians. With respect to social expectations, they argue,

> The disenchantment of government has continued unabated at another level, that is, in our tolerance for fate and misfortune as significant forces shaping our lives and the society we live in. There is a paradox here. At one level, we have grown more disappointed with government as the great problem solver. At the same time, however, our expectations concerning a life free from acts of God, nature's capriciousness, and other random forces beyond institutional control have continued to rise. As a result, the tragic dimensions of public life, not so long ago still accepted as an important feature of statecraft and governance, have faded from both popular discourse about politics and from the evaluation designs of policy analysts. Since we no longer accept misfortune as a cause of social ills, someone has to [be] blamed for them. . . . Government has become an ever more readily available scapegoat. (Bovens and 't Hart 1996, 147)

When evaluating public performance, citizens should consider the stereotypical appreciation of government in contrast to their personal experience with its employees. Politicians should make realistic rather than impossible promises. Not only do such promises deceive the electorate (some among them may wish to be deceived!), but they load the bureaucracy with an impossible task. Civil servants should not succumb to the public's and politicians' perception of big government.

Performance can be evaluated in a short-term and a long-term perspective but at the basis of evaluation are *criteria of good governance* (Bemelmans-Videc 1998, 7–8). These can also serve as criteria for selecting policy instruments. Criteria of good governance reflect the classical challenge of balancing democracy with efficiency. The criterion of *democracy* is concerned with the degree to which public action is in line with accepted values and norms regarding society as such and government-society relations. The second criterion on this side of the continuum is *legality*, which regards equity and the degree to which public action occurs within the existing formal rules and procedures. On the efficiency side of the continuum, we find *efficiency,* the relation between costs and benefits, and *effectiveness,* the relation between means and ends.

In the short-term perspective, policies are evaluated in terms of the degree to which they deliver immediate gratification. The literature on various evaluation techniques is extensive (Patton 1997; Posavec and Carey 1996; Rossi, Freeman, and Lipsey 1999; Shadish, Cook, and Leviton 1993; Wholey, Hatry, and Newcomer 1994). Here, I focus on the nature of policy evaluation. Looking at the criteria for good governance, it appears that policy analysis is often focused on the efficiency/effectiveness side because costs and benefits, and means and ends, seem easier to quantify than the more vague and ambiguous criteria of democracy and legality. What is more, evaluating democracy and legality requires, it seems, a more explicated choice of values held important than does the evaluation of efficiency and effectiveness. Indeed, is it possible to evaluate democracy and legality in the same manner as efficiency and effectiveness? There are several problems with the methods and focus of policy analysis and evaluation. One problem with much of the policy analysis and evaluation literature is that it focuses on the *measurable criteria.* Another problem is that it focuses most on evaluating the realization of *operational, short-term goals.* Of course, it is more difficult to evaluate the realization of strategic goals, given the middle-range term involved. And it is probably close to impossible to evaluate long-term goals in measurable terms, if only because the policy implementation process itself should be flexible enough to adapt to changing environmental circumstances. Third, policy analysts have hung a noose around their own necks by claiming to generate *usable knowledge.* If policy analysts have not been able to live up to the promise of generating usable knowledge, it is because of the one-sided and short-term focus of their research. This is in part a product of the political environment in which Western bureaucracies operate. Candidates for public office like to point to recent successes or to things they can make happen, and these usually include neither policies in a distant past nor visions with a long-term perspective. It is up to the bureaucrat to guard that long-term perspective both backward as well as forward in time. A fourth problem is that policy evaluation excludes one important arena—politics. Politicians are too little concerned with operational aspects of policy. And an even more important problem, which is also related to politics, is that elected officials, political executives, and civil servants at the summit have a very short tenure. The average tenure at the top of U.S. government is between one and a half and two years, which is hardly a period in which policies and programs can be pursued properly, let alone evaluated.

The performance of government can really be evaluated only in long-term retrospect (see also Sabatier and Jenkins-Smith 1993, 16). The knowledge to evaluate government policy over the past decades is available. If long-term evaluation is not pursued, it is because of lesser interest in understanding than in immediate problem solving. Citizens, bureaucrats, and politicians should ask themselves if they would like to go back to the society and government as they were 100 years ago. If the answer is no, it may very well be that the implicit theory holds that government performance nowadays is quite good. If argued that comparison over time is useless and that the experiences of earlier generations with government in their day are irrelevant when discussing experiences with government today, then anything considered useless right now can be thrown out. If this is the case, then any decision made or consideration expressed in the past, whether it is a commitment to (part of) the public or a commitment to public organizations, can be declared void at any time. If government is considered in contemporary terms only, the door is wide open to organizational anarchy and to whimsical government. Comparison with the situation in the past serves to highlight the democracy/legality side of policy evaluation and is thus able to focus on longer-term developments. Short-term analysis, with a focus on efficiency and effectiveness as well, is needed but should be combined with a longer-term analysis.

Such a long-term view of government performance was recently provided by Hicks (2000), who writes for Bridge News, and by Light (2000) of the Brookings Institution. Hicks looks back to the beginning of the twentieth century when most Americans lived in a house the size of a two-car garage, without running water, a central heating system, a flushing toilet, a washing machine, a refrigerator, a telephone, or electricity. Only 13 percent of the adults had completed high school education (today 80 percent); the average work week was about fifty-three hours (today forty-two hours); 63 percent of men over sixty-five worked (today 17 percent); life expectancy for whites was 50 percent greater than for blacks (today, only a 10 percent gap); and African Americans and women occupied few positions in elected office. The New Deal brought social security, farm subsidies, unemployment insurance, and Aid to Dependent Children. Government involvement in society expanded during and after World War II with medicaid and medicare, the GI bill (Mosch 1975), and environmental, health, occupational, and transportation safety measures, just to name a few.

Light conducted research on the fifty greatest achievements of federal government in the second half of the twentieth century, based on a survey among college and university professors of history and of government. There is little sense in listing all fifty, but the lessons derived from Light's work are worth mentioning. The first lesson is that while there are clearly breakthrough policies such as in the field of medicare and welfare reform, most federal policies were the outcome of policy making over a long period of time (cf. Lindblom's incremental model). By way of illustration, of the fifty achievements more than 80 percent took an average of nine statutes. It took twenty-one statutes to establish financial security in retirement, nineteen to stabilize agricultural price supports, and fifteen to provide assistance to the working poor. This supports the idea that most policy making is incremental by nature. The second lesson is that more than 80 percent of these achievements were the result of bipartisan commitment. And, third, most of these achievements involved a mix of policy strategies. A little over half of the achievements concerned federal spending as a policy tool, so as to provide health care to the elderly, increase home ownership, stabilize agricultural prices, strengthen the federal highway system, reduce disease (think, for instance, of the Polio Vaccination Act of 1955), and expand the right to vote. Some 40 percent involved regulatory policies, such as programs to improve air and water quality, end workplace discrimination, and make government more transparent to the public. A very important element of this third lesson is that less than 25 percent of the fifty achievements involved benefits for particular target groups, such as the elderly, poor, veterans, or racial minorities (i.e., distributive policy in Lowi's terms). Hence, the large majority of achievements spread benefits across society in general. What better illustration is there of the success of redistributive policy?

Light's evaluation also notes policy failures, especially in the areas of poverty among children and continuing urban sprawl, skepticism about the performance of government with respect to expanding job training and placement, improvement of mass transportation, advancing human rights, improving government performance, renewing poor communities, and increasing the availability of low-income housing. Nevertheless, Light writes that the survey suggests "that the federal government mostly picked important and difficult problems to solve, and often had success in doing so" (2000, 6; 2002). Given our discussion above on the measurability of policy performance and the criteria of good governance, three more of Light's lessons are significant. First, the top ten achievements involved relatively clear and measurable results. Second, federal government was at least partly focused on advancing a moral right, human equality, world peace and democracy, and honoring commitments to previous generations. Third, it appeared that government had been willing to act where the private and nonprofit sectors could not or would not (Light 2000, 11). We can, therefore, conclude that government considers both efficiency/effectiveness and democracy/legality objectives.

Light's report concludes with a troublesome observation that deserves to be quoted in full:

> Just as one can look back with considerable awe at what the federal government tried to accomplish over the past half century, so, too, can one look forward with considerable doubt about whether government will ever be so bold again. Are the nation's leaders so worried about losing their jobs that they will not take the risks embedded in the kind of inherently risky projects that reached the top ten list above? Are Americans so impatient for success that no program, however well designed and justified, can outlast the early difficulties that face so many innovative efforts? And are the media so addicted to stories of government failure, that no endeavor, however noble and well designed, can survive long enough to achieve results?
>
> These questions would not be so troublesome but for the fact that many of the most important problems identified in this report are still in need of solution. The nation has far to go in increasing access to health care, reducing the dangers of

nuclear war, improving air and water quality, reducing hunger, and so on. To the extent that the nation's leaders avoid the risky issues in favor of safe rewards, *the public demands instant gratification instead of long-term diligence*, and the media punishes the trial and error so essential to ultimate impact, the list of government's greatest achievements of the next half century will be short, indeed. (Light 2000, 11–12; emphasis added)

It is impossible to assess whether government policy in the future will be as bold and successful as it has been so far, nor whether political leaders are, indeed, less inclined to advance bold and innovative policies. What appears to be true is that there is generally more attention paid to policy failure than to success, and it is at least plausible that the public at large seeks instant gratification instead of long-term diligence. For a better understanding of this, we need to look at what we know today about policy and decision making (section 11.6), about the basis of policy making (section 11.7), and about the cultural features of policy making in Western society at large and in the United States specifically (section 11.8). Together, sections 11.6 to 11.8 provide a characterization of the Western conceptualization of policy and decision making.

11.6. Much Literature, Less Theory, Lesser Enlightenment?

As abundant as the substantive literature is, we could wonder what attention is paid to the degree to which policy makers consider the impact of their policy upon other directly or indirectly related policies. How much interpolicy coordination takes place? Is public policy making compartmentalized according to the various policy areas, or are attempts made at cross-policy understanding both in the practice as well as in the study of public administration? There is also ample literature that outlines the features of the policy-making process in theory and its use to analyze real cases. However, to what degree is there attention for possible variations of policy-making processes between policy areas? Is it possible that a generic policy-making process does not exist, because the openness and closedness of policy varies (e.g., think of iron triangles or issue networks, closed or open access for actors outside the political and administrative arenas)?

Frequent calls are heard for better use of theory from the social sciences at large rather than resort to so-called logic models or program theories (e.g., Birckmayer and Weiss 2000, 409). Some hope that the development and application of social science theory results in *social intervention theories* that encompass a wide range of categories to identify the general form of the policy process (e.g., Lipsey 1997, 9). It could be argued that we have a general idea of the stages of the policy-making process (problem definition; identification of criteria to evaluate alternative solutions; development and selection of alternative solutions; decision making; implementation; evaluation), but that such is not based on meticulous meta-analysis of hundreds of studies (Lipsey 1997, 13–15). An example of such a meta-analytical approach is the attempt to generate comparable data series on common pool resources (e.g., E. Ostrom, Workshop in Political Theory and Policy Analysis, Indiana University). In addition to this, there is more need for better measures, but given "the large number of variables that are implied in many theories of change, measurement error makes it difficult to identify significant associations among variables" (Weiss 1997, 51). This reminds us of Weber's sigh: "how is causal explanation of an individual issue at all possible. . . . The number and nature of causes of even an individual event are, after all, infinite" (Weber 1985, 177). Can it be true that we have circled around the same problem as Weber did, but have not come any closer?

We need more theory grounded in comparison of existing cases. We also need to study more cases. Third, we need to look at the interplay between social and bureaucratic engineering, for policy and decision making can be understood only if we pay attention to the interplay between substantive issues and the managerial processes involved. Finally, we need to study short-term policies in a longer-term perspective. We have seen above that many government achievements have been the products of step-by-step actions over a fairly long period of time, rather than of major policy changes. That long-term perspective combined with a realistic view of what can be achieved in the short term will improve not only the understanding of government but also the public's patience with results. In the words of Lindblom and Cohen, the social engineering approach to problem solving should, at least, be balanced by the function of enlightenment (1979, 73). Like so many before them, they point to the necessarily value-laden nature of, for instance, the analysis of policy- and decision-making processes. The following quotation is illustrative of their argument:

> Despite the accepted convention that pPSI [i.e., practitioners of Professional Social Inquiry] are engaged in the pursuit of conclusive fact and proof, they are instead engaged in producing inconclusive evidence and argument. Problem complexity denies the possibility of proof and reduces the pursuit of fact to the pursuit of those selective facts, which, if appropriately developed, constitute evidence in support of relevant argument. We do not mean here that evidence is manufactured without respect to data, or that contrary evidence is suppressed, or that argument is indifferent to such facts as can be established. We mean only to call attention to the inevitably incomplete character of attempts at proof, the consequent reduction of such attempts to informed argument, and the highly selective search for just those facts that bear on argument as evidence for or against the argued position. (81)

Lindblom and Cohen's observation that practitioners—and one could add scholars as well—continue to pursue conclusive fact and proof and are less inclined to admit to the inevitably incomplete character of such attempts is of immediate relevance to the next section.

11.7.   Numerical Data as the Basis of Policy and of Research

Almost since the beginning of large-scale society, governments have collected and stored data on the state and business revenues. Babylonian and Assyrian clay tablets of the nineteenth to the ninth century B.C.E. contain data on fluctuations in real wages. The Assyrian Doomsday Book holds information about the ownership and administrative status of farms and villages, lists of people by name, and lists of houses, animals, land, and so forth (Snooks 1993, 166). The English Doomsday Book compiled during the reign of William the Conqueror contains comparable information. These data were collected with an eye on revenue, not necessarily—if ever—with an eye on improving domestic policy. This would change in the early modern age.

From the seventeenth century onward, scientific knowledge became increasingly regarded as superior over mere judgment or opinion (Price 1965, 154–155). The modernist worldview so familiar to us, which embraces market values, individualism, secularism, and instrumental rationality, has its roots in the seventeenth century with the elevation of science and in the eighteenth century with the idea that society could be known only on the basis of systematic and objective measures that would enhance human control over the uncertainties of life (Yankelovich 1991, 185, 187). It is in the eighteenth century that people start to systematically collect data on the human condition and provide substance. Although the earliest population and food supply census in the Western world is that of Nuremberg in 1449, compiled when the city was under siege and obviously for distributive purposes, it is not until the late eighteenth century that governments start to collect demographic, social, and economic data (Boorstin 1985, 670). As early as the 1680s, Perry in England and Leibniz in Prussia had proposed the creation of a central statistical office (Hacking 1990, 18), but it was not until Article 1, Section 2 of the U.S. Constitution that the first legislation passed prescribing a public census every decade and thus requiring a national agency for it. On both sides of the Atlantic, governments collected data with a reformist purpose that was local in scope (Boorstin 1985, 641–642). The collection rationale was that with data on crime, suicide, prostitution, madness, disease, and so forth, one could unearth lawlike generalizations that, subsequently, could be used to improve and/or control deviant populations through substantive policy making (Hacking 1990, 3, 118).

In the course of the nineteenth century, the study of statistics mushroomed under the untiring pursuits of the Belgian mathematician Adolphe Quetelet. Many of these statistics consisted of nominal data, listings of particular demographic, social, and economic facts. The impact upon the functioning of government was enormous. A century ago

> there was no gross national product, no consumer price index, no infant mortality rate, no out-of-wedlock birth rate, no unemployment rate, no poverty line, no political polls, no consumer surveys, no focus groups, no crime rates. (Hicks 2000, B5)

Quetelet's legacy was that public numbers came to dominate public policy (Boorstin 1985, 675) and that our view of the world became statistical. The data that underlie much government policy look at (aspects of) society at an aggregate level (Murphy 1997, 153, 156). In a society where many policies are distributive by nature, this should be so, but it comes at a price. Decision makers have increasingly come to rely on statistical data and on more or less informed assessments of what they mean, while a decision made on the basis of practical experience and a vision about reality is increasingly regarded as an act of ignorance or blindness (Murphy 1997, 217). Statistical data provide information, and perhaps some understanding, but, as Lindblom and Cohen imply, they do not provide the decisive type of evidence that comes with discourse and philosophical argument (Winch 1986, 113–115).

It could be argued that advocating discourse and philosophical argument, in addition to statistics, as the basis for policy and decision making would limit the opportunity for normal citizens to participate. In Fraser's view, it is the nature of the information that limits broad participation. Talking about education, he mentions how computers favor testing for facts because factual questions are the only kind that can be answered more or less unambiguously. However, computer testing

> promotes rote memory rather than the learning of inference, analysis, interpretation, and the application of broad principles. The latter tasks, necessary to keep a modern society viable, are becoming the domain of a minority of people: those at the policy institutes of the government, at private foundations, in think tanks, at the top research libraries. (Fraser 1987, 327)

Fraser does not stand alone with this conclusion. Yankelovich has argued that policy makers generally believe that factual information is better than judgment or opinion and that more facts will lead to better decisions (1991, 191–192). Given the amounts of information stored as statistical data that are not necessarily easy to digest quickly, one can advance the argument that the majority of people are excluded from policy and decision making. Another troubling aspect of this situation is that the technical sophistication of bureaucracy and economic analysis is far greater today than in the more distant past, [but] knowledge by policy advisors about the nature of the economy and society is much less. This is of considerable significance because the quality of decision making is determined more by intelligence, imagination, and knowledge of the policy advisor, than by formal decision making instruments. (Snooks 1993, 105)

Hence, the people cannot digest the data and the policy makers cannot understand economy and society beyond these data. Societal development is determined by policies based on data that do not necessarily reflect reality in every locality or region.

Concerns in the 1950s about the gap between the public at large and the experts in government have not lost any of their relevance (Yankelovich 1991, 3). Yankelovich advocates that the public policy- and decision-making process should be supported by three ways of knowing (based upon Jürgen Habermas): empirical-analytical science (i.e., statistics), intersubjective understanding (which is associated with insight into people's motives, values, and worldviews), and knowledge with an emancipatory purpose (such as can be provided by history, literature, philosophy, religion, language, art, etc.) (1991, 213 and 235). Yankelovich believes that combining our sources of knowing will contribute to the art of self-governance (236).

One puzzling question remains. High-level bureaucrats are generally very well educated. Are they aware of the limited knowledge basis upon which government policies and decisions are made and implemented, and, if so, why does aggregate data continue to be as important as ever? Is the *art of judgment*, to borrow the title of Vickers's book, lost? To answer this question, or at least to shed some light on it, we need to look at why policy is conceptualized in the way it is. Once again, culture appears to be an important variable.

11.8. The Western Conceptualization of the Policy Process

In the almost completely new edition of his comparative study of democracy, Lijphart investigates, among other things, the relation between the degree of consensus democracy and government performance in macroeconomic management and violence control and the quality of democracy in terms of women's representation, equality, and voter participation (Lijphart 1999, xii, chapters 15 and 16). Many of the explanations he provides for the relation between different variables are a statistical. But toward the end of his study, (political) culture pops out as a plausible explanation for the conclusion that "a consensus-oriented culture often provides the basis for and connections between the institutions of consensus democracy" (306). He then concludes that public policy is kinder and gentler in a consensus democracy (such as those in Western Europe) than in a majoritarian democracy (such as the United States):

> It appears to be more plausible to assume that both consensus democracy and these kinder, gentler policies stem from an underlying consensual and communitarian culture than that these policies are the direct result of consensus institutions. (306–307)

This quotation confirms the conclusions about the quality of welfare state programs as analyzed by Esping-Andersen (1990) and by Goodin et al. (1999). It also seemingly supports Thomas Paine's observation that much order in society is not the result of government intervention. However, the role and position of government in society have changed significantly since the days of Paine. Yet the quotation from Lijphart is fitting in the opening of this section because it suggests that political culture is rooted in a larger societal culture (how could it be otherwise?) and that it is ultimately culture that helps us understand the nature of government in the Western world.

Various remarks throughout this chapter, when taken together, characterize public policy and decision making: it is conceptualized as a linear process, it is distributive by nature, it is based on aggregate data, and it is evaluated in terms of instant gratification. In the discussion of why this is so, we must work our way back through the chapter.

Public policy is legitimated by societal demand. That the public at large desires instant gratification is explained by the fact that in Western society *waiting time,* the time that people are prepared to wait for results, has decreased significantly. Especially in American society, change and novelty are appreciated much more than continuity, and short-term benefits are favored over longer-term benefits (Smith 1988, 39). Smith attributes this to the declining role of religion in the public realm, which was a consequence of the rise of scientific thought, industrialism, and mass education. In his words, religious grace and truth have been exchanged for political grace and truth; salvation is expected through politics and power rather than through religion. In this secular epoch, people not only tend to forget the degree to which their ancestors expressed and experienced their culture in religious terms, they also forsake the future by demanding immediate redistribution of economic and social benefits (41–45). In Smith's characterization of Economic Man and Political Man (92–94), the first is more likely to defer gratification than the second and

> most policy disputes over the proper role of government in the economy are in reality disagreements over the long run or the short run. (97)

Citizen demand has fueled *promissory politics*, which is fanned by competitive party organizations and the democratic ideology that government should provide services that reduce the uncertainty of life (102 and 169).

In the effort to deal with the ever increasing societal demand and in the hope of legitimating the policy choices ultimately made, governments have increasingly come to use aggregate data. However, besides the fact that many people appear to agree that statistics do not provide complete understanding of society, true redistributive policies, based on the values of greater equality, justice, and economic growth, cannot be developed on the basis of a more individualized perspective. In fact, the welfare state demands nothing less than that government redistributes income, grants subsidies, and regulates business and labor in order to increase welfare. Under these circumstances, it is no surprise that government officials use aggregate data. Smith writes that

> this highly instrumental view of public life coincides with the tendency to look to government to resolve many problems heretofore perceived as essentially private in nature. (102)

The uncertainties of life (ill health, poverty, unemployment, crime), so normal to previous generations and accepted by necessity, have been mitigated through government intervention. We have already discussed how much public policy has improved the standard of living and general welfare, but it is almost paradoxical that, despite past and present efforts, satisfaction with government policy appears to be low.

This has much to do with a worldview in which the present is condensed to a moving point in time between the past and the future. This is, for instance, expressed in the fact that the grammar of Western languages explicitly recognizes past, present, and future. Time is a tangible and measurable commodity, the value of which can be calculated in terms of time saved, spent, lost, and made up. By way of generalization, Western people embrace *monochronic time* (M-time), where people classify and schedule activity (Hall 1983, 34, 45–47). The official worlds of government and business in the Western world are dominated by M-time, in contrast to many cultures of the world where *polychronic time* (P-time: doing different things at the same time, much less strict with scheduling) is more characteristic. P-time people generally have an extraordinary knowledge of one another, and involvement with people is central to existence. In fact, one cannot conduct any business, cannot make any policy, cannot reach any decision, unless the knowledge each participant has of the other has established trust (Hall 1983, 46, 50). P-cultures, so Hall argues, are *high-context cultures* in which people work together on the basis of interpersonal knowledge. In *low-context cultures*, on the other hand, every bit of information needs to be spelled out. In high-context cultures, normal transactions in daily life do not require that in-depth and background information is spelled out; it is already internalized. In low-context cultures, people have compartmentalized personal lives and work to such large degrees that detailed background information is needed. High-context people are impatient and irritated when low-context people insist on more background information, and conversely low-context people are at a loss when high-context people do not provide enough information (Hall and Hall 1990, 9). One cannot generalize and say that M-time and low-context culture is characteristically Western and that P-time and high-context culture is characteristic for the rest of the world. Among Western countries, some are clearly more low-context (United States, northern European countries) and others more high-context (Mediterranean countries). Also, some are much more M-time oriented (United States, Germany), while others are more P-time oriented (Mediterranean countries).

Does this have a bearing upon the understanding of government's functioning? The 1990 study of Hall and Hall was written to specifically educate American business managers who were about to be deployed in France or Germany. Hall's 1983 study contains much more discussion of government bureaucracy. In a P-time culture, bureaucratic administration and control are a matter of job analysis to identify the activities of a subordinate's job. But the scheduling of the subordinate's activity is left to the individual. M-time bureaucracies are much more focused on scheduling activity, leaving the details of a job up to the individual. Bureaucracies in P-type cultures are generally smaller, depend on gifted people at the top, and are very slow and cumbersome when dealing with new or different challenges. Hall's observation that in French bureaucracies, the middle managers play an important role is consistent with Hofstede's and Stevens's findings about national organizational cultures. P-type cultures are also much more focused on the people than on the tasks in the organization. In M-type cultures, bureaucracies, on the other hand, tend to grow in size and be much more blind to the humanity of their employees (Hall 1983, 47–49, 101). In relation to the short- and long-term perspectives of people, it is in M-time cultures that the past becomes dim and recedes from view, so that what happened twenty years ago quickly becomes "ancient," and Hall carries his observation even a little further when arguing that the more one has buried the past, the faster the present will appear to move (130). Hall's distinction between high- and low-context cultures is equally relevant to public policy. In high-context cultures, information, context, and meaning are inextricably linked together, and the more information is shared (i.e., available prior to interaction), the higher the context. Recalling Etzioni's distinction between bit-by-bit and contextuating decisions, we can see better how the latter provides meaning to the day-to-day operational activities.

These operational activities and public policy and decision making at large are often conceptualized as a linear process in time that employs an instrumental rationality, that is scalar and taxonomical by nature, and that adopts an analytic-economic mode of thought. Once again, a linear conception of time is peculiar for the Western world, even though official business throughout the world is increasingly conducted on the basis of the standardized Western calendar and time zones. That, however, does not mean that societies all over the world hold to a linear view of time. In fact, older cultures commonly adhere to a cyclical view of time as expressed in the change of seasons and the changes of the tides (Legge 1995, 289–290). The Western sense of time dates back to the Hebrews, who were the first among the ancient civilizations to conceive of a historical time (the following is based on Gardet et al. 1976, 151–190, 234–237; Nisbet 1969; Nisbet 1986, 34–77). In the Hebrew worldview, the world was not created at once, nor was humanity created as subject to God. Instead, the Creation was a work in progress, not just from the first to the sixth day, but throughout time. In the Jewish theology, God created man free, thus introducing an element of risk and uncertainty when entrusting man with his creation. Christianity not only adopted this linear sense of time but also further refined it. Especially, St. Augustine (fifth century C.E.) hammered upon the fact that historical time is an essential part of the spiritual life and of consciousness. In his view, we should use our time purposefully in order to be prepared at any moment to die and appear before the Creator. In this linear conception of time, the past appears as a potential for the future and serves to explain past trajectories and future options. The currently popular notion of *path-dependency* in some of the new institutionalist literature is clearly in sync with this Judeo-Christian conception of time. Time is not to be wasted, but should be made useful (Gardet et al. 1976, 189) and serve continuous progress; this is what Hall called an M-time argument.

What does this mean and is this useful (in terms of usable knowledge) for the understanding of government? If usable knowledge is narrowly defined in instrumental terms, then, clearly, reflections upon the nature of Western public culture (i.e., as defined by worldview at large, organizational and policy-making culture, perceptions of time, etc.) are not useful. If, however, knowledge is defined in the wider sense of insight and wisdom, it is very useful, for it helps us identify and perhaps even accept the limitations of government's domestic and foreign policy.

There is, however, a more tangible reason why attention is given here to Western conceptualizations of policy. In the past ten years or so, it is striking to see how much the literature both in public administration and in business administration recognizes the limitations of a linear view of time. Characterizing decision-making styles in the public sector, Van Wart labels two of his three cognitive models as linear (the third model is nonlinear). Next, he points out that nonlinear theorists have shown that organizational and decision-making systems are much more complex and much less predictable and controllable than often admitted (1998, 206). Writing about the world of private corporations, Buchanan and Badham reference research clearly showing that sociotechnical change processes are not simple and linear in character but rather involve endless circles of change (Buchanan and Badham 1999, 160; Bryson 1995; Sabatier and Jenkins-Smith 1993, 3). The typical problem-solving process in business and industry is presented as rational, logical, linear, and stepwise, while in reality it seldom operates in a tidy and predictable manner (Buchanan and Badham 1999, 185–186).

Until the mid-1980s, much organization theory and decision- and policy-making theory embraced top-down perspectives. Recipes for organizational change and for policy making emphasized objectives, rationality, linearity, and steps. Since then, a processual perspective on organizational change and policy-making styles has been rapidly gaining ground. This includes, naturally, attention to the substance (new technology, new organizational structure, new pay system, etc.), but also considers the past, present, and future context (internal as well as external to organization) and the nature of the process (which tasks, activities, decisions: i.e., process management) and acknowledges the political nature of structuring and restructuring organizations and policies. In a processual perspective, the long-term view dominates (as in, e.g., Deming's view of Total Quality Management) and neither normal development over time nor developments during a transition period are expected to show continuous improvement. Instead, context and cultural sensitivity are highly prized (Buchanan and Badham 1999, 18, 42–43).

11.9.   The Managerial Trap: Some Closing Remarks

If the short-term perspective dominates, then public administration is a study that focuses on managerial values and draws upon business administration. A longer-term perspective develops and refines the sensitivity to the norms and values underlying public sector organizations and performance. Teaching public administration as if it were only a tool kit is rather shallow for perpetuating this image of a problem-solving discipline. Given the value-laden nature of public sector choices, whether it is about type of organizations, about styles of policy and decision making, or about the styles and techniques of policy implementation and evaluation, a focus on developing understanding and on the values underlying all public action is desirable (e.g., Hood 1991).

The study of public administration is not only a problem-solving but also an enlightening study, as Lindblom and Cohen argue (1979). Academics can help by providing more empirical research on the development of policy over time. Politicians can make a major contribution by presenting more realistic claims about future policy, thus closing the gap between promise and what bureaucracy can achieve. Finally, citizens can be sensitized to the difference between the perception of big government and the fact of well-performing government. It is my contention that the inclusion of cultural analysis as a standard element in policy and decision making may perhaps not improve the quality in terms of results or substance, but certainly improves the quality in terms of process and of understanding the embeddedness of government intervention in social and historical time. It will also enhance Western understanding of the fact that perfectly rational policies (in terms of objectives, policy instruments, and so forth) do not quite fit or do not work at all in different cultural settings.

PART IV

WHO GOVERNS? THE INDIVIDUAL (ACTOR) LEVEL

Throughout this book, I argue that the activity of governing is embedded in terms of time as well as in terms of levels of abstraction. With respect to the latter, we have seen several examples where authors have disaggregated their object of interest into a most abstract, a more concrete, and a most concrete level of analysis. In the four parts of this book, the notion of levels of analysis is not limited to a specific subject matter within public administration, but concerns the study of government at large. Together parts I, II, and III provide layers that explain the public arena in which public servants and citizens operate. Of the four parts of this book, only part IV specifically addresses individual actors. Ultimately, organizations are run by people, policies are developed and implemented by people, and decisions are made by people. In whatever capacity, it is people who govern, and so separate attention needs to be given to the three major groups that are involved in the business of government. Their actions can be explained in part by the time and context in which they work, which includes the dominant ideas about government (part I), the public services provided to society (part II), and the organizational environment (part III). However, I emphasize that these do not entirely explain the behavior of individuals or groups in the public realm since actions of public officials and of involved citizens are, in principle, not predetermined. Believing in predetermination would fly in the face of everything that Western democracy holds dear, especially the notion of freedom of choice. Instead, we should consider the constant interaction between individuals and groups and the ideational, societal, and organizational environment.

In this section I discuss elected officeholders and political executives (chapter 12), civil servants or bureaucrats (chapter 13), and interest groups (chapter

14). I discuss the role and position of political officeholders and civil servants in government in relation to society and the role and position of interest groups with respect to public policy and decision making. Given my focus on government, I do not discuss specific political and administrative institutions and processes nor do I discuss societal associations at large in great detail.

12 POLITICAL OFFICEHOLDERS AND POLITICAL APPOINTEES

The history of administration has been defined as service to some higher authority (Gawthrop 1997, 208). In Western democracy, with its appreciation for positive law and for negotiable authority, political bodies are invested with that highest authority in society. As a consequence of the rationalization process, politics and administration have been regarded as a dichotomy rather than as a continuum. This dichotomy serves analytical purposes but was never intended to reflect reality. The dichotomy reflects a juridical perspective in which law defines politics and administration as clearly different realms. In discussing the reality of the interaction between politicians and civil servants, a more sociological perspective must be adopted. Combined, the juridical and sociological perspectives provide the most complete understanding of government. But over the past five decades, many authors have pointed out that in reality a politics-administration dichotomy is maintained for practical purposes. As Gawthrop remarked:

> there are those who have argued that the common thread in politics is hypocrisy, but, unlike the rain that falls on the good and the bad alike, popularly elected executive

and legislative officials seem particularly well adept in insuring that the public's perception of hypocrisy falls mainly on the career public servants. (Gawthrop 1997, 209)

Hence, from a sociological point of view, it may be considered expedient to recognize different roles. Gawthrop's comment relates to the rhetoric of politicians about big, inefficient, and expensive government that is mainly the fault of bureaucrats. When discussing civil servants as a whole, it is not an image of the poor, helpless bureaucrat who falls victim to the malicious politician that first comes to mind. While recognizing that both groups, politicians and civil servants, have distinct responsibilities, it is also clear that the demarcation between politics and bureaucracy is obscure and, especially at the top or summit of the public realm, probably nonexistent from a sociological viewpoint.

I first briefly discuss the basis upon which the role and position of politics in society rest (section 12.1). Next, I consider the theories that have been developed about the role of politics in decision making (section 12.2). The focus in sections 12.1 and 12.2 is on politics and the political elite in the abstract. I discuss what is expected from politicians (when speaking of politicians I include the political executives) and what roles they can and do play in section 12.3. An interesting feature of contemporary politics is that it has become a profession. The phenomenon of career or professional politicians is relatively new to history. At the same time, the growth of government has caused politics to bureaucratize (section 12.4). In that process of the professionalization and bureaucratization of politics, the nature of the relation between it and the bureaucrats has changed significantly (section 12.5). In the concluding section, I reflect upon the bureaucratization of politics in relation to the politicization of societal demand.

12.1. The Primacy of Politics and the Authoritative Allocation of Values

Politics and administration are fundamental to any society. There are cultural differences between various societies with respect to the role and position of politics. The belief that contemporary society or civilization and its political institutions represent the best in all of history rests upon a teleological, linear worldview wherein society and polity develop from primitive to ever higher stages. This is often referred to as the civilization or modernization process. With respect to political modernization, Eisenstadt believes that this process was characterized by four elements that could be viewed as stages. In the first stage, the degree of differentiation in political roles and institutions increases and a centralized and unified policy develops. In the second stage, the activities of the central administration and its political organizations gradually extend into all aspects and regions of society. Potential power then starts to spread wider and wider until in the end it includes all people in society. And finally the power of the traditional elites dwindles, rational-legal authority takes over, and the rulers in this politically fully modernized society can be held accountable for their actions (Eisenstadt 1963b, 99). This developmental view is in line with Enlightenment thought about a pluralist equilibrium (see Buchanan and Tullock 1962, 288–289). At the same time, this developmental view is somewhat naive, for it assumes that all adults will eventually partake in the sharing of power. The views of Eisenstadt and of Buchanan and Tullock concern the ideal democracy in a large society that believes in representative government and its objectives of liberty, equality, and fraternity. That system works because of free elections, majority rule, protection of the minorities, assumed responsiveness of government to people's needs, and accountability to the public of incumbents in political office. In such a representative democracy, all share in government because all have the right to vote and the right to stand for election.

According to democratic theory, politicians in democratic systems of government exercise real power given to them by the people, which makes them also accountable to the people. Thus, ideally, politics is subject to the public. But at the same time, that does not mean that politics is continuously subjected to the public. Once elected to office, politicians have and take a responsibility of their own. Representation of the public is not synonymous with obedience to the public. In principle, politicians have the capability to operate independently from the public, and, if they stray too far from the flock, they will face the consequences during elections. Hence, politicians are simultaneously subjected and not subjected to the public. At election time, they will have to account for their performance, and they will be held politically responsible for the actions of government. They are accountable to the public, while civil servants are accountable to their political bosses. Politics serves as the link between society and administration, and its professionals can be held accountable for their decisions and are also the first to make decisions.

The *primacy of politics* doctrine is relevant to Western governance for four reasons. The first reason is that it refers to the *subordination of the bureaucracy or administration to politics.* This doctrine provides the basis for recognizing a politics-administration dichotomy, in which politicians and bureaucrats each have a particular role. But if bureaucracy is subordinate to politics in theory, we should also ask to which part of the practice of politics the bureaucrat should be subordinated? Should the bureaucrat be subordinate to the highest elected official in the organization (e.g., the minister, the undersecretary, the director)? Should the bureaucrat be subordinate to the highest elected official in the executive (e.g., the president, the governor, the mayor)? Should the bureaucrat be subordinate to the highest elected officials in the collegial bodies of government (e.g., Congress, the state legislature, the local council), which is, after all, where the legislature resides? Should the bureaucrat be accountable to the public at large? Or should the bureaucrat be accountable to all of the above? It will be clear that the theory of political primacy may make sense in a democracy, but the practice of it is more difficult because political authority is not invested in one body or person. Instead, it is dispersed, as befits an organizational structure of checks and balances intended to protect democracy.

This raises a very important issue. If politics is defined by the authoritative allocation of values, then where is the highest authority that can actually allocate? It is not and could not be in only one of the political bodies. In the American and in other Western systems of government, the highest authority in practice is not a political institution but the *compromise* or the *accepted outcome of a negotiation process* between the individuals that fill the political bodies. Our highest authority is negotiable, and the fact that *political office-holders are accountable to the public* is a second reason in which primacy of politics becomes manifest. Bureaucratic officeholders are only indirectly accountable toward the public at large.

What are the values that require political intervention and that cause politicians to negotiate? Various lists can be drawn up and all have merit. The list by Lasswell is not necessarily better or worse, but is abstract enough to encompass a large range of issues that citizens value and consider important (Table 12.1).

These eight broad value categories can be read as the "authoritative allocation" of power, wealth, well-being, skill, enlightenment, affection, rectitude, and respect. It is clear that government cannot support each of these values to the same degree. Some values (e.g., the distribution of power and of wealth, the right to education) may be considered more subject to political negotiation than others (e.g., the distribution of affection, the distribution of rectitude). Also, some values (e.g., distribution of wealth) require a proactive government, whereas others (e.g., respect) may be served better by example or by a reactive attitude.

Values are discussed here again because the choice of a proactive or reactive government is fundamentally a political choice that is ultimately a politician's responsibility. It does not make much sense to speak in favor of either a proactive or a reactive government. With so many politicians, there will be so many opinions, and even if one group of politicians finds common

Table 12.1

Societal Values Requiring Political Intervention and Negotiation

1. Power: a voice in the making of decisions
2. Wealth: economic goods and services
3. Well-Being: physical and psychic health
4. Skill: opportunity to acquire and exercise latent talent
5. Enlightenment: access to information and comment on which rational choices depend
6. Affection: congenial human relations
7. Rectitude: common standards of responsibility in theory and fact and
8. Respect: absence of discrimination on grounds other than merit

Source: After Lasswell 1968, 149.

ground, there is another group that holds to a different opinion. The alliances between politicians may shift with the policy under consideration. Also, politicians have to keep their electorate and certainly all those who are organized in interest groups, happy. We can thus see what Bagehot meant when he wrote that a constitutional statesman is someone with a common opinion—which denotes being both sound and sensible as well as in touch with the popular desires—and uncommon abilities. Hence, in this perspective there is every reason to respect and maybe even admire those who aspire to and occupy public political office, for it is by no means an easy job.

From the above, a third reason emerges why the primacy of politics doctrine is deemed important. Elected officeholders need to be accountable for their deeds, and those who aspire to political office will know that they will be held accountable. That is not all. In a realist perspective, the politician is just another human being. Politicians can make mistakes. Most do not have extraordinary qualities or vision, and they are as open and vulnerable to temptations as anyone. Hence, a third reason to advocate the primacy of politics is that accountability helps to *fight potential and real nepotism and corruption.* The Pendleton Act of 1883, Woodrow Wilson's article of 1887, Frank Goodnow's book of 1900, the reform movement (in the United States between the 1880s and the 1920s) in general, and the relatively recent attempts at developing codes of ethical behavior have all been inspired by that goal.

There is a fourth, and more cynical, reason why the primacy of politics is important. Some theorists have argued that politics is subject to a more real and less visible power elite that *seriously challenges the autonomy of politicians.* It is this cynical view of politics in democracy that comes to the forefront in the so-called elite theories of decision making and that has made at least one author argue that the primacy of politics ought to be reasserted (Dror 2001, 31).

12.2. The Power of Politicians: The Elitist and Pluralist Perspectives on Decision Making

What power do politicians really have? If they have less in practice than what they are constitutionally invested with, where is it then? To Max Weber (1864–1920), the answer as to where power resided was clear. He envisions an inexorable march forward of bureaucracy, and in that process of bureaucratization democracy would slowly be smothered. Bureaucracy would ultimately be the real power. Weber's analysis depends upon a distinction between politics and administration. Many of his contemporaries in Europe did not make such a distinction, instead focusing their attention on power elites as such. We need to discuss these elite theories at some length in this chapter. First, because elites have been recognized on both sides of the Atlantic as an important factor in policy and decision making (cf. Mills 1956; Schattschneider 1990). Individuals at the summits of industry and business all belong to an exclusive network in which each wields a real and substantial economic power that cannot be ignored by politicians. Second, because the industrial and business elites they refer to cannot adequately be classified as an interest group wherein individuals have combined forces in an identifiable organization.

Weber's Italian contemporaries, Mosca, Pareto, and Michels, perhaps less formidable than him but equally compelling, focused on the nature of power elites in society at large. Gaetano Mosca (1858–1941) was the first of these three to study elites. His earliest publications go back to 1883 and he continued to elaborate his theories well into the 1930s. Central to his thought is what he called the *political formula,* in which

> the political class justifies its power by leaning on some better belief or sentiment generally accepted in that epoch and in that nation. These beliefs could be, according to the situation, the presumed will of the people or of God, a consciousness of forming a distinct nationality or chosen people, traditional fidelity to a dynasty, or trust in an individual endowed with exceptional qualities. (Mosca 1972, 249)

He concludes that the best political regimes are those that mix autocratic and liberal government. The elitist viewpoint is apparent in his idea that the ability to rule and other personal qualities are the criteria for recruitment into public office. It is also clear in his view of elections. Mosca regards elections as a struggle between organized groups that have the means to influence the unorganized masses. Each group strives to mobilize mass support, and in doing so the elite is compelled to bow to some degree to the influence of the uninformed majority, which is less aware of the true needs of society (Mosca 1972, 253, 256). Mosca's ideal ruler is thus the king-philosopher.

Vilfredo Pareto (1848–1923) shares the same ideas. His elite theory, first published in 1915 and influenced by Marxism, holds that social change is a consequence of the struggle for power between groups. Periods of harsh rule by a victorious elite alternate with periods of benevolent rule by the same elite but now in decline. New governments change only ideology, not the underlying structure and functioning of society. In Pareto's view, the winners in this elite struggle for power are those who lie, who cheat, who use violence, and who appeal to the gullible public (Pareto 1935; Bottomore 1972, 198, 226–227, 295; Collins and Makowsky 1972, 170–172. Pareto's analysis of elite behavior demonstrates a Machiavellian perspective.

Robert Michels (1876–1936) was, according to Mosca's translator and editors an Italian and something of a protégé of Mosca (Mosca 1972, 267), according to Lipset a German sociologist and close friend of Weber (Lipset's introduction in Michels 1962, 15, 21), according to Bottomore a colleague and friend of Weber (Bottomore 1972, 159), and according to Collins and Makowsky a German historian (1974, 217, 221). Michels was very well acquainted with the work of Mosca, Pareto, and Weber. His elite theory expands upon their work and, in Weber's case, may also have influenced it (e.g., Weber 1980, 546). Michels's *Iron Law of Oligarchy,* which is the title of chapter 2 in part 6 of his book, is best summed up in his own words:

> society cannot exist without a "dominant" or "political class," and . . . the ruling class, while its elements are subject to a frequent partial renewal, nevertheless constitutes the only factor of sufficiently durable efficacy in the history of human development. According to this view, the government, or, if the phrase be preferred, the state, cannot be anything other than the organization of a minority. It is the aim of this minority to impose upon the rest of society a "legal order," which is the outcome of the exigencies of dominion and of the exploitation of the mass of helots effected by the ruling minority, and can never be truly representative of the majority. . . . Thus the majority of human beings, in a condition of eternal tutelage, are predestined by tragic necessity to submit to the dominion of a small minority, and must be content to constitute the pedestal of an oligarchy. (Michels 1962, 353–354)

Michels's law is a lawlike generalization in the best of traditions. Mosca, Pareto, and Michels had all been influenced to some degree by Marxism (Michels, however, turned in disappointment to fascism in his later years). The same type of reasoning, however, could be found at the right-wing side of the political spectrum.

Karl Mannheim (1893–1947), equally interested in the relation between the individual and society, was more of a conservative liberal (influenced especially by Weber and Michels). Like Weber, he argues that modern industrial society can only exist by the grace of large and centralized bureaucracies headed by small elites. In his view, the concentration of power in a small group is a consequence of the growing interdependence between various sectors and regions of modern society. Following Weber's ideas, Mannheim argues that these large organizations progress blindly on the basis of functional rather than substantive rationality. In other words, there is no guarantee that policy and decision making become more intelligent as a consequence of rationalization (cf. Simon). Rather, the contrary is the case. Mannheim develops three future scenarios for the modern world: first, a status quo in which we muddle through on the basis of functional rationality; second, a flight into the irrationality of fascist dictatorship; third, a society in which the organizations and institutions are engineered by an intelligent and humanistic elite trained in the social sciences (Mannheim, 1936; Collins and Makowsky 1972, 190–194). The first scenario, making the best of reality, especially received attention in decision- and policy-making studies. The second scenario is one that most people would like to avoid. The first and second scenarios identify elements of functional rationality and irrationality that were fairly unique to early-twentieth-century thought about the relation between politics and administration. The third scenario is not at all new, going back to ideas in antiquity about leadership by king-philosophers.

In the United States, ideas about public leadership, and what makes a good leader, were expressed by the Founders, as well as a century later by—for instance—Woodrow Wilson. From the eighteenth century until the early twentieth, the belief reigned that a good leader has a fine and upstanding character, is virtuous, is educated in the liberal arts, and follows the call of a civic duty to govern. The "social engineering" element in Mannheim's third scenario was an additional element characteristic for the twentieth century. Earlier leaders responded and guided; modern leaders have to be proactive in the shaping of society.

Mosca, Pareto, and Mannheim saw their studies translated into English during America's Red Decade (1930), when they found an interested public among intellectuals and the literary and artsy crowds. Michels and Weber were not translated until the late 1940s. Influenced by Mannheim's firm belief in salvation by the social sciences and by Pareto's belief in elite rotation, Lasswell advocated a central place for policy sciences in order to prevent a *garrison state*. In the garrison state, a concept Lasswell coined in a 1941 article, the military emerges as an influential political group in the making of national security policy (Perlmutter 1977, 5). We find the same ideas in C. Wright Mills's notion, also grounded in Mannheim, of the *military-industrial complex* (1956), in which industry, army, and government control all power. Like so many before him, Mills argues that ownership and control are intertwined in American industry, and he too sees the emergence of a mass society where power would be concentrated in the hands of the CEOs of large organizations in the economic field (Bottomore 1972, 141, 144).

The American interest in business elites has roots in earlier experiences with corporate power. The Sherman Anti-Trust Act of 1890 had been passed as a (somewhat lame) response to the perceived concentration of power in large industries (oil, steel, railroads), whose power and influence were resented by farmers, laborers, and owners of small business. The act was a pacifying gesture toward popular discontent. In the words of an American senator at the time, "something must be flung out to appease the restive masses" (quoted in the *New York Times* of October 12, 1998). Bismarck could not have said it better when he introduced social insurance in imperial Germany in the 1880s. The situation in the 1950s, when Mills wrote his book, was different: compared to that for the tycoons of the turn of the century, who were visibly present and proud to show their good fortune. The new tycoons of the 1950s were not so visible:

> There are some one thousand companies listed on the New York Stock Exchange. . . . In the great majority . . . the only large stockholders are institutional trustees for other people's money: investment trusts, pension funds, and banks. . . . By and large, these enormous holdings have been acquired in the past ten years. . . . Anonymity . . . is exactly what our new masters prefer. . . . They are certainly the soberest, least conspicuous, and most studious of all of our managerial groups. It is unlikely that the public at large has even heard the names of men like [etc.]. Even in the financial community they are barely known. . . . Yet they are the "New Tycoons." In financial importance and the impact of their decisions on the economy, they—and the other managers of large investors—represent more power than the tycoons of yesteryear ever dreamed of possessing. (Drucker 1957, 35–37)

Analyzing how leaders in industry oozed power and prestige in the late nineteenth and early twentieth century and comparing that to the mid-twentieth century, when such open display of power and prestige would have been considered distasteful and even outright stupid, the economist Galbraith observes about the old tycoons and the new CEOs:

> [the old tycoons] answered not only for their personal wealth but also for the behavior of their companies. As men of corporate power they also were exceedingly visible. Today shares of the corporations are still the foundation of several notable fortunes. But no sins of the corporations are visited on these individuals, for they do not manage the company and almost no one knows who they are. (Galbraith 1958, 77)

Like the European theorists whose works were translated in the 1930s and 1940s, the Americans convey the clear message that democracy was under siege. Whether bureaucracy was a threat, as Weber believed, or whether elites as such were a threat, as the Italian political theorists argued, or whether business elites were a threat, as some American observers reasoned, is not really important, because—in the end—it was one social-economic-political power group that European and American intellectuals alike warned against. These elite theories struck a chord in Europe because of the fairly quick emancipation of the masses. In the Europe of Mosca, Pareto, Michels, Weber, and Mannheim, mass society had forced the elites into partial acceptance of a socialist ideology that lay at the foundation of the welfare state. In view of the brief European experience with totalitarianism, C. Wright Mills argued that the ultimate consequence of the road toward mass society would be totalitarianism. It is important to distinguish here between political totalitarianism, which refers to a dictatorship under one ruler or party, and societal totalitarianism, which refers to the dominance of a political-social-economic elite in society. It is this chance for societal totalitarianism that struck a chord in the United States in the 1950s because of its experiences with it at the time of the Founders and the Reform Era (1880s to 1920s), but also because of the strong republican-individualist nature of American culture (Bellah et al. 1996, 29–30; Croly 1965). Paradoxically, the United States also developed as a welfare state. Thus, the emergence of a welfare state is not simply a function of elite response to popular demand; it is as much a function of increased population size and density in urban areas.

Elite theory has not lost any of its relevance. In Europe, the days of mass emancipation are past and socialism has basically achieved what it set out to do. In the United States, industrialization is perceived as a fact of life, no longer a threat, although American government continues to secure the general interest vis-à-vis the monopolization of market segments by corporate actors. The case against Microsoft is the most recent example of this. Also, the Cold War, background for Mills's writings, belongs to the past. And yet there is ample reason to take elite theory seriously, not in conspirational terms, but simply in the sober recognition that every society has had elites and that they are and always will be as much a part of society as anything or anyone. For conspiracy theory to hold up, there should be empirical evidence of interlocking between the world of corporate enterprise, the world of government, and the world of public interest (including mass media, prestigious law firms, major philantropic institutions, leading universities, and recognized national civic and cultural organizations). Such an empirical study would place the logical analysis of Buchanan and Tullock in a more realistic perspective.

Whether such interlocking existed was an issue of debate among American political scientists in the 1950s and 1960s. The *stratificationists* firmly believed in a power network that included political officials and entrepreneurs in business. Their views were opposed by those of the *pluralists,* who defended the idea that the major decisions in society reflected a balance between competing forces and interest groups. In their view, the elected officeholder governed through negotiation (Ehrenhalt 1991, 29). The debate ended, so Ehrenhalt argues, in a stalemate. With the advantage of retrospect, Ehrenhalt concludes that the stratificationists were right when it came to describing how politics had been in the past, while pluralists such as Dahl were right with respect to the future of politics, which has been a system of open access to office and power since the 1960s, at least in the United States (Ehrenhalt 1991, 30).

In the 1970s and 1980s Dye conducted empirical research into the existence of interlocking power. Interlocking is the phenomenon of one person holding more than one position in different sectors at one point in time (Dye 1979, 145; 1986, 164). Dye distinguishes between two different models (1979, 237–238; 1986, 160–161). The *hierarchical* or *elitist model* hypothesizes that increased internal and external organizational complexity requires higher degrees of coordination and thus a greater centralization of power. The *polyarchical* or *pluralist model,* argues that as a consequence of organizational differentiation, elites have become specialized and compartmentalized and are recruited through separate institutional channels. Dye's empirical work confirms neither of these theories. In fact, his findings indicate that there is more interlocking between public interest positions (such as in civic, cultural, and educational institutions) and government positions, as there is at the top within the corporate sector, than there is between the corporate sector and the government (1979, 150, 152, 179; 1986, 184). Equally important is his observation that some three-quarters of the top positions in the public sector in the United States are held by people who have experience in government positions or in the law. Only one-quarter of the top public officials have held high office in the corporate sector. This is not much different from the situation in Europe (Page and Wright 1999).

Whatever power various elites have, it is constrained to some extent by the existence of organized society and highly organized government. Industrial and political elites are important, but bureaucracy has become the political force that Weber and his contemporaries so feared. However, presently it seems that bureaucracy is no longer feared (just as organized society is no longer feared) but, instead, considered an important counterweight to political and special interests. Slowly, but surely, the meaning of a political understanding of public administration has been recognized (e.g., Hill 1992, 1–57; Meier 1997).

12.3.   Our Representatives Are Also the Bureaucracies' Bosses

We assume that Miles's law (where you stand depends on where you sit) is as relevant to politicians as it is to any other group of individuals in society. What citizens expect from politicians depends on the role and position of each individual citizen in society. What the politician expects from the politician may differ from individual to individual. What citizens expect from their political officeholders is generally that they serve as a model of morality. This is not a jibe against some of the behavior of political officeholders, but is more generally a reference to Thomas Jefferson's insight about the politician living in a glass house. Naturally, political leaders are and should be entitled to privacy, but they are visible by nature of the position they occupy. First, we expect top leaders to have a nose for selecting the right people for the right job. Presidents and governors have major impact on policy and decision making, if not directly, then certainly indirectly through the people they select to serve in their governments. Second, the head of a department has great influence through the kind of political executives appointed to top executive positions. And then, third, it is expected that political leaders have uncommon capabilities. They must present bold yet realistic visions for the future, and it is even better when they can actually make their visions happen.

What is expected from political leaders does not necessarily coincide with the roles they play. For analytical reasons, I distinguish nine such roles, but in reality they are likely to be mixed. The most fundamental role for the politician is being the *flagship in the myth of democracy*. The people do not rule, but their representatives do. The people elect and may reelect, but the politician in office knows that after the election, the power of the people is basically over. From the point of view of elite theory one could argue that democracy exists only at election time. And even then it is limited because political party machines present candidates for public office. It is not as if the population at large has much of a say about who those candidates will be. This is true for all Western countries. Looking specifically into the development of democracy and the administrative state in the United States, one recent study speaks of the American *myth of communal democracy* and of the American *democratic wish* that images the people as a single, united political entity, where citizens directly participate in politics, where the people agree with each other, and where they are focused on each other (Morone 1990, 4–5). Morone's compelling analysis shows how much the populist belief in a communal democracy has always provided the rationale for reforms that, paradoxically, enhanced the buildup of the administrative state.

The politician's second role is being the *representative of the people*. Here politicians face a daunting task. On the one hand, they represent the people, which essentially assumes an ability to weigh various interests carefully and decide after ample consideration. But in the actual behavior of politicians, there is less of the intellectual appraisal Mannheim and Lasswell so hoped for and much more of *piecemeal engineering*. The concept of piecemeal engineering refers to the desire to meet someone's or a specific group's need without much consideration whether that would disadvantage other groups (cf. Lowi's distributive policy). As representative of the people, the politician has to cater both to the individualist tugs, as well as to the collectivist pulls in society. The politician has to balance between "being a fashion designer," and "an interpreter," looking out for the accumulated individuals' desires, on the one hand, and being a wise ruler in the ancient sense of the word on the other, who is able to assess the impact of structural developments in society and the economy and who may have to make decisions that are not understood by all.

Third, the true representative is also a *visionary leader,* whose hopes for the future are both romantic enough to play upon people's emotions (as embodied in slogans such as the New Frontier, a Thousand Points of Light, Don't stop thinking about tomorrow, and compassionate conservatism), as well as realistic enough to play upon the inevitable practical side of human nature. If romantic enough, a political leader's vision can create a large following, awakening the demagogical qualities that ride and grow upon the cheers of the public, until the vision finally assumes a momentum of its own. And, if practical enough, the political leader's vision can outline realistic policies that will gain support among a politician's most important allies: the bureaucrats.

Fourth, once elected to public office, the politician may act as *mediator between society and bureaucracy.* The link to constituents should guarantee that individual voices can reach high in the policy agenda and are not marginalized by the larger, organized appeals of interest groups. The politician-mediator is also the interpreter of what sentiments prevail in society. The politician-mediator is sensitive to the political climate. Given the public's natural distrust of government in the United States, the politician-mediator plays upon such sentiments by bashing bureaucracy in general terms while at the same time defending particular public services. The explanations as to why politicians behave toward bureaucracy the way they do are summarized by Hill (1992, 4–26). The relationship between politicians and bureaucrats has assumed biblical proportions: you do not spare those you love most.

Fifth, whether the politician is only a visionary with a malicious opinion of bureaucracy or a visionary with a program and an appreciation for bureaucracy, he or she is a *decision maker* who carries the final political responsibility for success and failure of policies. Here the democratic perspective is no longer cynical, but necessary. And here the distinction between politics and administration is more than just of analytical relevance. The following quote points to the heart of the matter:

> Their intent [Wilson and Goodnow] . . . was that politicians, who are principally charged with making top-level policy, ought not to bring partisan considerations into the administrative process; if they do so, this would be a legitimate object of

study for scholars and reformers. At the same time, administrators, who are principally charged with making secondary-level policy designed to flesh out the top-level policy legitimated by politicians and with implementing both levels of policy, should be given broad authority to do so and should be held responsible for their performance. (Hill 1992, 31)

In light of Kuypers's three-level policy analysis, we could say that Wilson and Goodnow reserved the setting of ultimate goals for politics, the determination of intermediate goals and instruments for politicians and administrators, and left the selection of strict instruments for administrators only. We should keep in mind that Wilson and Goodnow wrote at a time when a legal, constitutional, and comparative approach to politics and public administration thrived. Perhaps we can better understand the politics-administration dichotomy in their perspective than in the managerial approach of Taylor or in the behavioralist approach used since the 1940s. The rediscovery of the meaning of law and of ethics for our understanding of the public realm may well be the salvation of the field of government and of the study of public administration.

Sixth, what is less realized when politicians are elected for a term in public office is that they can also be elected or selected as the *heads of bureaucracy*. It is striking that the politicians' visions for the future overshadow their leadership capabilities and relevant experience in large public organizations. A good demagogue is not necessarily a good manager. Again, the elite theory is relevant, for is it reasonable to conclude that the gullible public is interested only in visions and images instead of in facts and careful appraisals? Politicians apparently think so, because they rarely focus on their experience in leading a large organization by coordinating its various organizational units and integrating its various policy responsibilities.

In the seventh role, politicians are *puppets in the hands of true, corporate power,* who faithfully take whatever actions are expected by their powerful supporters. It is impossible to generalize about the degree to which politicians are marionettes. Some will find support among corporate CEOs, others seek their bases among labor unions, but seeking and acquiring (financial) support is not synonymous with loss of independence in decision making. There is interlocking of people, but not in the manner suggested by the stratificationists. From a psychological point of view, it is unavoidable that humans seek out peers, gather with like-minded people, and associate with people of their own station. It is a feature of all ages. From a political point of view, we may expect that in Western countries power concentrates not so much around authority, but around money and ambition.

This takes us to the eighth role of the politician, which is being a *member of a political party.* Of all roles politicians play, this is perhaps the one that has been eroded most. Both in the United States and in Europe, the relation between political party and political officeholder has changed significantly. In the United States in the nineteenth century, political parties were the only truly national organizations. They did not only play a role in the election process, but also had significant influence in the appointment of administrative officials, and they were important in local communities as providers of jobs. This changed in the past forty years as a consequence of the open primary process and under the influence of the media. Political campaigns are now centered on candidates rather than parties, and candidates with enough money, time, energy, and ambition can win office independent of party organization. This is not to say that political parties have become obsolete. Indeed, they still identify candidates for the electorate and are still an important source for policy ideas (Bosso, Portz, and Tolley 2000, 256–257; Ehrenhalt 1991, 18–22).

While the importance of political parties has eroded, what has eroded even more is the ninth role of political officeholders, which is being a *morally exemplary individual* who serves as an example to follow for the citizenry at large. Dror remarks that root corruption in the body politic is grounded in the vices of, especially, senior politicians. From such *Fürstenspiegel* as that of India's Kautilya or Florence's Machiavelli, rulers were made aware of vices to avoid and virtues to develop. Today's politicians pay little attention to this, and, perhaps even worse, performance in office and personal behavior are considered different spheres that do not influence each other (Dror 2001, 95–97). Jefferson and his contemporaries needed no reminder that official performance and personal behavior could not be separated. That politicians today appear to be little concerned with this rule prompts Dror to advocate a code of ethics for politicians! (Dror 2001, 102–103).

Comparing the role and position of American political parties and politicians with those in Europe reveals differences and similarities. While the focus of elections is nowadays much more on candidates than on parties in the United States, European political candidates are firmly held within the folds of their political party. Another difference is that in Europe the influence of politics upon nomination to top career civil service positions appears to have increased over time (Page and Wright 1999), while in the United States it has decreased since the early twentieth century. One similarity is that political officeholders of today cannot play upon political and religious ideology as much as their predecessors could. Both in Europe and the United States, the societal basis of political parties has eroded because many of the emancipatory objectives that parties supported have been achieved. Another similarity is that in many of the continental European countries, the multiparty system of old has been replaced by a system with two or three major parties and a few smaller parties. As in the United States and Britain, the large parties in continental Europe provide a home to politicians along a broad spectrum within the conservative, Republican and the more liberal, Democrat parties (Roskin 1995, 43, 105, 179).

12.4. Bureaucratization of Politics and the Depoliticization of Policy Making

With the exception of one, all these roles have characterized politicians from Antiquity up to the present. The exception is ironical, for the one role that politicians are willingly or unwillingly playing increasingly is being a head of bureaucracy and thus being something of a bureaucrat. The bureaucratization of politics stems from at least four interrelated sources that are all a consequence of the growth in scope and size of government. First, the political process itself has been rationalized and bureaucratized. The official meeting-grounds of politicians are highly regulated by rules and procedures that concern speaking time, voting, agenda formation, and so on. Thus, the behavior of politicians has become more and more constrained by formal action and a bureaucratic way of functioning.

This is, second, reinforced by the fact that politics is no longer an occupation of gentlemen, who live off the proceeds of the land or of their business and who enter politics as a civic duty that is expected of their stratum in society. The politicians of the past could afford to *live for politics*. In the twentieth century, politics has become a profession in which its representatives *live off politics* (the distinction between living *for* and living *off* politics is from Weber 1980, 829). Politics and government are no longer a gentleman's pastime, but a full-time commitment of career politicians (Ehrenhalt 1991, 273). The shift from amateur to professional or expert politician was accompanied by increased bureaucratization. The contemporary elected politician is not just the people's representative but also, and equally important, the bureaucracy's top administrator. Politicians are increasingly involved in the administrative process. Realization of their policy desires requires sensitivity to considerations of administrative rationality. This is inescapable. Once elections are over and they assume their new position, they will be encapsulated by the organization they lead. There is no malice here. It is only reasonable to expect that politicians will develop loyalty toward the organizations they lead, if not for friendly and productive relationships with the civil service, then at least because they need to defend, for instance, their organizations' budget against the claims made by their fellow political incumbents who head other public bureaucracies.

A third reason for the bureaucratization of politics is a direct consequence of the scope of government services nowadays. It is physically impossible for politicians to have detailed knowledge of all issues that their departments are responsible for. The more routine decisions there are, made in the bureaucratic antechambers rather than in the political meeting rooms, the less influence a political officeholder has.

This relates to the fourth reason, which is that the influence of civil servants upon policy and decision making is considerable. What is more, civil servants are assumed to have the expertise and the experience to develop concrete policies out of the political leader's vision. A smart bureaucracy will usually present a newly elected or appointed political officeholder with some scenarios from which to choose. The growth of public services has, paradoxically, forced politicians back into their role as visionary leaders with a focus on the broad outline of policy, while at the same time forcing them to develop enough detailed knowledge so as to make intelligible decisions.

To understand this paradox, we need to revive the politics-administration dichotomy and look at the interplay between the two at the level of both individual interaction and collective decision making involving both political and administrative institutions, as is forcefully suggested in the following quotation:

> The bureaucracy, by most objective standards, is performing fairly well while the electoral institutions seem to be deteriorating. To solve this problem, public administration needs to revisit its past and reincorporate the study of electoral institutions into the field. This suggests a normative orientation, with public administration concerned with how governance should be structured and operated rather than just how the bureaucracy should implement public policy. (Meier 1997, 197)

The calls for a marriage between postwar political science and postwar public administration have been heard and followed up. The calls for a more realistic view of the politics versus administration dichotomy have not yet been, and may never be, heeded (see Svara 1998).

12.5. Political-Administrative Relations

One of the few areas where political science and public administration interests could have met was political-administrative relations. It was mostly political scientists who pursued research into this topic, which, given its focus on such relations at the top of the political-administrative system, was explicitly driving at the understanding of power relations. The most well-known analytical attempts at understanding them were by Aberbach, Putnam, and Rockman (1981) and by Peters (1988, 1989).

Aberbach, Putnam, and Rockman characterized the possible relationships between politicians and administrators as a development over time from one end of a continuum—a perfect separation of the two in the beginning of the twentieth century—to the other end—a perfect fusion toward the end of the twentieth century (Aberbach, Putnam, and Rockman 1981, 21). Image 1 represents the theoretical position in which the politician leads and decides, and the civil servants dutifully execute. In Image 1 we may hesitantly link Mannheim's substantive rationality to the politician and functional (process) rationality to the civil servant. Reality is better depicted in Image 2, in which the politician makes the value judgments and the civil servant provides the expertise. This is the angle that Herbert Simon took. In this image, both groups are separated, yet they are closer together because both pay attention to substantive as well as functional rationality. In the third image, both politicians and civil servants are engaged in frequent interaction with interest groups; the politician provides the passionate vision while the bureaucrat looks at the budgetary realism. Finally, in Image 4, both roles are merged. In all fairness to Aberbach, Putnam, and Rockman we should mention that they believed Image 1 and 2 to be relevant for the lower levels in the administration, while Image 3 and 4 accurately described the interactions at the upper levels in the administration. The lack of empirical support for their thesis that political and bureaucratic roles were converging was not noticed at the time that their study was published (Page 1995, 136).

The analysis presented by Peters is more elaborate and appears to focus on the interactions and behavior patterns at the political-administrative summit only (1988, 162). The *formal-legal model* fits Weber's type of legal-rational authority. The *village life model* images the situation in the nostalgic past, when those in public office belonged to one elite governing a fairly small and self-sufficient community. The New England style of local government is a good example of this model. In the *functional village life model,* the elites are integrated along functional lines, and thus networks exist in which politicians, civil servants, and representatives of interest groups circulate. In the *adversarial model,* the interaction between both groups appears to be close to organized anarchy. Finally, in the *administrative state model,* it is civil service that governs. This is not an administrative state in Waldo's sense, but literally a state run by bureaus or bureaucracy. As far as we know, this situation existed only once in history: Nineteenth-century Norway was in practice run by civil servants, while in terms of sovereignty it was part of the Swedish crown.

Analytical models are useful when mapping different types of political-administrative relations and when outlining differences between the upper and the lower levels in the political-administrative arena. It is likely that the type of interaction at the summit and close to the summit is determined by the involvement of both politicians and civil servants in policy making and decision making, where all actors can be expected to be sensitive to the political ramifications of their actions. At the middle and lower levels in the administration, interaction is likely to be between bureaucrats only. The chance that a political executive will directly speak with someone in the lower hierarchy is not large. If it occurs, it is probably because the political or the administrative actor in question wishes to bypass the immediate subordinate or supervisor. Interaction at the middle and lower levels of the bureaucracy is likely to be concerned with matters of implementation (implementation gap, goal displacement) and only indirectly with political choices. We should not underestimate, though, the degree to which policy is made and value judgments are passed at the street level (Lipsky 1980). At the summit of public organizations, interaction is more politicized than in the lower hierarchical levels. Naturally, a model should also be coherent and consistent, drawing upon either a formal or an informal approach. And, finally, any model with analytical pretention should travel over time; if not, it is a mere description of a situation that once existed.

With these considerations in mind, it is easy to see the merits as well as the shortcomings of the Aberbach, Putnam, and Rockman and Peters models (Raadschelders and Van der Meer 1998, 26, 32). First, both Aberbach, Putnam, and Rockman and Peters combine a juridical focus that emphasizes formal interaction with a sociological angle that concerns interaction in reality. In Aberbach, Putnam, and Rockman, the juridical angle is evidenced in Image 1 while Images 3 and 4 reveal a more sociological perspective. Peters's formal-legal model is legal/juridical by nature, while his other four models are rooted in a more sociological perspective. Hence, both these analyses combine a normative-juridical and a descriptive-empirical dimension. While Aberbach, Putnam, and Rockman suggest that there was a development over time from an Image 1 to an Image 4, there is ample reason to argue that such has never been the case. From a normative and legal point of view, politics and administration were as separated in 1900 as they are today, while in a sociological perspective those that populate the summit have always come from one and the same elite. Obviously, Peters's model does not implicitly assume a development over time.

Cross-time empirical work (including the United States, Canada, Australia, and several northern and southern European countries) has shown that the political-administrative elite was always one and never separated, that the development from a village life to a functional village life interaction happened everywhere, and that the size and composition of the summit changed but not the degree and nature of the interaction (Raadschelders and Van der Meer 1998; Page and Wright 1999, 4). These conclusions support Pareto's idea that elites may swap ideology but at the same time they are all too happy with the underlying structure!

There is one other critique of both models that we need to mention and that is that they both appear to lump the entire bureaucracy into one category. Is it conceivable that the nature of political-administrative relations at the summit varies with type of organization, level of government, the policy concerned, political regime (individualist or collectivist), and type of democracy (majoritarian or consensus democracy)? If this sounds plausible, then we can only conclude that the model required to analyze such a variety cannot be developed, for politicians strive to meet both general needs and unique cases in a particular national and cultural context. The merit of the Aberbach, Putnam, and Rockman and Peters models is that they provide the kinds of generalizations that enable us to analyze real-life situations. The leap to declaring that these models also reflect historical development is impossible since their content reflects a particular time and context.

12.6. Concluding Remarks: Balancing Visionary Leadership and Micromanagement

At the conclusion of this chapter, it is fitting to quote Blau's implicit acknowledgment of the existence of power elites, his explicit appreciation of the power of bureaucracy, and his very cautious remark about how to study government:

> Totalitarianism is the polar case of such bureaucratic concentration of power that destroys democratic processes, but not the only one. The same tendency can be observed in political machines that transfer the power that legally belongs to voters to political bosses, in business corporations that vest the power that rightfully belongs to stockholders in corporation officials, and in those unions that bestow the power that rightfully belongs to the rank-and-file members upon union leaders. These cases lead some writers to contend that the present trend toward bureaucratization spells the doom of democratic institutions. This may well be too fatalistic a viewpoint, but there can be no doubt that this trend constitutes a challenge. To protect ourselves against this threat, while continuing to utilize these efficient administrative mechanisms, we must first learn fully to understand how bureaucracies function. . . . This is the reason why the study of bureaucratic organizations has such great significance in a democracy. (Blau 1963, 22)

In Blau's view, government needs to be studied in its political and administrative manifestations, but it is more important to recognize that bureaucracy is synonymous not with government, but with organized society; that each bureaucracy has its power elites; and that thus, in each bureaucracy, oligarchy is never far away.

For reasons analyzed in this chapter, twentieth-century politicians have become as much a victim of bureaucratization as any other group in government and society. At the same time, politicians have been forced to depart from grand visions if they do not contain proposals for concrete action. This is a consequence of the politicization of societal demand. Fewer and fewer interests in society are not organized, and politicians have to pay attention to what each interest seeks to advance. The politician who cannot balance the qualities of visionary leadership with the need for micromanagement is doomed to fail.

13 BUREAUCRATS AND THE CIVIL SERVICE: BETWEEN IMAGES AND FACTS

The.true bureaucrat is a man of really remarkable talents. He writes a kind of English that is unknown elsewhere in the world, and he has an almost infinite capacity for forming complicated and unworkable rules.
—Henry Mencken, 1930

The citizen blames "bureaucrats" and "politicians" because the basic ecological causes have not been clarified for him.
—John Merriman Gaus, 1947

Why would an instrument [bureaucracy] designed to be impersonal and calculating be expected to be effective in delivering sympathy and compassion.
—Dwight Waldo, 1980

And what is the place of courage? Do we want a bureaucracy populated with pusillanimous paper pushers, or should we seek the plucky, the spunky, and the nervy?
—Donald P. Warwick, 1981

While public opinion about government has appeared to wax and wane with the tide of the economy in the past 200 to 250 years, public opinion of bureaucracy at large has been consistently negative. Before the 1750s, the population at large generally viewed government as an oppressive force, a means to extract hard-earned wages through taxes, and the vehicle of elite interests. It has only been since the late nineteenth century that government has come to be associated with the provision of social services beneficial to the masses. Also, until the 1750s the public's discontent was with individual public officials (especially tax collectors), but since the coining of the concept of bureaucracy in the 1760s, public discontent has especially targeted bureaucratic officials at large. Until the second part of the eighteenth century, a distinction between government (or politics for that matter) and bureaucracy did not exist.

The growth of public services was a response to societal demand, and amid the rapid changes in the relation between government and society and in the structure and functioning of government itself, people embraced different viewpoints. Some favored a strong and proactive government; others espoused limited government. Since the days of Jefferson, support for and suspicion of big government in the United States have both increased and decreased (Furner 1997). Few have been as torn as the journalist and social critic H.L. Mencken. He sided with the Progressivists in the support of a rational, efficient, and honest government that served people's needs. He supported public health, urban home rule, administrative efficiency, executive leadership, and clean government (Williams 1998, 23), as the following quote illustrates:

> The extortions and oppressions of government . . . will come to an end when the victims begin to differentiate clearly between government as a necessary device for maintaining order in the world and government as a device for maintaining the authority and prosperity of predatory rascals and swindlers. (as quoted in Nolte 1968, 118)

Like so many of his contemporaries, Mencken was aware of the corruption, fraud, and spoils so normal in politics and government in the United States into the third quarter of the nineteenth century, which explains his support of the Progressivists. However, at the time that he was most productive, from the 1910s to the late 1930s, government had grown substantially, providing new opportunities for irregularities and for the creation of a new, bureaucratic upper class:

> Government has now gone far beyond anything ever dreamed of in Jefferson's day. It has taken on a vast mass of new duties and responsibilities; it has spread out its powers until they penetrate to every act of the citizen, however secret; it has begun to throw around its operations with the high dignity and impeccability of a state religion; its agents become a separate and superior caste. (as quoted in DuBasky 1990, 377)

While always suspicious of the potential of government corruption, Mencken was equally concerned about the consequences of popular democracy for efficient and effective public policy. He believed universal suffrage to be a cancer since the great mass of the people was against changes that involved risk and sacrifice (Williams 1998, 20–22). That type of reasoning was in line with a king-philosopher approach to government that simultaneously was highly critical of bureaucrats.

In a way, Mencken's seemingly contradictory views of government reflect the views individuals still hold. Some believe that government cannot be small enough, others are supportive of interventionist government for the good of society, but most have stereotypical, negative images of bureaucrats. In this chapter, I discuss images of bureaucrats and facts about civil servants. In the first section, a variety of conceptualizations and definitions of bureaucrats will be reviewed as found in the literature starting with Max Weber. Next, the different ways in which scholars have described and conceptualized the role of civil servants in the public arena at large are examined (section 13.2). These descriptions range from negative to theoretical and even positive. The one negative image that has continued to capture public opinion for more than 200 years will be discussed separately (section 13.3). More theoretical images have been provided by authors who, from a legalist (Weber) or economic perspective (Downs, Niskanen), were driven to warn against the power of bureaucracy (section 13.4). It is interesting to see that the basis for bureaucrat-bashing is wobbly, to say the least, when individual citizens are asked about their own experiences with bureaucrats. There is a monumental gap between perception and reality in the Western world (section 13.5). A more nuanced view of civil servants is served by some facts about the developments in the role and position of the civil service in society since the Middle Ages, about its professionalization in the nineteenth and twentieth centuries, and about its size in relation to the population (section 13.6). I pay separate attention to the recent developments in the relation between politics and bureaucracy (section 13.7). Given the importance of civil servants in policy and decision making, the question can be raised if this is right given the primacy of politics. I therefore make a case that the role of civil servants in the "authoritative allocation of values" is not only unavoidable, but should even be welcomed (section 13.8). Another aspect that requires separate discussion is representative bureaucracy, a theme of increasing importance in the second part of the twentieth century (section 13.9). In sections 13.6 to 13.9, bureaucracy is considered in relation to its environment. And in section 13.10, I look at developments in human resource management, which is an internal function of public organizations.

13.1. Bureaucrats: Weber's Second Batch of Dimensions and Other "Neutral" Characterizations

The analysis of public organizations in the twentieth century went beyond the study of mere managerial principles once parts of Max Weber's monumental *Economy and Society* were translated into English in the 1940s by Gerth and Mills (1946) and by Hendershot and Parsons (1947). These translations focused, among other topics, especially on Weber's sociology of power, the idealtypes of authority, and organization. This damaged the initial understanding of Weber's work and particularly highlighted Weber's warnings about the consequences of bureaucratization. Some of these misunderstandings were

Table 13.1

Dimensions of Bureaucracy as a Group of People

9. Office held by individual functionaries,
10. Who are subordinate, and
11. Appointed, and
12. Knowledgeable, who have expertise, and are
13. Assigned by contractual agreement
14. In a tenured (secure) position, and
15. Who fulfill their office as their main or only job, and
16. Work in a career system
17. Rewarded with a regular salary and pension in money
18. Rewarded according to rank, and
19. Promoted according to seniority, and
20. Work under formal protection of their office.

Source: Van Braam 1986, 216–220; Raadschelders and Rutgers 1996, 92.

rectified by Lipset (1963, 58–59), Mayntz (1965), and Mouzelis (1967, 43–46), but up to this day, the scholarship on Weber still suffers from the limited selection in the early translations. Reading Weber in incomplete translation more or less confirms the stereotypes of bureaucracy. In the stereotypical image of bureaucracy, the bureaucrats are formalistic, lazy pencil pushers who spend too much time around the coffee machine. Reading Weber's work in its entirety, however, we realize that he did not stereotype but attempted to understand bureaucratization as an expression of the rationalization process in the Western world. He was genuinely concerned about the relation between bureaucracy and democracy (cf. Waldo 1984). First and foremost, Weber was a taxonomist who, in the best of continental European traditions, defined his object of analysis before exploring social reality.

Bureaucracy was one of the social phenomena he defined in greater detail than what is generally provided in the public administration literature. Weber's idealtype of bureaucracy consisted of seventeen dimensions, and it has been expanded to twenty by Van Braam (1986). The first set of eight dimensions concerns the features of the bureaucratic organization. The second batch consists of twelve dimensions that characterize the functionaries (*bürokratischer Verwaltungsstab*) (Table 13.1).

Dimension 9 in Table 13.1 refers to the indivisibility of office, which was uncommon until the late eighteenth and early nineteenth centuries. The tenth dimension, which concerns the unity of command principle, refers to the authority and accountability in the manager-subordinate relation. What is also underlined in this set of dimensions is the fact that bureaucratic functionaries are appointed (dimension 11), not elected, and thus subordinate to politics. What is equally important to the idealtype is that appointment rests on expertise and has a contractual and voluntary basis (dimensions 12 and 13). Appointment and expertise together serve as a safeguard against the patronage, nepotism, and corruption that had been so normal in the government machinery up to the late eighteenth century in Europe and up to the late nineteenth century in the United States. Dimensions 14 to 20 deal with creating protected work conditions for civil servants and with establishing a neutral bureaucracy. Dimension 14 is a reminder that a civil servant cannot be fired upon political whim, nor be threatened with loss of job by a politician who stands to gain personally from such action. Fulfilling the office as the main or only job (dimension 15) creates the security not only that civil servants can spend their active work life in one job, but also that they are never in the situation of wearing two hats and succumbing to temptation because of it. The modern bureaucracy in Weber's eyes should provide incentives for individuals to stay. For one, if work is conducted satisfactorily in the eyes of supervisors, promotion in a career system is a reward (dimension 16). Also, one may expect to receive a regular salary, the amount of which can be reviewed at set intervals (e.g., annually) or upon promotion. Part of the salary is set aside as a pension (dimension 17). This is a means of creating loyalty to the organization, but it is also a means to keep the expertise that has been accumulated in the individual and in the organization. Working in a career system means, in the German empire of Weber, that reward is also provided by advancing someone from rank to rank (dimension 18) on the basis of seniority (dimension 19). Finally, civil servants work under formal protection of their office. They are protected by the democratic accountability of political officeholders and can be sanctioned internally (refusal of promotion, refusal of salary raise, etc.) only for misconduct. An exception to this is, of course, when by their actions civil servants place themselves outside the normal review arenas (because of treason, embezzlement of any financial nature, corruption, etc.).

In the Weberian juridical or legalist definition of bureaucrat, every civil servant is one, irrespective of rank and status. A public employee is someone who works for and is paid by government out of public funds, from street sweeper to director-general. In continental Europe, the juridical understanding of bureaucracy and bureaucrats dominates the academic literature. In addition to this juridical or legalist definition of bureaucracy, there is a more sociological understanding of it that emphasizes the rank and status of bureaucrats in relation to other public officeholders. In that sociological perspective, the civil servant is the white-collar worker, sitting behind a desk, doing work that requires some or much intellectual ability. The blue-collar worker does manual labor. The term "civil service" in England refers to the upper echelons in the public service. In general, the sociological understanding of bureaucrats dominates in the Anglo-American literature. This is also visible in the Anglo-American emphasis on different types of personnel systems, such as the general civil service (e.g., the top in England, the senior executive service (SES) in the United States), the professional career system (e.g., white-collar), the collective system of unionized employees (e.g., blue-collar), and the political executive system (Klingner and Nalbandian 1998, 7). This last category is the one in between pure political and elective office and pure administrative and appointed office. A political executive is appointed without tenure, usually has a limited term of office, and enjoys significant policy-making powers. At the federal level in the United States, there are some 3,000 positions of this nature, of which about 700 are in SES; the total number of SES positions is around 7,900 (Meier 2000, 32–34), and there are many more at the state and local levels. In a variety of European administrative systems, one can also find political executives officials, especially in France and Italy. In Germany and the Netherlands, the number of political appointees at the top of the bureaucracy is much smaller (Page and Wright 1999).

The legalist versus sociological approaches to civil servants are also relevant in relation to the expanding functions of government. Throughout the nineteenth century and well into the twentieth, top-level positions in government were filled by generalists with a liberal arts background (as in Britain) or a law background (as on the European continent). Given the fact that government policy has ventured into so many new areas, the question arises whether specialists are needed at the top of the civil service and how important it is that they have political sensitivity. Asked to supply the British Fulton Committee with recommendations about the role of the civil service in the modern state, Ridley edited a now classic volume in which the British tradition to separate *generalists* in administrative roles from *specialists* in advisory roles was compared with such traditions in Australia, France, West Germany, Sweden, and the United States (1968). In his concluding chapter, Ridley makes clear that the two sides in this debate really depart from different assumptions: the *generalists* consider administration an art while the *specialists* believe it is a science (Ridley 1968, 211; cf. Vickers 1965, chapter 11). The most important conclusion Ridley draws is that top-level positions can be held equally well by generalists (i.e., those with a liberal arts background) and by specialists (i.e., those with an education in one of the natural or social sciences) and that appointment depends basically "only on the administrative ability that a particular individual shows" (Ridley 1968, 205). A similar theme was picked up by Putnam, who distinguishes between *classical* and *political bureaucrats* (1973). The first regard their function as carrying out the orders of politics and are not involved with interest groups, while the latter actively participate in the "pluralistic process of political decision-making" and seek contact with outside interests (Page and Wright 1999, 4). As was argued in the last chapter, there is no empirical evidence that the roles of top-level civil servants have developed from being more "classical" to being more "political." If anything, top-level officeholders always must have had a sense of politics. We will see below that the theme of legalist versus sociological perspectives on bureaucrats also determines the images and appreciation of civil servants.

13.2. Images of Bureaucracy: Fourth Power, Third Force, Second in Line, First for Stereotyping

The word "bureaucracy" has an interesting etymology. The Greek suffix *krateoo* means as much as "to rule." Thus democracy is the rule of the people (*demos*), meritocracy is the rule of the deserving (*merites*), gerontocracy is the rule of the elders (*gerontes*), aristocracy is the rule of the best (*aristoi*), timocracy is the rule by the "propertied" class, ochlocracy is the rule by the mob, kleptocracy is the rule by thieves, and bureaucracy is then the rule of bureaus. The use of this suffix suggests a relation of bureaucracy to the classical three types of government as distinguished by Plato and Aristotle: rule by one person (monarchy or tyranny), rule by a few (aristocracy or oligarchy), and rule by many (polis or democracy). In this sense, bureaucracy is indeed a fourth power next to the other three.

The word "bureaucracy" as we know it was first used in the middle of the eighteenth century by Vincent de Gournay (1712–1759), a French civil servant and physiocrat (the phrase *laissez-faire, laissez-passer* is also attributed to him). We do not have it in his own printed words, but it is documented in a letter by Baron de Grimm (July 1, 1764) to Diderot:

> The late M. de Gournay . . . sometimes used to say: "We have an illness in France which bids fair to play havoc with us; this illness is called bureaumania. Sometimes he used to invent a fourth or fifth term of government under the heading of bureaucracy." (Albrow 1970, 16)

What is interesting in this remark is that in one sentence the Greek-style distinction is made between the good and the perverted type of rule. Bureaucracy is the good form, like monarchy, aristocracy, and polis. What de Gournay calls *bureaumania* is nowadays usually referred to as *bureaucratism* (Van Braam 1986, 219). Red tape, formalism, hierarchicalism, and laziness are all elements of bureaucratism, referring to bureaucracy in a pejorative connotation. As Weber used it, bureaucracy is a neutral concept, neither good nor bad, but referring to a particular type of rule (that of bureaus). Bureaucratism implies a value judgment. I will outline how value judgments cloud the popular perception of bureaucracy (section 13.3), and indeed how they may color and have colored research (section 13.4).

There is more to say on the etymology of "bureaucracy." "Bureau" in eighteenth-century French referred to an office where people worked as well as to a writing table. In earlier times, a writing table was covered with a coarse brown cloth called *la bure* (Kamenka 1989, 94–95). Bureaucracy as a fourth power can be linked to the separation of powers of Locke and of Montesquieu. Bureaucracy is not only a fourth power in abstraction, in addition to the triads distinguished by the Greek philosophers or Montesquieu; bureaucracy is also a real power, since the power sources of civil servants are substantial. Not only do they have formal authority and specified powers and jurisdictions, but their power also comes from continuity in office (vis-à-vis the political incumbent and the political executive), from expertise, from organizational memory, from control of information, from being indispensable in almost the entire policy- and decision-making process, from being monopoly providers of particular services, from having citizens depending on them (for entitlements, permits, licences, etc.), from having politics depend upon them for proper implementation, and so forth. More specific to the United States is the fact that fragmentation of political power enhances the chances of an influential bureaucracy.

So far, the characteristics of bureaucracy have been presented in relation to types of rule. As a phrase, the *power of bureaucracy* suggests a monolith, while in reality it is not. When bureaucracy is discussed as a fourth power, it usually refers to that small group that has the power to direct the bureaucracy from within: the higher and highest administrative officeholders. Heclo (1991) suggests a third force between bureaucratic man, the obedient civil servant subordinate to the political authority, and political man, the elected officeholder. That third force is the civil servant, who "is responsive to the legal authority of political heads" and "has a responsibility that is institutional and enduring" (1991, 42). In Heclo's conception, members of the third force serve as a bridge between pure politics and pure administration. Thinking of the civil service as a third force or a fourth power betrays a sociological approach to the concept of civil service. In a legalist perspective, the civil servant is always second in line to the political officeholder, while in a sociological perspective we recognize that the role and influence of civil servants vary with their rank and status in the organization. The legalist and sociological perspectives also play a role in the appreciation of bureaucrats. It appears that authors who emphasize the legalist perspective hold a far more negative judgment of bureaucrats than do those who take a more sociological view.

13.3. Negative Images and the Teutonic Tradition of Bureaucrat Bashing

Civil servants are not fortunate in how they are portrayed. Once the concept of bureaucracy was coined in the mid-eighteenth century, public attention and discontent moved from the individual officeholder (the tax collector, the mayor) to the abstraction of the concept. People working in bureaucracies had to be bureaucrats and what was held "true" in a monolithic conception of bureaucracy must therefore be true for the individual officeholders as well. Modern dictionaries usually define bureaucracy as rule by bureaus (the organizational aspect) and as a collective of civil servants, but also as formalism, officialism, and red tape. For a long time, though, bureaucracy was solely defined in terms of bureaucratism. Take, for instance, the definition of bureaucracy by Robert Von Mohl (a German scholar of public administration) in 1846:

> the false understanding of state tasks, filled with many, partially very mediocre members, who wallow in purely formal gestures and function in an organization of professional civil servants with much personal lack of manners. (as quoted in Kaltenbrunner 1976, 7)

One of the contributors to Kaltenbrunner's volume called bureaucracy an "elephant disease" (Eisermann 1976, 50), and another wrote that "civil servants [are] multiplying like rabbits" (Zehm 1976, 52). These characterizations of bureaucracy illustrate the familiar stereotype. The American journalist and social critic H.L. Mencken referred to the unnecessarily complicated language of bureaucrats and their reliance upon rules, and he also did not shy away from using irrelevant analogies that played upon popular notions about bureaucrats. Consider his following observation, written in 1933:

> Is government, then, useful and necessary? So is a doctor. But suppose the dear fellow claimed the right, every time he was called in to prescribe for a bellyache or a ringing in the ears, to raid the family silver, use the family toothbrushes, and execute the *droit de seigneur* upon the housemaid? Is it simply a coincidence that the only necessary functionaries who actually perform any comparable brigandage are the lawyers—the very men who, under democracy, chiefly determine the form, policies and acts of government? (as quoted in DuBasky 1990, 370)

The reference to the feudal lord's right to the first night is deceptive, for such practices in Europe had not only ceased to exist long ago, but, more importantly, also were never as widespread as has been suggested. Mencken also argued in a 1927 article that bureaucrats were mainly concerned with their own power, income, and prestige, instead of working for the public's interest:

All government, whatever its form, is carried on chiefly by men whose concern is for their offices, not for their obligations. Its primary aim is to keep this group in jobs that are measurably more comfortable and exhilarating than the jobs its members could get in free competition. They are thus always willing to make certain sacrifices of integrity and self respect in order to hold these jobs. (as quoted in DuBasky 1990, 377)

When we line up the elements of the stereotype, the vehemence is clear: bureaucrats are formalistic and have no manners (Von Mohl), they seek the bureau's expansion for self-serving purposes (Eiserman, Zehm, Mencken), they speak a complicated language (Mencken), and they even engage in improper behavior (Mencken). While writing in the more distant manner of a true academic, Weber fueled the inbred distrust of bureaucracy as a threat to political power. Indeed, his work was continued by contemporary German and Austrian scholars up to a point where Goodsell felt comfortable enough to speak of a Teutonic tradition in the study of bureaucracy (Goodsell 1985, 8). And this has proved to be a very persistent tradition carried on not only by German scholars, by people of German descent (such as Mencken), and by first-generation German emigrants such as Hummel (see below), but also in such phrases as "government is not the solution but the problem."

In Hummel's phenomenological approach to bureaucracy, the same stereotypical elements are emphasized. Bureaucracy is synonymous with excessive control, bureaucrats are brainless and heartless people, they have a secret language, and they deal with cases, not with people (1977, 3). In Hummel's analysis, those who come to work for a bureaucracy will be dehumanized, for they are trained not to attach affection to any person, to relate only to their own functions and the exercise of power. Hummel believes the bureaucratic type to be a personality type and not just a specific type of worker. In his view, one is a bureaucrat twenty-four hours a day, in personal, family, and intimate relationships as well as at work:

As a result, when the bureaucratic type engages in what used to be known as personal relations between the sexes, his behavior is characterized by (1) an absence of love, (2) a great deal of emphasis on, and attachment and affect to, technical performance in sexual intercourse, and (3) the narrowing of the range of affect to feelings of power—i.e., the replacement of love by sexual aggression. (Hummel 1977, 51)

This is the strongest and most vitriolic stereotyping of bureaucrats that I know. What makes it a stereotype is that Hummel argues that phenomenological analysis is empirical, based on the experience of people (Hummel 1977, 212). In the more traditional understanding of empirical research, personal experiences of people can be used but do not elevate prejudicial and biased perceptions to theoretical status. Hummel is unusually strong in his choice of words, but one can find the same Teutonic stereotypes in theoretical literature by authors from different cultural traditions. While German and Austrian scholars have greatly contributed to the stereotyping of bureaucracy, it cannot be said that it is solely a Teutonic culture (with its appreciation for hierarchy, formality, and application of rules) that has fed the stereotyping. In Anglo-American countries we find the same stereotyping that regards the bureaucrat as a personality type (a pathology). The word "bureaucrat" is more often used in a pejorative sense by Republican than by Democratic members of the U.S. Congress. Democrats are inclined to use the more neutral term "civil servant" (Hall 2002, 247).

13.4.   Theoretical Images: The "Anglo-American" Warning

A good illustration that the cultural background of authors is relevant in understanding their theories is the debate about the relation between politics and administration as conducted in the early 1940s by Carl Friedrich, a doctor of law who came from Germany to the United States in 1926, and Herman Finer, a British scholar of Romanian descent who also concluded his career in the United States (McSwite 1997, 29). Friedrich believed that the two realms of politics and administration could not be separated, and he exhibited trust in the human nature of administrators in that they would advance policy on the basis of scientific and technical knowledge and on the basis of Rousseau's general will. Finer, on the other hand, did not trust human nature and desired control mechanisms that would correct and punish administrators who overstepped their boundaries (McSwite 1997, 38–39). What is "German" about Friedrich's point of view is his trust in the bureaucrat as a good organizational citizen who will play by the rules. What is "English" about Finer's position is that the growth of government, and thus of bureaucracy, in Great Britain resulted in a state and administrative system in which the tradition of amateur government no longer sufficed. Finer warned against the encroachment upon politics and amateur government by bureaucracy.

Friedrich and Finer are both concerned with the interaction between political and bureaucratic power. It is but one element of political science's orientation toward bureaucracy, which also includes notions that the expansion of bureaucracy is mainly related to career advancement and personal and organizational aggrandizement. This aspect of the bureaucratic stereotype is also embraced by scholars with an economic approach to behavior and decision making, of which the American economists Downs and Niskanen are examples.

Downs's [1966] (1997) *Inside Bureaucracy* is among the most cited studies, if not the most cited, of bureaucracy. While his analysis is far more detached than Hummel's, the underlying assumption of self-interest is comparable. The fundamental premise of his theory is that bureaucracy grows mainly, though not solely, as a consequence of bureaucrats' behavior that is aimed at maximizing power, prestige, income, security, loyalty, and/or convenience (Downs 1997, 2, 17). This premise has deep roots in American history. On October 18, 1787, "Brutus" published his first essay in the *New York Journal* to counter the *Federalist*, and one sentence in it read as follows: "In so extensive a republic, the great officers of government would soon become above the control of the people, and abuse their power to the purpose of aggrandizing themselves, and oppressing them" (Ketcham 1986, 279). Downs distinguishes between five main bureaucratic types (climbers, conservers, advocates, zealots, and statesmen), plus a mixed motive type (92–110). While Downs acknowledges that these types are arbitrary, he defends them in the same breath by saying that simplification and arbitrariness are inescapable in all human knowledge and that particular forms of simplification and arbitrariness will help develop better forecasts of behavior (4). Of these five types, the climber, the conserver, and the zealot determine our perception of bureaucrats most (according to Hummel, these three types display near hysteria in their activities, [1977, 131]). Unlike Hummel, Downs is quick to acknowledge that

> Bureaucrats as individuals are neither more nor less efficient, honest, hard-working, thorough, public-spirited, and generally worthy of admiration than nonbureaucrats. (26)

What is puzzling about his hypothesis of self-seeking motives behind bureaucratic growth is that he also writes, "The major causes of growth, decline, and other large-scale changes in bureaus are exogenous factors in their environment, rather than any purely internal developments" (263). Here the individual bureaucrat appears as an actor who responds to environmental change instead of one who expands his bureau no matter what.

One problem with Downs's analysis is that his theory is not tested through empirical research. Obviously, that was not his intention. Downs desires to develop a formal theory of decision-making behavior in bureaucracy, much as Buchanan and Tullock developed a logical model of democratic decision making. What is more of a problem in my view, though, is that, while Downs explicitly recognizes the pejorative definition of bureaucracy, he nonetheless adopts one element of the stereotype (expansion for self-serving reasons) as a cornerstone of his theory.

The same approach is taken by Niskanen, who develops a mathematical model of decision making. In his economic theory of bureaucratic growth, Niskanen points out some characteristics that differentiate bureaucrats from other collectives, such as that bureaucrats maximize their personal utility (1973,

12, 20). Niskanen presents two explanations for this tendency (22–24). First, from a rational point of view, an increased budget will lessen the necessity that the bureau chief has to make painful choices. More budget is a source for salary increase, extra perks, and more power. Second, because of the will to survive, the leader of the bureau will provide increasing salaries for his subordinates.

Chapter 3 of Niskanen's 1973 study carries the intriguing title "The Behaviour of Bureaus," which suggests that he collapses the conceptions of bureaucracy as organization and as group of officials into one. He does, however, believe that bureaucracy as a whole is more capable of influencing policy than an individual bureaucrat can. In his words:

> it is *impossible* for a single bureaucrat to act in "the public interest," because of the limits of his information." (23)

In this quotation we hear an echo of Simon's "bounded rationality," but there is more to this remark. Is it true—that is, empirically proven—that individuals make no difference? Like Downs, Niskanen adopts a macroperspective on decision making, but this inhibits him from recognizing that some individuals may have influence. In this respect, Mouzelis makes a distinction between *single actors*, who do not have much influence on the macroinstitutional order, *collective actors*, who wield influence through interaction, and *mega-actors*, who are single individuals whose decisions, by virtue of their economic, political, or culturally based social power, have widespread consequences (Mouzelis 1991, 106–107). With the remarks about elite theory in mind, one cannot logically assume the nonexistence of such mega-actors. Each society, including the American, has them. Again, like Downs's, the study by Niskanen lacks empirical support.

The theories by Downs and Niskanen have also been used to explain *budget maximization.* This concept assumes that managers responsible for making the budget will know that they have to ask for more than they really need, because they never get what they ask. Also, by the end of the year, the entire budget must be spent because the manager knows that frugality is punished by budget cuts. As a concept, budget maximization appears to be the sole rational motive of one top official or of one decision-making unit. Reality, though, is more complex. Dunleavy has argued that there are at least four reasons why budget maximization cannot be the sole rational motive. First, there is competition for the budget between officials and units. Second, there are competing types of budgets (core, bureau, program, and superprogram), and the size of the budget and its component parts (more for the core expenditure such as personnel and buildings or for programs) vary with the type of bureau (e.g., regulatory versus service delivery agency). Third, budget maximization is greatest when there is a close relation between core, bureau, and (super)program budgets. Finally, senior officials will maximize their own welfare rather than the collective interests of the department as a whole. Hence, the direction of budget maximization varies with rank (Dunleavy 1991; see also Parsons 1995, 318). Dunleavy's conclusion is based on a study of the privatization craze in Great Britain in the 1980s. The models of Downs and Niskanen, developed in a period of bureaucratic growth, cannot explain the downsizing and cost-cutting of the 1980s throughout the Western world. Dunleavy argues that there was such low resistance against privatization and contracting out among senior officials because they were more focused on shaping their organization than on pursuing bigness. Dunleavy also calls attention to the fact that through shaping their departments, senior bureaucrats advanced their own interests in the same direction as politicians and the corporate sector (as discussed in Parsons 1995, 317).

Budget growth, budget freeze, or budget cuts are also in part a consequence of politicians' promises to the electorate, of media attention, or of powerful and active lobbying for particular issues. In view of the literature on *promissory politics,* iron triangles, and issue networks, it appears that bureaucrats alone are not the sole drivers of budgetary decisions. And as for motives of privatization, Meier argues that most empirical research shows that the public choice argument that private sector service delivery is better than public service delivery is not true, that privatization may increase corruption, and that public service delivery may have more legitimacy in the eye of the citizen (Meier 2000, 192). If anything, government officials, like "normal" people, do act in self-interest, but they are also honest (Klein 1994).

13.5. Realistic Images: The Abstract Government and the Concrete Bureaucrat

The common perception is that government is too big, inefficient, inaccessible, and perhaps even corrupt. In this perception, government is an abstraction, but its attributes also determine the perception of individual bureaucrats. Hummel wrongly assumes that the impersonal nature of bureaucracy as such must also have an effect on the personality of the individual bureaucrat. By the same token, government is not just big, it is big because individuals seek bigness (Von Mohl, Downs, Niskanen); government operates on the basis of formal rules and so its employees are formalistic and distant (Hummel); the legalistic language of bureaucratic texts is often incomprehensible, and so bureaucrats speak a secret language (Mencken, Hummel). The stereotype has so much clouded judgment that

Table 13.2

Perception and Reality in Our Appreciation of Government

	Abstract: government as a whole	Concrete: government as subunits (including individuals)
Perception	Big bureaucracy; inaccessible; inefficient; red tape; corrupt	Self-seeking bureaucrats; formalistic; distant; corruptible
	Authors: Mencken, politicians	Authors: Downs, Hummel, Niskanen
Reality	Balancing myriad and conflicting demands; largest single employer; largest possible clientele; huge degree of organizational differentiation	Proactive; citizen-oriented; concerned; professional
	Author: Weber	Authors: Katz et al., Lipsky, Goodsell, Hill

Kaufmann spoke of a raging pandemic (1981). Empirical research into these various elements of the stereotype since the mid-1970s has clearly shown the existence of a perception-reality gap (Table 13.2).

What helped to unravel the stereotype were studies that evaluated government performance in terms of citizen satisfaction with particular services. Among the earliest of such investigations was a pilot study conducted by Katz et al. (1975) on the basis of a nationwide survey. Of the 1,500 surveys sent out, 1,431 were returned (1975, 4). The researchers investigated seven service delivery areas: employment service, job training, workers' compensation, unemployment compensation, welfare services (for the blind, disabled, elderly poor, poor, and poor families with dependent children), hospital and medical benefits, and retirement benefits (7–8). They found that, overall, people were very satisfied with services, but there were differences. With 90 percent, retirement services were rated highest, the work-related agencies received a 75 percent rating, while less than 60 percent of the clientele was satisfied with welfare, and medical and hospital care agencies. Citizens rated not only particular services, but also their satisfaction with bureaucracy as such. Katz et al. found that the respondents did not perceive bureaucracy as inefficient, unfair, and so forth. Seventy-five percent of the respondents indicated that they had been treated fairly. Interestingly, demographic characteristics played a minor role in providing an explanation for these findings. Age was an exception: younger people were consistently less satisfied than older people (1975, 184–185).

The study by Katz et al. focuses on public services provided through face-to-face interaction between civil servant and citizen-as-client. Much previous theory about bureaucracy merely considered bureaucracy as a whole or focused only on top-level bureaucratic officials. The study by Lipsky on *street-level bureaucracy* (1980) makes clear that close to 70 percent of all those working in the public sector are, in fact, street-level bureaucrats and that their individual decisions on whether to act together amounts to agency policy (1980, 3–5). The growth of government since the 1950s had occurred among street-level bureaucrats, Lipsky writes, and the reality of their functioning differed from the idealtypical (Weber) or stereotypical (Hummel) impersonal bureaucrat. Street-level bureaucrats are not only found at lower levels in the bureaucratic hierarchy. In fact, all those public servants who engage in direct interaction with citizens are street-level bureaucrats. Among them are police officers, nurses, doctors, judges, social welfare workers, and teachers. Rather than an empirical investigation of street-level bureaucracy, Lipsky's study is a theory that hypothesizes about the nature of the relation between, for instance, bureaucratization and worker alienation. Street-level bureaucrats not only provide a service to people, but also judge people. In that action of judging, they exercise discretion and thus have major influence in the allocation of values, while at the same time they have little or no influence over definition or achievement of organizational objectives. Official agency policy provides a general rationale and standardized rules and forms for the application of policy to individual cases. This bureaucratization of policy and lack of influence over its content may alienate public workers from their task (Lipsky 1980, 74, 79–81).

Given the discretion of street-level bureaucrats, one might expect a fair amount of criticism or even dissatisfaction with services rendered. However, surveys in individual cities, states, and agencies, as well as surveys by the Harris poll on behalf of the Senate Subcommittee on Intergovernmental Relations (1973), the survey by Katz et al. (often referred to as the University of Michigan poll), and the Ohio State University Survey conducted in the early 1970s all pointed to high degrees of satisfaction. These surveys are discussed by Goodsell (1985, 22–33) in support of his argument that bureaucracy and bureaucrats perform quite well. He also presents data showing that bureaucracies do not continuously expand and that there is no significant relation between the age of an organization and its size and structure. Quite the contrary is the case; older organizations tend to be more flexible and operate with less standardized personnel procedures than new ones (Goodsell 1985, 120–122).

Hill reviews almost the same surveys as Goodsell and also provides three reasons why the perception-reality gap is so persistent. First, citizens are only interested in government when their daily life brings them into contact with it. Thus, only experience might change a stereotypical opinion. Second, there is a lot of misinformation about government. Third, stereotyping is fed by politicians who are a product of political culture (which, in the United States, regards bureaucracy as an adversarial actor), who play into public sentiment and thus draw positive attention to themselves, who consider bureaucracy a safe target in order to mask their own marginality, and who use bureaucracy as a scapegoat (Hill 1992, 23–28).

What can be done to change the public mind? Goodsell suggests that the study of public administration should develop more intellectual self-confidence by extending its body of knowledge, and that teachers and consultants play a crucial role in the education of citizens and (future) public servants (Goodsell 1985, 148–149; see also Meier 2000, 211–212). I concur with these sugges-tions, but also recognize that we have to keep pummeling at the stereotype *in saecula saeculorum.* A recent study of American public opinion about gov-ernment characterizes the public as "ideologically conservative" and "opera-tionally liberal," and the findings suggest that little has changed since the polls of the early 1970s (Cantril and Cantril 1999, 4).

13.6. The Development of the Role and Position of the Civil Service in Western Society

The concept of civil service is of very recent origin. With the exception of the last two centuries or so, those working in government were not considered civil servants. As a concept, it denotes four different meanings. The legalist/ juridical and the sociological meanings of the civil servant concept were dis-cussed in section 13.1. We can, however, also look at the adjective "civil." It can be used to distinguish public servants from those in a military function. In this section, though, "civil" also refers to the fact that government officials work to serve individual civilians and the citizenry. Hence, the concept of civil servant denotes a service role in society and places the bureaucrat in a subservient position to the elected officeholders who, after all, represent the civilian interest. It took several centuries before this meaning of government official became dominant.

In the Western world, the oldest type of government servant was the *per-sonal servant* to the king or ruler. The personal servant was employed in the ruler's household, which included both the domestic as well as state affairs, and provided clerical services. The personal servant was accountable to none other but the ruler. By the sixteenth and seventeenth centuries, the status of government servants had slowly changed. While they still served a particular ruler, that ruler was increasingly regarded as a servant of the state rather than as an owner of the state. Thus, government servants became *state servants.*

Their job description was increasingly limited to state affairs (upstairs), while the private household of the ruler had become a separate administration (downstairs). Following the change toward constitutional democracy, from the early nineteenth century onward government servants became truly *public servants* working for the public cause (*res publica*). While in earlier publications I distinguished a fourth and fifth phase in the development of the civil service (a protected service and a professional service) (Raadschelders and Rutgers 1996; Raadschelders 1998a, 152), I now believe that these last two types are really elaborations of the third type. The civil servant loyally supports the elected incumbent, and in return the civil servant's position is protected by law (see also Weber's dimensions 17 up to 20) and through political accountability.

The development in the role and position of government servants is generally the same in most countries. There are, however, national differences in when, for instance, a transition occurred from state to civil servants and in when the civil service became truly a professional career.

Literature in the United States about the development of the civil service is generally limited to the period of its independence. The most well-known discussion is that by Mosher (unless otherwise indicated, the following discussion is based on his work; 1982b, chapter 3). Mosher provides a developmental model consisting of six stages. The *guardian period,* from 1789 to 1829, was one of *government by gentlemen* or, as Cozzetto, Pedeliski, and Tipple call it, government by aristocracy (1996, 130). Public officials were appointed on the basis of character, ethical conduct, and competence and were, of course, able to accept public office because they had income from landed wealth, industry, or trade. Back then, public service positions were very much subject to political change. More than two-thirds of George Washington's appointees were replaced by John Adams. It is thus not quite correct that the second period, the *spoils period* from 1829 to 1883, is identified with the presidency of Andrew Jackson. He did open public positions for all citizens, hence Mosher's characterization of this period as *government by the common man.* The idea was now that if a president emerged from the class that earned a living rather than had an income from land, industry, or trade, then a salary for those occupying political or administrative office should compensate for loss of income. Indeed, the Jacksonians introduced a rudimentary bureaucracy to accommodate the rotation of common men in office, but did they really come to power? In view of the emergence of political parties and people's bureaucracies, the answer is affirmative, but in view of the concentration of wealth, it is not. In 1825 1 percent of the population owned 25 percent of all wealth, while in 1850 the same 1 percent held 50 percent of all wealth (Morone 1990, 25, 95). The spoils system opened further opportunities for bribery and fraud, especially because power transferred from one, fairly small group (the gentlemen, aristocrats, or gentry) to another much larger group (the political parties that included elites and common men). It has been reported that from the 1820s to the 1850s at least four senators (Thomas Benton of Mississippi, Henry Clay of Kentucky, John C. Calhoun of South Carolina, and Daniel Webster of Massachusetts) and three vice presidents not only accepted bribes but actually solicited them (Douglas 1952, 14–15), and there is no reason to believe that such corruption was any less among the bureaucratic ranks. The times were slowly changing; in 1844, President James Polk promised to remove dishonest employees from office (Ingraham 1995, 21).

From the 1850s on, the idea that merit should surpass spoils became increasingly important, as is illustrated by a variety of congressional actions (Ingraham 1995, 23–24). Also, between 1865 and 1883, several citizens lobbied for reform, for instance through the New York Civil Service Reform Association, created in 1877, and the National Civil Service Reform League, created in 1881. It was not until President James Garfield was murdered by a disappointed office-seeker that the pressure for reform actually materialized into reform. The *reform period* of 1883 to 1906 was characterized by Mosher as a period of *government by the good* (i.e., those who have relevant training and experience and are not corrupt). The 1883 Pendleton Act that established a civil service based upon open entry examinations and merit created a bipartisan Civil Service Commission (which in 1978 was replaced by the White House Office of Personnel Management and the Merit System Protection Board) with a duty to fill vacancies through open, competitive exams. The content of the Pendleton Act, while inspired by a comparison with English civil service reform, was uniquely American. One clause in the act required that civil service exams had to be practical in character. In England, a proper civil servant's preentry education was generally a combination of Latin, Greek, history, and other liberal arts. The emphasis in the United States on practical knowledge also provided the basis for a detailed system of position classification forty years later. It also made lateral entry possible in addition to starting at the bottom in public organizations. There was no special relation between public service and university education, as was the case in England. Finally, top executive positions were regarded as political. The reform movement attacked the spoils system and was concerned with the morality and efficiency of the public service. Its immediate impact upon spoils was limited. At first, the Pendleton Act and the Civil Service Commission controlled only some 10 percent of all federal positions. This had expanded to 25 percent by the time that Theodore Roosevelt became one of the commissioners, to 46 percent when he became president in 1902, and to 66 percent when he left office (White 2000, 711, based on figures provided by Hoogenboom 1961; Ingraham 1995; Van Riper 1958; see also White 1958). The limited effect of the Pendleton

Act upon patronage becomes clear from the fact that the number of federal patronage positions increased from 118,000 in 1883 to 150,000 in 1901 (the largest single group was that of the postmasters; White 2000, 700, 705). But at the same time, the Civil Service Commission gained support through increasing media attention.

The reform movement continued into the fourth period of civil service development, commonly referred to as the *scientific management period,* from 1906 to 1937. This period is also characterized as one of *government by the efficient* or *government by principles* (Cozzetto, Pedeliski, and Tipple 1996, 19). The study of public administration and the practice of government were increasingly influenced by organizational principles as elaborated in the context of private business. Efficiency was not only moral and left no room for corruption, but it was also neutral. In the public sector, the attention for efficiency started at the local level, and the creation of the New York Bureau of Municipal Research in 1906 often serves as the signature moment (Stivers 2000). This is the period of the advent of the city manager, a nonpolitical officeholder as counterweight to the mayor and local councils.

Other large cities also established research bureaus. Most bureaus incorporated the techniques and values of scientific business management into objectives of public sector reform. Public personnel administration (PPA) became a science that involved people who developed quantitatively oriented and detailed job descriptions, productivity measurements, training programs, examinations concerning job-related abilities, efficiency ratings, and position classifications. This latter reform had already started in the 1850s. In 1912 the city of Chicago, and shortly after that year the state of Illinois, established position classification systems. The first handbook in public administration concerned personnel administration, and the following quotation illustrates the perception of a public sector job and of the "science" of administration at the time:

> The job is the molecule of industry; and what molecular study has done for physics and chemistry, job study, with the aid of every possible instrument of precision, can begin to do for industry. (Tead and Metcalf 1920, 255)

In 1923 the Classification Act provided the capstone to the basic structure of the federal civil service.

The fifth period is known as the *administrative management period.* This is the period of *government by administrators.* Many academics in public administration entered public service. It was the New Deal that heralded a new view about the role of government. The public sector should be aggressive and proactive, and management became slightly more important than efficiency. PPA became more than mere efficiency. Increasingly it was recognized that public sector officials played a political and policy-making role as well as performing management functions. The 1937 Brownlow committee report marks the opening of this period, during which the politics-administration dichotomy became blurred, in which the acronym POSDCORB was coined by Gulick, and which provided the basis for an expansion of the executive functions of the presidency. The second Hoover commission of 1955, whose report foreshadowed the creation of the senior executive service in 1978, serves as the end of this period.

The sixth and last phase of civil service development, described in the 1982 edition of Mosher's study, contains two periods. The *professional period,* from 1955 to 1970, is one of government by professionals. Hitherto, PPA had not been very sensitive to the implications of growing professionalism. Since the 1930s, government had recruited not only lawyers but also, and increasingly, natural scientists, engineers, sociologists, educational scientists, political scientists, and public administrationists. In civil organizations, professionals came to occupy positions both in the line and in the staff. In the military, these professionals mainly serve in staff positions. Professionals in civil capacity in the military (such as lawyers, doctors, nurses, priests, ministers, industrial hygienists, and engineers) are nowadays referred to as "combat multipliers." At the start of the *professional public administration period,* from 1970 to the present, the National Association of Schools of Public Affairs and Administration (NASPAA) was created and a sixth Model Public Personnel Administration Law of 1970 was issued by the National Civil Service League that was quite different from its predecessors. This model has been very influential at state and local government levels. At the federal level, the 1978 Civil Service Reform Act listed merit principles, introduced a three-member Merit System Protection Board and the Office of Personnel Management (OPM), established an independent Federal Labor Relations Authority, and created the SES. Some 7,000 officials (currently 7,900) joined the SES. This act emphasized the importance of government by professional managers, already called for by the Brownlow committee report of 1937.

The growth of government at large has greatly influenced the size as well as the changes in the role and position of civil servants. Around 1930, the total public workforce in the United States amounted to some 3 percent of the population, rising to more than 7 percent by the early 1990s. A recent publication reports that all government levels in the United States collectively employ some 14.3 percent of the total labor force (Knoke 2001, 81). The absolute size of the public workforce increased sixfold in the 1930–1997 period while the population more than doubled. In absolute terms, the public workforce increased only by 15 million employees, from 3 to almost 19.5 million. The population increased in the same period by more than 145 million people! To

Table 13.3

The Total Number of Public Servants per 1,000 Inhabitants and Number of Citizens per Public Servant in the United States, 1929–1997

Year	Public workforce	Population size (in millions)	Public servants per thousand of population	Public servant–citizen ratio
1929	3,112	122,775*	25.3	39.5
1939	4,040	131,669*	30.7	32.6
1950	6,402	151,326	42.3	23.6
1960	8,808	179,323	49.1	20.4
1970	13,028	203,302	64.1	15.6
1980	16,191	226,542	71.5	14.0
1990	18,119	248,765	72.8	13.7
1997	19,540	267,744	72.9	13.7

Source: Statistical Abstract of the United States: 1999, tables 14 and 535.
Note: See also Table 8 in chapter 8 above.
Legend: *The first two figures for population size actually date from 1930 and 1940; they do not include figures for Alaska and Hawaii. The measurement date for all population figures is April 1.

what conclusion can these figures lead us? There is much support for the idea that government is too big, and, indeed, the absolute numbers seem to support that conclusion. However, we must also ask, "too big in relation to what?" In comparison to the private sector, only some 14 to 15 percent of the total workforce is employed in government. In a more positive light, one could also argue that the growth of government is an expression of its responsiveness to public needs. The number of public servants in the United States has increased from a little more than 25 to almost 73 civil servants per 1,000 citizens in the 1979–1997 period. In 1929, close to 40 citizens were served by one civil servant compared to a little less than 14 in 1997 (Table 13.3).

In comparison, the public workforce in the United States is as small or as large as in some European countries. As a percentage of the total workforce, the public sector in European Union countries in 1990 employed between almost 11 percent (Luxembourg) to almost 32 percent of the total workforce (Sweden). Figures for some other countries are as follows: Netherlands, 14.7 percent; Germany, 15.1 percent; Italy, 15.5 percent; United Kingdom, 19.2 percent; France, 25.2 percent; and Denmark, 30.5 percent (Raadschelders and Toonen 1999, 46).

One of the themes that is emphasized in the recent developments in Western civil service systems is that they have become professionalized.

Professionalization is visible in all levels of public bureaucracy, where relevant preentry education and possibly experience are instrumental in getting a civil service position. With respect to the middle and higher management levels in the bureaucracy, a law degree commonly provided an adequate preparation for a public career well into the twentieth century. However, from the middle of the last century onward, government has increasingly employed other professionals, such as doctors, engineers, chemists, psychologists, educational scientists, teachers, political scientists, and administrative scientists, who could provide expertise in the various policy areas that government had branched out into. A professional is defined as someone who has four or more years of college education and who brings a certain specialization to the job (Cozzetto, Pedeliski, and Tipple 1996, 24). Mosher calculates that almost 40 percent of public sector employees are professionals and technicians while only 11 percent of private sector positions can be labeled as such. Even when teachers are taken out of this figure, the number of professional and technical personnel is still nearly double that in the private sector (Mosher 1982b). In view of privatization and contracting out in many Western countries, we can expect that the percentage of the public workforce that is professional or technical has increased.

The professionalism of the contemporary civil servant is also evident in the fact that loyal support is no longer equivalent to blind following of the political leader but rather takes the form of sound advice, including attempts to restrain the leader's political desires (the civil servant's right or obligation to resist). This is especially relevant in the higher levels of the civil service. A professional civil servant's most important function may be intellectual appraisal, the concept coined by Self (1979, 192). Intellectual appraisal involves the collection of information, the weighing of alternatives, sensitivity to the political climate, and, finally, the development of some scenarios to be presented to the political leadership. The political leader may then choose in accordance with his or her political conscience and promises made. The council manager in U.S. local government is an example of a civil servant who is continuously engaged in intellectual appraisal. What is interesting about this role is that the political environment forces the manager into a political role (Franklin 1998).

The civil servant's professionalization is usually approached in terms of training for the job. Pre- and post-entry training for public servants has increased enormously in the twentieth century. There are complete undergraduate and graduate curricula in public administration on the one hand and crash courses over the weekend on new developments on the other hand. It is hard to measure this kind of professionalization. To be sure, measurement is not necessary, unless it will draw our attention to something that would otherwise not be noticed. In the context of this section, a measure of professionalization is the citizen–civil servant ratio (cf. Raadschelders 1995, 620). We know that the number of public servants has grown exponentially in response to growing desires and demands in the societal environment. But professionalization goes hand in hand with the politicization of bureaucracy.

13.7.   Marginalization of Politicians and Politicization of Bureaucracy: General Trends and Cultural Differences

In light of the growth of public employment, it is no surprise that the relative number of political officeholders has seriously decreased. Research in the Netherlands regarding the administrative development of four municipalities between 1600 and 1980 reveals that so-called auxiliary functionaries (i.e., lower administrative personnel) and political officeholders were the largest two groups in the early seventeenth century. As local government functions increased, so did the number of workers and the number of citizen servants (i.e., citizens working as volunteers or conscripted on the basis of civic duty). By the end of the eighteenth century, those who could be categorized as political officeholders had already experienced serious decline in numbers relative to administrative officeholders. With the advent of the national state, the incorporation of public utilities, the fast growth of public schools, and the emergence of the welfare state, the bureaucracy continued to increase in size, whereas the political top experienced very little change at all in absolute numbers (Raadschelders 1994). Although the developments in four Dutch towns can hardly be generalized, it is reasonable to assume that more or less comparable developments occurred elsewhere. In the first decade of independence, the American federal government employed some 200 gentleman administrators and fewer civil servants (Morone 1990, 4). Currently, in the United States there are 17.9 million people in appointed positions, while the approximately 0.5 million elected officeholders constitute 2.8 percent of the public workforce (Nice and Frederickson 1999, 239). Thus, a first indicator of the marginalization of politics is the relative decline of political officeholders in relation to the public workforce as a whole.

Another, and far more important, indicator of the declining importance of political officials has to do with what is expected of civil servants and with the influence of civil servants upon policy and decision making. In the Weberian perspective, *neutral civil servants* are expected to be rational, politically neutral, and acting in compliance with the rules. They are expected to be models of integrity and cautiousness and at the same time dynamic, proactive, anticipating, and innovative. Anyone interested in a public career should consider the following remark carefully:

> Public sector managers are expected—by chief executives, legislators, and the body politic—to be efficient in their administrative capacities *and* effective in achieving the goals and objectives of the programs assigned to them. Moreover, they are expected to be responsible to their executive branch superiors *and* accountable to the appropriate legislative bodies *and* responsive to the needs of their clientele groups. Finally, they are expected to be dedicated to the standards of their professions *and* politically astute enough to appreciate the pragmatic political realities of life *and* committed fully to a life of service in the name of democracy. (Gawthrop 1998, 130)

Who in their right mind would apply for such a job? Civil servants are not only loyal to politics. They are also supposed to be sensitive to the political atmosphere and mood of the environment, testing the waters by pushing the boundaries of the possible in public policy (Majone 1989, 35). They must also be loyal to the citizen (client just does not sound right) and loyal to themselves as citizens. As *policy brokers* or *harmonizers*, they try to keep the level of political conflict within acceptable limits (Sabatier and Jenkins-Smith 1993, 27) and are assumed able to outline compromise and consensus wherever possible. They also can be *propagandists of values* and *advocates* of certain interests (Majone 1989, 34, 36). Finally, they are *interpreters* of vague, ambiguous, and/or contradictory legislative mandates (Majone 1989, 26). Perhaps the best characterization of civil servants is that they must know their *craft.* Craft knowledge is less general and explicit than theoretical knowledge, but is also not as idiosyncratic as pure intuition. Craft includes a body of skills (advocacy, interpretation, brokerage, testing, etc.) that can be used to produce useful service, that assures careful attention to quality of service, and that balances responsibility to the citizens, the profession, the organization, and the public sphere. Successful performance depends upon intimate knowledge of materials and tools and on quality interaction (with politics, with citizens) (Majone 1989, 44–45).

This is a set of role expectations that contains potential conflict. A dynamic and innovative civil servant may be less cautious and willing to run some or much risk. What is expected from civil servants is ambiguous. At the higher levels, the most important function, irrespective of how they perform within their position (active and innovative, or rule-bound and formal, etc.), is *intellectual appraisal.* That provides the higher civil servant with a very important power source. Given the growth of public services and the enhanced role that civil servants have come to play in the preparation of policy (i.e., arguing for and against choices) and actual service delivery (i.e., street-level bureaucrats), one can say that in the twentieth century a *politicization of bureaucracy* has taken place. Bureaucrats have substantial influence on policy and decision making. They initiate contact with and respond to relevant societal interests. They are expected to assess which objectives of a political incumbent are politically feasible, and they should have a feeling for political reality and relations. Politicization is also visible in the fact that political officeholders are frequently recruited from among the ranks of the civil service. In European countries, this has become quite a normal phenomenon; the percentage of parliamentarians with a prior career in the ranks of the civil service has substantially increased in the past 150 years. In the United States, crossing over from the civil service into a political position is equally common (Heady 2001, 236). However, members of Congress and political officeholders (in appointed ranks: ministers, ambassadors, political executives) are also drawn from among those who financially or otherwise supported a political office-holder. But, as far as career civil servants are concerned and in whatever country they are, they may have a (professed or not) political identity as long as it does not interfere blatantly with their support of the policies of the elected or appointed political official.

Obviously, the position of civil servants in different countries varies. Heady contrasted the "classic" administrative systems of France and Germany with the "civic culture" systems of the United Kingdom and the United States. In France, the *grand corps* officials are the major decision makers. They are far removed from those who are affected by their decisions. Citizen participation in decision making is limited. High civil servants also enjoy high social status. In the eyes of Crozier (1964), they are the change agents, while Suleiman (1984) argues that they are an integral part of the system that is resistant to change and linked to the centralized state. Thus, in France there is still a very powerful and homogeneous power elite (Heady 2001, 198–202). Unlike in the past, German officials no longer enjoy such social prestige as their French colleagues. They are no longer recruited from among the aristocracy and the highest middle classes, but on the basis of competitive examination. Putnam found that in the higher levels in Germany's civil service, the political bureaucrat dominated over the classical bureaucrat, but they cannot escape political control (Heady 2001, 207–213). What both these classic countries and various other continental European countries (Austria, Belgium, Ireland, Italy, the Netherlands, Switzerland, and, to a lesser extent, the Scandinavian countries) have in common is the existence of a professional civil service with specialized training and the recognition that bureaucracy has a constitutional obligation to uphold the law (Heady 2001, 214).

The civic cultures, on the other hand, are much more participative, pluralist, and communicative. Reporting the work by Almond and Verba, Heady writes the United Kingdom has a deferential civic culture while the United States has a more participant civic culture. In England, civil servants play a traditionally neutral role. They will change colors like a chameleon when the opposition party comes to power. At the same time, behind closed doors they exercise influence in policy making and implementation and in advising the minister. High civil servants in England enjoy substantial social status, but not as much as in France. In the United States, civil servants do not enjoy high social status and they operate not in secrecy, as in the United Kingdom, but very much in the public eye. The American civil servant who earns high and lasting prestige becomes a public figure (e.g., Secretary of State Colin Powell, Federal Reserve Chairman Alan Greenspan). What connects the civic cultures is that the civil service was much slower to professionalize than on the European continent (Heady 2001, 223–236).

Having said that bureaucrats play a variety of important and influential roles, what does it mean for political officeholders? Those in political office are marginalized not only by growing bureaucracy and by the politicization of bureaucracy. Politicians themselves, or their spin doctors, have something to do with it as well. They marginalize the substance of what they have to offer and at the same time blow up imagery and catchphrases. The nature of political campaigning has changed considerably. For example, visual aids have become more important than language in conveying policy objectives. In the Netherlands, posters printed in the face of upcoming elections in the 1920s and 1930s would usually show a number (the party with the largest number of members of Parliament would be no. 1, the second largest no. 2, and so forth), a symbol that was related to the party (a red rose for socialists, a hammer and sickle for communists, a cross for Catholics, etc.), and a list of issues and choices the party stood for. The number was in small print, the symbol somewhat larger, and the list of issues in large print. After World War II, the number grew in size, a small photograph of the party leader could be included, and the list of issues appeared in smaller print. Political campaign posters and pamphlets today print the politician's face and the party name large. Substantive issues are mentioned less often on posters and discussed more often during televised debates. This development may be attributed as much to politicians as to citizens who do not want to take the time to get acquainted with the merits and objectives of every candidate's policies.

13.8.   Is It Right That Bureaucrats Have Power?

A marked difference between the United States and European countries is that in the latter, government and the state are generally perceived in a rather positive light. True, Western European populations (including the British) are not free from stereotyping bureaucrats, but at the same time, they do not distrust government or state as much as their American cousins do. As a consequence, in Europe there is not too much debate about the proper role of civil servants in policy making. In the United States, however, it appears that after two centuries of antistatism and democratic myth, the people and their political and administrative representatives still have to come to terms with the administrative state. In recent years, authors have argued that the old fear of government should be reappraised (e.g., Morone 1990, 333) and that more bureaucracy would not be so bad (Meier 1997). America faces, so argues Morone, a variety of major challenges in the twenty-first century (in the fields of international trade, deficits, education, health care, homelessness, etc.) that can be tackled only through judgments made by a competent, coherent, and independent state. This is difficult, since

> in a nation that insistently subordinates administration to democracy, the constant touchstone is bureaucracy without reflection; administration by inexorable, autonomous forces rather than the deliberation of elders. (Morone 1990, 128)

It is ironic that in the civic culture of American bureaucracy, the Weberian, impersonal bureaucrat thrives. What is needed instead is

> a new political environment [that] would require public officials with a far richer set of skills and a far greater discretion—bluntly, more power—than Americans have ever been willing to concede to their public officials. (Morone 1990, 332)

In view of such theories as the primacy of politics and of such stereotypes as the secrecy of antechamber decision making, it has been argued that the fourth power of bureaucracy should be constrained. However, a case has been made that this would not at all serve the needs of society today. Meier suggests that the system of checks and balances in the United States could be redesigned after the example of the more unified political structures in Europe, that the electoral cycle should be extended so that public policy making could operate in a longer time frame, and that the number of political appointees should be restricted or even eliminated. At the same time, we should carefully determine which services could be offered through public and which through private organizations, critically review the agencies' effective contribution to policy making, balance the ideology of efficiency with that of public philosophy, and train administrators in politics and administration both (Meier 1997, 197). Meier's suggestions for recasting the political system in the United States are probably intended to stir up some reflection and are perhaps unrealistic—but he does have a point.

Perhaps the political system need not be revised and we merely need to make a case that it is ethical, responsible, and justifiable that bureaucrats play an important role in public policy and decision making. Yates advances the following observation:

> If bureaucrats do not illuminate, analyze, and educate citizens about value conflicts, what other institutions will? The simple point is that . . . it is clearly not in the standard operating procedure of other major political institutions to perform this normative role. (Yates 1981, 46)

He argues that members of the U.S. Congress do not weigh values, but attend to distributive policy and benefits for their own constituents. The presidency is supposed to represent all people and thus advances policies and programs that merge, blend, and accommodate different values in the hope of acquiring broad national support. The U.S. Supreme Court, frequently used to make and enforce value decisions, is by design the least democratic of institutions (Yates 1981, 46–47). Yates then presents four reasons why it is good that the major responsibility for public value decisions should rest with the bureaucracy. First, bureaucrats are not as directly subject to the intense political pressure of the electoral cycle. At some distance from the political battles, they can actually engage in some careful and thoughtful value clarification. Second, professional neutrality and detachment are important preconditions for useful value analysis. Bureaucrats can also afford to develop a longer-term perspective. Third, they have the personnel, informational, and analytical resources and are in the best position to observe how the relation between normative values and actual programs develops. Finally, placing the burden of value analysis and clarification openly upon bureaucrats directly attacks bureaucracy as a fourth power. Indeed, they should be forced to justify their decisions publicly (Yates 1981, 47–48).

Recognizing the power of bureaucrats and the potential for deviant behavior (bribery, corruption, and so forth), bureaucracies and professional associations of public servants have embraced codes of ethics (e.g., American Society for Public Administration). Paper is patient, though, and does not change behavior. At the same time, and in contrast to the world of practice, scholars of public administration have advocated that public servants need to be reacquainted with the high road of ethics and morality. It was observed of the latter,

> of little value are the many treatises advocating universal moral virtues and strength of character as guarantors of ethical behavior. Prudence, justice, temperance, fortitude, loyalty, integrity, honor, and similar qualities are assuredly assets for the public official, but their implications for resolving dilemmas of discretion are often not obvious. (Warwick 1981, 113)

Instead, Warwick argues, we should work with what exists and enhance what we need. What exists is respect for procedures and restraint on the means. What we need is a public orientation and interest, reflective choice, and veracity. The idea that civil servants should have a public orientation is not the same as that they have to be emptied of personal, bureaucratic, or constituency interests. Indeed, the public is served best when civil servants make explicit their own values. Reflective choice invites civil servants to publicly deliberate their own values and those of others which, together, underlie public policy. Veracity includes truthfulness in the discharge of official responsibilities, but also respect for the ability of others to gather and present information (Warwick 1981, 115–121).

Authors such as Meier, Morone, Warwick, and Yates not only defend the bureaucrat's role in contemporary society as necessary, but also advocate that bureaucrats have to be "plucky, spunky, and nervy," for the future of America may very well depend upon the degree to which its people are able to embrace government (Morone 1990, 337). There is yet another way that the power of bureaucracy can be constrained from within.

13.9.   Representative or Expert Bureaucracy?

The combined processes of democratization of politics and politicization of bureaucracy have enhanced our sensitivity toward the power of bureaucracy. In the light of emancipation of the masses and of equal opportunity for everyone, the representativeness of bureaucracy has become an important issue (Kingsley 1994). This is not only relevant to the twentieth century. Even as far back as the start of the Jacksonian era (1829–1883), representativeness was considered an issue, and populism was a response to elitist government. In modern democratic theory, everyone should be represented. The first question is why? The second question is how this can be organized. And the third question concerns the willingness to accept the consequences.

Van Braam (1986, 191) advances three arguments why representativeness is important. Under the *political legitimacy argument,* he reasons that when bureaucracy is representative, society recognizes itself in bureaucracies' actions. Thus, the legitimacy of government action is enhanced. The *political loyalty argument* emphasizes that a representative civil service is in tune with the variety of political values in society and is thus likely to be more responsive. The question remains, of course, to whom the civil servant is responsive: the citizen, the political officeholder, the interest group, or all of the above? Finally, the *political reward argument* points to the fact that equal opportunities for women, the disabled, African Americans, and other groups are presumably enhanced if the composition of the civil service is proportionate to the size of the various groups in society.

These motives or arguments have a bearing upon the definitions of representativeness. Mosher (1982b) makes a distinction between *active* and *passive representativeness.* The first type concerns the active pursuit of objectives in relation to a particular clientele. Following Van der Meer and Roborgh (1996, 225–230), active representation can be further elaborated. In the case of *opinion representativeness,* a political congruence is sought between the views and values held in society and in bureaucracy. In the case of *interest representativeness,* the civil servant may act as sponsor of a particular interest, which is the most active type of representativeness. The problem is, of course, that what people say (opinion) is not necessarily the same as what they need, do, expect, and hope (interest). Passive representativeness is merely the situation where the civil service is a mirror of society in terms of the personal characteristics of its employees. This may also be called *demographic representativeness,* based on gender, ethnicity, education, language, geographic origin, religion, political affiliation, social-economic background, and so forth. Demographic representativeness is also known as *mirror image representativeness,* and as such is to be distinguished from *equal opportunity representativeness.* This last type seeks to establish impartiality in the process of recruiting candidates for vacant positions. The question of who is the best candidate for the job should not take the applicants' demographic characteristics into account. The question that needs to be raised, though, is how important demographic (personal) background is in comparison to enculturation or socialization in a bureaucracy? With respect to demographic representation, we should consider the fact that a relation is assumed between demographic characteristics (gender, color, etc.) and how a job will be done. To what degree do demographic characteristics matter after one has become employed in the civil service? As time goes by, enculturation or socialization processes may very well line up the newcomer with the organizational culture and its goals. They may also line up the individual with a different group of interests than those with which he or she entered the organization. Research has shown that similar social origins do not necessarily lead to comparable socialization experiences and that the link between social origins and values held is not strong because socialization continues throughout life (Meier 2000, 177).

Has the composition of the U.S. civil service become more representative in the past few decades? The tables that follow provide some indication. In Table 13.4, the composition of the total population is broken down in percentages according to sex and race/ethnicity. These data speak for themselves.

In Table 13.5 the data indicate that federal policies of affirmative action and equal employment opportunity have borne fruit to some degree. With respect to race, it appears that African Americans are overrepresented. Hispanic Americans are underrepresented, but the data indicate a tendency to correct for that.

At the state and local level we can see the same basic trend. Already in the 1970s, African Americans were overrepresented and Hispanic Americans were clearly underrepresented. The percentage of African American government employees has steadily grown, while the percentage of Hispanic American public employees has doubled. The percentage of white civil servants in state and local government declined by 8.3 percent in the 1980–1997 period, while the percentage of white citizens relative to the total population declined by only 3.2 percent in that same period.

The state and local government figures also indicate that female representativeness has significantly increased in the past twenty-five years. Given that

Table 13.4

Population Size of the United States, 1980–1997 Showing Gender and Race/Ethnicity as Percentages of the Total Population

Year	Total population (in millions)	Male	Female	White	Black	Hispanic
1980	226,546	48.6	51.4	85.9	11.8	6.4
1990	248,765	48.7	51.3	83.9	12.3	9.0
1995	262,765	48.8	51.2	83.0	12.6	10.3
1997	267,744	48.8	51.2	82.7	12.7	10.9

Source: Statistical Abstract of the United States: 1999, table 12.

Table 13.5

Federal Executive Branch (Nonpostal) Employment in Total Absolute Numbers and Percentages by Race

Year	Total	White	Black	Hispanic
1990	2,150,359	72.7	16.6	5.4
1995	1,960,577	71.1	16.7	5.9
1997	1,830,300	70.7	16.6	6.3

Source: Statistical Abstract of the United States: 1999, table 568.
Note: The *Statistical Abstract* does not provide the same information about federal employees (i.e., composition of workforce according to gender) as it does about state and local employees.

Table 13.6

State and Local Government Full-Time Employment by Sex and by Race/Ethnic Group

Year	Total (in millions)	Male (%)	Female (%)	White (%)	Black (%)	Hispanic (%)
1975	3,899	62.5	37.6	79.6	15.4	3.7
1980	3,987	58.9	41.1	78.9	15.5	4.1
1985	4,742	58.8	41.2	75.1	17.6	5.2
1990	5,374	57.2	42.8	72.9	18.5	6.1
1995	5,315	55.7	44.3	71.1	18.7	7.1
1997	5,205	55.7	44.3	70.6	18.7	7.5

Source: Statistical Abstract of the United States: 1999, table 537.
Note: These data do not include school systems and educational institutions and a sample of county, municipal, township, and special district jurisdictions that employ fifteen or more non-elected and nonappointed full-time employees.

the data in Tables 13.5 and 13.6 do not include the total workforce at federal, state, and local levels, we could cautiously conclude that it appears that positive discrimination in the public workforce at large has resulted in overrepresentation of African Americans, has not (yet) resulted in a demographically correct representation of Hispanic Americans, and has not (yet) resulted in a female workforce proportional to the percentage of women in the total population. However, women and minorities are generally better represented at lower levels in the organization than at the higher managerial levels. At the federal level, the percentage of female managers has steadily increased but is not even near the mark of the federal female workforce at large (Wooldridge and Maddox 1995, 186). We can assume that the percentage of black and Hispanic managers is quite a bit lower than that of the black and Hispanic workforce at large. With respect to the upward mobility of women, a variety of barriers exist. *Glass ceilings* (invisible barriers) prevent a woman from moving to the higher managerial ranks. Another barrier is the *sticky floor* job, essential to the organization but difficult to escape from. These jobs are often occupied by women. Finally, the term *trapdoors* refers to challenges (sexual harassment, close scrutiny of performance, age) that women experience once they have broken through the glass ceiling (Guy 1995, 233–235). The glass ceiling and the sticky floor barriers are certainly relevant to understanding why not only women, but also minorities are underrepresented at the managerial level.

13.10. Managing the Human Resource

In section 13.6 an outline of the development of the public service at large was provided. In sections 13.7 and 13.8, specific changes with respect to role and position of bureaucracy versus politics and of composition of the public workforce were discussed. These changes, together with the information provided in earlier chapters on the development of government in terms of services, organizational structure and culture, and styles of decision and policy making, provide the intellectual background for understanding why intuitive and subjective methods of recruitment were replaced by the standardized approach of "old PPA," as Garvey calls it (1997, 32), which very much emphasized standardized instruments and procedures. In this section, I explore how the tone and content of human resource management in the public sector has changed in the past five decades. The general development is more or less comparable among Western countries. The examples in this section concern the changes in the United States civil service only.

For centuries, recruitment of civil servants was based on personal acquaintance, family relationship, and so forth. In the course of the nineteenth century, attempts were made to categorize individual qualities on the basis of visual appearance. In the latter part of the nineteenth century, L.N. Fowler developed the science of *phrenology,* aimed at providing a scientific basis for recruitment. The ideal model that he developed showed a person's head, divided in sections, each of which is marked with a particular characteristic. By using the model, the manager could determine whether a candidate was, for instance, quickly inclined to stress or able to work efficiently. Thus, phrenology was a policy instrument. In view of the century that has passed since, and given the enormous progress in the area of human resource management, we may believe that the days of phrenology, when subjective and visual aids ruled the recruitment process, are over. This is unfortunately not the case. Books are still being published that present particular facial features as representative for a particular psychological condition. They also serve as instruments for recruitment (see, for instance, Whiteside, Stokes, and Callaway 1996). The least one can say is that the rationalization of society did not diminish the importance of visual and simplistic agents.

Phrenology was followed by an approach known as "old PPA," which emphasized the use of standardized instruments (application forms, job descriptions, job classifications, career system, etc.) to diminish the influence of personal and subjective opinion. The "old PPA" has been described as masculine and as a *manpower planning* approach. So dominant was this approach to personnel management that shortly after World War II, Wallace Sayre (1948) sighed that technique had triumphed over purpose.

That the times were changing had already become clear in the years immediately prior to World War II. The following quotation, taken from Mosher's analysis of the Brownlow committee report, captures the beginning of a new style of PPA (Barnard 1938):

> Personnel was seen as a principal, if not major, tool of management. [It] should be organized as a staff aid integral to the operating organization, not as a semi-independent agency. . . . It should operate primarily as a service to managers up and down the line, not as a watchdog and controller over management. . . . At the top level [personnel management] should be concerned with the development of standards and policies. Personnel operations . . . should be decentralized and delegated to bring them into more immediate relationship with the middle and lower managers whom they serve. *Personal and interpersonal considerations should be reintroduced into personnel administration, even if they cost some degree of objectivity and of scientific technique.* (Mosher 1982, 82; emphasis added)

After World War II, the tone of personnel management became more personal, with an eye for human relations and more attention to the nature of the interaction between manager and subordinate. Rules and procedures continued to be important, but under the new concept of *human resource management* (HRM or new PPA), attention to organizational mission and to individual employee needs was more balanced. HRM attempted to better balance the demands of efficiency and legality with those of democracy. And, finally, personnel management not only concerned lower- and middle-ranked employees, but increasingly encompassed all levels in the organization. Popular concepts at present, such as employee empowerment, Total Quality Management (TQM), and strategic management, are indicative of an understanding of personnel or human resource management that is quite different from old PPA.

This new personnel philosophy had major consequences for how the role and position of individual employees were defined. Under old PPA, theory about manager-employee relations was dominated by what McGregor called *theory X* (1960). The employee had to be supervised because he was essentially lazy. What motivated the employee were pay and promotion. In the labor relationship, the emphasis was on duty. The employer "bought" your time between 9 and 5, which meant that as soon as you walked into your office you ought to have left domestic worries behind. Of course, reality was not like this, but the theory did have very practical consequences for personnel management. Given the emphasis on duties, given clearly defined tasks, and given fairly detailed job descriptions, the educational focus, for instance, was on training for specific skills. The focus of recruitment was on specific skills. Legislative activity relevant to the work conditions mainly concerned statutory law that regulated job description and classification, pay, hours, and benefits (e.g., the 1883 Pendleton Act, the 1923 Classification Act, and the 1938 Fair Labor Standards Act).

From the 1960s on, the emphasis shifted to a combination of duties and rights. Manager-employee relations were now interpreted as *theory Y* without forgetting the teeth of theory X (after Aristotle: laws must have teeth). The employee was internally motivated to do the job and derived satisfaction from more than just the pecuniary rewards. The new employee allegedly desired responsibility and recognition. And, again, this theory had practical consequences. The recruitment focus turned to a combination of acquired skills, knowledge, and abilities (SKA) with a potential for the future. The educational focus turned toward a combination of training and learning. That regular universities developed advanced programs for professional categories is a feature of only the past three decades. Motivation enhancement beyond financial compensation was not really an issue before World War II. Since the war, though, a variety of minor structural modifications to the work situation (e.g., job rotation, work modules, project and task forces) have been developed. From the 1970s on, work conditions as well as manager-employee relations became the objects of major structural modifications (job enrichment, shorter workweek, flextime, employee empowerment, TQM, etc.). Together, temporary or more lasting minor and major structural modifications have served to enhance morale and to strengthen loyalty to the organization.

Legislative activity reflects that the employee is not only the incumbent of a job or a position, but an individual who needs to be protected from unsavory work conditions and whose constitutional rights have to be observed. Presidents John Kennedy, Richard Nixon, and William Clinton used the executive order (i.e., regulatory law) to slowly expand public employees' rights to collective bargaining. As important as these regulatory actions are, all of the legislation passed by Congress that aims at protecting the constitutional rights of the employee both in the public and the private sector needs to be considered. Many of these acts are concerned with protecting people against discrimination (on the bases of gender, race, age, physical ability, and so forth). The oldest act of that type of legislation was the Equal Pay Act of 1963. That act and many since emphasize that we are all equal as citizens not only in the eyes of the law but in terms of opportunity in public employment. The impact that this legislation had on personnel management is clear. Workforce diversity no longer applies only to employees' professional or educational backgrounds, but also to representative bureaucracy (at least in terms of the composition of the population). The personnel manager will proactively develop plans to hire people that are labeled a minority through Title VII of the 1964 Civil Rights Act (affirmative action, equal employment opportunity). Managing workforce diversity is considered one of the greatest challenges to modern HRM both in the public as well as in the private sector (Knoke 2000, 17). Increased sensitivity to the demographic makeup of society prior to recruitment is visible in various ways. Equal employment opportunity and affirmative action programs assure some proactive enhancement of representativeness. The Professional and Administrative Career Examination (PACE) system that was used between 1974 and 1982 was terminated because of cultural bias. Also, some public organizations (e.g., U.S. Air Force) no longer require that job applicants include a photograph or indicate their race on the application form. And, of course, during employment the protection of employee rights and sensitivity to diversity are apparent in the sexual harassment case law, as in the Pregnancy Discrimination Act of 1978 and the Family and Medical Leave Act of 1993.

In all of these changes in the role and position of individual employees in the public sector, one recognizes the influence of public pressure. Before World War II, the societal environment was not really relevant in the perception of public managers. Representativeness was a nonissue since workforce homogeneity required little sensitivity to it. Given that the organization had to do the most efficient job possible, employee needs were subordinate to that end. Morale and ethics were interpreted at the level of bureaucratic responsibility.

The organization did not care too much for outside pressure such as that from labor unions. Freedom of association was not considered applicable to those that worked in the public sector. The focus on collective bargaining was thus that of a pluralist (conflictual) model. And certainly in the public sector, wages, hours, and fringe benefits were nonnegotiable, for they fell to the authority of the Civil Service Commission. Finally, the public generally had respect for people in the public service, even more so in Western Europe. Certainly in Western Europe, the idea that working for the government was a privilege (and a civic duty in the eyes of some) was strong until the late 1950s. Beyond the major reforms government instigated around 1900, the public at large did not appear to have much interest in the structure and functioning of its government.

All this changed from the 1960s on. Public opinion strongly desired a more representative bureaucracy. Since the late 1970s, public opinion also desired a smaller government. In general, some cutbacks have been achieved, especially at the level of blue-collar jobs and middle management positions. Privatization and contracting out have resulted in a more bureaucratized workforce in the sense that the relative number of white-collar workers has increased. It is interesting, though, that this "bureaucratization" of the public workforce has not resulted in a significant decline in labor union membership. In the United States, overall union membership peaked at 32 percent in the 1950s. It dropped in the private sector to 13.2 percent in 1999. In the public sector, however, union membership throughout the 1990s was around 37 percent (Knoke 2001, 296) or 43 percent (Berman et al. 2001, 297, 300). The same trend in unionization (overall decline, but increase in the public sector) has been observed in Britain (Legge 1995, 251, 266). Union membership is especially strong among teachers in public schools. While unions are thus still important in the public sector, collective bargaining is increasingly perceived in the light of a unitary (consensual) model in which disagreements between management and employees are preferably solved through one-on-one interaction or through mediation rather than through union involvement. Especially the higher ranked and white-collar employees in government are generally well educated and able to take care of themselves. Also, in higher positions, financial and other types of compensation are negotiable up to a point, which would have been inconceivable even thirty years ago. Developments in public sector pay generally lag behind the private sector, not to mention the fact that pay for highly educated and experienced professionals in the public sector is on average lower than in the private sector, where compensation for American CEOs is thirty-four times that of lower-level employees (in the United Kingdom, twenty-four times; in France, fifteen times; in Germany, thirteen times; in Japan, eleven times) (Knoke 2001, 264). After all, public sector pay is taxpayers' money. Hence, in this sense too, the pressure of the environment has consequences for personnel management. Finally, government jobs are no longer fulfilled on the grounds of civic duty or privilege. Rather, public sector jobs are a right, based on merit (the best person for the job) and on notions of equality of opportunity (i.e., as reparation for past injustice) and/or of patronage (certainly for political appointees).

13.11. Concluding Remarks

The first part of this chapter addressed definitions and perceptions of bureaucracy. It became clear that no single theory can help to explain or understand government and bureaucracy. Especially the discussion in sections 13.3 to 13.5 demonstrated that facts will not always—if ever—replace fiction. The second part of this chapter provided a discussion of various developments in the civil service and in human resource management. The study of public administration has developed to such an extent that its graduates at both the bachelor's and master's levels can be certain that they have acquired a set of skills that will enable them to embark upon a professional career in the public sector, in the nonprofit sector, or—as experts in "government knowledge"— in the private sector. The progressive reform era in the United States and in, for instance, the Netherlands and Germany (1880s–1920s) led to a revival of the study of public administration that emphasized practical skills in addition to theoretical insights. Government, especially local government, desperately needed reliable—that is, noncorruptible—and specialist public servants. In preentry and in-service training, the emphasis was very much on the expert with practical skills. Durant, who argued along the same lines in the 1920s, had no reservations about whether he should revise his opinions in the 1963 edition of his book in light of the changes since its first publication (1929). Thus, Durant also advocated a highly trained bureaucracy, checked by a reliable democracy. And yet, the 1930s and 1940s, the decades of the Great Depression and World War II, brought about great changes in the role and position of government in state-society. Dwight Waldo was among the early authors who recognized the need for a different type of public servant, or at least for another type of public servant next to the legal or personnel specialist that was trained in the earlier part of the century. In other words, Waldo argued that the administrative state needed generalists:

> there has emerged from the general notion of permanence, capacity, and expertise in government service a concept of a distinct and definable function of "general administration," not merely a skill in the employment of government, but a skill *in* or *of* government. (Waldo 1984, 92)

What makes a generalist is, of course, not so easy to determine because it is dependent upon the specific qualities the leaders of government should have and whether they operate in a political or administrative role. Despite all possible differences, there are probably at least two characteristics that the contemporary top manager will need. The first, as old as mankind itself, is life experience, which includes such qualities as wisdom, restraint, the ability to separate work and work-related issues from other compartments of life (or other communities to which top managers belong), vision, and open-mindedness. These qualities can only be trained for in an indirect manner—hence the popularity of curricula in leadership for midcareer professionals. But the second characteristic is something that we can learn, and that is to become knowledgeable in more than one body of knowledge, which among other things may very well serve to make us wiser and more open-minded. The curricula in public administration should be tailored to meet this requirement. The generalist in the public service operates as the go-between in the continuum between democracy (the political leadership and its electorate) and bureaucracy (the civil service). This defies a separation of policy making and policy execution, which certainly is irrelevant at the summit of public organizations, as Waldo so clearly voiced as early as the late 1940s:

> if abandonment of the politics-administration formula is taken seriously, if the demands of present world civilization upon public administration are met, administrative thought must establish a working relationship with every major province in the realm of human learning. (Waldo 1984, 203)

14 ORGANIZED SOCIETY: CITIZENSHIP, INTEREST GROUPS, AND CITIZEN PARTICIPATION

All government is evil, and the parent of evil. . . . The best government is that which governs least.
—John L. O'Sullivan, 1837

I heartily accept the motto, "That government is best which governs least"; and I should like to see it acted up to more rapidly and systematically. Carried out, it finally amounts to this, which I also believe,—"That government is best which governs not at all."
—Henry David Thoreau, 1849

It by no means follows, however, that because the state may unwisely interfere in the life of the individual, it must be pronounced in itself and by nature a necessary evil. It is no more evil than is society itself. It is the organic body of society.
—Woodrow Wilson, 1892

With the advent of representative democracy, the meaning of citizenship changed significantly in the nineteenth and twentieth centuries. In Europe, following two centuries of mercantilist policies, early nineteenth-century governments withdrew into what at the time was believed to be their core tasks: police, justice, taxation, and defense of the territory. This was the era of the nightwatch state, when government was—at least when compared to today— small and when bureaucracy was perceived as potentially evil. In the United States, fitting a traditional suspicion of too much centralization, ideas such as those of John O'Sullivan and Henry Thoreau were widely held in the nineteenth century. In the United States, a fair amount of distrust against government existed from the start of its independence. Half a century later, Woodrow Wilson advanced the idea that government could be as evil, and by implication, as good as society itself. Organic state theory held that government was an expression of society.

Since the second half of the nineteenth century, the social geography of society changed, slowly at first and accelerating in the twentieth century. Together, industrialization, urbanization, demographic growth, democratization, but also the alienation from original habitats and the decline of the village community had major impact upon society-government relations and upon the meaning of citizenship. Society consisted no longer of a series of more or less autonomous, self-contained, and geographically demarcated villages. Instead, it became increasingly based on interests organized along functional rather than geographical lines. In the twentieth century, interest groups have mushroomed, and by now there are not many interests that have no voice at all. As government has proliferated into an intricate network of hundreds of thousands of organizations, society has differentiated into many, many interest groups. Since the second part of the nineteenth century, interest groups have become a powerful force in policy and decision making (Skocpol, Ganz, and Munson 2000) The labor unions and women's associations are examples. At the beginning of the twentieth century they were of such influence that they attracted academic interest. A.F. Bentley was the first to study interest groups (1908), but the flow of studies really began in the 1920s and 1930s. In Europe, academic attention to interest groups did not emerge until the 1950s and 1960s.

Interest groups are extremely important to contemporary governance. They are considered an alternative to the distrusted and disappointing political parties of old. While political parties claim to represent aggregated and thus potentially competitive interests, interest groups are usually focused on a particular and coherent set of issues. Political parties also exist to secure positions of public authority for prolific members, whereas interest groups are more programmatic in orientation. Interest groups in general are a powerful political force, and some are formally incorporated in the political-administrative policy- and decision-making system (Wilson 1990).

Contemporary governance and democracy, of which interest groups are one expression, cannot function without a notion of active citizenship. In this chapter, I first discuss the changing meaning of citizenship and of citizen participation (section 14.1). Next, I briefly discuss definitions and types of interest groups (section 14.2). In section 14.3 the origin and development of interest groups in Western society are outlined. What distinguishes them from earlier societal associations is that they are based on voluntary participation and cooperation between interest groups and government (section 14.4). Interest groups serve as an intermediary between particular societal interests and government and can be regarded as an example of self-government. There is at least one other example of self-government, which assumes that humanity is not faced with the Hobbesian choice between market and state. Indeed, in voluntary cooperation, it appears that there is a middle way possible with respect to the delivery of public services and will be discussed in section 14.5. Finally, now that civil society is such an important concept, appropriately and inappropriately used to point to civic duty and civil responsibility, we should wonder about the meaning of civil society: Are some interest groups adequately equipped to take over some services from government? In the concluding section 14.6 we will see if civil society is an alternative to government, and if so, what kinds of organizational forms are available.

14.1. Changing Notions of Citizenship

Although citizenship was discussed at some length in chapter 4, we need to look at it again in this chapter since the evolution of citizenship provides a useful context for better understanding the emergence of interest groups in Western society.

A citizen is not just someone who by reason of birth is the inhabitant of a city (as in ancient Greece or Rome) or a national of a particular country. From the ancient Greeks on, citizenship had been defined in terms of the *good citizen,* who has to have the knowledge and capacity to rule as well as to be ruled. To the Greeks, citizenship was a bond that was forged between people and between people and their government, through voluntary participation in public affairs. While this sounds familiar as a theory, it is only 150 years old as a practice. For most of history, those who could exercise their rights of citizenship were few in comparison to the size of the population at large. Generally, the elites governed as part of their civic duty. The population at large, and certainly the male population, participated as well but more often than not on the basis of conscription. The notion that, in principle, all people could be citizens and thus engage in voluntary contractual relations with one another and with government was advanced by John Locke and fell on fertile grounds in the American colonies (Heater 1990, 30). By the end of the eighteenth century, citizenship as a right for all had become a full-fledged theory. As common practice in government, however, it evolved more slowly.

The classic study on the development of citizenship from the late eighteenth century to the present is that of Marshall (1965). In the modern world, citizen rights developed in three stages (Marshall 1965, 91). The first were the *civil rights*, such as freedom of speech, the right to own property, the right of association, and so forth. The institution that monitored the civil and legal rights of individuals was the court system. The notion of participative citizenship was enhanced through the expansion of the *political rights*. Most important among these were the expansion of the franchise, which not only allowed

Table 14.1

The Development and Elaboration of Citizenship in the Western World

Right	Content	Institution
Civil	Legal rights of individual	Courts
Political	Participation	Parliament, local councils
Social	Welfare, social security	Educational system, social services

Source: After Marshall 1965, 78.

ever larger portions of the adult population to vote, but also allowed them to be voted into public office. Obviously, parliaments and councils of subnational jurisdictions were the prime monitors of political rights. Finally, the capstone of *citizen rights* was provided in the development of welfare and social rights, initially rooted in the local communities of towns and guilds, from the beginning of the twentieth century on. Various public organizations share responsibility for the protection of these social rights (Table 14.1).

Citizenship developed in the context of the process of nationalization, during which separate parts of a sovereignty became fused together as one polity. One of the main vehicles of strengthening citizenship was civics education. In the course of the nineteenth century, educational systems in all Western countries helped socialize individuals into citizens through civics classes and classes in national history and government (Heater 1990, 88). Ideally, education for citizenship promoted open-mindedness, toleration, and respect for different viewpoints, thus serving as counterweight to the more closed-minded socialization provided by private institutions such as churches (Heater 1990, 202–203). Hence, citizenship is a type of identity that emphasizes high moral authority and behavior and thus not only overlaps, but transcends specific secular and religious identities as well as identities rooted in gender, race, language, region, and so forth.

Citizenship nowadays is conceptualized in a generic manner, but is experienced differently according to geographical context (Heater 1990, 318). As citizens, individuals often identify with a particular locality or region. Local government is the school of democracy, so John Stuart Mill argued, and it is there that citizenship can be most directly experienced and come to fruition. Citizenship is also experienced at the national level—for some people very concretely, as elected representatives in political bodies or as citizen members in consultative organizations, for others more as an abstraction, as an American, a Canadian, a Nigerian, and so forth. However, citizenship today is much less *only* identified with local and national governments and communities, for citizens increasingly engage, as individuals and as members of supranational associations, in the international community. The most abstract level is therefore that of global citizenship. Ideally, and in stable polities, these three levels are harmoniously linked (Heater 1990, 319). It is not only for ideological but also for practical reasons that citizenship is perceived as a multilevel phenomenon. Loyalty to the local environment is practical, for what is good for the national state is not always good for the locality. Conversely, loyalty to the state is practical, for what is good for the state may not always be good for the locality. And, finally, ever since the Club of Rome report in 1972 about the future of our planet, loyalty to the human species at large has become a very practical matter (Heater 1990, 324). Multilayered citizenship breaks through the traditional Weberian connection between the state's monopoly over the use of violence and the support of government by the people (Albrow 1996, 179). Thus, in the European Union, such citizenship places the national government's power in an arena with local/regional and supranational powers. It is in this type of state-fragmenting and state-transcending polity that *performative citizenship,* as Albrow calls it (Albrow 1996, 175), is no longer limited to many at the local level and to few at the national level. It is also in this context that legal, political, and social rights are no longer limited to citizens of a nation, but increasingly advanced as human rights at large on a global scale. Hence, Aristotle's notion of participative citizenship—based on a link between sovereign and citizen—is giving way to a performative or *global citizenship* that transcends physical and conceptual boundaries (Albrow 1996, 4), is focused on the future of the planet, and operates through open networking. Participation in the emergent interest groups and networks at local/regional and national levels has prepared the citizen for this new role.

14.2. Types of Interest Groups and Networks of Interaction: General and Country-Specific Observations

Interest groups can be classified in various ways. Given that they are assumed to have some degree of influence in politics, they can be distinguished according to their role and position in relation to the authoritative allocation of values. Drawing upon the early American literature, de Jong (1958, 17–19) distinguishes between three types of associations. In *constitutional associations,* action is based on law or in some type of governmental decision. Within this group, he distinguishes between codeciding bodies (e.g., Congress, state senate and house, local councils), executive bodies (e.g., implementing bodies such as deconcentrated agencies), and neutral associations (part of government, but not involved in making or implementing policy). The second main type is *politically active associations* in the environment of government. Within this generic type, the *politically active integral associations* in principle address a complete range of issues concerning the redistribution of values (e.g., political parties, churches). *Politically active sectoral associations* are more limited to the value distribution of a set of related issues (e.g., labor unions, the Automobile Association of America [AAA], professional associations, political action committees). The third subcategory in this group is the *politically active unitary associations*, which are focused on one issue only (e.g., Society for the Prevention of Cruelty to Animals). The third major type, that of the *apolitical associations*, is far removed from the political process (e.g., the family, a sports club, a small business).

Also in the 1950s, Almond presented his categorization of interest groups based on the degree to which political parties and interest groups were demarcated or intertwined and linked to particular geographic areas (Almond 1968b, 229–231). In the Anglo-American type, the function of political parties and interest groups is strongly demarcated. Interest groups articulate a particular demand, seek support, and try to get their demands on the public agenda, while political parties aggregate a variety of demands. In the developing world, the second type, neither political parties nor interest groups are fully differentiated. They may exist in the urbanized areas, but in the larger parts of the country they play little or no role. In the third type, of which France and Italy are examples, both parties and interest groups are bureaucratized (as in the Anglo-American type) but they are not autonomous. Rather, they are highly related and control each other up to a point. In Almond's fourth type, political parties aggregate demand (as in the Anglo-American type), while at the same time political parties (or, rather, their representatives in the legislature) and interest groups have developed a consensual style of policy making. In this respect, Lijphart speaks of consensus or consociational societies (1984, xiv). Examples of this fourth type are the Scandinavian countries, Belgium, and the Netherlands. Lijphart specifically mentions Belgium, where one part, Wallonia, of that recently federalized country (1994) has features of the French-Italian type, while the other part, Flanders, has features of the fourth type. Germany, he argues, moved in the direction of the fourth type and is now, thirty years after Almond's analysis, most certainly a fourth type country.

In addition to De Jong and Almond, a third way of looking at interest groups is presented by Peters (1989, 157–175), whose categories focus on the nature and types of interaction between interest groups and bureaucracy. In the *legitimate interaction* type, some interest groups have become an institutionalized part of the decision-making process and, as a legal requirement, will have to be consulted in specified cases. An example is the mandatory consultation of labor unions when collective labor contracts are negotiated between employers and employees. Another example is the frequent, and often mandatory, consultation of governmental bodies with representatives of business and labor in the development of social-economic policy. Peters makes the following interesting remark:

> societies that have had the most positive conceptions of the public bureaucracy—Germany, the Netherlands, and the Scandinavian countries—have been much more successful in accommodating the role of pressure groups in policy making than have political systems that have a less exalted conception of their civil servants. (Peters 1989, 156)

This is interesting because, even though the United States public holds a less exalted conception of their civil servants, American government has been very successful in accommodating interest groups. One specific variant of an accommodating and consensual polity with legitimate interest groups is corporatism. While interest group association is generally believed to be voluntary, Lowi observes, with respect to legitimate interaction, that an interest group ceases to exist as an ordinary lobby once it has become part of the interior decision-making process. The more influence an interest group has, the less voluntary its membership. He refers to this phenomenon as *sponsored pluralism* (Lowi 1979, 60).

Peters's next two types, those of *clientela* and of *parantela,* are taken from a study by Joseph LaPalombara on interest groups in Italy. Under *clientela* interaction, the relationship to bureaucracy is pursued by the interest group and accepted as legitimate representation of that particular interest in society. In many countries, the best examples are agricultural associations. Governmental agencies tend to consult with clientela interest groups, but such consultation is not necessarily required by law. Interaction between interest group and bureaucracy is still direct. Examples of countries where this type is found are the United States, France, and Italy. In the case of *parantela*, the interaction between interest group and government is based on "kinship" or close fraternal ties and often travels via the political parties. Hence, interaction between interest group and bureaucracy is indirect. This is found in several western and southern European countries (generally the Latin or Mediterranean countries: France, Italy, Spain, Greece), as well in Latin American and African states and especially in single-party countries (e.g., the Soviet Union before 1991) where a *parallel hierarchy* exists (each level in the bureaucratic hierarchy is complemented with a controlling/monitoring level in the political party system from the local up to the national level). Finally, *illegitimate interaction* concerns all attempts at influencing policy making outside the normal political channels and by other means such as demonstration and violence.

Yet another way of gauging the role of interest groups in government and

Table 14.2

Taxonomy of Policy Networks

Dominant actor	Few members	Many members
State (collective)	Bureaucracy, clientela or corporatist networks	Pluralist networks
Society (individual)	Participatory-statist, captured statist, triadic networks	Issue networks

Source: Howlett and Ramesh 1998, 470. Reprinted with permission from the Policy Studies Organization.

policy making is by considering the culture-specific nature of the interaction between bureaucrats and interest groups. In the United States and Germany the

> executive leadership, whether by officials or politicians is substantially constrained by the constellation of outside pressures . . . [while in Britain and France] the potential for either political leadership or *Beamtenherrschaft* is greater since the executive has greater discretion over which interest groups it negotiates with and . . . when. (Page 1992, 119)

Of these four countries, the French high civil servant is farthest removed from the people and is rarely pressured into consulting with interest groups. The civil service regards itself as serving the public interest and sees itself as a counterweight to the special pleading of self-interested groups. English government officials have a consultative style but also retain the capacity to determine key issues as nonnegotiable. German public policy has been strongly influenced by interest since the 1950s in the attempt to move away from the totalitarian state. Finally, in the United States, the issue networks and interest are as strong if not stronger than in Germany (Page 1992, 108–118).

Peters's categories of interaction provide a continuum from frequent and institutionalized interaction in the case of legitimate interest groups on the one hand to the ad hoc and noninstitutionalized interaction of illegitimate interest groups on the other hand. What all interest groups share is the effort to lobby for what they (claim to) represent. In most Western countries, the number of interest groups and independent professional lobbies has grown enormously. The exchange of information is the most minimal type of lobbying. The maximum type of lobbying is the informal but intensive efforts to influence public officeholders, whether in a political or bureaucratic position. Lobbying requires knowledge about participants and the crucial actors among them, about options and chances and the risks of each, and about the various arenas, the various conflicts, the various agendas, and so forth, so it is no wonder that lobbying has become a professional endeavor. It is certainly not an activity that one could do in spare time and yet expect to be successful. Successful lobbying requires not only professional commitment and knowledge, but also that one seeks to wield influence at the earliest possible moment in the policy-making process and at the lowest possible hierarchical level (Andersen and Eliassen 1991, 180). The later one starts lobbying, the more difficult it will be to move the decision-making process in the desired direction. This is because most decisions at later stages have already been the result of a consensus-seeking and hence a negotiation process. Also, the more progressed a particular decision-making process is, the higher the level at which the conflicts of interests will have to be ironed out. It is much more difficult to gain access to the top decision makers than to those who start out collecting and weighing the information upon which the higher echelons will make decisions.

Lobbying may also be more effective when various interest groups support each other's objectives. In fact, in highly organized societies, one-on-one relations and interactions are extremely rare. Many organizations operate in a network. One of the earliest conceptualizations of networks was as *iron triangles,* the intricate relationship between government, military, and industry. Iron triangles are closed and segmented and involve a fairly limited number of actors. *Issue networks,* on the other hand, involve many actors and are more open and fragmented (Heclo 1992). It is very difficult to define the boundaries of an issue network, because it may shift from dormant to active, its membership may shift between levels of government, and it may involve a variety of interest groups. Van Waarden (1992a, 31) argues that the most general concept to characterize public-private relations is the *policy network* (cf. Majone's *policy space* [1989, 158–159]), of which the issue network is a component. Van Waarden distinguishes among eleven types of policy networks: statism and pantouflage (in France, when civil servants move to positions in industry yet still identify with civil service values); captured statism; clientelism; pressure pluralism; parantela relationships; iron triangles; issue networks; sectoral corporatism; macrocorporatism and intersectoral concertation; state corporatism; and sponsored pluralism (Van Waarden 1992a, 42–49). Some of these were mentioned above (iron triangle, issue network, clientela, parantela, sponsored pluralism). Corporatism will be discussed below, and statism has been addressed in chapter 7.

Van Waarden distinguishes seven dimensions (actors, function, structure, conventions of interaction, institutionalization, distribution of power, strategies of public administration). Six of these have three to eight characteristics scoring on each of the eleven network types (Van Waarden 1992a, 39–41). His classification is extremely complex. Howlett and Ramesh (1998) classify networks into four main groups (Table 14.2).

Their taxonomy is based on who takes the initiative in the network, state and/or individual actors in society, and on the exclusiveness of the network. In exclusive networks, the membership is well defined; hence Howlett and Ramesh speak of "few" members. More open networks are characterized by changing membership. Some networks, such as military organizations and the defense industry, are quite closed. Other networks are much more open, such as is the case with a whole range of welfare services.

14.3. From One to Many Interest Groups

The oldest types of large-scale societal interest groups (other than church-related associations) were the professional business organizations known as guilds (Van Waarden 1992c, 527). Guilds are usually associated with medieval Western Europe; they existed there until the end of the eighteenth century. But guilds were also found in various Islamic countries, in the Byzantine Empire, in China until the beginning of the twentieth century, and in Babylon, India, and ancient Greece and Rome (Olson 1982, 147–148, 156). The advent of the guilds represents a phase in the development of organizational capacities that is characterized by the concentration of wealth, resources, and rights in the hands of particular groups in society (Kieser 1989, 545). Some guilds were created solely for religious, charitable, or cultural reasons. The most well-known are the trade guilds and the craft guilds. These guilds organized a monopoly of a specific product and/or craft. Nonmembers were excluded from actively pursuing the particular trade or craft of a guild. The trade and craft guilds functioned as a training system for apprentices, guaranteed a minimum product quality, and fulfilled a very important function of social cohesion, which was strengthened by symbols and rituals that served to create moral bonds between members. There was no separation of work and private life. This is important if we want to understand the magnitude of the change from the early nineteenth century on when work and private life became separated. In addition, guilds worked in close cooperation with (local) government, ensuring rules of product quality, serving as first-line collectors of excises and taxes, and generally monitoring economic relations in the market. The influence of the guilds declined with the increasing functional specialization in the production process (mass production in factories), with the loss of monopoly and the advent of the free market, and with the separation of production (the goal of the organization) and livelihood (individual motive to work). This last element emphasizes the separation between work and private life (Kieser 1989, 546–547).

As the advocates for free market economies gained ground in the eighteenth century, the guilds were abolished (in England in 1762; Tuscany, 1770;

France, 1791; the Netherlands, 1798; Prussia, 1810; Sweden, 1846; Italy, 1864) (Crouch 1986, 192, 197). With their disappearance, one of the most important guarantees of regulated interaction between consumers and producers was lost. Government withdrew from any direct control of product quality.

The medieval guilds can best be compared to the modern business interest organizations. The development of interest groups was such that a situation with "one" type of organization changed to one with many different interest groups. In Europe, the legitimacy for modern interest groups is partially found in corporatism. In the United States their legitimacy is yet another expression of the checks and balances built into the state and administrative system. The reasons for their emergence, though, were the same on either side of the Atlantic.

During a large part of the nineteenth century, the idea dominated that the market and its "invisible hand" provided the best foundation for economic order. In that economic order, prices were established via unlimited competition between supply and demand. This view came increasingly under siege in the second half of the nineteenth century. Demographic growth generated a mass demand for products that could be met by industrialization and technological innovation. Standardization of production processes became a necessity, but this required huge capital investments so enterprises strived to limit the risks involved. Thus they tried to limit competition and, preferably, establish a monopoly. That, in turn, led to price increases and a limitation upon free production, which was not in the interest of the consumer and the employee. Governments responded with actions such as the Sherman Anti-Trust Act of 1890 in the United States, or, as in Western Europe, with attempts to align employers and employees in the formulation of social-economic policy. Society responded to the growing organizational capacities of government and industry with its own organization of interests. Among these in Europe from the 1860s on were political parties and labor unions. In the same period, however, other types of interests became as organized: housewives, car owners, medical doctors, town clerks, accountants, teachers, vegetarians, et cetera, et cetera.

Van Waarden (1985, 232, 259) distinguishes four phases in the development of the organizational capacity of society. The first phase is dominated by the guilds already mentioned. In the second phase, local interest organizations emerged in the middle of the nineteenth century and proliferated enormously around the 1900s. This is an indication of the degree to which private individuals had come to regard organization as the means to pursue their collective interest. In the third phase, local and regional interest groups united in national organizations. This occurred in the first half of the twentieth century. From the middle of the twentieth century, these national interest groups engaged in institutionalized relations with government: the fourth phase. Societal associations are able to institutionalize their interaction with government and other organized interests only if political stability is a fact (Olson 1982, 40–41).

It may appear that the discussion above is basically relevant to Europe since, as both Olson (1982, 94) and Van Waarden (1992b, 151) remind us, the United States had no special interest organizations and traditions with medieval origins. More important to both Western Europe and the United States is that the similarities between the medieval and early modern guilds and the modern interest groups are superficial and trivial, and the guild is really not a medieval predecessor of our contemporary interest group. The differences between the medieval guilds and the modern interest group associations (of whatever kind) are by far larger than the similarities. The guilds fulfilled both economic and social functions. They operated in a situation in which government did not stimulate or channel self-organization (as in the nineteenth and twentieth centuries) and in which it was interested only in the taxes and excises it could collect via the guilds. The guilds were highly hierarchical organizations, in which no equality existed between master and apprentice. Guilds held a monopoly within their craft or trade, but were extremely fragmented for lacking an external (i.e., overarching) organization. This brief discussion of guilds highlights how different the interest groups of modern society are from the medieval and early modern guilds. It also shows that, despite the differences in historical development in early modern United States and Western Europe, the developments of interest groups in the modern era have been quite the same, for they emerged at the same time on both sides of the Atlantic in response to comparable changing social, economic, and therefore political conditions. In one sense, the remote past did have impact, at least in Western Europe. Guilds played an important role in the regulation of relations between consumers and producers and in controlling the economy. That regulatory function fell away around the 1800s and created a vacuum that came to be filled by interest groups and government. With respect to North America, one can also argue that the emigrants of the seventeenth and eighteenth century brought experience with or at least a collective memory of guilds with them. Those who had settled in the colonies that were to rebel against monarchical and aristocratic rule chose not to regulate economic life through a coproduction of government and guild. In this sense, the tradition of social-economic association through guilds and its abolishment is a common heritage in the Western world.

In addition to the church and affiliated institutions, the guilds were the only other significant societal association in Europe for centuries. They disappeared in a matter of decades. In the entire Western world, new types of societal association emerged: political parties, labor unions, associations of professionals, employer unions, associations of like-minded people (reformers), associations of people with a shared experience (veterans, disabled, survivors of cancer, etc.), sports clubs, and so forth. Society in all its aspects, in all its appearances, and at all levels has become organized to a degree that we would not have fathomed even a hundred years ago. The voluntary nature of their membership and the noninvolvement of government as far as the creation of interest groups is concerned (subsidies, obviously, represent some involvement) call for a different type of relationship between government and citizen. Government can call upon a citizen's sense of duty, but it can hardly oblige a citizen to do anything the law does not prescribe.

14.4. Citizen Participation: Voluntary Associations, Coproduction, and Public-Private Partnership

Citizen participation is a concept that can be approached in at least two ways. The first is concerned with the degree to which citizens are able to organize themselves and is thus focused on self-governance. Is society at large conducive to the establishment of voluntary groups in which citizens associate for the collective good? Or is society stratified in such a way that individual citizens can be excluded from participation and/or prevented from creating their own associations? With respect to the medieval guilds, the first question can be answered with an unequivocal "no" and the second one can be affirmed. After all, if not the guild, then the church would channel any type of participation and cooperation for the common good. The answers to both questions for modern society are the reverse from the answers to these questions for the Middle Ages. It is, in fact, characteristic for democracies that participation in terms of citizen (voluntary) association, nonprofit organization, and third sector activity is possible (for discussion of these three types, see Lohmann 1992, 40–43). Autocratic regimes will be much less inclined to stimulate the self-governance capacities of their citizens.

The second way in which citizen participation has been defined concerns notions of citizen participation in the production of and possibly decision making about public services. With respect to participation in service delivery, a distinction between *voluntary* and *compulsory participation* should be made (I address this below in more detail in the context of coproduction). Participation in terms of actual citizen involvement in decision making is the one that dominates the Western conceptualization of participation and is either direct (for instance, through referenda) or indirect (political parties, interest groups, voting). Lane and Ersson argue that indirect participation has become the more common form (1987, 210–211).

If indirect participation has become the more common form, it does not also mean that the number of voluntary associations has decreased. The broader conception of *citizen participation in society* and the more limited conception of *citizen participation in government* are really not very well related. In fact, the number of voluntary associations has increased rapidly in the twentieth century. There are marked differences between countries, though. If all memberships are included, then the United States is clearly a nation of joiners, with more than 72 percent of respondents to a survey indicating membership in some association. If church membership is excluded, then the United States is more or less comparable to the United Kingdom, the Netherlands, and Australia. But if both church membership and union membership are excluded, then, for instance, Australia and the Netherlands rank quite a bit higher than the United States (Curtis, Grabb, and Baer 1992, 143–145). In other words, the American people may be a nation of joiners but they like their individual freedom even more; the Dutch may pay tribute to individual freedom (they live in a very densely populated country), but they appreciate associating even more. The degree to which voluntary associations appear in a society is, however, dependent on the degree to which government is centralized (Rose 1954; as reported in Curtis, Grabb, and Baer 1992, 150).

That voluntary associations have grown so much in numbers is testimony to the idea that problems of cooperation can be overcome. Jordan (1989, 24–25) mentions at least four such problems: no common interest in modern society; different desires among the people; limited quantities of natural resources and of time and energy; no single system of coordination that works for every good and all citizens. This list, however, provides an incomplete analysis. There can be neither a common interest nor a people wanting the same thing, if only in view of the size of most populations. There are, however, so many people that there is always something that someone can identify and thus associate with. Quantities of natural and human resources will always be limited, which is thus a real problem. A single coordination system is really not necessary in a situation where networks and interactions are fluid and where, by some magical process, interest groups, political parties, and government officials somehow manage to meet.

Like Lane and Ersson, Elinor Ostrom argues that scholars are very much focused on indirect participation, given that citizen participation is defined as "contacting leaders, organizing interest groups and parties, and voting" (Ostrom 1998, 18). She is correct in observing that the educational system produces cynical citizens, instead of teaching them skills and knowledge that would help them solve social dilemmas (e.g., free-rider problem, tragedy of the commons, prisoner's dilemma, etc.; Ostrom 1998, 1–2). I explore some of the possible solutions to social dilemmas in the next section. In this section, I conclude by discussing two ways in which government has sought to utilize the associative capacity in society.

Public-private partnership usually refers to ways in which government engages in productive interaction with private and profitable enterprises. *Coproduction*, a very popular concept in the 1980s, refers to any type of interaction between government and (groups of) citizen(s). Brudney and England provide a stipulative definition of coproduction that is fairly complete:

> Coproduction consists of citizen involvement or participation (rather than bureaucratic responsiveness) in the delivery of urban services. These outcomes are intended to have a positive (rather than negative) impact on service delivery patterns. Coproduction stems from voluntary cooperation on the part of the citizen (rather than compliance with laws or city ordinances) and involves active (rather than passive) behaviors. Both groups and individuals may engage in coproduction, but the more important participants from both practical and equity standpoints are collectivities. (1983, 63)

Brudney and England do not think that coproduction can be compulsory, but they do believe that an act of noncompliance (vandalism, littering) should be labeled negative coproduction. If this is so, then an act of compliance, such as the compulsory membership of a nightwatch in early modern times, is certainly an example of positive coproduction. With that in mind, coproduction can be defined as the

> voluntary or compulsory active conjunction of personally and/or functionally involved citizens and public officials in the care-taking of common interests. Whether this coproduction takes the form of policy formulation, policy implementation, or the production of goods and/or services is irrelevant. (Raadschelders 1988, 268)

In the past, governments could easily resort to compulsory types of coproduction. While the elites had a moral duty to be involved in government, they only did so on a voluntary basis. The lower income groups were simply forced to participate (conscripted) in the nightwatch, the firewatch, the waterwatch, and so forth (Raadschelders 1988, 269–272; 1998a, 179–181). Currently, as far as we know, compulsory coproduction is unheard of in Western societies.

14.5.   Between State and Market: Collective Action, the Commons, and Corporatism

In a way, coproduction may appear to be a convenient solution to a particular problem at a given moment. To what degree more institutionalized forms of cooperation between (groups of) citizen(s) only and between them and government are considered desirable depends on issue, time, and civic mentality. In most scenarios, some degree of government involvement is considered inevitable. This is based on the idea that people, when confronted with a choice between self-interest and collective interest, will choose the first, thus necessitating government intervention in those areas where the market does not care. Combined, theories such as those of Hardin on the tragedy of the commons, of Olson on the limits of collective action, and of the prisoner's dilemma provide us with a sobering analysis of human behavior. Hardin (1968) argues that human beings are focused on the individual short-term gain they can make and will thus deplete the natural resource upon which their livelihood as a collective depends. What is more, people who care about the resource and seek ways to protect its regenerative capacities will have to accept that others who have not contributed to this goal will profit from their effort (free riders). Olson (1965) argues that only small groups can successfully engage in the development and delivery of collective services and that, by nature, people are not inclined to cooperate:

> unless the number of individuals is quite small, or unless there is coercion or some special device to make individuals act in their common interest, rational, self-interested individuals will not act to achieve their common or group interests. (1965, 2)

And, finally, the prisoner's dilemma game provides a more formal presentation of the outcome of tension between self-interest and cooperation (Ostrom 1990). All three theories point to market failure as a consequence of selfishness and provide a possible justification for a government takeover. The classic choice is thus one between the total anarchy of the market or the Hobbesian absolutism of the state.

It is the achievement of Elinor Ostrom that we have been reminded that throughout the ages, many societies have had and continue to have organizations that operate between state and market and that traditional political theory and political science have been focused on the extreme choices or solutions. She calls that type of organization a *common pool resource* (CPR) *arrangement*. CPR arrangements are most certainly societal associations, but they differ from the more generic voluntary associations in that they can actually impose sanctions upon those that do not comply with the rules. Like voluntary associations, their emergence and development are a bottom-up rather than a top-down process. CPR arrangements are established after three initial questions have been addressed. First, is formal organization necessary and, if so, what would be the best? Second, how can credible commitment to agreements be generated in light of the human inclination to free rider behavior? And, third, how can mutual monitoring of conformity to established rules be arranged? (Ostrom 1990, 42–45). In the course of her research and that of others at or through the Workshop in Political Theory and Policy Analysis at Indiana University, hundreds if not thousands of such CPR arrangements have

Table 14.3

Comparison of Commons, Market, and State on Five Dimensions

	Market	Commons	State
Participation	Uncoerced	Uncoerced	Coercive
Purpose	Maximization (private goods)	Shared (common goods)	Authoritative (public goods)
Resources	Private	Common	Public
Reciprocity	Quid pro quo	Mutuality	Equity
Social relations	Caveat emptor	Fairness	Law

Source: Lohmann 1992, 60. Reprinted with permission from the author.

been identified throughout the world. They can certainly not be regarded as a secondary phenomenon in the world of governance, because they not only perform important public functions but also tend to exist for long periods of time. Just a few examples: The *huerta*-irrigation systems have existed in Spain since 1435. The common management arrangements of alpine meadows and forest in Switzerland have a history going back to 1483. At least since 1630, irrigation communities have existed in the Philippines (Ostrom 1990, 58–88). The traditional common lands in Japan have been managed on a CPR basis since at least the thirteenth century (McKean 1992, 63–98). The waterboards in the western part of the Netherlands have existed since the early eleventh century. In the course of time, however, and especially since the nineteenth century, the Dutch waterboards have been completely incorporated into the state and administrative system. Under what conditions CPR systems continue to exist next to the state and under what conditions they are incorporated into the state is not clear.

The differences between market, state, and commons have been analyzed from various angles, which are summarized in Table 14.3 above.

Clearly market and state are presented as the extremes, with the commons as a middle way. The commons, I argue, represent an example of direct participation, more common than some authors realize. It has been said that indirect participation is much more common (neighborhood councils, task forces, community action committees, etc.) and not very satisfactory. Among the authors who share that opinion, Streeck and Schmitter (1985, 8) state that neither community (spontaneous solidarity), market (competition), nor state (hierarchy) generates adequate problem-solving capabilities. They define the alternative of *private interest government* (PIG) as

> arrangements under which an attempt is made to make associative, self-interested collective action contribute to the achievement of public policy objectives. (17)

In this sense, the concept of private interest government does not differ much from what characterizes CPR arrangements. Both emphasize combined individual effort, embedded in but not determined by the state and administrative system. The difference between CPRs and PIGs is in the "achievement of public policy objectives" when these objectives are identical to government policy. In this case, PIG is an example of corporatism, which has been defined as

> a resolution to the problem of social order [where] the state, rather than superimposing a structure of autocratic authority, tries to succeed by sharing its public order functions with organized groups in civil society. (Hemerijck 1992, 77)

This is reminiscent of the legitimate interaction between government and interest groups. Corporatism is the institutionalized (i.e., organized, frequent, and mandatory) consultation of interest groups by government; as with the commons, it represents a situation of mutual reciprocity. The interest groups have a good chance of influencing public policy and government has a good chance of legitimating its policy choices. Corporatism attracted much attention in the 1980s among Western European scholars, especially those in Britain and the northwestern European consensual states. In a situation of *societal* or *neocorporatism*, all sorts of societal organizations have the opportunity to shape issues of a general and private interest within a structure of consultation and decision making established by government. In the best tradition of corporatism, government operates as mediator between various organized interests, such as in wage negotiations between labor unions and employers' associations. This is bottom-up corporatism. The top-down variant is known as *state corporatism*, of which fascist Italy is a good example. In general, in corporatist theory, (professional) groups rather than individuals are considered the most important constituting components of state and society, and this is rooted in Christian notions about the relation between state and society. In its Catholic version, it is known as *subsidiarity*, which emphasizes that government intervention is justified when societal mechanisms and associations (such as charity and the church) of just distribution of welfare are insufficient. Protestant denominations speak of *sovereignty in one's own circle*, emphasizing societal association as a civic duty. State intervention is more limited in this Protestant approach. Neocorporatism has been presented by Streeck and Schmitter and many others as the solution to government's limited problem-solving capabilities (see also Grant 1985; Landauer 1983).

A discussion of corporatism is more relevant to the United States than one would perhaps assume. What Dahl and Lindblom call *polyarchy* is basically a democracy in which "non-leaders exercise a high control over governmental leaders" (1953, 277). At the same time, they warn against the dangers of national bargaining on the part of "gigantic organizations" (498) for these would jeopardize the sovereignty of the people (i.e., equality). And yet the United

States is a prime example of a pluralist polity, in which institutionalized inter-actions occur between societal organizations and government. The difference between European corporatism and American pluralism is that in the former, government tends to invite representatives of societal associations to partici-pate in policy making and decision making (legitimate interaction) and tends to act as mediator rather than as initiator. The possibility that interest groups pursue "manipulative purposes" (Dahl and Lindblom 1953, 506) may appear to be larger in pluralist and federal polities such as the United States than in the unitary states of Western Europe. However, what is important is not so much the unitary or federal makeup of the administrative system, but rather the culture of its interaction with interest groups. In France and Britain, the executive power has much more discretion over whom it wishes to negotiate with than in, for instance, the United States or Germany. While both these latter states are federal states, it is not the federated system but, rather, the relative openness of their civil services to interest groups that determine the latter's influence (Page 1992, 119). Thus, the Netherlands is a decentralized-unitary state but in many areas of public policy, individual citizens and/or societal associations are actively involved in policy making.

14.6.   Concluding Remarks: Civil Society as Utopian or Realistic Alternative for Public Services

In terms of academic interest, neocorporatism appeared to be short-lived, al-most a fashion, for it disappeared from the journals and book titles after the 1980s. During the 1990s, the concept of civil society gained ground. What combines the scholarly interest in corporatism and in civil society is that both bodies of literature assume that citizen participation and voluntary associa-tions have declined and that corporatism and civil society ought to be re-vived. Both assumptions are wrong, of course, for there is abundant evidence to the contrary (Ferris 1984; Chubb and Moe 1988; Lohmann 1992; Curtis, Grabb, and Baer 1992). In fact, it has been demonstrated that the quality of government (at the local level) is highly dependent upon the degree to which citizens are involved in their community (voting, reading newspapers, but also as members of neighborhood associations etc.) (Follett 1920; Putnam, Leonardi, and Nanetti 1993). From an ideological point of view, *civil society* is a way to revitalize the citizen as an active member of government. In a more cynical mood, one could argue that civil society is just a way to soften the blow that must come when government retreats from directly providing all sorts of welfare services. It is not a coincidence that civil society is de-fended at the same time that reform of the welfare state is seriously consid-ered. Like third sector bodies, neocorporatism, and coproduction, civil society is merely another way of expressing the hope that individuals will take up their responsibility as citizens and combine to fill the vacuum left as a consequence of welfare state reforms.

Ever since society went beyond tribal organization, it has been the challenge of governments to balance between the needs of the individual and those of the collective. That balancing act is avoided in the extreme cases of pure individualism or pure collectivism. In modern democracies, however, it is impossible to avoid balancing, and the balancing act itself has been named coproduction, public-private partnership, voluntary association, corporatism, checks and balances, and civil society. And, of course, these are all types of organization; more specifically, they are types of organized interaction between citizen and government. Modern society could not do without this intricate network of organized interests. Plato's preference for mixed government should not be considered only the combination of aristocracy and democracy. As far as our time is concerned, mixed government is the situation in which public organizations share responsibility for collective tasks with societal organizations. The way in which they do so varies from culture to culture and from era to era. Again, modern governance requires more than ever a balancing between individual and collective interests. And the difference between the two is perhaps less clear than in the early twentieth century.

CONCLUSION

15 A HOLISTIC PERSPECTIVE ON GOVERNMENT AND GOVERNANCE

[The public administrator] will not merely represent one government agency or be a legal or technical specialist but rather be a center of social coopera-tion and able to command and utilize broad knowledge, deep understanding, and human sympathy in a synthesis of social wisdom.
—Louis Brownlow, 1934, as quoted in Richard Stillman, 1991

While substantial advantages exist from academic specialization, sweeping prescriptions based on stylized notions of the institutional arrangements studied by other disciplines are negative fallouts of overspecialization.
—Elinor Ostrom, 1997

Profession-bent students should be helped to understand that in the twenty-first century the world will not be run by those who possess mere information alone. . . . We are drowning in information, while starving for wisdom. The world henceforth will be run by synthesizers.
—Edward O. Wilson, 1998

Governance and government today are more complex than ever before. This complexity stems, for instance, from the values shared in society yet inter-preted differently in terms of their meaning for public action, from the mul-tiple and conflicting demands upon government, from the existence of so many public organizations and so many societal associations, and from the multitude of interactions between individual actors of various institutional and professional allegiance. The sheer size of government in terms of rev-enue and expenditure, personnel, and the scope of its activities makes it such a complex social phenomenon that the study of a specific aspect rather than of the whole is inviting. While the understanding of governance and govern-ment is, without doubt, advanced through specialized inquiry, it is at the same time impaired when various bodies of knowledge are not brought together in a holistic framework.

The compartmentalization of knowledge in general has been a continuous concern ever since the early seventeenth century, but it has gained increased attention in the course of the twentieth century in the slipstream of unprecedented specialization of government functions and of academic disciplines (Raadschelders 2000a). Before World War II practitioners and academics in public administration embraced specialization in the pursuit of efficiency and responsiveness. But at the same time, practitioners such as Louis Brownlow advocated a desire for wisdom. In academe, the study of public administration emerged as a specialization in the expectation that it would provide practice with usable knowledge. After World War II, specialization continued. At the universities, the wave of specialization was balanced from the early 1980s by a more generalist and reflective approach (e.g., Minnowbrook I and II, the Blacksburg Manifesto). Currently, consensus appears to be growing that practitioners are as much if not more served by generalist perspectives on governance and government, that academics cannot develop usable prescriptions for reality if these are based only on specialists' perspectives, and that students preparing for a career in the public sector or in academe need an integrative framework in which the various specializations begin to make sense.

In this book, a holistic perspective on government has been developed. The dominant approach to government in the study of public administration in the past century was instrumentalist and technocratic. In this tradition, government was studied in terms of techniques and principles of budgeting, management, organization, personnel policy, policy- and decision-making processes, and so forth. To be sure, these specializations are necessary and important elements in the training of future civil servants and academics. However, if the study of government does not go beyond them, chances are that the novice public servant will quickly discover that the mere knowledge and application of a tool kit does not suffice when attempting to develop and legitimate public policy. Modern public managers will have to

> be encouraged to develop the higher order, reflective competencies to analyse, synthesise, judge and reflect, not in some narrow rational-functional way, but one that takes account of the wider social, moral, cultural and political relationships and interdependencies which have consequences for their actions. (Beardwell and Holden 1997, 456)

An academic interested in government and solely pursuing theory without regard for policy and societal relevance will not reach the practitioners' audience, instead merely confirming the stereotype that scholars work in ivory towers. The generalist practitioner or pracademic (to borrow Waldo's phrase) who does not reflect upon the nature of government and merely searches for ready-made and quick-and-dirty solutions to societal problems may well be a danger to society. The specialist practitioner who is not forced to gauge and explain in lay terms what possible societal consequences specific innovations might have is equally dangerous to society (Snow 1971).

15.1. Once Again: Observations on the Framework of This Book

This book is holistic and multidisciplinary in its approach to government since this complex social phenomenon can be fully understood neither in a monodisciplinary perspective nor in the framework of traditional public administration. The framework in this book is one of differentiated integration. To be more specific, the book provides a metaframework that organizes and relates different bodies and sources of knowledge concerning government. I believe that this metaframework enhances the theory competence of practitioners because it provides them with a way for viewing and for understanding a situation. That frame consists of a variety of perspectives, thus encouraging flexibility of attention (i.e., the ability to see a wide range of potential angles for understanding and of a wide range of solutions) as well as modesty about possible lines of action (i.e., the ability to engage with and listen to others) (McSwite 2001, 112). This metaframework is nothing more, nothing less than a bookcase. Katz and Kahn call their open system theory of organizations a metatheory since it does not present testable cause-effect hypotheses but does provide "an approach and conceptual language for understanding and describing many kinds and levels of phenomena" (1966, 452). Their metatheory is more than a bookcase framework for it provides a basis for studying the dynamics that shape organizational life. Mine is a metaframework that cannot be but a bookcase since it holds knowledge from different studies and contains a variety of theoretical insights. The content of each of the bookshelves is determined by the fact that it has to do with government. What I place on the bookshelves, however, is subject to differences of opinion.

This latter observation must be elaborated. Herbert Simon took the lead in attacking the prewar science of administration and advocated a positivist approach. Hood and Jackson dryly remark that positivist administrative science has borne little fruit, as evidenced by the fact that very few of the old proverbs have been laid to rest, that fifty years of administrative science in the "Simonian" mode have had remarkably little effect on the practice of administrative argument, and that positivism as research methodology even in the United States commands less respect today than it did at the time of Simon's early work (1991, 20–21). Public administration is thus an interpretative science that must allow for different opinions. On a positive note, one can say that, in spite of the positivist's pressure, the study of public administration continues to strive to be relevant to government at all levels.

Table 15.1

The Metaframework for the Study of Government

	Individualism	Collectivism	
Juridical perspective	**Institutions** *Ideational level*: People need government; legal constitution of society; moral and ethical constitution of society		Historical perspective
Sociological perspective	*Societal level*: Democracy; justice and social justice; traditional services; welfare services **Actors** *Organization level*: Efficiency; organizational structures and cultures; decision and policy making *Individual level*: Political actors; bureaucratic actors; citizen actors and interest groups		Contemporary perspective
	Abstract level	More concrete level	Concrete level

In this concluding chapter, I summarize the holistic and multidisciplinary approach in this book by combining Tables 1.1 and 1.2 in chapter 1 into a metaframework for the study of government. What I consider to be part of the public realm not only includes public officials, citizens, public organizations, and a variety of public policies, but explicitly encompasses also the democratic superstructure (i.e., the political theory of representative democracy and of central-local or intergovernmental relations) and the values that constitute society at large. Each of these subjects can be analyzed in terms of the perspectives (Table 15.1).

At a very abstract level, Western countries are comparable to each other in terms of the basic features of the relationship between society and government and in terms of the basic features of the structure and functioning of government. I explore these in section 15.2. In the next four sections, the different perspectives upon government are discussed. The first two of these angles emphasize that government should be studied in terms of continuums rather than of dichotomies. The third and fourth of these angles emphasize that government must be understood as a layered phenomenon and that we must penetrate beyond the immediate and visible by digging for deeper levels of meaning and by positioning the present firmly in the past.

The first angle stresses that public officials are always challenged to balance the needs of a collection of individuals with those of communities of people through a government of citizens. This continuum of *individualism and collectivism* poses public officials with a, if not the, major political challenge (section 15.3).

The second angle, that of the continuum from *juridical to a sociological approach,* shows how much public officials are required to balance fairness from a legal and abstract point of view (e.g., due process and equality before the law) with fairness from a social and more concrete standpoint (e.g., discretion in determining government support relative to individual need) (section 15.4).

Both these angles highlight that governing is not an activity that provides clear-cut solutions for equally clear-cut problems. Presenting problems of government in a dichotomous fashion (public or private, politics versus administration, centralization or decentralization, vertical or flat organizations, bigger or smaller government, etc.) and with clearly defined ways and instruments of intervention suggests an "either-or" mind-set that is not very helpful in the real world. It is extremely important to understand that neither the social sciences nor, for instance, history, philosophy, and theology can be concerned with the unraveling of *mechanisms* such as exist in the natural sciences (natural selection with human intervention as ceteris paribus condition, gravity, magnetism, etc.) or with the development of *universal axioms and language* such as exist in mathematics, physics, and chemistry. Society and the way in which we think about the relation between human beings is bound not only by forces of nature but also by interpretations of culture. The sciences that deal with the human mind and human interaction can begin their analysis only in the cultural context within which thought and interaction acquire meaning. This is why dichotomies are nothing but helpful agencies in analyzing reality—which is subject to interpretation and thus negotiation. The notion of a continuum with extremes is thus more useful in capturing the nature of government's challenges and balances as the mix that it is.

That mix in reality is a consequence of choices varying by policy, by organization, by type of interest(s) involved, by politicians, by tradition, and so on. Taken as a whole, government has to perform a balancing act between competing policies, organizations, interests, and political parties. But even within each policy, organization, interest, and political party, that balancing act has to be performed. Let us assume for the sake of the argument that a fundamental choice can be made for a more individualist or a more collectivist society. Once such a choice is made at the ideological level, it is not automatically transposed to a more concrete level of policy, organization, or interest formation. Each step of the way, from the founding principles in a given time down to the most operational level, a choice has to be made about the particular mix desired.

The third and fourth angles emphasize that government is a multilayered phenomenon. First, we can understand government in terms of levels of meaning or abstraction (from abstract to concrete; section 15.5). Second, we can understand contemporary government in terms of its embeddedness in the past (the contemporary and historical aspects; section 15.6). These four perspectives together emphasize the balancing act that the citizen, the bureaucrat, the politician, and the academic have to perform when attempting to understand reality. These four perspectives are relevant to the understanding of all Western governments. Throughout this book, however, I have also emphasized that national traditions and cultures of government and administration play an important role in determining how these challenges play out in practice. There may be a *global public administration* emerging in terms of concepts and theories, but once applied to a specific national or even regional and local case, it quickly becomes clear how different the various traditions and cultures are (section 15.7). In fact, in chapter 10, we have seen an example of how national tradition and culture influences the development of organizational theory. I suggest that, with respect to government and the study of public administration, a *global theory* is truly trivial and general, and that we must therefore recognize the degree to which our concepts and theories are shaped by the culture we are part of. In chapter 11, we have seen how the Western conceptualization of the policy process is particularly influenced by a linear conception of time that is, once beyond the professional and business world, foreign to much of the rest of the world. Hence, the metaframework in this book begets meaning only in a conceptualization of the role and position of a particular government in its society. An integral theory of government cannot be developed.

The generalist public servant and by implication the master's of public administration (MPA) student and future academic or practitioner must be knowledgeable in the general (i.e., global as in worldwide) body of literature on government as well as intimately acquainted with the national tradition and culture to which that general body of knowledge can be applied. In view of the degree of compartmentalization of knowledge and of activity, we can only conclude that the generalist public servant of today must have uncommon if not uncanny capabilities when trying to understand the role and position of government in society and acting in accordance with the multiple needs he or she is confronted with (section 15.8).

15.2. Structural Similarities Between Western Societies and Governments

At the most abstract level, Western governments in their societies can be lumped together as one case. They are all democracies that developed in the early modern and modern period and they share at least four characteristics:

    a. *a Rechtsstaat* tradition;

b. a tradition of deep but conflictual appreciation of freedom, equality, and fraternity;

c. a tradition of negotiated authority; and

d. a tradition of deep and conflicting appreciation of the rationalist's calculus of cost-benefit and the philosopher's understanding of right and wrong.

The *Rechtsstaat* or constitutional state tradition is perhaps the most fundamental of these traditions. With the exception of the United Kingdom, all Western governments have a formal constitution. This foundational legal document is the formal expression of the Western political theory of democracy, and from it emanates legislation that determines central-local or intergovernmental relations (IGR). Together, democracy theory and IGR provide the democratic superstructure of Western societies and governments. Other, policy-specific legislation and regulation is reviewed in the context of this democratic superstructure, whether by means of formal judicial review, as in the United States and Germany, or through parliamentary debate, as in most Western European countries.

The Western political theory of democracy also includes a deep appreciation for the values of liberty, equality, and fraternity. The importance of liberty is stressed in terms of the position of the individual vis-à-vis fellow human beings and government. Liberty or freedom is often understood in terms of individual freedom. The existence of government is legitimated by the fact that it protects and where possible advances the life, liberty, and property of the individual. In this Lockean list of values, the value of equality is missing. As important as liberty is, equality has become as important. Weighing liberty and equality, one could say that contemporary government protects the life, liberty, and property of the advantaged individual and tries to advance the life, liberty, and property of the disadvantaged. Equality is minimally defined as "opportunity" and maximally as "condition." The union of citizens that is presupposed in the constitution or other constituting documents materializes when policies are developed that actually advance brotherhood. While governments have come a long way since the Atlantic Revolutions in serving liberty, equality, and fraternity, it is equally clear that the closing hymn of Beethoven's ninth symphony, *Alle Menschen werden Brüder,* still contains a major challenge. Is fraternity best expressed in terms of neighborly choice or in terms of civic duty gently but firmly advanced through government? The answer to this question is influenced by how circumstances in context and time are evaluated by the observant individual. Aldous Huxley and George Orwell expressed deep fear of totalitarian government and expanded upon developments on the European continent at the time. Mark Twain and Emile

Zola saw government as the champion of social legislation and as the institution that could correct the evils brought about by industrialization and urbanization and thus protect society as a community of people. John Steinbeck conceptualized self-governance as rooted in the community of people who organized the tent camps during the migration of the dust bowl era. For Ayn Rand, self-governance was rooted in absolute individualism, where government exists merely to protect society as a collection of individuals. Few people would disagree with the basic idealism of brotherhood, but there is very little consensus about what it means in terms of actual public policy.

Public policy is the object of much negotiation and compromise. In fact, the constitutional framework of Western democracies itself is the product of negotiation and compromise. The great weakness of democracy, negotiable authority, is also its strength, for there is no one so powerful that all other authorities and concerns can be subjugated. This is certainly the case in the United States with its cultivation of an *adversarial method* of governance (Barber 1986, 45). In general, though, wherever a separation of powers is realized under positive law we have a situation of *negotiable authority.*

In developing constitutional frameworks and public policy, Western governments steer between factual rationalism and value judgment. Increasingly, public policy in the twentieth century rooted in facts, analyzed data, and "scientific" conclusions that together supported a claim for a more or less objective and neutral government. In most recent decades, however, it appears that calls for explicit value judgment and wisdom are on the rise. Would the citizenry be content in the pursuit of happiness when government is legitimated, for instance, only through the sophisticated economic modeling of decision making in democracy, or only through the equally sophisticated philosophy of Rawlsian advantageous inequalities, or only through the much older sense of social justice? Is it realized fully what it means when the idea of social justice is reduced to the Bismarckian pragmatics of pacifying the masses? Could it be that the welfare state is nothing else but the modernist opium of the people, having displaced religion from that doubtful honor? The *realpolitiker* is probably more at home with Bismarck, while the political idealist will sooner identify with the egalitarian conception of social justice. Both the realist and idealist are kept in check by the people who do have the power to elect political officeholders and thus also have the power to force them out of public office. The question then becomes in what we can find the legitimacy to call power to order? Legitimacy is provided through calculated rationalism based on "science" and through judgment based on ethical considerations which, in turn, are grounded in secular and/or religious worldviews. The great political controversies in the United States (slavery, segregation, abortion, euthanasia, the Vietnam war, welfare services, etc.) and other Western countries have been fought on the battlegrounds of fundamental ethical secular and/or religious beliefs about what is right and wrong. Naturally, citizens of the modern era consider cost and benefit of public services because they are taxpayers. They are also, however, members of a community that protects civilization as they know it. The current reappreciation of civil society, preferably organized locally and functioning organically, is an indication that the existence and advancement of individualism needs to be balanced with a sense of community and collectivism. Consider the following:

> the introduction of the old communal tradition of Common Work . . . requires of citizens participation not only in the deliberation and decision-making processes but also in the implementation of public policy decisions. (Barber 1986, 59)

To be sure, there was certainly a communal tradition in many Western countries in the early modern period, but it was imposed through social control (for instance, the civic duty of the elites to govern) and local ordinance (for instance, the conscription of male adults into the nightwatch). Citizen participation was thus hardly voluntary. Somehow, that does not seem to fit well in our present day and age.

15.3. The Balancing of Challenges I: Individualism and Collectivism

Of the four angles in my framework, the first one is perhaps the least understood. To varying degrees, individualism is highly valued in Western society. The more individualism is valued, the more suspicious people are about notions of collectivism. The strong state tradition in Western European countries makes its populations more accepting and even trusting of government, but no Western European citizen would accept collectivism with a totalitarian slant. In fact, governments in Western Europe are regarded not only as protectors of general welfare but also as mediators between various societal interests. A collectivist society under representative democracy seeks to advance the welfare of the population as a whole. The American citizen, on the other hand, is by nature much more suspicious of government, and notions of collectivism are more readily equated with communism or socialism. This being so, Americans fail to recognize the degree to which their society and government have become collectivist. In fact, American society would not be where it is today without large-scale government intervention in society and economy on behalf of the welfare of the entire population. In Table 15.2 I have contrasted characteristics of Western-style individualism and Western-style collectivism.

Table 15.2

The Challenge to Balance the Individualist and Collectivist Extremes

	Individualism	Collectivism
Values	Freedom	Equality; fraternity
Democracy	Direct	Indirect
Role of government	Repressive; reactive	Preventive; proactive
Degree of government intervention	Nightwatch state	Welfare state
Type of taxation	Proportional taxation	Progressive taxation
Nature of justice	Procedural; fragmented	Substantive; concentrated
Role of tradition	Burden; here and now	Experience; intergenerational morality
Efficiency	Cost; means; market	Benefits; ends; state
Decision-making style	Decentralized	Centralized
Organization; structure of bureaucracy	Horizontal	Vertical
Policy-making style	Distributive	Redistributive
Role and position of politician	Representative	King-philosopher
Functioning of bureaucracy	Discretionary freedom; flexibility	Control; standardization
Role and position of civil servant	Expertise; specialist	Loyalty; generalist
Role and position of interest groups and citizens	Voluntary association; civil rights; performative citizenship	Conscription; civic duties

In the case of individualism, freedom is defined as individual freedom, equality is defined in terms of opportunity, and fraternity is defined in terms of neighborly choice. Democracy is as direct as possible, and government's role is repressive and reactive (or protective). Government intervention in society is as limited as possible, will occur at the lowest possible level (the principle of subsidiarity), and be based on direct consultation with citizens (for instance, through referendum). The decision-making style is as decentralized as possible, and the organizational structure of bureaucracy is horizontal or flat. Public activities are financed through proportional taxation, a system by which each citizen pays a flat rate based on income. The administration of justice is limited to procedural application of rules and is fragmented. The judicial system is certainly not used for substantive policy making. An emphasis on individualism also negates the role of tradition. The individualist is inclined to consider the here and now, looks ahead, and considers the past as a burden. Under individualism, efficiency is regarded in terms of costs and means, and best provided through the market or market-type mechanisms. Policies are targeted to particular groups and thus distributive by nature. The politician is a representative of a particular constituency and supports pork-barrel politics of a distributive nature. Obviously, this is the case in political systems with district representation. Civil servants provide the politician with information in "their" area of expertise, are not necessarily concerned with other policies, and at the same time enjoy a fair amount of discretion and flexibility in the administration of their duties. Finally, citizenship is voluntary by nature. In an individualist perspective, one cannot be forced to be a citizen and engage in association. Performative citizenship is a choice that is rooted in civil rights.

Western-style collectivism is quite different. Freedom is understood in terms of the Golden Rule, by which the freedom of others should not be inhibited by an individual's actions. Equality is defined in terms of condition, which in many Western societies is measured by the gap between rich and poor. Fraternity is not just voluntary but also understood as a civic duty. Under collectivism, democracy cannot but be more indirect. Authority is centralized in national government so as to guarantee that all parts of the polity can equally benefit from public services. To be sure, collectivism in Western democracies does not preclude decentralization, for central government needs the input and cooperation of subnational governments to a large extent. Government intervention serves both nightwatch state and welfare state objectives. In the good society, government protects as well as advances individual welfare. Under collectivism, taxation is generally progressive by nature. While the degree to which a taxation system is progressive varies from country to country, all Western countries have a progressive taxation system, the revenue of which is used to finance distributive and redistributive policies. Justice is thus more than mere adjudication. In a collectivist perspective, a strong sense of intergenerational morality exists. The past is regarded as a source of experience that provides guidance for the future. Efficiency is defined in terms of benefits and ends, and is with respect to collective services best protected by government. With respect to policy-making style and the functioning of bureaucracy, government officials balance between discretionary freedom that allows for an assessment of individual cases and a legal framework or centralized control system that prescribes standardized options to be applied irrespective of individual circumstance. This is a consequence of the emphasis on equality of condition. In the extreme collectivist case, which is totalitarianism, the choice for equality becomes a straitjacket, inflexible and rigid, inexorably leading to a vicious circle of bureaucracy. Under collectivism, the politician serves as a representative of all the people and is expected to be a king-philosopher. This type of politician is generally found in political systems with proportional representation. Civil servants are loyal to the political system of which the elected officeholders are temporary representatives. At the higher levels, they are also—first and foremost—generalists. Finally, citizenship under collectivism acknowledges civil rights as well as civil duties (for instance, the duty to vote), and citizens can even be conscripted to help provide services.

Table 15.2 makes clear that a choice between individualism and collectivism is illusory. Neither one of the extremes can be achieved to the fullest extent possible, and, more important, neither extreme would be very desirable. Determining the role and position of government in society is not a simple zero-sum game in which government size and intervention can be decreased through privatization, contracting out, separating policy making from execution, and so forth. In reality, governments perform a delicate balancing act between individualism and collectivism. It is ironic to see to what extent the individualist society par excellence of the United States has become a collectivist administrative state; its people are still struggling to come to terms with this. It is equally ironic to see that in the more collectivist societies of Western Europe, individualism has not been submerged and is served through, for instance, neocorporatism. No Western government can afford to sacrifice the rights of the individual for the needs of the collective. At the same time, no Western government can afford to sacrifice the needs of the collective for the rights of the individual. The pure totalitarian societies of Huxley and Orwell and the pure individualist society of Ayn Rand serve as warnings against either extreme.

One can even argue that individualism and collectivism are inherent in each other. Individualism assumes freedom, yet too much freedom calls for some degree of control. Collectivism, on the other hand, assumes a fair degree of control and thus calls for a certain amount of freedom. While I disagree with McSwite's characterization that the study of public administration is crazy, I do agree with the reasoning immediately following that remark:

[public administration] faces so directly the central contradiction posed to human beings by collective life: the dual, conflicting necessities of control and freedom. (McSwite 2002, 96)

15.4. The Balancing of Challenges II: Juridical and Sociological Modes of Action

The distinction between a juridical or legalist and a sociological perspective, however inadequate these labels are, is much less controversial than the first perspective. Basically, it emphasizes the need to balance between a formal and impersonal application of rules and a more informal style of action based on personal judgment (Table 15.3).

In the legalist perspective, values are defined as precisely as possible and solidified in the constitution and other laws. Government serves first and foremost as a legislator whose activities are expressed in uniform statute and Roman law. Government intervention is determined by the constraints of the law, just as justice is limited to using the law as yardstick in the evaluation of individual cases. The past is of limited importance; past legislation and jurisprudence serve as the framework for present action and, in fact, can be replaced when present concerns deem such necessary. The efficiency of government action is determined as much as possible in terms of measurable indicators. The organizational structure is hierarchical, for unity of command provides a clear demarcation of authorities and competencies. Policy making is conceptualized in terms of rule making, with an eye for detail. The politician is a member of the highest authoritative body in the national or a subnational jurisdiction, and as such, is responsible for developing visions for the future. As consequence, civil servants are subordinate and take their cue from the politicians. Finally, in the truly legalist perspective, citizens are regarded as subjects, for no one is above the law.

In a more sociological perspective, values are ambiguous and contested. While the uniform legal foundations of society and government are considered important, the societal norms and values are even more important because they reflect diversity. This is expressed in a more executive role of government. Government intervention is determined by social demand and is more expansive since it is defined in terms of social justice. The impact of the past is more important in this perspective because past practices, memories, and experiences are as important as past legislation. The efficiency of government performance is evaluated not only in terms of measurable indicators but certainly and even more so in terms of wisdom and judgment. Emphasizing interaction instead of hierarchy is also conducive to more cooperative decision-making styles and flatter organizations. Policy making is expressed

Table 15.3

The Challenge to Balance Juridical and Sociological Modes of Action

	Juridical mode	Sociological mode
Values	Preciseness	Ambiguity
Democracy	Constitution; legal foundations	Norms and values
Role of government	Legislator	Executive
Degree of government intervention	Determined within constraints of statute and Roman law	Determined by social demand
Understanding of justice	Limited; adjudication	Expanded; social justice
Role of tradition	Low; past legislation	High; past practices
Determination of efficiency	Measurable indicators	Judgment; wisdom
Decision-making style	Unity of command	Cooperative
Organization; structure of bureaucracy	Hierarchy	Flatter organization
Policy-making style	Regulatory; eye for detail	Broad strokes; vision
Role and position of politician	Ultimate authority; provide vision	One among many authorities
Functioning of bureaucracy	Formal	Informal
Role and position of civil servant	Subordinate; takes orders	Coequal; provides facts and vision
Role and position of interest groups and citizens	Citizens as subjects	Citizens as partners

in rules but based on broad, visionary strokes that serve as framework for elaboration according to local needs. The politician is one among many who hold authority, and the civil servant is a coequal who provides facts as well as vision. Finally, in the truly sociological perspective, citizens are seen as partners who help to define policy.

As with the first perspective, viewing legalist and sociological modes of action as a continuum clarifies the degree to which Western governments balance between both. Again, the notion of choice is nonsensical. No contemporary Western government can afford to apply a purely legalist perspective when defining its role and position in society, for that would, in the minimal case, result in a nightwatch state that is inadequate to meet the challenges of today and, in the extreme case, would result in an absolutist state that would be at odds with the current understanding of democracy. At the same time, no Western government can afford to have its role and position defined solely by popular demand. Perhaps the better contrast of legalism is populism. Extreme populism (whether catering to a power elite or to an entire population) has been a breeding ground for nepotism, favoritism, and corruption. Once again, the best circumstances are those in which legalism and populism are balanced and bound to each other.

15.5.   The Balancing of Challenges III: Abstract and Concrete Layers of Understanding

It is striking to see how much the present understanding of government's structure and functioning is expressed in terms of embeddedness. The subject of interest can be management, reform, rules, citizenship, policy, planning, organization, culture, ethics, and so forth, but the understanding of these is increasingly approached in terms of levels of abstraction, from a most concrete and visible level to a most abstract and less visible level. Generally, authors have settled for three levels of abstraction (Table 15.4).

Each of the topics mentioned in the left column of Table 15.4 has been discussed at some length in the chapter(s) indicated. In this chapter, it is useful to point out how much the understanding of each of these topics is enhanced when considered as layered and when related to the others. The embedded nature of each of the topics has been advanced by very different authors. Most readers will have no difficulty accepting that the concrete is embedded in the more abstract.

It is more challenging to consider that the content of each of the second, third, and fourth columns of this table is not logically consistent yet is coherent. Government in its most concrete and visible manifestation is concerned with operational rules and responsibility. It emphasizes managerial values and, given a short-term focus, engages in operational planning. At the most concrete level, that of day-to-day practice, politics and administration are highly interdependent, and citizens acknowledge that they want government for they express appreciation for the quality and quantity of public services provided. A focus on management and reforms at the suborganizational and primary work level will guarantee citizen satisfaction with public services. At the most abstract level, the longer-term perspective dominates, and with it a focus on intergovernmental constitution, macrosocietal issues, and normative planning. At this abstract level, politics and administration are clearly

Table 15.4

The Challenge to Balance the Abstract with the Concrete

	Most abstract	Intermediate	Most concrete
Time (Braudel; ch. 1)	Long-term	Middle range	Short-term
Constitution of society (chs. 3, 4)	Type of authority	Institutional structure	Balancing individual and collective needs
Rules and choices (Kiser and Ostrom; chs. 3, 11)	Constitutional rules and choices	Collective rules and choices	Operational rules and choices
Ethics (Rohr; ch. 4)	Ethics of societal responsibility	Ethics of bureaucratic responsibility	Ethics of operational responsibility
Morality reasoning (Kohlberg; ch. 4)	Postconventional	Conventional	Preconventional
Citizenship (Heater; chs. 4, 15)	International/ global	National	Local/regional
Government structure and functioning (Deil S. Wright, Agranoff; ch. 5)	Intergovernmental constitution	Intergovernmental relations	Intergovernmental management
Public management values (Hood; ch. 9)	Lambda-type values	Theta-type values	Sigma-type values
New public management values (Ventriss; ch. 9)	Macrosocietal level	Organizational level	Suborganizational level

separated, each with its own set of responsibilities. Also, in the most abstract or stereotypical sense, government is considered bad for it is a breeding ground of bureaucratisms. At this deepest level, the societal and public sector values together produce a constitutional framework for the good society.

Much of the mainstream literature in the study of public administration and the perspective of practitioners in the field have focused on the most concrete level. It is not only the easiest to measure, but also the easiest target for reform. To be sure, a focus on the measurable is neither a choice out of laziness nor an attempt to avoid the more difficult philosophical questions and challenges. Governments deal with calculating citizen-taxpayers who demand a demonstration of the quality of public sector performance and who evaluate value for money rather than value for society. Other literature in the study of public administration (for instance, on ethics) as well as in, for instance, history, philosophy, and theology seeks to understand government at the most abstract level, where, ideally, judgment and wisdom reign supreme and where change is much more the consequence of unplanned and long-term

Most abstract	Intermediate	Most concrete	
Focus of reform (ch. 9)	(Civil) society	Political-administrative decision-making system	Structure and functioning administration
Organization of governance (Talcott, Frederickson; ch. 10)	Institutional level: rules, boundaries, regime values, type of authority	Organizational or managerial level: public organizations, nongovernmental organizations	Primary work level: discretion, performance measures, civil service functioning
Organizational culture (Schein; ch. 11)	Underlying basic assumptions	Patterns of behavior	Artifacts
Policy analysis (Kuypers; ch. 11)	Ultimate goals: politics	Intermediate goals/ instruments: politics + administration	Strict instruments: administration
Policy layers (Sabatier and Jenkins-Smith; ch. 11)	Deep core	Policy core	Secondary aspects
Planning (Jantsch; ch. 11)	Normative planning	Strategic planning	Operational planning
Politics-administration (Goodnow; ch. 12)	Separate in juridical sense	Interdependent in sociological sense	Separate and interdependent both
Perception of government (Goodsell; ch. 13)	Stereotype: government is bad	Government is necessary	We want government

structural societal developments than of planned and short-term governmental interventions. As Nisbet observes:

> There is no historical evidence that macro-changes over time are the cumulative results of small-scale, linear micro changes. (Nisbet 1969, 288)

While this is true in general, I also recognize the fact that the incremental changes in public policy since the 1880s have resulted in a society that is very different from that of a century ago. Government policy that developed in response to citizen demand may have been mostly incremental by nature, but the cumulative effect constitutes nothing less than a macrochange in a fairly short span of time. In the light of Table 15.4, abstract notions about the good society and the good government guided actions at the more concrete levels.

Obviously, the holistic understanding of government is served by connecting the levels of abstraction for each of the topics or angles relevant. Today's public administrator, whether elected or appointed, cannot but balance between the more concrete and the more abstract levels of understanding.

Choices made at the most concrete level, for particular rules or particular instruments, can be legitimated only when related to more abstract considerations. The most concrete and operational choices can be justified when their embeddedness in deeply held values is demonstrated.

15.6. The Balancing of Challenges IV: The Past as Present for the Future

In recent years, a variety of authors have increasingly come to recognize that embeddedness is not simply a matter of abstraction in space but also a matter of being layered in time. Throughout this book, I have demonstrated that the contemporary focus on government is served by a historical—that is, developmental—perspective. A historical approach is not simply one that catalogs events from the past to the present. While a chronology of events is necessary, it is meaningless without a developmental perspective. What does it mean to the contemporary practitioner in and the scholar of government to know that our political theory is Greek, that our administrative practices are Roman, and that our perspective on policy is linear and thus Hebrew in origin? A true historical perspective uses dates and data to document and trace the origin and development of the Western worldview at large in order to show how this has shaped the present practices of governance and government. It does not document the development of government in a present-minded or anachronistic way, and certainly does not demonstrate that the present represents the pinnacle of civilization, but seeks to explore how the present came to be. In the Western world, the past is often used to provide contrast to the present and to demonstrate that we have made progress. In other words, the process of civilization is one of continuous progress. However, the

> idea of continuity is amusing since the documentary record is generally filled with events and changes recorded because of their lack of continuity. (Nisbet 1969, 290)

Certainly, the government of the contemporary welfare state as such is ample illustration of lack of continuity with the distant past, when government in the perception of people was situated above them. Even within the time frame of the welfare state (say, the 1880s to the present), the various policies developed and the variety of acts adopted are testimony to the simultaneous manifestation of continuity, diversity, and change.

The fourth angle provides understanding of the degree to which governments need to balance the present with the past on behalf of the future. In the *History Is Efficient* model (Figure 15.1a), the past is not an issue, for the

Figure 15.1   **The Challenge to Balance the Present with the Past**

a) The "History is Efficient" Model

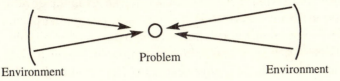

b) The "History as Linear Process" Model

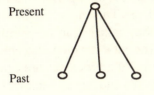

c) The "History as Nonlinear Development" Model

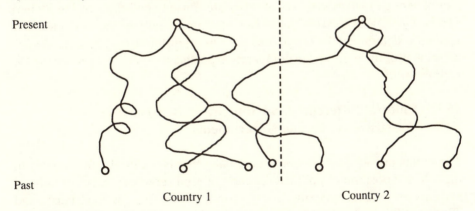

model defines a contemporary problem in terms of the immediate social-economic environment. The characteristics of this environment determine both the definition of the problem as well as the public policy solution for it. As far as we can tell, no Western government has ever discarded the impact of the past in its attempt to address problems for the future. This is not simply because past legislation cannot be ignored. More importantly, it is because the past provides continuity in the midst of contemporary change.

The *History as Linear Process* model is far more relevant to the understanding of Western government, for its conceptualization of the historical process is distinctly linear (Figure 15.1b) and emphasizes convergence rather than divergence, and similarities rather than differences in the developments between countries. Bureaucratization, for instance, is a global phenomenon because it has happened everywhere. Linearity is also visible in the conceptualization of decision- and policy-making processes as logical stages or phases. Thus, this model is highly abstracted from reality. It is, however, interesting and encouraging to see that public administration literature increasingly recognizes the importance of the more reality-based cyclical and process perspectives that emerge in the developmental perspective of the *History as Nonlinear Development* model (Figure 15.1c). In this model, development is as much a result of rational planning as it is of experimental trial and error and of unintended consequences of policies. This model emphasizes the differences in developments between countries rather than the similarities. Hence, bureaucratization occurred everywhere but it developed according to national culture. Also, policy- and decision-making processes are characterized by leaps, backtracking, and cycles. In this model, governments copy practices from other governments but at the same time adapt these to the local circumstances. Dorman Eaton did not transplant the British civil service system to the United States, but used its sense of loyalty and neutrality to create a civil service system that was appropriate for the conditions of the United States. The degree to which practices of other countries can be copied and applied is determined by the particular cultural differences. Thus, good government is defined through a comparative perspective with a refined nose for national culture.

15.7. Cultural Differences and Similarities Between Western Societies and Governments

The comparative literature about national—that is, cultural—differences in the role and position of political regimes, of civil service systems, of judicial systems, of taxation systems, and so forth, is rich (e.g., Bekke, Perry, and Toonen 1996; Blondel 1990; Farazmand 1991; Heady 1996; Page 1992; Peters 1991; Pierre 1995; Roskin 1995). In the comparative public administration of the 1950s and 1960s, the contrast between the developed and the developing world dominated. Indeed, comparative administration became synonymous with the study of non-Western government. Throughout this book, I have presented illustrations of the importance of balancing our understanding of the structure of government with an understanding of the culture of its functioning. There is no need to rehash what has been said on this in various chapters, but two main conclusions can be drawn.

The first conclusion is that culture is a very important explanatory variable for understanding government. While the organizational structure of bureaucracies is more or less comparable, their functioning varies from country to country. In all Western countries, civil servants are legally subordinate to politics, but how they actually interact with politics is more revealing. Likewise, national traditions of state and government determine the role and position of civil servants vis-à-vis citizens. The existence of cultural differences stands in the way of a global—that is, world encompassing—theory of government. The challenges of government may be conceptualized in terms used all over the globe (e.g., accountability, civil service reform, corruption, management, efficiency, decentralization), but how they are interpreted varies with cultural setting. In fact, some of these conceptualizations (e.g., efficiency, accountability) that are particularly valued in Western societies are meaningless in a non-Western setting. At the practical level of day-to-day government, convergence of traditions is unlikely for there are clear differences between different types of public organizations within one country. Comparing countries, convergence of administrative traditions is equally unlikely because of different national state and administrative culture traditions.

The second and more important conclusion is that the development of theory about government is bound by culture. At the most general level, Western governments are rooted in a combination of Judeo-Christian conceptions of social justice and of linear time on the one hand, and in Greco-Roman theories about and practices of government on the other hand. This sets the Western world apart from other parts of the world. We have also seen in a variety of chapters how much Western governments differ from each other. In fact, we have seen that theory development is to some degree determined by the time and context in which the scholar lives. Public administration theories and definitions of concepts are thus not timeless, but determined by political, bureaucratic, and societal culture at large. One can argue that public administration theory chases fashions, but at the same time that it is an expression of the degree to which the study responds to political, social, and economic change and to the different perceptions citizens, politicians, and civil servants develop of government.

Despite the differences between administrative traditions and cultures, Western countries are currently rather similar in their appreciation of government. We live in an age in which government is considered too big. In the United States and in Western Europe, governments have pursued reductions in personnel size and in expenditure for two decades. The nature of these reforms suggests attempts to bring government closer to the people (for instance, decentralization), to reduce government to a decision-making role (for instance, contracting out the production of services), to make government focus on the larger picture (for instance, framework legislation instead of detailed legislation and regulation, or block grants instead of specific grants), and literally to abolish public provision and production of services (for instance, privatization). Many of these reforms concern the federal or national level, and their consequences trickle down to the subnational levels. Big government, however, is not situated at the national level. Certainly, national or federal governments hold the larger share of total public sector revenue and expenditure. Also, national or federal governments have major impact on subnational levels in terms of legislation and regulation. But measured by personnel size, big government is really found at state or regional and local levels. It is at the subnational level that government actually does things. Government as a whole is one of the most important institutions, if not the most important, through which we can come to agreement about how we wish to pursue the values we hold dear and the degree to which government should play an initiating role. However, as Putnam points out, government is not simply an institution for mediating between conflicting societal interests. Some values held dear in society are best pursued through government, which means that government actually provides services. Indeed,

> We want government to *do* things, not just *decide* things—to educate children, pay pensioners, stop crime, create jobs, hold down prices, encourage family values, and so on. We do not agree on which of these things is most urgent, nor how they should be accomplished, nor even whether they are all worthwhile. All but the anarchists among us, however, agree that at least some of the time on at least some issues, *action* is required of government institutions. (Putnam, Leonardi, and Nanetti 1993, 8–9)

The challenge for incumbents in public office is to have the courage to determine which action best balances the competing demands of individualism versus collectivism and of legalism versus populism, and subsequently to legitimate these actions in terms of philosophical, political theoretical, and historical considerations.

Government has not only become an integral part of Western culture, it increasingly defines Western culture. Whether in the collectivist and strong-state traditions of continental Europe or in the individualist and weak-state tradition of the United States, the size of government is a concern. With all due respect to political officeholders and citizens alike, the strong notion of big government emphasizes to what degree stereotypical thinking dominates a proper assessment of the role and position of government in society. DeIulio and Kettl recently observed that the question of whether American government needs to be "razed or reinvented, devolved or downsized" is not for them to say, but that, in view of the importance of government for society, it is more necessary than ever before that policy elites and average citizens are educated about government and that they "rediscover government" (DeIulio and Kettl 2000, 327). In their words:

> No one who understands what it actually takes to translate complicated public policy mandates into administrative action; alter out-moded government personnel or procurement practices; foster and maintain cooperation among disparate public and private bureaucracies; promote effective leadership and build productive organizational cultures within the public sector; coordinate a network of federal, state, and local agencies, private contractors, and non-profit organizations; institutionalize meaningful ways of measuring and evaluating government performance; or devise ways of cutting "red tape" without destroying democratically enacted procedural safeguards, knows that *none of these things can be done without lots of political foresight and forbearance, plenty of hard work by public administrators, and no shortage of sheer good luck.* (emphasis added; De Iulio and Kettl 2000, 325)

Government and governing are complex; therefore it is imperative that we teach them as a normal element in the general education during high school and college years. Yes, we need to rediscover government, but we also need to redefine government. The governments at the time of the Atlantic Revolutions and of the nightwatch state are no more, and—save some major natural or human-made disaster—will be no more. Wherever we live in the Western world, there is no turning back to the age of small or smaller government. We live in an age and society that can no longer operate without a fairly sizable government, and it is time to come to terms with this fact. Redefining government as a necessary and central institution in Western society and culture provides a more realistic basis for determining which collective interests should be pursued through the public sector. The division of labor between society and government should not be determined on the basis of conservative ideology and stereotypical thinking, but on the basis of serious reflection about where government should stand and act.

15.8. Compartmentalization and the Uncommon Public Servant

Whether in a political or administrative capacity, public servants today make such difficult decisions that they may well be people of "common opinion and uncommon capabilities," as Bagehot suggests. History, however, tends to remember the uncommon and has little attention for the far larger contingent of citizens with common opinions and common capabilities. The idea that most public servants must have common capabilities does not imply support of de Tocqueville's observation that democratization resulted in the decline of quality in American political life (2000, 188). Perhaps this was the case during the years of "government by the common man" but it is no longer relevant. In the world of today, the link that once may have existed between the rise of the common man and the decline of the intellectual quality of political life is no longer confirmed by empirical evidence (Brans 1999, 84–92). And how could it be? In the twentieth century, public servants at large of common descent increasingly had to have uncommon capabilities and great intellectual quality. And of these public servants we can probably mention more politicians than civil servants, if only because the first are much more visible.

Upon what grounds can we argue that public servants must have uncommon capabilities? First, there are many different needs that merit attention and support. A politician or administrator speaking out in favor of a particular policy, group, or approach can quickly be branded as discriminatory. In an atmosphere of political correctness in society and in government, the only people who can actually speak out are the zealots who seek to convince society that what they believe is right. It is expected of public servants that they respect us and that they are politically correct. This means they have to be vague and noncommittal. In American society, political correctness undermines the government of citizens because it separates the citizens from their government. How can a particular group of citizens demand a "politically correct" attitude toward them from a government that is required to treat everybody as equals? How can government be politically correct if what is right and wrong differs from group to group? How can government choose between abortionists and antiabortionists, between creationists and evolutionists, between pacifists and gun-owners, without a yardstick? The civil religion of flag, anthem, and monument does not provide that kind of yardstick. Here emerges the first reason why I believe that today's public servant has to have more uncommon abilities than his predecessors at the time of Bagehot. There are at least two other reasons as well.

The second reason why today's public servants have to have more uncommon capabilities is that they are expected to serve an imagined community of people. Yes, H.G. Wells is correct when observing that democracy dies five miles from the parish pump, but he does not speak of "the" democracy but of the "democracy of the parish pump." The democracy of the parish pump is one of association and direct governance, and that was left behind a long time ago. Contemporary democracy is one of indirect governance and is based on contract. That is why it can span an entire continent in the case of the United States or entire countries in Western Europe. The geographical size of the country is no longer an issue, since with today's width of social time 5 miles is the same distance as 5,000 miles. In this extended and indirect democracy, it is the public servant who has to serve an imagined community while the various collections of individuals united in interest groups cannot but operate on the basis of association. In contemporary political theory, government at large cannot and may not associate with one particular group or interest. The public servant must therefore be flexible in order to balance various interests and to muster the courage to choose carefully.

The third reason has to do with the degree to which life is compartmentalized. The separation of church and state, two powers demarcating their turf practically and legally, is one example. Another example is that citizens compartmentalize as well. We may belong to an imagined community, but also experience a more tangible fraternity in the various associations we declare membership. But there is a beginning and an end to associating; we depart from and return to our private lives. We are engaged in piecemeal associating. We engage in multiple associations, the membership of which only partially overlap. Are citizens always aware of the fact that their lives are compartmentalized? How can a public servant be less compartmentalized than the citizenry? In the imagined community, public servants too are first and foremost individuals and citizens. In view of the fact that government is sizable whatever indicator we use, those working in government cannot but compartmentalize. To do so is a fact of life in large-scale, indirect democracies that seek to serve an imagined community of people. Whether appreciated or not, a government with thousands of more or less compartmentalized organizations is a bare necessity because, without it, we must wonder which societal institution should have the authority to protect and advance stability in a democracy with such large populations. Government caters to thousands of fraternities while not forgetting about freedom, equality, and equity. Government serves an imagined community of people as well as catering to all of the associations held so dear. Public servants have to walk a fine line between individualism and collectivism, between legalism and flexibility, and they have to justify every action. This is a lot to ask for, and so I believe that, more than ever before, *public servants need uncommon abilities to be common.*

Just as we need very capable and enlightened public servants, we also need enlightened citizens. I do not assume that every citizen wishes to be enlightened about the intricacies and complexities of contemporary government and governance. We should, however, give all citizens better access to knowledge about public affairs in order to "counter-balance the anti-enlightenment effects of the mass media and a cyber-sphere driven by audience ratings and marketing considerations" (Dror 2001, 107). Finally, we need enlightened politicians who subject themselves to a code of ethics just as much as civil servants are expected to adhere to a professional code of ethics (Dror 2001, 102–103).

We need enlightened citizens, civil servants, and politicians because only then can we move beyond efficiency, that misguided twentieth-century shortcut to success, and view human relations as the core of the public administration challenge. McSwite's concluding remark in the recent *Invitation to*

Public Administration concerns public administration both as a study as well as government:

> Public administration, properly construed, is not about efficient service as much as it is about building and maintaining an inclusive sense of social relationship—relationship between people, between people and institutions, between groups, between groups and institutions. Where such relationship is achieved, concerns with efficiency recede into the background, where they take care of themselves. (2002, 113)

To be sure, moving beyond efficiency is not the same as allowing efficiency to recede into the background where it is cared for by an invisible hand. Democracy and efficiency are as inseparable as individualism and collectivism. McSwite rather implies that once social relationship is considered central to the construction of the public realm, which, in turn, implies trust, people will find the most acceptable solution to each problem and will be less inclined to measure efficiency according to some neutral standard external to themselves.

15.9. Concluding Remarks

Underneath the choices government is required to make lies a fundamental continuum of individualism and collectivism—the challenges of which can be resolved in a more legalist or more sociological mode of action, and which actions must be legitimated in terms of fundamental value and in terms of tradition. This is an issue of moral conscience, and they can only be seen as complementary to each other. As philosophies of life, both the extreme individualist and extreme collectivist perspectives are totalitarian, not in terms of political system, wherein we could impose such a worldview on citizens, but in terms of total commitment to one worldview only. Although the appeals and approaches of John Steinbeck and of Ayn Rand are both attractive for their simplicity, in the real world life is not so simple. Indeed, living the extreme would probably create greater or lesser unpleasantness for fellow human beings, of whom Ayn Rand herself is an example (Branden 1986). The simplicity is one of choice, not one of consequences. Being consistent in terms of consequences is very complex, because complexity comes from the impact of time, depends on the issue(s) at hand, and depends upon the range of opinions.

With respect to time, in real life we not only have to deal with the present ramifications of past decisions, but we must also be aware of our responsibility to the future. And we must realize that what citizens desire and expect from government changes over time. Regarding the issue at hand, our conscience may well advise us to adopt a more individualistic choice for the one policy, and a more collectivistic choice for the other. Generally, the so-called nightwatch state tasks are still considered public, and they are considered in a collectivist perspective. After all, we recognize the need for government-controlled policies on police, justice, taxation, and military matters. Where we waver and flow with the tide or the fashion of the day is with the so-called welfare tasks, sometimes appraised in a collectivist, sometimes in an individualist perspective. The balance is highly dependent on culture. By tradition, Americans have explored the collectivist approach to welfare in a culture that espouses individualism. Welfare states in continental northwestern Europe developed individualist solutions to welfare problems in a culture that is collectivist in outlook. I realize full well that this is an immense simplification and that it does not do justice to the complexity of reality. If, indeed, reality cannot be reduced to simple dichotomies, we should accept the consequence of that line of reasoning. Democracy then cannot do without bureaucracy or efficiency.

In the same breath, we must accept the inevitability of compromise between the needs of the individual and the needs of the collective. We must accept the idea of walking the middle ground. We should not accept seemingly clear-cut, one-way solutions offered by those whom we elect. Nor should we allow ourselves to be deluded or seduced by simplistic and vague statements. Instead, in addition to a willingness for compromise (the core feature of negotiable authority), we should take time to weigh our alternatives and develop an awareness of where we are prepared to negotiate and where we draw the line. We are not always for sale. In sum, we must accept the consequences of realizing that life's challenges and problems cannot be overcome by relying on the truth of such simplistic dichotomies as "I will have to take care of myself, otherwise no one will" versus "government will take care of me, why should I bother to make an effort?" We should be true citizens and true public officials, able to weigh our personal needs in relation to the larger societal needs. Our sense of citizenship has matured when we are able to walk the fine line between individualist and collectivist solutions with a clear conscience, when we are willing to combine legalist with sociological modes of action, and when we are reflective.

If this is a lame, middle-of-the-road approach to the challenges of government, then so be it. The utilitarian desire to establish the greatest happiness for the greatest number will fall with the tyranny of the majority and the philosophy of greed, but will thrive with the democracy of compromise or negotiable authority and the attitude of sharing. It is the government that citizens want and create alone that has the authority and the resources to pull off that balancing act.

BIBLIOGRAPHY

Aberbach, Joel D.; Putnam, Robert D.; and Rockman, Bert A. 1981. *Bureaucrats and Politicians in Western Democracies*. Cambridge, MA: Harvard University Press.

Abrahamsson, Bengt. 1972. *Military Professionalization and Political Power.* Beverly Hills, CA: Sage.

Adamolekun, Ladipo, ed. 1999. *Public Administration in Africa: Main Issues and Selected Country Studies*. Boulder, CO: Westview Press.

Adams, Guy B. 1992. "Enthralled with Modernity: The Historical Context of Knowledge and Theory Development in Public Administration." *Public Administration Review* 52, no. 4: 363–373.

Adams, Guy B., and Balfour, Danny L. 1998. *Unmasking Administrative Evil.* London: Sage.

Agranoff, Robert. 1990. *Frameworks for Comparative Analysis of Intergovernmental Relations*. (Occasional paper no. 26, series edited by Randall Baker). Bloomington: School for Public and Environmental Affairs, Indiana University.

Albrow, Martin. 1970. *Bureaucracy.* London: Pall Mall Press.

———. 1996. *The Global Age: State and Society Beyond Modernity.* Cambridge: Polity Press.

Aldrich, Howaard E. 1972. "Technology and Organizational Structure: A Reexamination of the Findings of the Aston Group." *Administrative Science Quarterly* 17, no. 1: 26–43.

———.1979. *Organizations and Environments.* Upper Saddle River, NJ: Prentice-Hall.

Allison, Graham T., Jr. 1982. "Public and Private Management: Are They Fundamentally Alike in All Unimportant Respects?" In *Current Issues in Public Administration,* 2d ed., ed. Frederick S. Lane, 13–33. New York: St. Martin's Press.

Almond, Gabriel A. 1968a. "Comparative Political Systems." In *Comparative Politics. Notes and Readings,* ed. Roy C. Macridis and Bernard E. Brown, 55–66. Homewood, IL: Dorsey Press.

———. 1968b. "Interest Groups and the Political Process." In *Comparative Politics: Notes and Readings,* ed. Roy C. Macridis and Bernard E. Brown, 227–234. Homewood, IL: Dorsey Press.

Almond, Gabriel A., and Verba, Sidney. 1963. *The Civic Culture: Political Attitudes and Democracy in Five Nations.* Princeton, NJ: Princeton University Press.

Alt, James E.; Levi, Margaret; and Ostrom, Elinor, eds. 1999. *Competition and Cooperation: Conversations with Nobelists about Economics and Political Science.* New York: Russell Sage Foundation.

Andersen, Svein A., and Eliassen, Kjell A. 1991. "European Community Lobbying." *European Journal of Political Research* 20, no. 1: 173–187.

Anderson, Benedict. 1995. *Imagined Communities: Reflections on the Origin and Spread of Nationalism.* 2d ed. London: Verso.

Anderson, Charles W. 1977. *Statecraft: An Introduction to Political Choice and Judgment.* New York: John Wiley.

Applbaum, Arthur Isak. 1999. *Ethics for Adversaries: The Morality of Roles in Public and Professional Life.* Princeton, NJ: Princeton University Press.

Archer, Margareth S. 1979. *The Social Origins of Educational Systems.* Beverly Hills, CA: Sage.

Armstrong, Karen. 1993. *A History of God: From Abraham to the Present: The 4000-Year Quest for God.* London: Mandarin Books.

Arnold, Peri E. 1998. "The Development of Administration at the Summit in the United States." In *Administering the Summit* (Cahier d'Histoire de l'Administration no. 5), ed. Jos C.N. Raadschelders and Frits M. van der Meer, 133–161. Brussels: International Institute of Administrative Sciences/Ets. Bruylant.

Arnold, R. Douglas. 1979. *Congress and the Bureaucracy: A Theory of Influence.* New Haven, CT: Yale University Press.

Bachrach, Peter S., and Baratz, Morton S. 1962. "Two Faces of Power." *American Political Science Review* 56, no. 5: 1947–1952.

———. 1963. "Decisions and Non-Decisions: An Analytical Framework." *American Political Science Review* 57, no. 2: 641–651.

———. 1970. *Power and Poverty, Theory and Practice.* New York: Oxford University Press.

Badie, Bertrand, and Birnbaum, Pierre. 1983. *The Sociology of the State.* Chicago: University of Chicago Press.

Barber, Benjamin R. 1986. "The Compromised Republic: Public Purposelessness in America." In *The Moral Foundations of the American Republic,* 3d ed., ed. Robert H. Horwitz, 42–61. Charlottesville: University Press of Virginia.

Barker, Lucius J., and Barker, Twiley W., Jr., eds. 1978. *Civil Liberties and the Constitution: Cases and Commentaries.* Englewood Cliffs, NJ: Prentice-Hall.

Barnard, Chester I. 1938. *The Functions of the Executive.* Cambridge, MA: Harvard University Press.

Barth, Thomas J., and Green, Mark T. 1999. "Public Administration Handbooks: Why, How, and Who?" *Public Administration Review* 59, no. 6: 535–544.

Beardswell, Ian, and Holden, Len, eds. 1997. *Human Resource Management. A Contemporary Perspective.* 2d ed. London: Pitman.

Bekke, Hans A.G.M.; Perry, James L.; and Toonen, Theo A.J., eds. 1996. *Civil Service Systems in Comparative Perspective.* Bloomington: Indiana University Press.

Bell, Daniel. 1961. *The End of Ideology: On the Exhaustion of Political Ideas in the Fifties.* New York: Collier Books.

Bellah, Robert M. 1975. *The Broken Covenant: American Civil Religion in a Time of Trial.* New York: Seabury.

Bellah, Robert M.; Madsen, Richard; Sullivan, William M.; Swidler, Ann; and Tipton, Steven M. 1996. *Habits of the Heart: Individualism and Commitment in American Life.* 2d ed. Berkeley: University of California Press.

Bemelmans-Videc, Marie Louise. 1998. "Policy Instrument Choice and Evaluation." In *Carrots, Sticks and Sermons: Policy Instruments and Their Evaluation,* ed. Marie Louise Bemelmans-Videc, Ray Rist, and Evert Vedung, 1–18. New Brunswick, NJ: Transaction.

Bemelmans-Videc, Marie Louise, and Vedung, Evert. 1998. "Conclusions: Policy Instruments Types, Packages, Choices, and Evaluation." In *Carrots, Sticks and Sermons: Policy Instruments and Their Evaluation,* ed. Marie Louise Bemelmans-Videc, Ray Rist, and Evert Vedung, 249–273. New Brunswick, NJ: Transaction.

Bentley, Arthur F. 1908. *The Process of Government: A Study of Social Pressures.* Chicago: University of Chicago Press.

Berman, Evan M.; Bowman, James S.; West, Jonathan P.; and Wart, Montgomery van. 2001. *Human Resource Management in the Public Service.* Thousand Oaks, CA: Sage.

Berman, Harold. 1983. *Law and Revolution: The Formation of the Western Legal Tradition.* Cambridge, MA: Harvard University Press.

Berns, Walter. 1986. "Religion and the Founding Principle." In *The Moral Foundations of the*

American Republic, 3d ed., ed. Robert H. Horwitz, 204–229. Charlottesville: University Press of Virginia.

Birckmeyer, Johanna D., and Hirschon Weiss, Carol. 2000. "Theory-Based Evaluation in Practice." *Evaluation Review: A Journal of Applied Social Research* 24, no. 4: 407–431.

Birkland, Thomas A. 2001. *An Introduction to the Policy Process: Theories, Concepts, and Models of Public Policy Making.* Armonk, NY: M.E. Sharpe.

Bivin Raadschelders, Julie. 1995. Development Aid Policy Rationales: Durability and Change, 1960–1993. Ph.D. dissertation, Indiana University.

Blau, Peter M. 1963. *Bureaucracy in Modern Society.* New York: Random House.

Blau, Peter M., and Schoenherr, Richard A. 1971. *The Structure of Organizations.* New York: Basic Books.

Blondel, Jean. 1973. *Comparative Legislatures.* Englewood Cliffs, NJ: Prentice-Hall.

———. 1990. *Comparative Government. An Introduction.* New York: Philip Allen.

Boin, Arjen. 1998. *Contrasts in Leadership: An Institutional Study of Two Prison Systems.* Delft: Eburon.

Bok, Derek C. 1996. *The State of the Nation: Government and the Quest for a Better Society.* Cambridge, MA: Harvard University Press.

Boorstin, Daniel J. 1985. *The Discoverers.* New York: Vintage Books.

Borch, Herbert von. 1954. *Obrigkeit und Widerstand: Zur politischen Soziologie des Beamtentums* [Government and resistance: A political sociology of the civil service]. Tübingen: J.C.B. Mohr.

Bosso, Christopher J.; Portz, John H.; and Tolley, Michael C. 2000. *American Government: Conflict, Compromise, and Citizenship.* Boulder, CO: Westview Press.

Bottomore, Tom B. 1972. *Sociology: A Guide to Problems and Literature.* New York: Random House.

Boulding, Kenneth E. 1953. *The Organizational Revolution. A Study in the Ethics of Economic Organization.* New York: Harper and Brothers.

Bovens, Mark, and Hart, Paul 't. 1996. *Understanding Policy Fiascoes.* New Brunswick, NJ: Transaction.

Bozeman, Barry. 1979. *Public Management and Policy Analysis.* New York: St. Martin's Press.

Branden, Barbara. 1986. *The Passion of Ayn Rand.* Garden City, NY: Doubleday.

Brans, Marleen. 1999. Public Office—Private Awards: The Dynamics of Material Reward Systems for Legislators: A Comparative Study of Material Rewards for Legislators in the Netherlands and Belgium. Ph.D. dissertation, European University, Florence.

Braudel, Fernand. 1958. "Histoire et les sciences sociales: La longue durée." *Annales* 13: 725–753.

Brown, Ronald G.S., ed. 1978. *Approaches to the Study of Public Administration. Part 3: The Administrative Process as Incrementalism.* Milton Keynes: Open University Press.

Bruce, Willa. 1995. "Ideals and Conventions: Ethics for Public Administrators." *Public Administration Review* 55, no. 1: 111–116.

Brudney, Jeffrey L., and England, Robert E. 1983. "Toward a Definition of the Coproduction Concept." *Public Administration Review* 44, no. 1: 59–65.

Bryson, John M. 1995. *Strategic Planning for Public and Nonprofit Organization.* San Francisco, CA: Jossey-Bass.

Buchanan, David, and Badham, Richard. 1999. *Power, Politics, and Organizational Change: Winning the Turf Game.* London: Sage.

Buchanan, James M., and Tullock, Gordon. 1962. *The Calculus of Consent: Logical Foundations of Constitutional Democracy.* Ann Arbor: University of Michigan Press.

Burns, Nancy. 1994. *The Formation of American Local Governments: Private Values in Public Institutions.* New York: Oxford University Press.

Burns, Tom, and Stalker, George M. 1961. *The Management of Innovation.* London: Tavistock.

Cann, Steven J. 1995. *Administrative Law.* Thousand Oaks, CA: Sage.

Cantril, Albert H., and Davis Cantril, Susan. 1999. *Reading Mixed Signals. Ambivalence in American Public Opinion about Government.* Washington, DC: Woodrow Wilson Center Press.

Carnevale, David G. 1995. *Trustworthy Government: Leadership and Management Strategies for Building Trust and High Performance.* San Francisco, CA: Jossey-Bass.

Carnoy, Martin. 1984. *The State and Political Theory.* Princeton, NJ: Princeton University Press.

Chandler, Alfred D., Jr. 1977. *The Visible Hand: The Managerial Revolution in American Business.* Cambridge: Harvard University Press.

Chandler, Ralph Clark. 1987. *A Centennial History of the American Administrative State.* New York/London: Free Press/Collier Macmillan.

Chase, William C. 1982. *The American Law School and the Rise of Administrative Government.* Madison: University of Wisconsin Press.

Chubb, John E., and Moe, Terry M. 1988. "Politics, Markets, and the Organization of Schools." *American Political Science Review* 82, no. 4: 1065–1087.

Cohen, Michael; March, James G.; and Olsen, Johan P. 1972. "A Garbage Can Model of Organizational Choice." In *Administrative Science Quarterly* 17, no. 1: 1–25.

Collins, Randall, and Makowsky, Michael. 1972. *The Discovery of Society.* New York: Random House.

Condrey, Stephen E., ed. 1998. *Handbook of Human Resource Management in Government.* San Francisco, CA: Jossey-Bass.

Coontz, Stephanie. 1992. *The Way We Never Were. American Families and the Nostalgia Trap.* New York: Basic Books.

Cooper, Terry L. 1992. *Handbook of Administrative Ethics.* New York: Marcel Dekker.

———. 1998. *The Responsible Administrator: An Approach to Ethics for the Administrative Role.* 4th ed. San Francisco, CA: Jossey-Bass.

Cooper, Philip J., and Newland, Chester A., eds. 1997. *Handbook of Public Law and Administration.* San Francisco, CA: Jossey-Bass.

Corwin, Edward S. 1955. *The 'Higher Law' Background of American Constitutional Law.* Ithaca: Cornell University Press.

———. 1990. The "Higher Law" Background of American Constitutional Law. In *Classic Readings in American Politics,* ed. Pietro S. Nivola and David H. Rosenbloom, 431–435. New York: St. Martin's Press.

Council of Europe. 1994. *Colloquy on the Size of Municipalities, Efficiency and Citizen Participation: Summary Report on the Situation in Member States.* Budapest: Steering Committee on Local and Regional Authorities, April 7–8.

Cozzetto, Don A.; Kweit, Mary Grisez; and Kweit, Robert W. 1995. *Public Budgeting: Politics, Institutions, and Processes.* White Plains, NY: Longman.

Cozzetto, Don A.; Pedeliski, Theodore B.; and Tipple, Terence J. 1996. *Public Personnel Administration: Confronting the Challenges of Change.* Upper Saddle River, NJ: Prentice-Hall.

Cramton, Robert S. 1982. "Judicial Law Making and Administration." In *Current Issues in Public Administration,* 2d ed., ed. Frederick S. Lane, 149–155. New York: St. Martin's Press.

Croly, Herbert. 1914. *Progressive Democracy.* New York: Macmillan.

———. 1965. *The Promise of American Life,* ed. A.M. Schlesinger, Jr. Cambridge, MA: Belknap.

Crouch, Colin. 1986. "Sharing Public Space: States and Organized Interests in Western Europe." In *States in History,* ed. John Hall, 179–201. Oxford: Basil Blackwell.

Crozier, Michel. 1964. *The Bureaucratic Phenomenon.* Chicago: University of Chicago Press.

Crozier, Michel; Huntington, Samuel P.; and Watanuki, Joji. 1975. *The Crisis of Democracy: Report on the Governability of Democracies to the Trilateral Commission.* New York: New York University Press.

Crozier, Michel, and Friedberg, Ernst 1980. *Actors and Systems: The Politics of Collective Action.* Chicago: University of Chicago Press.

Curtis, James E.; Grabb, Edward G.; and Baer, Douglas E. 1992. "Voluntary Association Membership in Fifteen Countries: A Comparative Analysis." *American Sociological Review* 57, no. 2: 139–152.

Dahl, Robert A. 1947. "The Science of Public Administration: Three Problems." *Public Administration Review* 7, no. 1: 1–11.

Dahl, Robert A., and Lindblom, Charles E. 1953. *Politics, Economic, and Welfare: Planning and Politico-Economic Systems Resolved into Basic Social Processes.* New York: Harper and Row.

Debbasch, Charles. 1989. *Science Administrative, Administration Publique.* Paris: Dalloz.

De Iulio. John J. 1991. *No Escape: The Future of American Corrections.* New York: Basic Books.

De Iulio, John J., and Kettl, Donald F. 2000. "Hooking Leviathan—or Rediscovering Government?" In *American Intergovernmental Relations: Foundations, Perspectives, and Issues,* 3d ed., ed. Laurence J. O'Toole, Jr., 320–328. Washington, DC: CQ Press.

Dekker, Paul. 1989. *Overheidsplanning in West-Europa.* Rijswijk: Sociaal-Cultureel Planbureau.

DeMarco, Edward J., and Rist, Ray C. 1998. "Government-Sponsored Enterprises as a Credit Allocation Tool in the United States." In *Carrots, Sticks and Sermons: Policy Instruments and Their Evaluation,* ed. Marie Louise Bemelmans-Videc, Ray Rist, and Evert Vedung, 185–210. New Brunswick, NJ: Transaction.

Deming, W. Edward. 1994. *W. Edward Deming: The Prophet of Quality* (Broadcast by UNC-TV). Silver Spring, MD: Wootton Productions.

Denhardt, Robert B. 1984. *Theories of Public Organization.* Pacific Grove, CA: Brooks/Cole Publishing.

Dente, Bruno, and Kjellberg, Francesco, eds. 1988. *The Dynamics of Institutional Change: Local Government Reorganization in Western Democracies.* London: Sage.

De Long, Bradford J. 1988. "Productivity Growth, Convergence, and Welfare: Comment." *American Economic Review* 78, no. 5: 1138–1159.

De Swaan, Abram. 1988. *In Care of the State: Health Care, Education and Welfare in Europe and the USA in the Modern Era.* Oxford: Polity Press.

Diamond, Martin. 1986. "Ethics and Politics: The American Way." In *The Moral Foundations of the American Republic,* 3d ed., ed. Robert H. Horwitz, 75–108. Charlottesville: University Press of Virginia.

Dimock, Marshall E.; Dimock, Gladys O.; and Fox, Douglas M. 1983. *Public Administration.* 5th ed. New York: Holt, Rhinehart and Winston.

Dinan, John. 2000. "State Government Influence in the National Policy Process: Lessons from the 104th Congress." In *American Intergovernmental Relations: Foundations, Perspectives, and Issues,* 3d ed., ed. Laurence J. O'Toole, Jr., 130–142. Washington, DC: CQ Press.

"Divining the God Factor: Are Americans Really Undergoing a Spiritual Revival?" 2000. *Newsweek,* October 23, 22.

Douglas, Paul H. 1952. *Ethics in Government* (The Godkin Lectures at Harvard University, 1951). Cambridge, MA: Harvard University Press.

Downs, Anthony. 1966. *Inside Bureaucracy.* Boston, MA: Little, Brown. (Reprint, Prospect Heights, IL: Waveland Press, 1994).

Dror, Yehezkel. [1964] 1978. "Muddling Through—'Science' or Inertia?" In *Approaches to the Study of Public Administration: Part 3: The Administrative Process as Incrementalism,* ed. R.S.G. Brown, 76–80. Milton Keynes: Open University Press.

———. 2001. *The Capacity to Govern: A Report to the Club of Rome.* London: Frank Cass.

Drucker, Peter F. 1957. *America's Next Twenty Years.* New York: Harper and Brothers.

DuBasky, Mayo. 1990. *The Gist of Mencken: Quotations from America's Critic.* Metuchen, NJ: Scarecrow Press.

Duganne, Augustine J.H. 1860. *A History of Governments Showing the Progress of Civil Society and the Structure of Ancient and Modern States.* New York: Robert M. De Witt.

Dunleavy, Pataricia 1991. *Democracy, Bureaucracy and Public Choice: Economic Explanations in Political Science.* Hemel Hempstead: Harvester Wheatsheaf.

Durant, Will. [1929] 1963. *The Pleasures of Philosophy.* New York: Simon and Schuster.

Dye, R. Thomas. 1979. *Who's Running America? The Carter Years.* 2d ed. Englewood Cliffs, NJ: Prentice-Hall.

———. 1986. *Who's Running America? The Carter Years.* 4th ed. Englewood Cliffs, NJ: Prentice-Hall.

Dyson, Kenneth H.F. 1980. *The State Tradition in Western Europe: A Study of Idea and Institution.* Oxford: Martin Robertson.

Easton, David J. 1965a. *A Systems Analysis of Political Life.* Englewood Cliffs, NJ: Prentice-Hall.

———. 1965b. *A Framework for Political Analysis.* Englewood Cliffs, NJ: Prentice-Hall.

———. 1968. "The Analysis of Political Systems." In *Comparative Politics: Notes and Readings,* ed. Roy C. Macridis and Bernard E. Brown, 86–96. Homewood, IL: Dorsey Press (excerpts from Easton's article in *World Politics* 9, no. 3: 383–400).

Easton, David J., and Easton, Dennis, J. 1969. *Children in the Political System: Origins of Political Legitimation.* New York: McGraw Hill.

Eaton, Dorman. 1880. *Civil Service in Great Britain. A History of Abuses and Reforms and Their Bearing upon American Politics.* New York: Harper.

Ehrenhalt, Alan. 1991. *The United States of Ambition: Politicians, Power, and the Pursuit of Office.* New York: Random House.

Eisenstadt, Shmuel N. 1963a. *The Political Systems of Empires: The Rise and Fall of Historical Bureaucratic Societies.* New York: Free Press.

———. 1963b. "Bureaucracy and Political Development." In *Bureaucracy and Political Development,* ed. Joseph LaPalombara, 97–119. Princeton, NJ: Princeton University Press.

Eisermann, G. 1976. "Auf dem Weg zur Parteibuch-Republik" [On the way to a Party-Republic]. In *Der Apparatschick. Die Inflation der Bürokratie in Ost und West* [Bureaucrats: The inflation of bureaucracy in east and west], ed. G.K. Kaltenbrunner, 37–51. München: Hercler.

Elazar, Daniel J. 1966. *American Federalism: A View from the States.* New York: Thomas Y. Crowell.

———. 1993. "The Scope of Cooperation." In *American Intergovernmental Relations: Foundations, Perspectives, and Issues,* 2d ed., ed. Laurence J. O'Toole, Jr., 49–56. Washington, DC: CQ Press.

Elias, Norbert. [1939] 1982. *The Civilizing Process.* New York: Blackwell.

Elmore, Richard. 1982. "Backward Mapping: Implementation Research and Policy Decisions." In *Studying Implementation,* ed. W. Williams Chatham, 89–98. London: Chatham House.

"Emerging Market Indicators: Corruption." 1998. *Economist,* October 3, 120.

Emerson, Ralph Waldo. [1841] 1972. "Self-Reliance." In *Documents in the History of American Philosophy,* ed. Morton White, 172–177. New York: Oxford University Press.

Emery, Fredric E., and Trist, Eric L. 1965. "The Causal Texture of Organizational Environments." *Human Relations* 18, no. 1: 21–32.

Esping-Andersen, Gøsta. 1990. *The Three Worlds of Welfare Capitalism.* Oxford: Polity Press.

Etzioni, Amitai. 1967. "Mixed Scanning: A 'Third Approach' to Decision-Making." *Public Administration Review* 27, no. 5: 385–392.

Eurostat Yerbook. 1995. Luxembourg: Office for Official Publications of the European Communities.

Farazmand, Ali, ed. 1991. *Handbook of Comparative and Development Public Administration.* New York: Marcel Dekker.

———. 1999. "Globalization and Public Administration." *Public Administration Review* 59, no. 6: 509–522.

Fayol, Henri. 1987. *General and Industrial Management.* Belmont, CA: David S. Lake.

Federalist Papers, The, by Alexander Hamilton, James Madison, and John Jay. 1982. Introduction and commentary by Gary Wills. New York: Bantam Books.

Feeley, Malcolm, and Rubin, Edward L. 1998. *Judicial Policy Making and the Modern State: How the Courts Reformed America's Prisons.* Cambridge, UK: Cambridge University Press.

Fernandez, Denise Rotondo; Carlson, Dawn S.; Stepina, Lee P.; and Nicholson, Joel D. 1997. "Hofstede's Country Classification 25 Years Later." *Journal of Social Psychology* 137, no. 1: 43–55.

Ferris, James E. 1984. "Coprovision: Citizen Time and Money Donations in Public Service Provision." *Public Administration Review* 44, no. 4: 324–333.

Finer, Samuel E. 1975. *The Man on Horseback: The Role of the Military in Politics.* 2d ed. Harmondsworth, UK: Penguin Books.

———. 1997. *The History of Government from the Earliest Times.* Oxford: Oxford University Press.

Fleishman, Joel L. 1981. "Self-Interest and Political Integrity." In *Public Duties: The Moral Obligations of Government Officials,* ed. Joel L. Fleishman, Lance Liebman, and Mark H. Moore, 52–92. Cambridge, MA: Harvard University Press.

Flora, Peter, and Heidenheimer, Arnold J. eds. 1990. *The Development of Welfare States in Europe and America.* New Brunswick, NJ: Transaction.

Follett, Mary Parker. [1918] 1920. *The New State: Group Organization the Solution of Popular Government.* New York: Longmans, Green.

Fowler, Robert Booth, and Hertzke, Allen D. 1995. *Religion and Politics in America: Faith, Culture, and Strategic Choices.* Boulder, CO: Westview Press.

Franklin, Aimee. 1998. The Unfulfilled Promise of the Council Manager Plan. Paper presented at the annual meeting of the ASPA Association for Budgeting and Financial Management, November 5–7, 1998.

Fraser, Julius T. 1987. *Time: The Familiar Stranger.* Amherst: University of Massachusetts Press.

Frederickson, H. George. 1980. *New Public Administration.* University: University of Alabama Press.

———. 1994. "Can Public Officials Correctly Be Said to Have Obligations to Future Generations?" *Public Administration Review* 54, no. 5: 457–464.

———. 1997. *The Spirit of Public Administration.* San Francisco, CA: Jossey-Bass.

———. 1999. "Public Administration as Governance." Paper presented at the annual conference of the American Society for Public Administration, Orlando, FL, April 9–14, 1999.

———, ed. 1993. *Ethics and Public Administration.* Armonk, NY: M.E. Sharpe.

Friedman, Benjamin M. 1998. "The New Demon." *New York Review of Books* 45, no. 15: 32–36.

Fry, Brian R. 1989. *Mastering Public Administration: From Max Weber to Dwight Waldo.* Chatham, NJ: Chatham House.

Fukuyama, Francis. 1991. *The End of History and the Last Man.* New York: Free Press.

Furner, Mary O. 1997. "Downsizing Government: A Historical Perspective." *USA Today* (November): 56.

Galbraith, John K. 1958. *The Affluent Society.* Boston, MA: Mentor Books.

Gardet, L.; Gurevich, A.J.; Kagame, A.; Larre, C.; Lloyd, G.E.R.; Neher, A.; Panikkar, R.; Pàttaro, G.; and Ricoeur, P. 1976. *Cultures and Time.* Paris: UNESCO Press.

Gargan, John J., ed. 1997. *Handbook of Local Government Administration.* New York: Marcel Dekker.

Garnett, James L. 1980. *Reorganizing State Government: The Executive Branch.* Boulder, CO: Westview Press.

Garnett, James L., and Kouzmin, Alexander, eds. 1997. *Handbook of Administrative Communication.* New York: Marcel Dekker.

Garvey, Gerald. 1997. *Public Administration: The Profession and the Practice: A Case Study Approach.* New York: St. Martin's Press.

Gaus, John Merriman. 1947. *Reflections on Public Administration.* University: University of Alabama Press.

Gawthrop, Louis C. 1997. "Democracy, Bureaucracy, and Hypocrisy Redux: A Search for Sympathy and Compassion." *Public Administration Review* 57, no. 3: 205–210.

———. 1998. *Public Service and Democracy. Ethical Imperatives for the 21st Century.* New York: Chatham House.

Gerth, Hans H., and Mills, C. Wright. 1946. *From Max Weber: Essays in Sociology.* New York: Oxford University Press.

Geus, Marius de. 1989. *Organisatietheorie en de Politieke Filosofie.* Delft: Eburon.

Giddens, Anthony. 1989. *The Constitution of Society: Outline of the Theory of Structuration.* Cambridge: Polity Press.

Gil, Moshe. 1976. *Documents of the Jewish Pious Foundations from the Cairo Geniza.* Leiden: E.J. Brill.

Golembiewski, Robert T. 1962. "Organization as a Moral Problem." *Public Administration Review* 22, no. 1: 51–58.

———. 1977a. *Public Administration as a Developing Discipline: Part 1—Perspectives on Past and Present.* New York: Marcel Dekker.

———. 1977b. *Public Administration as a Developing Discipline: Part 2—Organization Development as One of a Future Family of Miniparadigms.* New York: Marcel Dekker.

———. 1992. "Organization *Is* a Moral Problem: Past as Prelude to Present and Future." *Public Administration Review* 52, no. 2: 99–103.

———, ed. 2000. *Handbook of Organizational Consultation.* New York: Marcel Dekker.

Goodin, Robert E.; Headey, Bruce; Muffels, Ruud; and Dirven, Henk-Jan. 1999. *The Real Worlds of Welfare Capitalism.* Cambridge: Cambridge University Press.

Goodnow, Frank J. 1900. *Politics and Administration: A Study in Government.* New York: Macmillan.

Goodsell, Charles T. 1985. *The Case for Bureaucracy: A Public Administration Polemic.* 2d ed. Chatham, NJ: Chatham House.

———. 1993. "Reinvent Government or Rediscover It?" *Public Administration Review* 53, no. 1: 85–87.

Gordon, George J., and Milakovich, Michael E. 1998. *Public Administration in America.* 6th ed. New York: St. Martin's Press.

Gore, Al. 1993. *Creating a Government That Works Better and Costs Less: The Gore Report on Reinventing Government.* Washington, DC: The White House.

Grant, Wyn, ed. 1985. *The Political Economy of Corporatism.* London: Macmillan.

Green, Richard T., and Hubbell, Lawrence. 1996. "On Governance and Reinventing Government." In *Refounding Democratic Public Administration,* ed. Gary L. Wamsley and James F. Wolf, 38–67. Thousand Oaks, CA: Sage.

Greenfeld, Liah. 1992. *Nationalism: Five Roads to Modernity.* Cambridge, MA: Harvard University Press.

Greiner, Larry E. 1972. "Evolution and Revolution as Organizations Grow." *Harvard Business Review* (July–August): 37–46.

Grindle, Merilee S. 1980. "Policy Content and Context in Implementation." In *Politics and Policy Implementation in the Third World,* ed. Merilee S. Grindle, 3–34. Princeton, NJ: Princeton University Press.

Gulick, Luther. 1967. "Science, Values, and Public Administration." In *Basic Issues in Public Administration,* ed. Donald C. Rowat, 3–9. New York: Macmillan.

Gulick, Luther, and Lyndall F. Urwick, eds. 1937. *Papers on the Science of Administration.* New York: Institute of Public Administration.

Guy, Mary E. 1995. "Women, Public Administration, and the Personnel Function." In *Public Personnel Administration: Problems and Prospects,* 3rd ed., ed. Steven W. Hays and Richard E. Kearney, 232–246. Englewood Cliffs, NJ: Prentice-Hall.

Hacking, Ian. 1990. *The Taming of Chance.* Cambridge: Cambridge University Press.

Hall, Edward T. 1983. *The Dance of Life: The Other Dimension of Time.* Garden City, NY: Anchor Press/Doubleday.

Hall, Edward T., and Hall, Mildred Reed. 1990. *Understanding Cultural Differences.* Yarmouth, ME: Intercultural Press.

Hall, Richard H. 1977. *Organization, Structure, and Process.* London: Prentice-Hall.

Hall, Thad E. 2002. "Live Bureaucrats and Dead Public Servants: How People in Government Are Discussed on the Floor of the House." *Public Administration Review* 62, no. 2: 242–251.

Hannan, Michael T., and Freeman, John H. 1978. "The Population Ecology of Organizations." In *Environments and Organizations,* ed. Marshall W. Meyer and Associates, 131–171. San Francisco, CA: Jossey-Bass.

Hardin, Garret. 1968. "The Tragedy of the Commons." *Science* 162, no. 4: 1243–1248.

Hart, David K. 1972. "Theories of Government Related to Decentralization and Citizen Participation." *Public Administration Review* 33, no. 3: 603–621.

Hart, Paul 't. 1990. *Groupthink in Government: A Study of Small Groups and Policy Failure.* Amsterdam: Swets and Zeitlinger.

Hays, Steven W., and Kearney, Richard E., eds. 1995. *Public Personnel Administration: Problems and Prospects.* 3d ed. Englewood Cliffs, NJ: Prentice-Hall.

Heady, Ferrel. 1996. *Public Administration. A Comparative Perspective.* 5th ed. New York: Marcel Dekker.

———. 1998. "Comparative and International Public Administration: Building Intellectual Bridges." *Public Administration Review* 58, no. 1: 32–39.

Heater, Derek. 1990. *Citizenship. The Civic Ideal in World History, Politics and Education.* London: Longman.

Heclo, Hugh. 1991. "The Idea of Civil Service: A Third Force?" In *Classics of Public Personnel Policy,* 2d ed., ed. Frank J. Thompson, 41–50. Belmont, CA: Wadsworth.

———. 1992. "Issue Networks and the Executive Establishment." In *Public Administration. Concepts and Cases,* ed. Richard J. Stillman II, 429–439. Boston, MA: Houghton Mifflin.

Heffron, Florence. 1982. *Organization Theory and Public Organizations. The Political Connection.* Englewood Cliffs, NJ: Prentice-Hall.

Heilbroner, Robert L. 1962. *The Making of Economic Society.* Englewood Cliffs, NJ: Prentice-Hall.

Held, David. 1985. "Central Perspectives on the Modern State." In *States and Societies,* ed. David Held. Oxford: Basil Blackwell in association with The Open University.

———. 1987. *Models of Democracy.* Cambridge: Polity Press.

Hemerijck, Anton. 1992. The Historical Contingencies of Dutch Corporatism. Ph.D. dissertation. Balliol College, Oxford University.

Hendershot, Alexander M., and Parsons, Talcott. 1947. *The Theory of Social and Economic Organization.* New York: Oxford University Press.

Henry, Nicholas. 1999. *Public Administration and Public Affairs.* 7th ed. Upper Saddle River, NJ: Prentice-Hall.

Hertzke, Allen D. 1987. "American Religion and Politics: A Review Essay." *Western Political Quarterly* 41, no. 4: 825–837.

———. 1995. "Sin Boldly: Lowi, Liberalism, and the Love of God." *Public Administration Review* 55, no. 5: 481–486.

Hesse, J. Jens. 1991. "Local Government in a Federal State: The Case of West Germany." In *Local Government and Urban Affairs in International Perspective: Analysis of Twenty Western Industrialised Countries,* ed. Joachim Jens Hesse, 353–385. Baden-Baden: Nomos Verlagsgesellschaft.

Hicks, Louis. 2000. "Numbers Chart American History from 1900 to 2000: Surprising Trends of America's 20th Century." *Norman Transcript,* December 24, B5.

Hill, Dilys M. 1974. *Democratic Theory and Local Government.* London: Allen and Unwin.

Hill, Larry B. 1991. "Who Governs the American Administrative State? A Bureaucratic-Centered Image of Governance." *Journal of Public Administration Research and Theory* 1, no. 3: 261–294.

———. 1992. "Taking Bureaucracy Seriously." In *The State of Public Bureaucracy,* ed. Larry B. Hill, 15–57. Armonk, NY: M.E. Sharpe.

———. 1995. "Is American Bureaucracy an Immobilized Gulliver or a Regenerative Phoenix? Reconsidering the Alleged Demise of Federal Bureaucratic Power." *Administration and Society* 27, no. 3: 322–360.

———. (forthcoming). *Bureaucracy and Governance*. White Plains, NY: Addison Wesley Longman.

Hirschman, Albert O. 1982. *Shifting Involvements*. Princeton, NJ: Princeton University Press.

"History: We're Losing It." 1999. *Newsweek*, July 12, 47.

Hobbes, Thomas. 1987. *Leviathan or the Matter, Forme & Power of a Common-Wealth Ecclesiastical and Civil*. London: Penguin Books.

Hofstadter, Richard. 1955. *The Age of Reform: From Bryan to F.D.R*. New York: Vintage Books.

———. 1968. *The Progressive Historians: Turner, Beard, Parrington*. New York: Alfred A. Knopf.

———. 1986. "The Founding Fathers: An Age of Realism." In *The Moral Foundations of the American Republic*, 3d ed., ed. Robert H. Horwitz, 62–74. Charlottesville: University Press of Virginia.

Hofstede, Geert. 1980. *Culture's Consequences: International Differences in Work-Related Values*. Beverly Hills, CA: Sage.

———. 1997. *Cultures and Organizations: Software of the Mind*. 2d ed. New York: McGraw Hill.

Hogwood, Brian W., and Gunn, Lewis A. 1989. *Policy Analysis for the Real World*. Oxford: Oxford University Press.

Holden, Matthew, Jr. 2000. "The Competence of Political Science: 'Progress in Political Research' Revisited." *American Political Science Review* 94, no. 1: 1–19.

Holzer, Marc. 2000. "For President or for Government? President's Column." *PA-Times* 23, no. 11: 13.

Hood, Christopher. 1986. *The Tools of Government*. Chatham, NJ: Chatham House.

———. 1991. "A Public Management for All Seasons?" *Public Administration*, 69, no. 1: 3–19.

———. 1998. *The Art of The State: Culture, Rhetoric, and Public Management*. Oxford: Clarendon Press.

Hood, Christopher, and Jackson, Michael. 1991. *Administrative Argument*. Aldershot: Dartmouth Publishing.

Hoogenboom, Ari. 1961. *Outlawing the Spoils*. Urbana: University of Illinois Press.

Howe, Louis E. 1998. "The Designated Mourner: The Future of Public Administration's Past." *Studies in the Social Sciences* 35, no. 2: 45–58.

Howlett, M., and Ramesh, M. 1998. "Policy Subsystem Configurations and Policy Change: Operationalizing the Postpositivist Analysis of the Politics of the Policy Process." *Policy Studies Journal* 26, no. 3: 466–481.

Hugo, Victor. 1987. *Les Miserables*. London: Penguin Books.

———. 1997. "Voltaire (1694–1778)." In *The Book of Eulogies. A Collection of Memorial Tributes, Poetry, Essays, and Letters of Condolence*, ed. Phyllis Theroux, 183–187. New York: Scribner.

Hummel, Ralph P. 1977. *The Bureaucratic Experience*. New York: St. Martin's Press.

Huntington, Samuel P. 1957. *The Soldier and the State: The Theory and Politics of Civil-Military Relations*. Cambridge, MA: Harvard University Press.

———. 1996. *The Clash of Civilizations and the Remaking of the World Order*. New York: Simon and Schuster.

Hurst, James W. 1977. *Law and Social Order in the United States*. Ithaca: Cornell University Press.

Huxley, Aldous. [1932] 1996. *Brave New World*. Groningen: Wolters-Noordhoff.

Immergut, Ellen M. 1992. *Health Politics: Interests and Institutions in Western Europe*. Cambridge: Cambridge University Press.

Ingraham, W. Patricia. 1995. *The Foundation of Merit: Public Service in American Democracy*. Baltimore, MD: Johns Hopkins University Press.

———. 1999. "A Laggard's Tale: Civil Service and Administrative Reform in the United States." In *Research in Public Administration*, ed. James L. Perry, 173–187. Stamford, CT: JAI Press.

Jacoby, Henry. 1976. *The Bureaucratization of the World.* Berkeley: University of California Press.

Janis, Irving L. 1972. *Groupthink: Psychological Studies of Policy Decisions and Fiascoes.* Boston, MA: Houghton Mifflin.

Janowitz, Morris. 1971. *The Professional Soldier: A Social and Political Portrait.* 2d ed. New York: Free Press/Collier Macmillan.

Jantsch, Erich, ed. 1969. *Perspectives of Planning.* Paris: Organization for Economic Cooperation and Development.

Johnston, Les. 1992. *The Rebirth of Private Policing.* London: Routledge.

Jones, Trevor, and Newburn, Tim. 1998. *Private Security and Public Policing.* Oxford: Clarendon Press.

Jong, Johannes J. de. 1958. *Pressiegroepen: De Invloed der Georganiseerde Groepen op het Maatschappelijk en Politiek Leven* [Pressure groups: The influence of organized groups on societal and political life]. Amsterdam: Nederlandse Federatie van Universitaire Studieverenigingen in de Sociale Wetenschappen.

Jordan, Bill. 1989. *The Common Good. Citizenship: Morality, and Self-Interest.* Oxford: Basil Blackwell.

Jurkovich, Ray. 1974. "A Core Typology of Organizational Environments." *Administrative Science Quarterly* 19, no. 3: 380–394.

Kalat, James W. 1996. *Introduction to Psychology.* 4th ed. Pacific Grove, CA: Brooks/Cole Publishing.

Kaltenbrunner, Gerd-Klaus, ed. 1976. *Der Apparatschick: Die Inflation der Bürokratie in Ost und West* [Bureaucrats: The growth of bureaucracy in east and west]. Munich: Hercler.

Kamenka, Eugene. 1989. *Bureaucracy.* Oxford: Basil Blackwell.

Kanter, Arnold. 1983. *Defense Politics: A Budgetary Perspective.* Chicago: University of Chicago Press.

Karl, Barry Dean. 1976. "Public Administration and American History: A Century of Professionalism." *Public Administration Review* 36, no. 5: 489–503.

———. 1983. *The Uneasy State: The United States from 1915 to 1945.* Chicago: University of Chicago Press.

Kast, Fremont E., and Rosenzweig, James E. 1996. "General Systems Theory: Applications for Organization and Management." In *Classics of Organization Theory,* ed. Jay M. Shafritz and J. Steven Ott, 302–315. Fort Worth, TX: Harcourt Brace College Publishers.

Katz, Daniel, and Kahn, Robert L. 1966. *The Social Psychology of Organizations.* New York: John Wiley.

Katz, Daniel; Gutek, Barbara A.; Kahn, Robert L.; and Barton, Eugenia. 1975. *Bureaucratic Encounters: A Pilot Study in the Evaluation of Government Services.* Ann Arbor: Institute for Social Research, University of Michigan.

Kaufmann, Herbert. 1981. "Fear of Bureaucracy: A Raging Pandemic." *Public Administration Review* 41, no. 1: 3–12.

Ketcham, Ralph. 1986. *The Anti-Federalist Papers and the Constitutional Convention Debates.* New York: Penguin Books.

Kettl, Donald F. 2000a. *The Global Public Management Revolution. A Report on the Transformation of Governance at Century's End.* Washington, DC: Brookings Institution Press.

———. 2000b. "The Transformation of Governance: Globalization, Devolution, and the Role of Government." *Public Administration Review* 60, no. 6: 488–497.

Kettl, Donald F., and Milward, H. Brinton, eds. 1996. *The State of Public Management.* Baltimore: Johns Hopkins University Press.

Kieser, Alfred. 1989. "Organizational, Institutional, and Societal Evolution: Medieval Craft Guilds and the Genesis of Formal Organizations." *Administrative Science Quarterly* 34, no. 4: 540–564.

King, Martin Luther, Jr. 1992. *I Have a Dream: Writings and Speeches That Changed the World.* San Francisco, CA: Harper.

Kingdon, John W. 1984. *Agendas, Alternatives, and Public Policies.* Boston, MA: Little, Brown.

Kingsley, John D. 1944. *Representative Bureaucracy.* Yellow Springs, OH: Antioch.

Kinneging, Andreas A.M. 1994. *Aristocracy, Antiquity, and History: An Essay on Classicism in Political Thought.* Delft: Eburon.

Kiser, Lawrence L., and Ostrom, Elinor. 1982. "The Three Worlds of Action: A Metatheoretical Synthesis of Institutional Approaches." In *Strategies of Political Inquiry,* ed. Elinor Ostrom, 179–222. Beverly Hills, CA: Sage.

Klein, Daniel B. 1994. "If Government Is So Villainous, How Come Government Officials Don't Seem Like Villains?" *Economics and Philosophy* 10, no. 1: 91–106.

Klingner, Donald E., and Nalbandian, John. 1998. *Public Personnel Management: Contexts and Strategies.* 4th ed. Upper Saddle River, NJ: Prentice-Hall.

Knoke, David. 2001. *Changing Organizations: Business Networks in the New Political Economy.* Boulder, CO: Westview Press.

Koch, Koen. 1993. *Over Staat en Statenvorming* [On the state and state making]. Leiden: DSWO-Press.

Kuypers, Guy. 1980. *Beginselen van Beleidsontwikkeling: Basistheory* [Principles of policy developments]. Muiderberg: Dick Coutinho.

Landauer, Carl. 1983. *Corporate State Ideologies: Historical Roots and Philosophical Origins.* Berkeley, CA: Institute of International Studies.

Lane, Jan-Erik. 1994. "Will Public Management Drive Out Public Administration?" *Asian Journal of Public Administration* 16, no. 2: 139–151.

———. 1996. *Constitutions and Political Theory.* Manchester: Manchester University Press.

Lane, Jan-Erik, and Ersson, Svante O. 1987. *Politics and Society in Western Europe.* Beverly Hills, CA: Sage.

———. 1994. *Comparative Politics: An Introduction and a New Approach.* Cambridge, MA: Polity Press.

Lang, Kurt. 1965. "Military Organizations." In *Handbook of Organizations,* ed. James G. March, 838–878. Chicago: Rand McNally.

Lasswell, Harold D. 1930. *Psychopathoogy and Politics.* Chicago: University of Chicago Press.

———. 1941. "The Garrison State and Specialists on Violence." *American Journal of Sociology* 46, no. 1: 455–468.

———. 1948. *Power and Personality.* New York: W.W. Norton.

———. 1968. "The World Revolution of Our Time." In *Comparative Politics: Notes and Readings,* 3d ed., ed. Roy C. Macridis and Bernard E. Brown, 148–160. Homewood, IL: Dorsey Press.

Lawrence, Paul R., and Lorsch, Jay W. 1967. *Organization and Environment: Managing Differentiation and Integration.* Cambridge, MA: Harvard University Press.

———. 1970. *Studies in Organizational Design.* Homewood, IL: Irwin-Dorsey.

Lazarus, Edward. 1998. *Closed Chambers: The First Eyewitness Account of the Epic Struggles Inside the Supreme Court.* New York: Times Books.

Leeds, Christopher; Kirkbride, Paul S.; and Duncan, Jim. 1994. "The Cultural Context of Europe: A Tentative Mapping." In *Human Resource Management in Europe: Perspectives for the 1990s,* ed. P.S. Kirkbride, 11–27. London: Routledge.

Legge, Karen. 1995. *Human Resource Management: Rhetorics and Realities.* New York: Palgrave.

Light, Paul C. 2000. *Government's Greatest Achievements of the Past Half Century.* Washington, DC: Brookings Institution Press.

———. 2002. *Government's Greatest Achievements: From Civil Rights to Homeland Defense.* Washington, DC: Brookings Institution Press.

Lijphart, Arend. 1968. *The Politics of Accommodation: Pluralism and Democracy in the Netherlands.* Berkeley: University of California Press.

———. 1977. *Democracy in Plural Societies: A Comparative Exploration.* New Haven, CT: Yale University Press.

————. 1984. *Democracies: Patterns of Majoritarian and Consensus Government in Twenty-One Countries.* New Haven, CT: Yale University Press.

————. 1999. *Patterns of Democracy: Government Forms and Performance in Thirty-Six Countries.* New Haven, CT: Yale University Press.

Lindblom, Charles E. 1978. "The Science of 'Muddling Through.'" In *Approaches to the Study of Public Administration: Part 3: The Administrative Process as Incrementalism,* ed. R.S.G. Brown, 66–76. Milton Keynes: Open University Press.

————. 1980. *The Policy-Making Process.* Englewood Cliffs, NJ: Prentice-Hall.

Lindblom, Charles, and Cohen, David K. 1979. *Usable Knowledge: Social Science and Social Problem Solving.* New Haven, CT: Yale University Press.

Lippmann, Walter. 1961. *Drift and Mastery: An Attempt to Diagnose the Current Unrest.* Introduced and annotated by William E. Leuchtenburg. Englewood Cliffs, NJ: Prentice-Hall.

Lipset, Seymour M. 1963. *Political Man: The Social Bases of Politics.* Garden City, NY: Anchor Books.

————. 1979. *The First New Nation: The United States in Historical and Comparative Perspective.* New York: W.W. Norton.

Lipsey, Mark W. 1997. "What Can You Build with Thousands of Bricks? Musings on the Cumulation of Knowledge in Program Evaluation." In *Progress and Future Directions in Evaluation: Perspectives on Theory, Practice, and Methods* (*New Directions for Evaluation: A Publication of the American Evaluation Association*), no. 76, ed. Debra J. Rog and Deborah Fournier, 7–23. San Francisco, CA: Jossey-Bass.

Lipsky, Michael. 1980. *Street-Level Bureaucracy: Dilemmas of the Individual in Public Services.* New York: Russell Sage Foundation.

Little, Roger W. 1971. *Handbook of Military Institutions.* Beverly Hills: Sage.

Locke, John. 1986. *Two Treatises of Government.* London: Dent.

Lockyer, Roger. 1982. *Tudor and Stuart Britain 1471–1714.* London: Longman.

Lohmann, Roger A. 1992. *The Commons: New Perspectives on Nonprofit Organizations and Voluntary Action.* San Francisco, CA: Jossey-Bass.

Lowi, Theodore J. 1972. "Four Systems of Party Politics and Choice." *Public Administration Review* 32, no. 4: 298–310.

————. 1979. *The End of Liberalism: The Second Republic of the United States.* 2d ed. New York: W.W. Norton.

————. [1964] 1990. "Distribution, Regulation, Redistribution: The Functions of Government." In *Classic Readings in American Politics,* ed. Pietro Nivola and David S. Rosenbloom, 512–523. New York: St. Martin's Press.

Magruder, Frank A., and Seckler-Hudson, Catherine. 1936. *Our National Government: An Introductory Course for Colleges.* Boston, MA: Allyn and Bacon.

Majone, Giandomenico. 1989. *Evidence, Argument, and Persuasion in the Policy Process.* New Haven, CT: Yale University Press.

Maletz, Donald J. 1998. "The Union as Idea: Tocqueville on the American Constitution." *History of Political Thought* 19, no. 4: 599–620.

Maletz, Donald J., and Herbel, Jerry. 1998. Some Paradoxes of Government Ethics Revisited. Paper presented at the Annual Meeting of the American Political Science Association, September 3–4.

Malitza, Mircea. 2000. "Ten Thousand Cultures, a Single Civilization." *International Political Science Review* 21, no. 1: 75–89.

Mannheim, Karl. 1936. *Ideology and Utopia.* New York: Harcourt, Brace.

Mansfield, Harvey C., Jr. 1993. *America's Constitutional Soul.* Baltimore, MD: Johns Hopkins University Press.

March, James G., and Olsen, Johan P. 1982. "The New Institutionalism: Organizational Factors in Political Life." *American Political Science Review* 78, no. 3: 738–749.

————. 1989. *Rediscovering Institutions.* New York: Free Press.

————. 1995. *Democratic Governance.* New York: Free Press.

March James G., and Simon, Herbert. 1958. *Organizations*. New York: John Wiley.

Marini, Frank, ed. 1994. "Echoes from No-Person's Land: Reflections on the Political Theory of Some Recent Dialogue." *Administrative Theory and Praxis* 16, no. 1: 1–14.

———. 1971. *Toward a New Public Administration: The Minnowbrook Perspective*. Scranton, PA: Chandler.

Marshall, Thomas H. 1965. *Class, Citizenship, and Social Development*. Garden City, NY: Anchor Books.

Martin, Daniel W. 1987. "Déjà Vu: French Antecedents of American Public Administration." *Public Administration Review* 47, no. 3: 297–303.

———. 1988. "The Fading Legacy of Woodrow Wilson." *Public Administration Review* 48, no. 2: 631–635.

Mayntz, Renate. 1965. "Max Weber's Idealtypus der Bürokratie und die Organisationssoziologie" [Max Wber's ideal type of bureaucracy and organization sociology]. In *Kölner Zeitschrift für Soziologie und Sozialpsychologie* 17, no. 4: 493–501.

———. 1978. *Soziologie der Öffentlichen Verwaltung* [Sociology of government]. Heidelberg/Karlsruhe: C.F. Müller Juristischer Verlag.

McCurdy, Howard E. 1987. "How Novelists View Public Administration." In *A Centennial History of the American Administrative State,* ed. Ralph Clark Chandler, 543–574. New York/London: Free Press/Macmillan.

McGraw, Thomas K. 1992. "The Public and Private Spheres in Historical Perspective." In *Public Administration. Concepts and Cases,* ed. Richard J. Stillman II, 454–472. Boston, MA: Houghton Mifflin.

McGregor, Douglas. 1960. *The Human Side of Enterprise*. New York: McGraw-Hill.

McKean, Margaret A. 1992. "Management of Traditional Common Lands (*Iriaichi*) in Japan." In *Making the Commons Work: Theory, Practice, and Policy,* ed. Daniel W. Bromley, 63–98. San Francisco, CA: Institute for Contemporary Studies.

McNeill, William Hardy. 1999. *A World History*. New York: Oxford University Press.

McSwite, O.C. 1997. *Legitimacy in Public Administration: A Discourse Analysis*. Thousand Oaks, CA: Sage.

———. 2001. "Theory Competency for MPA-Educated Practitioners." *Public Administration Review* 61, no. 1: 111–115.

———. 2002. *Invitation to Public Administration*. Armonk, NY: M.E. Sharpe.

McWilliams, Wilson Carey. 1986. "On Equality as the Moral Foundation for Community." In *The Moral Foundations of the American Republic,* 3d ed., ed. Robert H. Horwitz, 282–312. Charlottesville: University Press of Virginia.

Meier, Kenneth J. 1997. "Bureaucracy and Democracy: The Case for More Bureaucracy and Less Democracy." *Public Administration Review* 57, no. 3: 193–199.

———. 2000. *Politics and the Bureaucracy: Policymaking in the Fourth Branch of Government*. Fort Worth, TX: Harcourt Brace College Publishers.

Meyers, Ray T. 1998. *Handbook of Government Budgeting*. New York: Marcel Dekker.

Michels, Robert. 1966. *Political Parties. A Sociological Study of Oligarchical Tendencies of Modern Democracy*. Introduction by S.M. Lipset. New York/London: Free Press/Collier Macmillan.

Miewald, Robert D. 1984. "The Origins of Wilson's Thought: The German Tradition and the Organic State." In *Politics and Administration: Woodrow Wilson and American Public Administration,* ed. Jack Rabin and James S. Bowman, 17–30. New York: Marcel Dekker.

———. 1994. "European Administrative History and American Public Administration." *Jahrbuch für Europäische Verwaltungsgeschichte* 6: 319–328.

Mikesell, John L. 1991. *Fiscal Administration: Analysis and Applications for the Public Sector.* 3d ed. Pacific Grove, CA: Brooks/Cole Publishing.

Mill, John S. 1984. *Utilitarianism, On Liberty, Considerations on Representative Government,* ed. H.B. Acton. London: Dent.

Miller, Maureen. 1983. "From Ancient to Modern Organization: The Church as Conduit and Creator." *Administration and Society* 15, no. 3: 275–293.

Miller, Trudi C., ed. 1984. *Public Sector Performance: A Conceptual Turning Point.* Baltimore, MD: Johns Hopkins University Press.

Mills, C. Wright. 1956. *The Power Elite.* New York: Oxford University Press.

Mintzberg, Henry. 1979. *The Structuring of Organizations. A Synthesis of the Research.* Englewood Cliffs, NJ: Prentice-Hall.

———. 1983a. *Structure in Fives. Designing Effective Organizations.* Englewood Cliffs, NJ: Prentice-Hall.

———. 1983b. *Power in and Around Organizations.* Englewood Cliffs, NJ: Prentice-Hall.

———. 1994. *The Rise and Fall of Strategic Planning: Reconceiving Roles for Planning, Plans, Planners.* New York: Free Press.

Moe, Terry M. 1980. *The Organization of Interests.* Chicago: University of Chicago Press.

Mooney, Paul. 2002. "Do Your Homework. Did Confucius Say That? Lots of Chinese Think So." *Newsweek,* May 27, 51.

Moore, Mark H. 1997. *Creating Public Value: Strategic Management in Government.* Cambridge, MA: Harvard University Press.

Morone, James A. 1990. *The Democratic Wish: Popular Participation and the Limits of American Government.* New York: Basic Books.

Mosca, Gaetano. 1972. *A Short History of Political Philosophy.* New York: Thomas Y. Crowell.

Mosch, Theodore R. 1975. *The G.I. Bill: A Breakthrough in Educational and Social Policy in the United States.* Hicksville, NY: Exposition Press.

Mosher, Frederick C. 1982a. "Public Administration." In *Current Issues in Public Administration,* ed. Frederick S. Lane, 4–13. New York: St. Martin's Press.

———. 1982b. *Democracy and the Public Service.* 2d ed. New York: Oxford University Press.

Mosher, Frederick C., and Poland, Orville F. 1969. *The Costs of American Governments: Facts, Trends, Myths.* New York: Dodd, Mead.

Mouzelis, Nicos P. 1967. *Organisation and Bureaucracy: An Analysis of Modern Theories.* Chicago: Aldine.

———. 1991. *Back to Sociological Theory: The Construction of Social Orders.* New York: St. Martin's Press.

Murphy, W. Timothy 1997. *The Oldest Social Science? Configurations of Law and Modernity.* Oxford: Clarendon Press.

Neiman, Max. 2000. *Defending Government: Why Big Government Works.* Upper Saddle River, NJ: Prentice-Hall.

Nelson, Michael. 1982. "A Short Ironic History of American National Bureaucracy." *Journal of Politics* 44, no. 3: 747–778.

Nettl, J. Peter. 1968. "The State as a Conceptual Variable." *World Politics* 20, no. 4: 559–592.

Neustadt, Richard E., and May, Ernest R. 1986. *Thinking in Time: The Uses of History for Decision-Makers.* New York/London: Free Press/Collier Macmillan.

Nice, David C., and Frederickson, Patricia. 1999. *The Politics of Intergovernmental Relations.* Chicago: Nelson-Hall.

Niebuhr, Reinhold. 1944. *The Children of Light and the Children of Darkness.* New York: Scribners.

Nietzsche, Friedrich. 1980. "The Transvaluation of Values." In *Great Traditions in Ethics,* ed. Ethel M. Albert, Theodore C. Denise, and Sheldon P. Peterfreund, 275–300. New York: D. Van Nostrand.

Nigro, Felix A., and Nigro, Lloyd G. 1989. *Modern Public Administration.* 7th ed. New York: Harper and Row.

Nisbet, Robert A. 1969. *Social Change and History: Aspects of the Western Theory of Development.* New York: Oxford University Press.

———. 1975. *Twilight of Authority.* New York: Oxford University Press.

————. 1986. *The Making of Modern Society.* Brighton: Wheatsheaf Books.

Niskanen, William A. 1971. *Bureaucracy and Representative Government.* Chicago: Aldine/Atherton.

————. 1973. *Bureaucracy: Servant or Master? Lessons from America.* London: Institute of Economic Affairs.

Nolte, William H. 1968. *H.L. Mencken's Smart Set Criticism.* Ithaca, NY: Cornell University Press.

North, Douglass C. 1990. *Institutions, Institutional Change and Economic Performance.* Cambridge: Cambridge University Press.

OECD. 2000. *Trust in Government: Ethics Measures in OECD Countries.* Paris: OECD.

Olson, Mancur. 1965. *The Logic of Collective Action: Public Goods and the Theory of Groups.* Cambridge, MA: Harvard University Press.

————. 1982. *The Rise and Decline of Nations: Economic Growth, Stagflation, and Social Rigidities.* New Haven, CT: Yale University Press.

Orwell, George. 1961. *1984* (with an afterword by Erich Fromm). New York: New American Library.

Osborne, David, and Gaebler, Ted. 1992. *Reinventing Government: How the Entrepreneurial Spirit Is Transforming the Public Sector.* Reading, MA: Addison-Wesley.

Ostrom, Elinor. 1990. *Governing the Commons: The Evolution of Institutions for Collective Action.* Cambridge: Cambridge University Press.

————. 1997. *The Comparative Study of Public Economies.* Acceptance paper as the recipient of the Frank E. Seidman Distinguished Award in Political Economy. Memphis, TN: P.K. Seidman Foundation.

————. 1998. "A Behavioral Approach to the Rational Choice Theory of Collective Action." *American Political Science Review* 92, no. 1: 1–22.

Ostrom, Vincent. 1974. *The Intellectual Crisis in American Public Administration.* 2d ed. University: University of Alabama Press.

————. 1987. *The Political Theory of a Compound Republic: Designing the American Experiment.* Lincoln: University of Nebraska Press.

Ostrom, Vincent; Bish, Robert; and Ostrom, Elinor. 1988. *Local Government in the United States.* San Francisco, CA: ICS Press.

O'Toole, Laurence J., Jr., ed. 2000. *American Intergovernmental Relations. Foundations, Perspectives, and Issues.* Washington, DC: CQ Press.

Ott, J. Steven. 1989. *The Organizational Culture Perspective.* Chicago: Dorsey Press.

Overman, E. Sam, and Foss, Linda. 1993. "The Ethics of Physicians and Citizens: An Empirical Test of the 'Separatist Thesis.'" In *Ethics and Public Administration,* ed. H. George Frederickson, 121–135. Armonk, NY: M.E. Sharpe.

Oxford Library of Words and Phrases, Part I, Quotations. 1990. London: Guild Publishing.

Page, Edward C. 1991. *Localism and Centralism in Europe: The Political and Legal Bases of Local Self-Government.* Oxford: Oxford University Press.

————. 1992. *Political Authority and Bureaucratic Power: A Comparative Analysis.* 2d ed. New York: Harvester Wheatsheaf.

————. 1995. "Comparative British Public Administration." *Public Administration* (UK) 73, no. 1: 123–141.

————. 2001. *Government by Numbers: Delegated Legislation and Everyday Policy-Making.* Oxford: Hart Publishing.

Page, Edward C., and Goldsmith, Michael J., eds. 1987. *Central and Local Government Relations: A Comparative Analysis of West European Unitary States.* London: Sage.

Page, Edward C., and Wright, Vincent, eds. 1999. *Bureaucratic Elites in Western European States.* Oxford: Oxford University Press.

Paine, Thomas (no date; originally 1794). *Age of Reason being an Investigation of True and Fabulous Theology.* New York: Wiley Book.

Palmer, Robert R., and Colton, Joel. 1971. *A History of the Modern World.* New York: Alfred A. Knopf.

Pareto, Vilfredo. 1935. *The Mind and Society.* New York: Harcourt, Brace.

Parker, Geoffrey. 1988. *The Military Revolution: Military Innovation and the Rise of the West, 1500–1800.* Cambridge: Cambridge University Press.

Parsons, Talcott. 1966. *Societies: Evolutionary and Comparative Perspectives.* Englewood Cliffs, NJ: Prentice-Hall.

Parsons, Wayne. 1995. *Public Policy: An Introduction to the Theory and Practice of Policy Analysis.* Cheltenham, England: Edward Elgar.

Patton, Michael Q. 1997. *Utilization-Focused Evaluation.* 3d ed. Newbury Park, CA: Sage.

Perlmutter, Amos. 1977. *The Military and Politics in Modern Times: On Professionals, Praetorians, and Revolutionary Soldiers.* New Haven, CT: Yale University Press.

Perrow, Charles. 1979. *Complex Organizations: A Critical Essay.* 2d ed. Glenview, IL: Scott, Foresman.

Perry, James L., ed. 1996. *Handbook of Public Administration.* 2d ed. San Francisco, CA: Jossey-Bass.

Perry, James L., and Kraemer, Kenneth L. 1986. "Research Methodology in the Public Administration Review, 1975–1984." *Public Administration Review* 46, no. 3: 215–226.

Peters, B. Guy. 1987. "The United States: Absolute Change and Relative Stability." In *Public Employment in Western Nations,* ed. Richard Rose, 228–261. Cambridge: Cambridge University Press.

———. 1988. *Comparing Public Bureaucracies: Problems of Theory and Method.* Tuscaloosa: University of Alabama Press.

———. 1989 *The Politics of Bureaucracy.* 3d ed. New York: Longman.

———. 1991. *The Politics of Taxation: A Comparative Perspective.* Cambridge, MA: Blackwell.

———. 1993. *American Public Policy: Promise and Performance.* 3d ed. Chatham, NJ: Chatham House.

———. 1996. *The Future of Governing: Four Emerging Models.* Lawrence: University Press of Kansas.

———. 1999. *Institutional Theory in Political Science: The "New Institutionalism."* London: Pinter.

Peters, B. Guy, and Pierre, Jon. 2003. *Handbook of Public Administration.* Thousand Oaks, CA: Sage.

Peters, Ronald M., Jr. 1990. *The American Speakership: The Office in Historical Perspective.* Baltimore, MD: Johns Hopkins University Press.

Peters, Thomas J., and Waterman, Robert H. 1982. *In Search of Excellence.* New York: Harper and Row.

Pfiffner, John M., and Sherwood, Frank P. 1960. *Administrative Organization.* Englewood Cliffs, NJ: Prentice-Hall.

Pierre, Jon, ed. 1995. *Bureaucracy in the Modern State: An Introduction to Comparative Public Administration.* Aldershot, England: Edward Elgar.

Plumb, John H. 1980. *England in the Eighteenth Century.* Harmondsworth: Penguin Books.

Posavec, Emil J., and Carey, Raymond D. 1996. *Program Evaluation: Methods and Case Studies.* 5th ed. Englewood Cliffs, NJ: Prentice-Hall.

Pressman, Jeffrey L., and Wildavsky, Aaron. 1984. *Implementation: How Great Expectations in Washington Are Dashed in Oakland.* 3d ed. Berkeley: University of California Press.

Presthus, Robert. 1978. *The Organizational Society,* rev. ed. New York: St. Martin's Press.

Price, Don K. 1965. *The Scientific Estate.* Cambridge, MA: Belknap Press of Harvard University Press.

PUMA 2000. *Building Public Trust: Ethics Measures in OECD Countries.* PUMA Policy Brief no. 7. Paris: OECD.

Putnam, Robert D. 1973. "The Political Attitudes of Senior Civil Servants in Western Europe: A Preliminary Report." *British Journal of Political Science* 3, no. 3: 257–290.

Putnam, Robert; Leonardi, Robert; and Nanetti, Raffaella Y. 1993. *Making Democracy Work: Civic Traditions in Modern Italy.* Princeton, NJ: Princeton University Press.

Quinn, Robert E. 1988. *Beyond Rational Management: Mastering the Paradoxes and Competing Demands of High Performance.* San Francisco, CA: Jossey-Bass.

Raadschelders, Jos C.N. 1988. "Co-Production in Historical Perspective: Initiative and Participation at Local Government Level." In *Public Infrastructure Redefined,* ed. L.J. Roborgh, R.R. Stough, and Th. A.J. Toonen, 265–280. Bloomington/Leiden/Rotterdam: School for Public and Environmental Affairs, Indiana University/Departments of Public Administration, Universities of Leiden and Rotterdam.

———. 1994. "Understanding the Development of Local Government: Theory and Evidence from the Dutch Case." *Administration and Society* 25, no. 4: 410–442.

———. 1995. "Rediscovering Citizenship. Historical and Contemporary Reflections." *Public Administration* (UK) 73, no. 4: 611–625.

———. 1997a. "The Progress of Civil Society: A 19th Century American History of Governments." *Administration and Society* 29, no. 4: 471–489.

———. 1997b. "Size and Organizational Differentiation in Historical Perspective." *Journal of Public Administration Research and Theory* 7, no. 3: 419–441.

———. 1998a. *Handbook of Administrative History.* New Brunswick, NJ: Transaction.

———. 1998b. "Evolution, Institutional Analysis, and Path Dependency: An Administrative-Historical Perspective on Fashionable Approaches and Concepts." *International Review of Administrative Sciences* 64, no. 4: 565–582.

———. 1999. "A Coherent Framework for the Study of Public Administration." *Journal of Public Administration Research and Theory* 9, no. 2: 281–303.

———. 2000a. "Understanding Government in Society: We See the Trees, but Could We See the Forest?" *Administrative Theory and Praxis* 22, no. 2: 192–225.

———. 2000b. "Administrative History of the United States: Development and State of the Art." *Administration and Society* 32, no. 5: 499–528.

———. 2002a. Public Administration: Toward a Study of Government or Public Affairs for Civil Society. Lecture for the Inaugural Event of the Henry Bellmon Chair of Public Service, College of Arts and Sciences, University of Oklahoma, April 8.

———, ed. 2002b. *State and Church in Europe in an Administrative History Perspective (19th/ 20th c.).* Vol. 14 of the Yearbook of European Administrative History. Baden-Baden: Nomos Verlagsgesellschaft.

Raadschelders, Jos C.N., and Meer, Frits M. van der. 1998. "Administering the Summit: A Comparative Perspective." In *Administering the Summit* (Cahier d'Histoire de l'Administration no. 5), ed. Jos C.N. Raadschelders and Frits M. van der Meer, 13–33. Brussels: International Institute of Administrative Sciences/Ets. Bruylant.

Raadschelders, Jos C.N., and Rutgers, Mark R. 1996. "The Evolution of Civil Service Systems." In *Civil Service Systems in Comparative Perspective,* ed. Hans A.G.M. Bekke, James L. Perry, and Theo A.J. Toonen, 66–99. Bloomington: Indiana University Press.

Raadschelders, Jos C.N., and Toonen, Theo A.J. 1999. "Public Sector Reform for Building and Recasting the Welfare State: Experiences in Western Europe." In *Research in Public Administration,* vol. 5, ed. James L. Perry, 39–62. Stamford, CT: JAI Press.

Rabin, Jack; Vocino, Thomas; Hildreth, W. Bartley; and Miller, Gerald J., eds. 1995. *Handbook of Public Personnel Management.* New York: Marcel Dekker.

Rabin, Jack; Hildreth, W. Bartley; and Miller, Gerald J., eds. 2000. *Handbook of Strategic Management.* New York: Marcel Dekker.

Rainey, Hal G. 1997. *Understanding and Managing Public Organizations.* 2d ed. San Francisco, CA: Jossey-Bass.

Rand, Ayn. 1957. *Atlas Shrugged.* Garden City, NY: International Collectors Library.

———. 1964. "The Nature of Government." In *The Virtue of Selfishness,* ed. Ayn Rand. New York: Signet.

Rawls, John. 1971. *A Theory of Justice.* Cambridge, MA: Belknap Press of Harvard University Press.

———. 1980. "Ethics and Social Justice." In *Great Traditions in Ethics,* ed. Ethel M.

Albert, Theodore C. Denise, and Sheldon P. Peterfreund, 430–451. New York: D. van Nostrand.

Rhodes, Rod A.W., and Wright, Vincent, eds. 1988. *Tensions in the Territorial Politics of Western Europe.* London: Frank Cass.

Ridley, Frederick F., ed. 1968. *Specialists and Generalists: A Comparative Study of Professional Civil Service at Home and Abroad.* London/New York: Allen and Unwin/Barnes and Noble.

Riggs, Fred W. 1964. *Administration in Developing Countries: The Theory of Prismatic Society.* Boston, MA: Houghton Mifflin.

———. 1998. "Public Administration in America: Why Our Uniqueness is Exceptional and Important." *Public Administration Review* 58, no. 1: 22–31.

Robbins, Stephen P. 1980. *The Administrative Process.* Englewood Cliffs, NJ: Prentice-Hall.

Roberts, Michael. 1955. *The Military Revolution 1560–1660.* Belfast: Marjory Boyd.

Rochefort, David A.; Rosenberg, Michael; and White, Deena. 1998. "Community as a Policy Instrument: A Comparative Analysis." *Policy Studies Journal* 26, no. 3: 548–568.

Rodgers, Robert, and Rodgers, Nanette. 2000. "Defining the Boundaries of Public Administration: Undisciplined Mongrels versus Disciplined Purists." *Public Administration Review* 60, no. 5: 435–443.

Rohr, John A. 1989. *Ethics for Bureaucrats: An Essay on Law and Values.* New York: Marcel Dekker.

Rokkan, Stein. 1970. *Citizens, Elections, Parties: Approaches to the Comparative Study of the Processes of Development.* Oslo: Universitetsforlaget.

———. 1975. "Dimensions of State-Formation and Nation-Building: A Possible Paradigm for Research on Variations within Europe." In *The Formation of National States in Western Europe,* ed. Charles Tilly, 562–584. Princeton, NJ: Princeton University Press.

Rokkan, Stein, and Urwin, Derek W. 1982. *The Politics of Territorial Identity: Studies in European Regionalism.* London: Sage.

———. 1983. *Economy Territory Identity: Politics of West European Peripheries.* London: Sage.

Rose, Richard. 1987. "The Significance of Public Employment." In *Public Employment in Western Nations,* ed. Richard Rose, 1–53. Cambridge: Cambridge University Press.

———. 1989. *Understanding Big Government: The Programme Approach.* London: Sage.

Rosemond, John. 1998. "Kids Are Seeing Therapists, and It's All the Parents' Fault" In *The Norman Transcript,* December 4, A4.

Rosenbloom, David H. 1983. "Public Administration Theory and the Separation of Powers." *Public Administration Review* 43, no. 3: 219–227.

———. 1998. *Public Administration: Understanding Management, Politics, and Law in the Public Sector.* 4th ed. New York: McGraw-Hill.

Roskin, Michael G. 1995. *Countries and Concepts: An Introduction to Comparative Politics.* 5th ed. Englewood Cliffs, NJ: Prentice-Hall.

Rossi, Peter H.; Freeman, Howard E.; and Lipsey, Mark W. 1999. *Evaluation: A Systematic Approach.* 6th ed. Newbury Park, CA: Sage.

Rousseau, Jean-Jacques. 1986. "A Discourse on the Origin of Inequality." In *The Social Contract and Discourses*, ed. Jean-Jacques Rousseau, 31–126. London: Dent.

Rubin, Irene S. 1998. *Class, Tax, and Power: Municipal Budgeting in the United States.* Chatham, NJ: Chatham House.

Rutgers, Mark R. 1994. "Can the Study of Public Administration Do Without a Concept of the State? Reflections on the Work of Lorenz von Stein." *Administration and Society* 26, no. 4: 395–412.

———. 1997. "Beyond Woodrow Wilson: The Identity of the Study of Public Administration in Historical Perspective." *Administration and Society* 29, no. 3: 276–300.

———. 1998. "Paradigm Lost: Crisis as Identity of the Study of Public Administration." *International Review of Administrative Sciences* 64, no. 3: 553–564.

———. 2003. *Retracing Public Administration.* Vol. 7, Research in Public Administration. Amsterdam: JAI Press.

Ryan, Mick, and Ward, Tony. 1989. *Privatization and the Penal System.* New York: St. Martin's Press.

Sabatier, Paul, and Jenkins-Smith, Hank C., eds. 1993. *Policy Change and Learning: An Advocacy Culture Coalition Approach.* Boulder, CO: Westview Press.

Sancton, Andrew. 2000. *Merger Mania: The Assault on Local Government.* Montreal/Kingston: McGill-Queen's University Press.

Sayre, Walace. 1948. "The Triumph of Techniques over Purpose." In *Public Administration Review* 8, no. 2: 134–139.

Schattschneider, Elmer E. 1990. "The Scope and Bias of the Pressure System." In *Classic Readings in American Politics,* ed. Pietro Nivola and David H. Rosenbloom, 241–254. New York: St. Martin's Press.

Scheb, John M., and Lyons, William. 2000. "The Myth of Legality and Public Evaluation of the Supreme Court." *Social Science Quarterly* 81, no. 4: 928–940.

Schein, Edgar H. 1980. *Organizational Psychology.* Englewood Cliffs, NJ: Prentice-Hall.

———. 1993. *Organizational Culture and Leadership.* San Francisco, CA: Jossey-Bass.

Scholten, Ilja, ed. 1987. *Political Stability and Neo-Corporatism: Corporatist Integration and Societal Changes in Western Europe.* London: Sage.

Schreiber, Harry N. 2000. "The Condition of American Federalism: An Historian's View." In *American Intergovernmental Relations: Foundations, Perspectives, and Issues,* ed. Laurence J. O'Toole Jr., 66–73. Washington, DC: CQ Press.

Self, Peter. 1979. *Administrative Theories and Politics: An Enquiry into the Structure and Processes of Modern Government.* London: Allen and Unwin.

Shadish, William R.; Cook, Thomas D.; and Leviton, Laura C. 1993. *Foundations of Program Evaluation: Theories of Practices.* Newbury Park: Sage.

Shafritz, Jay M. 1988. *Dictionary of American Government and Politics.* Chicago: Dorsey Press.

Shafritz, Jay M., and Ott, J. Steven. 1996. *Classics of Organization Theory.* 4th ed. Fort Worth: Harcourt Brace College Publishers.

Shafritz, Jay M., and Russell, E.W. 2000. *Introducing Public Administration.* 2d ed. White Plains, NY: Addison Wesley Longman.

Shaw, Malcolm N. 1986. *International Law.* 2d ed. Cambridge: Grotius Publications.

Simon, Herbert A. 1957. *Administrative Behavior: A Study of Decision-Making Processes in Administrative Organization.* 2d ed. New York/London: Free Press/Collier-Macmillan.

———. [1958] 1961. "The Decision-Making in Schema: A Reply." In *Basic Issues in Public Administration,* ed. Donald C. Rowat, 85–91. New York: Macmillan.

———. 1969. "The Proverbs of Administration." In *Readings on Modern Organizations,* ed. Amitai Etzioni, 32–49. Englewood Cliffs, NJ: Prentice-Hall.

Simon, Herbert A.; Smithburg, D.W.; and Thompson. V.A. 1964. *Public Administration.* New York: Alfred A. Knopf.

Skocpol, Theda; Ganz, Marshall; and Munson, Ziad. 2000. "A Nation of Organizers: The Institutional Origins of Civic Voluntarism in the United States." *American Political Science Review* 94, no. 3: 527–546.

Skocpol, Theda, and Somers, Margaret. 1980. "The Uses of Comparative History in Macrosocial Inquiry." *Comparative Studies in Society and History* 22, no. 2: 174–197.

Smith, Alexander T. 1988. *Time and Public Policy.* Knoxville: University of Tennessee Press.

Smith, Brian C. 1985. *Decentralization: The Territorial Dimension of the State.* London: Allen and Unwin.

Smith, Toulmin. 1851. *Local Self-Government and Centralisation: The Characteristics of Each; and Its Practical Tendencies, as Affecting Social, Moral, and Political Welfare and Progress.* London: J. Chapman.

Snooks, G. Donald. 1993. *Economics Without Time. A Science Blind to the Forces of Historical Change.* Ann Arbor: University of Michigan Press.

Snow, Charles P. 1971. *Public Affairs.* New York: Charles Scribners Sons.

Solomon, Robert C., and Higgins, Kathleen M. 1996. *A Short History of Philosophy.* New York: Oxford University Press.

Sørensen, Georg. 1998. *Democracy and Democratization: Processes and Prospects in a Changing World.* Boulder, CO: Westview Press.

Sorokin, Pitirim. 1962. *Social and Cultural Dynamics.* Vol. 4. Basic Problems, Principles, and Methods. New York: Westminster Press.

Spicer, Michael W., and Terry, Larry D. 1993. "Legitimacy, History, and Logic: Public Administration and the Constitution." *Public Administration Review* 53, no. 3: 239–246.

Spong, John Shelby. 1998. *Why Christianity Must Change or Die: A Bishop Speaks to Believers in Exile.* San Francisco, CA: HarperCollins.

Starling, Grover. 1998. *Managing the Public Sector.* 5th ed. Fort Worth, TX: Harcourt Brace College Publishers.

Statistical Abstract of the United States: 1997, 1999. Washington, DC: U.S. Department of Commerce.

Steinbeck, John. 1957. *The Grapes of Wrath.* Garden City, NY: International Collectors Library.

Stewart, Debra W., and Sprinthall, Norman A. 1993. "The Impact of Demographic, Professional, and Organizational Variables and Domain on the Moral Reasoning of Public Administrators." In *Ethics and Public Administration,* ed. H. George Frederickson, 205–2189. Armonk, NY: M.E. Sharpe.

Stillman, Norman A. 1975. "Charity and Social Services in Medieval Islam." *Societas: A Review of Social History* 5, no. 2: 105–115.

———. 2000. "*WAQF* and the Ideology of Charity in Medieval Islam." In *Hunter of the East: Studies in Honour of Clifford Edmond Bosworth,* ed. Ian R. Netton, 357–372. Leiden: Brill.

Stillman, Richard J., II. 1991. *Preface to Public Administration: A Search for Themes and Direction.* New York: St. Martin's Press.

———. 1992. *Public Administration: Concepts and Cases.* 5th ed. Boston, MA: Houghton Mifflin Company.

———. 1998. *Creating the American State: The Moral Reformers and the Modern Administrative World They Made.* Tuscaloosa: University of Alabama Press.

Stivers, Camilla. 2000. *Bureau Men, Settlement Women: Constructing Public Administration in the Progressive Era.* Lawrence: University Press of Kansas.

Stone, Deborah. 2002. *Policy Paradox: The Art of Political Decision Making.* 3rd rev. ed. New York: W.W. Norton.

Strayer, Joseph R. 1975. "The Development of Bureaucracies." *Comparative Studies in Sociology and History* 17, no. 4: 504–509.

Streeck, Wolfgang, and Schmitter, Philippe C. 1985. *Private Interest Government: Beyond Market and State.* Beverly Hills, CA: Sage.

Suleiman, Ezra N., ed. 1984. *Bureaucrats and Policy Making: A Comparative Overview.* New York: Homes and Meier.

Sullivan, Kathleen M. 1998. "Behind the Crimson Curtain." In *New York Review of Books* 45, no. 15: 15–18.

Svara, James H. 1998. "The Politics-Administration Dichotomy Model as Aberration." *Public Administration Review* 58, no. 1: 51–58

Szymanski, Ann-Marie. 1999. "Dry Compulsions: Prohibition and the Creation of State-Level Enforcement Agencies." *Journal of Policy History* 11, no. 2: 115–146.

Taylor, Frederick. 1996. "The Principles of Scientific Management." In *Classics of Organization Theory,* ed. Jay M. Shafritz and J. Steven Ott, 66–79. Fort Worth: Harcourt Brace College Publishers.

Tead, Ordway, and Metcalf, Henry C. 1920. *Personnel Administration: Its Principles and Practice.* New York: McGraw-Hill.

Thelen, Kathleen, and Steinmo, Sven. 1992. "Historical Institutionalism in Comparative Politics."

In *Structuring Politics. Historical Institutionalism in Comparative Analysis,* ed. Sven Steinmo, Kathleen Thelen, and Frank Longstreth, 1–32. Cambridge: Cambridge University Press.

Thompson, Dennis F. 1992. "Paradoxes of Government Ethics." *Public Administration Review* 52, no. 3: 254–259.

Thompson, Frank J. 2002. *Classics of Public Personnel Policy.* Florence, KY: Thomson/Wadsworth.

Thompson, James Dennis. 1967. *Organizations in Action.* New York: McGraw-Hill.

Tilly, Charles, ed. 1975. *The Formation of National States in Western Europe.* Princeton, NJ: Princeton University Press.

———. 1990. *Coercion, Capital, and European States A.D. 900–1990.* Cambridge: Blackwell.

———. 1994. "Entanglements of European Cities and States." In *Cities and the Rise of States in Europe: A.D. 1000 to 1800,* ed. Charles Tilly and Wim P. Blockmans, 1–27. Boulder, CO: Westview Press.

Tocqueville, Alexis de. 1984. *Democracy in America* (abridged), ed. Richard D. Heffner. New York: Penguin Books.

———. 2000. *Democracy in America,* ed. Harvey C. Mansfield and Delba Winthrop. Chicago: University of Chicago Press.

Toonen, Theo A.J. 1990. *Internationalisering en het Openbaar Bestuur als Institutioneel Ensemble. Naar een Zelfbestuurskunde* [Internationalization of government as institutional arrangement: Toward self-government]. Den Haag: VUGA.

Tönnies, Ferdinand. [1887] 1940. *Fundamental Concepts of Sociology* (Gemeinschaft und Gesellschaft) *by Ferdinand Tönnies,* trans. Charles P. Loomis. New York: American Book.

Tugwell, Rexford Guy; Munro, Thomas; and Stryker, Roy E. 1930. *American Economic Life and the Means of Its Improvement.* 3d ed. New York: Harcourt, Brace.

Van Braam, Aris (in cooperation with Marie Louise Bemelmans-Videc). 1986. *Leerboek Bestuurskunde* [The study of public administration]. Muiderberg: Coutinho.

Van der Meer, Frits M., and Roborgh, Renk L.J. 1996. "Civil Servants and Representativeness." In *Civil Service Systems in Comparative Perspective,* ed. A.J.G.M. Bekke, J.L. Perry, and Th.A.J. Toonen, 119–133. Bloomington: Indiana University Press.

Van Riper, Paul. 1958. *History of the United States Civil Service.* Evanston, IL: Row, Peterson.

———. 1997. "Some Anomalies in the Deep History of U.S. Public Administration." *Public Administration Review* 57, no. 3: 218–222.

———. 1999. Why Public Administration? When Not to Privatize. Senior scholar session at the annual conference of the American Society for Public Administration, Orlando, FL, April 9–14.

Van Vree, Wilbert. 1994. *Nederland als Vergaderland: Opkomst en Verbreiding van een Vergaderregime* [The Netherlands as a meeting country: Genesis and growth of a meeting style]. Groningen: Wolters-Noordhoff.

Van Waarden, Frans. 1985. "Regulering en Belangenorganisatie van Ondernemers." [Regulation and interest organization of entrepreneurs]. In *De Nederlandse Samenleving sinds 1815: Wording en Samenhang* [Dutch society since 1815: Making and unity], ed. F.L. van Holthoon et al., 229–260. Assen: Van Gorcum.

———. 1991. "Introduction: Crisis, Corporatism, and Continuity." In *Organizing Business for War: Corporatist Economic Organizations During the Second World War,* ed. Wyn Grant, Jan Nekkers, and Frans van Waarden, 1–19. Providence, RI: Berg Publishers.

———. 1992a. "Dimensions and Types of Policy Networks." *European Journal of Political Research* 21 no. 1: 29–52.

———. 1992b. "The Historical Institutionalization of Typical National Patterns in Policy Networks Between State and Industry: A Comparison of the USA and The Netherlands." *European Journal of Political Research* 21, no. 1: 131–162.

———. 1992c. "Emergence and Development of Business Interest Associations: An Example from The Netherlands." *Organization Studies* 13, no. 4: 521–562.

Van Wart, Montgomery. 1998. *Changing Public Sector Values.* New York: Garland.

Vedung, Evert. 1998. "Policy Instruments: Typologies and Theories." In *Carrots, Sticks and*

Sermons: Policy Instruments and Their Evaluation, ed. Marie Louise Bemelmans-Videc, Ray Rist, and Evert Vedung, 21–58. New Brunswick, NJ: Transaction.

Verbon, Harrie. 1988. On the Evolution of Public Pension Schemes. Ph.D. dissertation, University of Amsterdam.

Vickers, Sir Geoffrey. 1965. *The Art of Judgment: A Study of Policy Making.* London: Chapman and Hall.

Vincent, Andrew. 1987. *Theories of the State.* Oxford: Basil Blackwell.

Wagenaar, Pieter. 1997. "The 'Waardgelders' of Den Haag." In *Exercise of Arms: Warfare in the Netherlands, 1568–1648,* ed. Marco van der Hoeven, 211–230. Leiden: Brill.

Waldo, Dwight. 1968. "Scope of the Theory of Public Administration." In *Theory and Practice of Public Administration: Scope, Objectives, and Methods,* ed. James C. Charlesworth, 1–26. Philadelphia, PA: American Academy of Political and Social Science.

———. 1980. *The Enterprise of Public Administration.* Novato, CA: Chandler and Sharp.

———. 1984. *The Administrative State: A Study of the Political Theory of American Public Administration.* 2d ed. New York: Holmes and Meier.

———. 1987. "Politics and Administration: On Thinking About a Complex Relationship." In *A Centennial History of the American Administrative State,* ed. Ralph Clark Chandler, 89–112. New York: Free Press/Collier Macmillan.

———. 1992. "Public Administration and Ethics: A Prologue to a Preface." In *Public Administration: Concepts and Cases,* ed. Richard J. Stillman II, 460–471. Boston, MA: Houghton Mifflin.

Wallace, Michael, and Singer, J. David. 1970. "Intergovernmental Organizations in the Global System." *International Organization* 24, no. 2: 239–287.

Wamsley, Gary L.; Bacher, Robert N.; Goodsell, Charles T.; Kronenberg, Philip S.; Rohr, John A.; Stivers, Camilla M.; White, Orion F., and Wolf, James F. 1990. *Refounding Public Administration.* Newbury Park: Sage.

Wamsley, Gary L., and Wolf, James F., eds. 1996. *Refounding Democratic Public Administration: Modern Paradoxes, Postmodern Challenges.* Thousand Oaks, CA: Sage.

Warner, W. Lloyd. 1962. *The Corporation in the Emergent American Society.* New York: Harper and Brothers.

Warwick, Donald P. 1981. "The Ethics of Administrative Discretion." In *Public Duties: The Moral Obligations of Government Officials,* ed. Joel L. Fleishman, Lance Liebman, and Mark H. Moore, 93–127. Cambridge, MA: Harvard University Press.

Webber, Carolyn C. 1980. "Development of Ideas About Balanced Budgets." In *How to Limit Government Spending,* ed. Aaron Wildavsky, 163–180. Berkeley: University of California Press.

Webber, Carolyn, and Wildavsky, Aaron. 1986. *A History of Taxation and Expenditure in the Western World.* New York: Simon and Schuster.

Weber, Max. 1980. *Wirtschaft und Gesellschaft: Grundriss der Verstehenden Sozioogie* [Economy and society: Foundation of an understanding sociology]. 5th ed. Tübingen: J.C.B. Mohr.

———. 1985. *Gesammelte Aufsätze zur Wissenschaftslehre* [Collected essays on epistemology]. 6th ed., ed. J. Winckelman. Tübingen: J.C.B. Mohr.

Weilenmann, Hermann. 1966. "The Interlocking of Nation and Personality Structure." *Nation-Building,* ed. K.W. Deutsch and W.J. Foltz, 33–55. New York: Atherton Press.

Weiss, Carol H. 1997. "Theory-Based Evaluation: Past, Present, and Future." In *Progress and Future Directions in Evaluation: Perspectives on Theory, Practice, and Methods (New Directions for Evaluation: A Publication of the American Evaluation Association),* no. 76, ed. Debra J. Rog and Deborah Fournier, 41–55. San Francisco, CA: Jossey-Bass.

White, Jay D.; Adams, Guy B.; and Forrester, John P. 1996. "Knowledge and Theory Development in Public Administration: The Role of Doctoral Education and Research." *Public Administration Review* 56, no. 5: 441–452.

White, Richard D. 2000. "Theodore Roosevelt as Civil Service Commissioner: Linking the Influence and Development of a Modern Administrative President." *Administrative Theory and Praxis* 22, no. 4: 696–713.

White, Leonard D. 1958. *The Republican Era: 1869–1901: A Study in Administrative History.* New York: Macmillan.

Whiteside, Daniel; Stokes, Gordon; and Callaway, Candice. 1996. *Under the Code.* Burbank, CA: Three in One Concepts.

Wholey, Joseph S.; Hatry, Harry P.; and Newcomer, Kathryn E., eds. 1994. *Handbook of Practical Program Evaluation.* San Francisco, CA: Jossey-Bass.

Whyte, William H., Jr. 1956. *The Organization Man.* New York: Simon and Schuster.

Wildavsky, Aaron. 1964. *The Politics of the Budgetary Process.* Boston, MA: Little, Brown.

Williams, Daniel W. 2000. "Reinventing the Proverbs of Government." *Public Administration Review* 60, no. 6: 522–534.

Williams, William H.A. 1998. *H.L. Mencken Revisited.* New York/London: Twayne Publishers/Prentice Hall International.

Wilson, Edward O. 1998. *Consilience: The Unity of Knowledge.* New York: Alfred A. Knopf.

Wilson, Graham K. 1990. *Interest Groups.* Oxford: Basil Blackwell.

Wilson, Woodrow. 1892. *The State: Elements Historical and Practical Politics.* 2d ed. Boston, MA: D.C. Heath.

———. 1913. *The New Freedom: A Call for the Emancipation of the Generous Energies of a People.* Garden City, NY: Doubleday, Page.

———. 1992. "The Study of Administration." In *Public Administration: Concepts and Cases,* ed. Richard J. Stillman II, 6–17. Boston, MA: Houghton Mifflin.

Winch, Peter. 1986. *The Idea of a Social Science and Its Relation to Philosophy.* London/Atlantic Highlands, NJ: Routledge and Kegan Paul Humanities Press.

Wittfogel, Karl A. 1957. *Oriental Despotism: A Comparative Study of Total Power.* New Haven, CT: Yale University Press.

Wolin, Sheldon S. 1989. *The Presence of the Past: Essays on the State and the Constitution.* Baltimore, MD: Johns Hopkins University Press.

Wood, Gordon S. 1986. "The Democratization of Mind in the American Revolution." In *The Moral Foundations of the American Republic,* ed. Robert H. Horwitz, 109–135. Charlottesville: University Press of Virginia.

Wood, James E., Jr. 1991. "Introduction: Religion and Public Policy." In *The Role of Religion in the Making of Public Policy,* ed. James E. Wood, Jr. and Derek Davis, 5–21. Waco, TX: J.W. Dawson Institute of Church-State Studies, Baylor University.

Wooldrige, Blue, and Maddox, Barbara Clark. 1995. "Demographic Changes and Diversity in Personnel: Implications for Public Administrators." In *Handbook of Public Personnel Management,* ed. Jack Rabin, Thomas Vocino, W. Bartley Hildreth, and Gerald J. Miller, 183–215. New York: Marcel Dekker.

"The World Is Watching: A Survey of Human-Rights Law." 1998. *Economist,* special insert, December 5, 3–16.

"World Law and World Power." 1998. *Economist,* December 5, 16.

Wren, Daniel A. 1972. *The Evolution of Management Thought.* New York: Ronald Press.

Wright, Deil S. 1988 *Understanding Intergovernmental Relations.* 3d ed. Pacific Grove, CA: Brooks/Cole.

———. 1990. "Federalism, Intergovernmental Relations, and Intergovernmental Management: Historical Reflections and Conceptual Comparisons." *Public Administration Review* 50, no. 2: 168–178.

Wright, Vincent, ed. 1994. *Privatization in Western Europe: Pressures, Problems and Paradoxes.* London: Pinter Publishers.

———. 1995. Privatizations in Western Europe: Paradoxes and Implications for Institutions. Paper presented at the annual conference of the Netherlands Institute of Government, Oosterbeek, November 9–10.

Wunder, Bernd, ed. 1995. *The Influences of the Napoleonic "Model" of Administration on the Administrative Organization of Other Countries* (Cahier d'Histoire de l'Administration no. 4). Brussels: International Institute of Administrative Sciences.

Yankelovich, Daniel. 1991. *Coming to Public Judgment: Making Democracy Work in a Complex World.* New York: Syracuse University Press.

Yates, Douglas T., Jr. 1981. "Hard Choices: Justifying Bureaucratic Decisions." In *Public Duties: The Moral Obligations of Government Officials,* ed. Joel L. Fleishman, Lance Liebman, and Mark H. Moore, 32–51. Cambridge, MA: Harvard University Press.

Zehm, G. 1976. "Der Hohle Staat und der Dicke Apparat." In *Der Apparatschick: Die Inflation der Bürokratie in Ost und West* [Bureaucrats: The growth of bureaucracy east and west], ed. G.K. Kaltenbrunner, 52–61. Munich: Hercler.

Zimmerman, Louis J. 1987. *Politieke Economie van Plato tot Marx* [Political economy from Plato to Marx]. Groningen: Wolters Noordhoff.

Zuckert, Michael P. 1986. "Locke and the Problem of Civil Religion." In *The Moral Foundations of the American Republic,* ed. Robert H. Horwitz, 181–203. Charlottesville: University Press of Virginia.

AUTHOR AND NAME INDEX

SUBJECT INDEX

A

Administrative man, 256–257
Administrative management, 72, 195, 215, 262, 329
Advisory Committee Intergovernmental Relations, 233
Affirmative action, 345
Agency
    administrative, 133–135
    independent, 134–135
    regulatory, 231
Amalgamation, 74, 232
American Society for Public Administration, 338
Anarchy, 18, 364
Anti-Federalists, 18, 321
Antiquity, influence of, 45, 61, 76–77, 80, 88–90, 93, 124, 388, 391
Antitrust, 131, 297, 359
Apartheid, 138
Aristocracy, 316
Army, 147–151
    feudal, 147
    mercenary, 148
    standing, 148
Assimilation, 78, 353–355
Association, 78, 353–355
    professional, 338
    public administration as science of, 16
    societal, 360
    voluntary, 9, 41, 43, 361–362, 366
Authority, 53
    charismatic, 54
    coordinate, 114

Authority *(continued)*
    distribution of, 210
    expendable, 58
    inclusive, 114
    legal–rational, 54, 57, 63, 140
    moral, 7
    negotiable, 50, 57–59, 62–63, 119, 289, 292, 378, 397
    overlapping, 115
    secular, 66, 77
    spiritual, 66. 77
    traditional, 54, 57, 94
    universal, 57, 61–62, 89–90
Autonomous man, 208

B

Balance of power, 136
Behavioralism, 22
Bill of Rights, 62, 137
Blacksburg Manifesto, 26, 372
Brotherhood, 108, 381
Budget(ing), 175–179
    balanced, 176
    for results, 178
    executive, 177
    line-item, 176, 178
    maximization, 256, 260, 321–323
    zero-base, 178, 257
    performance, 178
    Planning Programming System, 149, 178
    target-base, 178
    top-down, 178
Bundesrat, 115

435

Jos C.N. Raadschelders is professor of Public Administration and holds the Henry Bellmon Chair of Public Service at the University of Oklahoma. His research interests include administrative history, the study of public administration, and comparative government. Prior to his appointment in the United States, he worked at the University of Leiden in the Netherlands (1983–98). He is the author and coauthor of several books, articles, and chapters on a wide range of topics within public administration.